SCOTT'S

Fingerprint Mechanics

SCOTT'S
Fingerprint Mechanics

By

ROBERT D. OLSEN, SR.

Special Agent in Charge
Latent Fingerprint Division
United States Army
Criminal Investigation Laboratory
Fort Gordon, Georgia

With a Foreword by

WALTER R. SCOTT

Retired Lieutenant in Charge
Criminal and Photographic Laboratory Division
Police Department
San Diego, California

CHARLES C THOMAS • PUBLISHER
Springfield • Illinois • U.S.A.

Published and Distributed Throughout the World by

CHARLES C THOMAS • PUBLISHER

Bannerstone House

301-327 East Lawrence Avenue, Springfield, Illinois, U.S.A.

©1978, by CHARLES C THOMAS • PUBLISHER
ISBN 0-398-03730-2 (cloth)
ISBN 0-398-06308-7 (paper)
Library of Congress Catalog Card Number: 77-12985

Library of Congress Cataloging in Publication Data

Scott, Walter R.
　　Scott's Fingerprint mechanics.

　　Bibliography: p.
　　Includes index.
　　1. Fingerprints. I. Olsen, Robert D. II. Title.
III. Title: Fingerprint mechanics.
HV6074.S34 1977　　　364.12′5　　　77-12985
ISBN 0-398-03730-2. — ISBN 0-398-06308-7 (pbk.)

Printed in the United States of America

C-1

The views of the author do not purport to reflect the position of the Department of Defense, the Department of the Army, or the U.S. Army Criminal Investigation Command.

To

Law Enforcement Officers

and

Their Profession

Foreword

THE WORD *fingerprint* brings to mind two concepts: (1) the presence of natural ridge patterns on the skin of the undersides of the tips of the fingers and (2) the reproduction of those ridge patterns for purposes of visibility and identity.

Nature has supplied an abundance of ridges with unlimited variations on the skin of the fingers, and it is a recognized fact that no two fingers bear identical ridge patterns. These facts make it possible to use the ridge patterns for easy, simple, and positive identification.

The pages of this book are intended to describe and illustrate the various methods and techniques which have been found applicable and effective in recovering or reproducing latent finger impressions, as well as to identify the person whose finger made the impression.

Included in the text at the end of each chapter is supplemental classroom instructional material in the form of true-false questions and completion sentences to place additional emphasis on points covered in the text.

Walter R. Scott
San Diego, California

Preface

Fingerprint Mechanics, written by Lieutenant Walter R. Scott of the San Diego Police Department, was published in 1951, by Charles C Thomas, Publisher. The book has been acknowledged as one of the most outstanding texts pertaining to fingerprinting that has ever been published. In 1971, a reviewer made the following statement about the book: "Fingerprint Mechanics is a well-written, easy-to-understand 'how to' and 'why' book. The author tells it like it is without useless and non-productive theory." Mr. Scott's book gained wide recognition because it was practical and provided the information essential to good fingerprint work.

It is a great responsibility to write a revision of a book which has been long recognized as a classic in its field. Considerable revision has been made because of the development of new and improved techniques and equipment in the intervening twenty-six years, but, hopefully, the same practical approach has been maintained.

The purpose of this book is to provide the basic knowledge of fingerprint identification and latent fingerprint techniques necessary to recover latent prints at crime scenes. Everyone, from the first officer on the crime scene to the prosecutor in court, must be conscious of the value of fingerprint evidence. Physical evidence has become increasingly important in our criminal justice system. Fingerprint evidence must be considered as having particular significance, because it can positively establish the identity of a specific individual in a case.

Regarding physical evidence, the most important person in any investigation is the officer at the crime scene responsible for collecting and preserving the physical evidence. It is hoped that all investigators, those just beginning their careers as well as experienced investigators, will find the material in this book of value in their daily activities. Some of the latent fingerprint techniques listed are experimental today, but twenty-six years ago many techniques now commonly in use were not even dreamed of.

R.D.O.

Acknowledgments

T HIS BOOK is a product of the accumulative experience of thousands of investigators, police officers, and laboratory personnel, as reflected in professional and technical journals. Students and investigators who wish to increase their knowledge of fingerprint identification and to keep abreast of new developments should subscribe regularly to professional and technical journals pertaining to forensic science. Each new generation of investigators is fortunate to have the collective knowledge of previous generations of investigators at its disposal in the available technical literature.

I have received much help and kindness during the writing of this book, and I wish it were possible to acknowledge everyone who has graciously contributed to it. However, only a partial listing is possible. Much information was gained from informal conversations with many members of the American Academy of Forensic Sciences and the International Association for Identification. I am grateful to all those who have shared their knowledge and experiences with me.

I am especially indebted to Mr. Walter Scott and Mr. Payne Thomas for the opportunity to write this revised edition of Mr. Scott's book. I am deeply indebted to Andrew J. Brooks, Jr., of the Chicago Police Department, who has contributed immeasurably to this book. Andy's assistance has been indispensable.

I am much indebted to the following for the use of copyright material: R. E. Stockdale, editor of the *Journal of the Forensic Science Society* (P.O. Box 41, Harrogate, North Yorkshire, England HG1 2LF), for permission to reprint the article appearing in Section 107, and Michael A. Prieto, CAREERCO Institute of Applied Science and James A. Roberts, San Diego Police Department (retired), for permission to reprint the article appearing in Section 132. It is particularly gratifying to have a contribution by Mr. Roberts, as he and the San Diego Police Department were involved in the preparation of the original text by Mr. Scott.

I gratefully acknowledge the assistance of the following personnel of the U.S. Army Criminal Investigation Laboratory System: Charles E. Cooper, Gideon Epstein, Curtis L. Flood, Larry L. Flinn, Edward R. German, Roy E. Haas, Ernest D. Hamm, Kenneth J. Hoag, Paul E. Llewellyn, Jr., Edward B. Mizelle, Paul M. Norkus, Harold V. Page, Daniel W. Smith, Jr., Paul F. Spangler, James H. Stopper II, Thomas J. Tomich, Jr., Ralph T. Turbyfill, Arthur J. Varriale, and John C. Wilson.

I owe a particular debt of gratitude to my wife, Pamela, without whose assistance as reviewer, typist, and critic, this book could not have been written. I am also grateful to my children, Malcolm, Robby, Pam, and Beth, who donated much of their time with their father in order that he may write this book.

R.D.O.

Contents

Page

Foreword ix
Preface xi
Acknowledgments xiii

CHAPTER I
FINGERPRINT IDENTIFICATION

Section

1. WHAT ARE FINGERPRINTS? 5
2. THE PAPILLARY SYSTEM 7
3. FRICTION RIDGES ARE THE BASIS OF IDENTIFICATION . . . 9
4. EVERY FINGER BEARS ITS OWN TRADEMARK 11
5. FINGERPRINT TERMINOLOGY 14
6. RIDGE DAMAGE AND DESTRUCTION 15
7. FINGERPRINT CLASSIFICATION 17
8. SPACE VALUES ON FINGERPRINT CARDS 19
9. FINGERPRINT PATTERNS ARE COMPLEX YET SIMPLE . . . 20
10. IDENTICAL AND SIMILAR FINGERPRINTS 21
11. THE SCIENCE OF FINGERPRINT IDENTIFICATION 24
12. CHARACTERISTICS AND POSITION OF CHARACTERISTICS . . . 25
13. NUMBER OF CHARACTERISTICS REQUIRED FOR IDENTIFICATION. 27
14. POROSCOPY AND EDGEOSCOPY 30
15. PALMPRINTS ARE USED TO ESTABLISH IDENTITY 36
16. PATTERN AREAS, FLEXION, AND TENSION CREASES OF THE PALMS 39
17. FOOTPRINTS 43
    QUESTIONS: True-False and Completion 46

CHAPTER II
TAKING FINGER-, PALM-, AND FOOTPRINTS

18. THE IMPORTANCE OF LEGIBLE FINGERPRINTS 55
19. ELIMINATION OF FINGERPRINT EVIDENCE 56
20. THE FINGERPRINT CARD 59

Section   *Page*

21. Two Kinds of Inked Impressions 60
22. Taking Fingerprints Means Just That 63
23. How to Take Fingerprints 64
24. Stance for Taking Prints 69
25. Major Case Prints 70
26. Taking Palmprints and Footprints 72
27. Errors in Taking Fingerprints 76
28. Occupational Damage and Bad Skin Condition . . . 80
29. Techniques for Taking Problem Prints 82
30. Postmortem Fingerprinting 84
31. Ink Methods for Taking Fingerprints 90
32. Inkless Fingerprint Techniques 92
33. Copying of Fingerprint Cards 99
    Questions: True-False and Completion 101

CHAPTER III
LATENT FINGERPRINTS AND CRIME SCENE PROCEDURES

34. Value of Fingerprint Evidence 111
35. Latent Fingerprints 114
36. Palmar Sweat Differs From Other Skin Secretions . . 115
37. Factors Affecting Latent Fingerprints 117
38. How Long Do Latent Fingerprints Last? 123
39. Latent Fingerprint Techniques 125
40. Preservation of Fingerprint Evidence 126
41. Use of a Strong Light in Fingerprint Work 127
42. Points to Remember in a Fingerprint Search 129
43. Collection and Identification of Fingerprint Evidence . 133
44. Special Laboratory Considerations 135
45. Packaging Fingerprint Evidence 139
46. Fingerprint Photography 141
    Questions: True-False and Completion 151

CHAPTER IV
FINGERPRINT EQUIPMENT

47. The Fingerprint Kit 161
48. Seventeen Items That Make Up a Serviceable Finger-
    print Kit 164

Section   *Page*

49. FINGERPRINT BRUSHES 168
50. FINGERPRINT POWDERS AND PHOSPHORS 170
51. FINGERPRINT MAGNIFYING GLASSES 171
52. FINGERPRINT LIFTING MATERIALS 175
53. THE FINGERPRINT CAMERA 177
54. EQUIPMENT FOR TAKING FINGER- AND PALMPRINTS . . . 182
55. LIGHTBOXES 184
56. ULTRAVIOLET LIGHT SOURCES 185
57. A STRONG LIGHT SOURCE 187
58. MORTAR AND PESTLE 189
59. FUMING CABINETS 190
60. IODINE FUMING PIPE 194
61. CHEMICAL EXHAUST HOODS 195
62. GLOVEBOXES 196
63. HUMIDITY CABINETS 197
64. CLEAN EQUIPMENT 199
65. LIST OF MANUFACTURERS OF FINGERPRINT EQUIPMENT . . 201
    QUESTIONS: True-False and Completion 202

CHAPTER V
LATENT FINGERPRINT POWDER TECHNIQUES

66. WHY POWDER LATENT FINGERPRINTS? 209
67. LOOK FOR LATENT PRINTS BEFORE POWDERING 210
68. WHEN IN DOUBT, MAKE TEST PRINTS 211
69. FINGERPRINT POWDERS 212
70. USING FINGERPRINT BRUSHES 215
71. PHOTOGRAPHING LATENTS BEFORE POWDER DEVELOPMENT . 218
72. THE EFFECT OF BRUSHING POWDER ON PAPER 219
73. POWDER TECHNIQUES FOR LARGE AREAS 221
74. MAGNETIC FINGERPRINT POWDER TECHNIQUES 223
75. THERMOPLASTIC POWDERS 227
76. LEAD SULFIDE TECHNIQUES 229
77. FLUORESCENT AND PHOSPHORESCENT FINGERPRINT POWDERS . 229
78. DYESTUFFS AS FINGERPRINT POWDERS 231
79. PREPARING FINGERPRINT POWDERS 232
80. FINGERPRINT POWDER FORMULAS 233
    QUESTIONS: True-False and Completion 235

CHAPTER VI
LATENT FINGERPRINT PHYSICAL TECHNIQUES

Section   *Page*

81. Iodine Development of Latent Fingerprints 243
82. Fixing and Intensifying Iodine-Developed Prints . . 250
83. Clearing Paper Treated With Iodine 255
84. Chlorine and Bromine Fuming Techniques 256
85. Bacteriological Techniques 258
86. Heat as a Latent Fingerprint Technique 259
87. Flame Techniques 260
    Questions: True-False and Completion 263

CHAPTER VII
LATENT FINGERPRINT CHEMICAL TECHNIQUES

88. The Chemical Composition of Latent Fingerprint Resi-
    due 271
89. Chemical Formulas 274
90. The Ninhydrin Technique 276
91. Ninhydrin Clearing Solutions 290
92. Silver Nitrate Technique 291
93. Silver Nitrate Clearing Solutions 302
94. Osmium Tetroxide Techniques 308
95. Ruthenium Tetroxide Technique 309
96. Hydrogen Fluoride Techniques 310
97. Chemical Techniques for Brass Surfaces 311
98. Calcium Sulfide Technique 319
99. Tannic Acid Technique 321
100. Ink, Dye, and Stain Techniques 322
101. Techniques for Latent Prints in Blood 323
102. Fluorogenic Chemical Techniques 329
103. Autoradiography 331
     Questions: True-False and Completion 332

CHAPTER VIII
LATENT FINGERPRINT ELECTRONIC TECHNIQUES

104. Electronics 343
105. X-ray Techniques 344

Section

Page

106. LASER TECHNIQUE 347
107. SCANNING ELECTRON MICROSCOPE TECHNIQUE
G. E. Garner, C. R. Fontan, and D. W. Hobson 348
108. THE METAL-EVAPORATION TECHNIQUE 351
109. MICROWAVE VACUUM-DRYING TECHNIQUE 352
110. IMAGE-ENHANCEMENT TECHNIQUES 353
111. COMPUTER IDENTIFICATION OF LATENT FINGERPRINTS . . . 355
QUESTIONS: True-False and Completion 357

CHAPTER IX
LATENT FINGERPRINT LIFTING TECHNIQUES

112. LIFT LATENT PRINTS ONLY WHEN NECESSARY 369
113. THREE TYPES OF LIFTING DEVICES 370
114. TRANSPARENT AND OPAQUE LIFTS 374
115. WHAT SIZE LIFT TO USE 374
116. APPLYING LIFTS TO POWDERED PRINTS 376
117. LIFTING POWDERED PRINTS 379
118. USING FINGERPRINT LIFTS AS NEGATIVES 383
119. LIFTING IODINE-DEVELOPED LATENT PRINTS 387
120. CHEMICAL SOLUTIONS FOR LIFTING LATENTS 389
121. LIFTING VISIBLE AND PLASTIC FINGERPRINTS 390
QUESTIONS: True-False and Completion 395

CHAPTER X
FINGERPRINT CASES

122. REPRESENTATIVE FINGERPRINT CASES 403
123. FINGERPRINTS ON CLOTH 405
124. FINGERPRINTS ON TAPES 406
125. FINGERPRINTS IN DUST 408
126. FINGERPRINTS ON GLASS AND METAL 411
127. FINGERPRINTS ON WOOD 417
128. FINGERPRINTS ON PLASTIC 419
129. FINGERPRINTS ON PAPER 420
130. FINGERPRINTS IN DRUG CASES 423
131. FINGERPRINTS ON SKIN 426

Section   *Page*

132. IMAGE ENHANCEMENT OF A BLOODY PRINT

    J. A. Roberts   429

133. USE OF NEW TECHNIQUES   435

134. FINGERPRINT COURT EXHIBITS   437

    QUESTIONS: True-False and Completion   442

Bibliography   449

Index   457

SCOTT'S
Fingerprint Mechanics

Chapter I

Fingerprint Identification

1
WHAT ARE FINGERPRINTS?

FINGERPRINTS are the most positive means of identifying individuals. Of all the methods of identification, fingerprinting alone has proved to be both infallible and practical. Fingerprint identification is best known to the general public for its application in criminal investigations; however, that is only one aspect of its usage. Fingerprinting may also provide the means for positive identification of deceased persons and disaster victims in cases where injury or other circumstances preclude visual identification. Footprinting of infants may assist in the identification of babies when parents claim errors in hospital maternity wards. Fingerprints on documents may assist in establishing the authenticity of the documents in civil actions.

Fingerprints are impressions made by the end joints of the fingers and, therefore, are reversed reproductions of the skin surface details. The palmar surfaces of the hands and the plantar surfaces of the feet have ridged skin formations called *papillary* or *friction ridges*. The characteristics and their position and relationship to each other vary from person to person and even between fingers on the same hand.

Fingerprints are permanent. The papillary ridges of the hands and feet form on the fetus before birth and, except for size, remain unchanged throughout life and even after death, until decomposition of the skin destroys them. Injury and disease may damage or alter the ridges, but only if the underlying dermis is damaged and even then not normally to the extent of preventing identification.

Fingerprint evidence is fragile. Fingerprint evidence is perhaps the most sought-after evidence encountered in criminal investigations. It is evidence of the most delicate nature; it is highly destructible; it may be cleverly developed, improved, and intensified, or just as easily destroyed. Success in recovering fingerprint evidence depends not only on the equipment used, but upon the experience, imagination, interest, knowledge, skill, and versatility of the person working with the evidence.

A fingerprint technician must know which method is best in each situation as it arises and what technique to apply and when. The technician must be quick to recognize the point at which a latent print is developed to its peak, so that it will not be inadvertently or unwittingly destroyed.

The first officer at a crime scene must be *fingerprint conscious.* That officer must have knowledge of the value and possibilities of fingerprint evidence if it is to be preserved and protected for investigators who follow.

Every fingerprint technician who has developed latent fingerprints has most likely experienced the misfortune depicted in Figure 1. Good latents are easily brushed away. A valuable lesson is learned when this happens; the technician's attitude toward latent prints is more respectful thereafter. Experience is a good teacher—with fingerprint evidence it is the best.

Figure 1. Fingerprint evidence is the most common type of physical evidence encountered in criminal investigations. It is extremely delicate: It may be improved or intensified, or it may be brushed away.

2

THE PAPILLARY SYSTEM

The *papillary* system of glands, ducts, ridges, and pores evolved perhaps because of the necessity of increasing friction where it was most needed, on the palms of the hands and the soles of the feet. The ridges of the palmar and plantar surfaces are commonly referred to as *papillary* or *friction* ridges. The word *papillary* is derived from *papilla* meaning a small, elongated, nipple-shaped protuberance, as the papillae of the tongue, or in this instance, the protuberances of the dermis forming the ridges of the skin on the fingers, palms of the hands, and soles of the feet.

A dry, hard, smooth, ridgeless skin surface affords little or no friction, whereas skin elevated into ridges continuously moistened by glandular activity affords maximum natural friction. Friction ridges make it possible for the fingers and palms to hold objects; they increase the friction between the skin and the object handled; they make for better contact. Without the moistened friction ridges, it would be difficult to pick up or hold light objects. Friction ridges are found on the palmar and plantar skin surfaces of all primates.

Friction ridges begin to form on the human fetus during the third and fourth months of fetal life, when the fetus is at least 90 mm in sitting height (Miller, 1968). The ridges begin as raised apertures around the pores and then are joined together into rows forming the ridges. The pores may open anywhere across the ridge surface, but they are most often found near the midline. A pore near the edge is the exception. Pores may also open on the skin surface apart from the ridges, with only a single raised aperture. A single pore appears as a dot in a fingerprint. In some instances, only two or three pore apertures may fuse together, forming a short ridge.

Pores are the openings of the sweat gland ducts and number about 2,700 per square inch on the palmar and plantar surfaces of the body. The depressions between the ridges are called *furrows*. They appear in an inked fingerprint as the white or blank spaces between the lines made by the ridges. Figure 2 is a diagrammatic sketch of a cross section of a friction ridge. The furrows are the sloping edges on either side of the ridge which, as a rule, are flat.

When the skin is damaged to the extent that both the epidermis and the dermis are disturbed, a permanent scar may result with attendant alteration of the ridges involved. A permanent scar may be recognized in a fingerprint by the characteris-

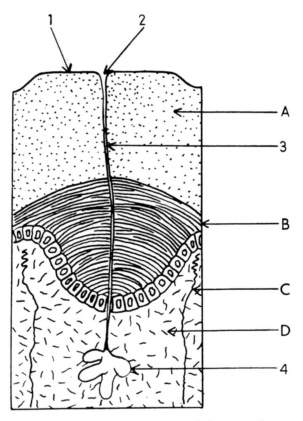

Figure 2. Diagrammatic sketch of a section of skin. Papillary system: (1) ridge surface, (2) pore, (3) duct, and (4) sweat gland. Papillary skin: (A) epidermis, (B) stratum mucosum, (C) nerve, and (D) dermis.

tic curl or puckering of the ridge endings on either side of the scar. The ridge endings on either side of a temporary scar or crease end abruptly and are straight, with the ridge endings pointing toward the continuation of the ridges on the other side of the temporary scar or crease. Scars provide additional and valuable means of identification. They may have a bearing on classification, depending upon the extent of damage to the ridges and to the pattern area upon which classification is based.

3
FRICTION RIDGES ARE THE BASIS OF IDENTIFICATION

The friction ridges of the fingers form patterns divided or classified into three major groups of patterns: arches, loops, and whorls. About 60 percent of all fingerprint patterns are loops, 35 percent whorls, and 5 percent arches. Classification of fingerprints by pattern types is only one stage in the process of identification. Pattern types are class characteristics, as all fingerprints within a particular pattern-type grouping meet the classification requirements for that group.

Positive identification, or elimination, of fingerprints is dependent upon the individual ridge characteristics in a fingerprint, their relative position to each other, and whether or not there are any dissimilar characteristics that cannot be explained. Figure 3 is a line-drawing sketch of the different types of individual ridge characteristics upon which an identification may be based.

There is no common agreement among authorities in the field of fingerprint identification of the different types of ridge characteristics or their terminology. The Standardization Committee of the International Association for Identification recommended that only five types of ridge characteristics be accepted as standard: ridge endings, bifurcations, short ridges, enclosures, and islands (dots). Osterburg (1964) recommends ten types of ridge characteristics which, in addition to the aforementioned, are: deltas, bridges, double bifurcations, trifurcations, and spurs

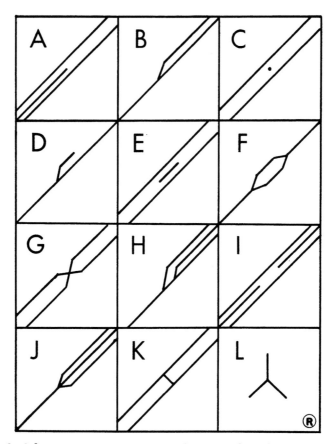

Figure 3. Schematic representation of friction ridge characteristics. (A) ridge ending, (B) bifurcation, (C) dot, (D) spur, (E) short ridge, (F) enclosure, (G) ridge crossing, (H) double bifurcation, (I) ridge break, (J) trifurcation, (K) bridge, and (L) triradius.

(hooks). Others may wish to include prominently diverging ridges, recurving ridges, and incipient, or nascent, ridges as additional types of ridge characteristics.

Basically, there are only three types of ridge characteristics; all other characteristics are combinations of one or more of these three basic types. The three basic types of ridge characteristics are ridge endings, bifurcations, and dots. Thus, a short ridge is two ridge endings, and a spur is a bifurcation and a ridge ending. However, a spur is certainly more uncommon than either a ridge ending or a bifurcation. Consideration must be given to characteristics that are less common than others.

The terminology for the different ridge characteristics is as varied as the choice of types of characteristics. One fingerprint examiner may call a ridge that splits into two ridges a bifurcation, while another may term that particular characteristic a forking ridge. The differences of opinion regarding the types and terminology of ridge characteristics need not be a matter of any great concern. The resulting conclusion of whether or not a particular print was made by a specific individual is the same, regardless of terminology or definitions of type of characteristics. Essentially, all characteristics, including scars and creases, which appear consistently from one fingerprint to another made by the same finger may be used for identification.

4

EVERY FINGER BEARS ITS OWN TRADEMARK

Each of the ten fingers on every person's hands bears its own individual and distinctive trademark in its ridge pattern and characteristics. No two leaves on a tree are found to be exactly identical in every detail, and no two fingers have ever been found identical in their ridge patterns and characteristics. The basis for this fact may be found in the principle of biological variation, proposed by Charles Darwin, that no two living things are ever exactly alike. This principle is supported by the science of statistics and theories of probability.

The ridges that constitute each person's trademarks go unnoticed in everyday life; they receive no particular attention, but they play a very important role in identification, both civil and criminal. Ironically, the occasions that the attention of the average person is directed towards their trademarks are for the most part associated with criminality and law enforcement and, subconsciously, with the stigma of guilt. However, in many instances, fingerprints may establish innocence.

Figure 4, a photograph of a finger, symbolizes the science of fingerprints and the methods and techniques involved in using

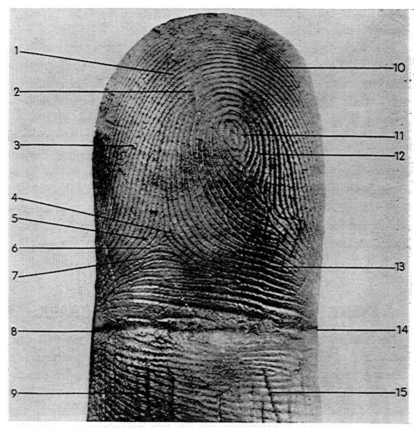

Figure 4. Photograph of a fingertip showing ridge characteristics or "trademarks" by which identification is made. Characteristics pointed out by numbered lines are described in the text.

the ridges to establish identity. The object of the photograph is to create at this early stage a fingerprint consciousness and familiarity in the minds of those whose duty is to search out and recover fingerprint evidence. A number of ridge formations and characteristics are pointed out by the numbered lines around the photograph; the points are explained in the following pages.

FINGER TRADEMARKS

The finger in Figure 4 displays a central pocket loop-type whorl pattern. Characteristics or trademarks are as follows:

1. The ridge patterns on the side of the finger go up one side, around the tip, and down the other side.

2. Skin damage, which is temporary in character and which will not leave a scar, is present.

3. A prominent ridge is broken into segments.

4. A short independent ridge is crowded between two prominent ridges.

5. The upper-type line ridge forms the *upper-type line* in an inked impression. It "tends to surround" the pattern area in an upward direction.

6. The *delta* is a specific point established by definite rules. Deltas are found in all fingerprint patterns except plain arches. They are found between the upper and lower type lines in an inked impression.

7. *Lower-type line* is formed by this ridge in an inked impression. Like the upper-type line, it tends to surround the pattern area in the opposite direction.

8. The *flexion crease* or *fissure* is the most prominent crease in the skin which shows on the face of the finger. There may be one or two or more prominent flexion crease lines at a joint; they are caused by extreme creasing or folding of the skin at the joint to accommodate joint movement.

9. A prominent *tension crease* in the skin. Tension creases below the flexion creases usually are prominent. They may be as characteristic and individualistic as ridge structure.

10. *Counterclockwise bifurcation*. Some ridges divide or fork and make two ridges where one existed before. They are named or described according to the direction they turn: clockwise or counterclockwise.

11. *Central pocket loop*, a small recurving ridge, is seen in the pattern area by which it is determined that the pattern is a central pocket loop-type whorl.

12. *Clockwise bifurcation* or forking of a single ridge to the right. The two forks stop abruptly in front of a ridge at a sharp angle.

13. A *short ridge* is between two long ridges.

14. A *flexion crease* crosses the finger at the joint.

15. Below the flexion crease, the *tension creases* are usually at right angles to the flexion creases and are prominent.

5

FINGERPRINT TERMINOLOGY

The fingerprint pattern in Figure 5 is a *right-slant loop* of *sixteen counts*. It is considered a right-slant loop because both ends of the "innermost recurving ridge" (12) enter and leave the pattern from the same or right side in this instance. The pattern is a sixteen-count loop because sixteen ridges cross an imaginary line between the delta (4) and the core (11) indicated by the

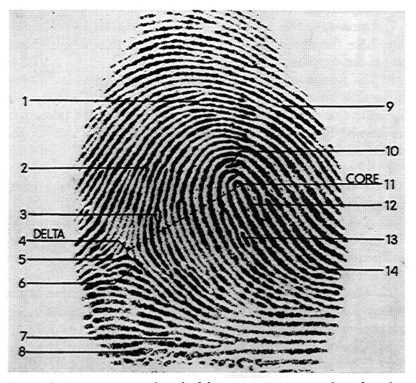

Figure 5. Fingerprints are described by appropriate terms for ridge characteristics. Variations are unlimited in different patterns. Characteristics pointed out by numbered lines are described in text.

broken line C to D. Neither the delta nor the core are included in the count.

The names of the points indicated by numbers in Figure 5 are listed:

1. Clockwise bifurcation
2. Counterclockwise bifurcation
3. Enclosure
4. Delta
5. Lower type line
6. Independent ridge
7. Ridge dot
8. Broken ridge
9. Counterclockwise bifurcation
10. Spur
11. Core
12. Innermost recurving ridge
13. Short ridge
14. Ridge ending

The points named are not to be construed as a complete list of all points appearing in all types of fingerprint patterns. This particular pattern was chosen because it shows many common points used in classification and comparison, and it will familiarize the reader with technical terms.

The delta and core are arbitrary points selected in certain fingerprint patterns according to the type of pattern and the definite rules that apply to the science of classification. Their locations vary in different patterns according to the rules.

6

RIDGE DAMAGE AND DESTRUCTION

Ridge patterns and characteristics are formed on the human fetus before birth, and they remain after death until destroyed by decomposition of the skin. As an individual develops through childhood to maturity, ridge formations and characteristics remain the same, but patterns increase in size as the hand grows. The process may be likened to making contact and projection prints from the same negative—the two prints, contact and projection, remain identical as to detail but differ in size. So do fingerprints during a normal life span. The thickness and clarity of the ridges also increase with maturity but decrease again during old age.

Ridge formation in life is changed only by accident, injury, burns, disease, or other similar causes—or in rare instances, intentionally (Fig. 6). Ridges may be worn or impaired temporarily by occupational pursuits that form callouses or cause wear or damage to the ridges (*see* Fig. 25, Sec. 28). Chemists, photographers, carpenters, bricklayers, electricians, and machinists are but a few whose occupations may result in temporary ridge damage, but the wear or damage is corrected within a reasonable time if given an opportunity.

One case that occurred during World War II is recalled in which a discontented member of a branch of the military forces sandpapered the ridges from all of his fingers. When he was satisfied that it was impossible to obtain classifiable prints, he enlisted in another branch of the service under an assumed name. The artifice worked and he was fingerprinted and accepted in the new branch. Since the prints taken at the time of the second enlistment were unclassifiable, the recruit was fingerprinted about three weeks later after the skin damage had healed. The recruit's past quickly caught up with him.

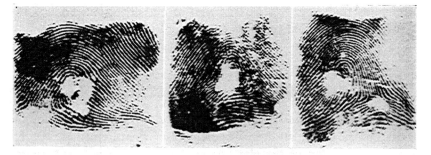

Figure 6. Fingerprints are changed intentionally in rare cases. John Dillinger had all ten fingers mutilated in an effort to conceal his identity—the attempt was a failure. Location of scars would lead one to believe a deliberate attempt was made to eradicate cores and deltas.

Other attempts to deliberately alter and obliterate fingerprints have proved equally unsuccessful though somewhat painful for the person making the attempts. John Dillinger, the notorious criminal of the Great Depression, tried to remove his fingerprints with acid while others have tried intentional scarring, skin grafting, and surgical planing ("The Question of Print Removal by Surgical Planing," 1958). The absence of fingerprints serves only to arouse immediate suspicion and marks the individual as unique. Other identification methods may then be employed to tentatively identify the individual, and positive identification may be effected by comparison of the ridge characteristics on the second joint of the finger with those in the plain impression blocks of the fingerprint card.

7
FINGERPRINT CLASSIFICATION

It is not the purpose of this book to explain or to make a study of the science of fingerprint classification. That is a specialized study best learned from a manual or textbook on classification. There are several excellent and authoritative manuals, textbooks, and correspondence courses to aid the beginner on fingerprint classification. However, as in any field or endeavor, practical experience is essential for accuracy and speed. Anyone desiring a sound, practical knowledge of fingerprints should, in addition to their studies, attend the fingerprint classification course of the Federal Bureau of Investigation. This forty-hour course is periodically scheduled at the request of local law enforcement agencies at various locations in each state.

The first English language text on classification was a book written by Sir Edward Richard Henry, titled *Classification and Uses of Fingerprints* (1901), in which the *Henry system* of classification is explained. The present system of classification used in the United States is based on the Henry system, but it has been found necessary to develop many extensions and refinements to properly handle the increased number of fingerprint records on file today. The purpose of a classification system is to facilitate the filing, searching, and retrieval of fingerprint records. The Henry system is based on the classification of an individual's ten fingers; therefore, many agencies also maintain five-finger and single-finger systems as a means of identifying latent fingerprints from crime scenes.

Automation of the tasks of classifying, searching, storing, and retrieving fingerprint information has been a goal long sought by agencies with extensive fingerprint files. Recent advances in electronic data processing has added emphasis to the research in automation. The concepts in automation range from computerized storage and retrieval systems to computerized systems that would also include classification, searching, and optical pattern recognition techniques to identify single fingerprints. Realization of a fully automated system still remains in the future; however, advances such as the *Automated Identification Division System* (AIDS) of the Federal Bureau of Investigation, indicates that future is not too far distant.

A person who is thoroughly familiar with classification of fingerprints and knows the rules or steps involved in classification makes a better fingerprint technician than one who knows noth-

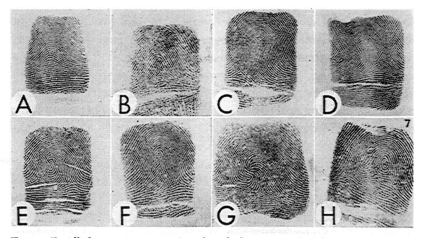

Figure 7. All fingerprints may be classified in one of eight pattern types, which are shown: (A) arch, (B) tented arch, (C) right-slant loop, (D) left-slant loop, (E) plain whorl, (F) central pocket loop, (G) double loop, and (H) accidental.

ing of classification. If he knows what constitutes a fingerprint and what is required for classification, he will obtain better fingerprint impressions. This fact is readily recognized by examining prints taken by a person unfamiliar with classification. The best inked impressions are obtained under circumstances where the person who takes the impressions is responsible for their proper classification. Such impressions are invariably of better quality and they are taken with much greater care.

8
SPACE VALUES ON FINGERPRINT CARDS

For purposes of classification, the ten individual spaces on a standard fingerprint card are given arbitrary values. The values have no significance in the mechanics of fingerprints or fingerprint processes, but in the study of fingerprints, *space value* is often mentioned, and it is important that the technician know the meaning of the term.

Under the Henry system of classification, which is used by most law enforcement departments in the United States, the primary division of the classification is determined by assigning arbitrary values to certain types of patterns when they appear in particular spaces on a fingerprint card. Classification or description of any group of objects, whether they are fingerprints or firearms, are dependent upon descriptive values which apply thereto; for example, caliber, make, number, type, and finish, etc., may be applied to firearms, whereas fingerprints are classified by other and different values. One of those used in fingerprint classification is an arbitrary value assigned to certain types of patterns called *whorls*. The value changes according to the position or space occupied on the fingerprint card.

It is worthwhile for a fingerprint technician who is not fully familiar with classification to know how the primary division of the classification is deduced. It is sufficiently simple that a novice can pick it up in a few minutes.

There are ten spaces for individual rolled impressions on a fingerprint card, and if a whorl appears in either the right thumb or right index finger space, the space is given a value of *sixteen*. If any other type of pattern appears in those two spaces, the value is considered as nil—no value. If a whorl-type pattern appears in either of the next two spaces, the right middle and ring fingers, the spaces are given an arbitrary value of *eight*. Values are given by *pairs* of fingers; right little and left thumb, value of *four*; left index and middle, value of *two*; and finally, the last two fingers, the left ring and little have a space value of *one*. If no whorls appear, the value of any space is zero. By totaling the space value where whorls appear, using every other finger, fingers numbered 1, 3, 5, 7, and 9 and adding an arbitrary 1, the denominator of the primary classification is found. By totaling the space values of the even-numbered fingers 2, 4, 6, 8, and 10 where whorl-type patterns appear, and again adding the arbitrary 1, the numerator of the primary division of the classification is found.

A fingerprint technician should be as well informed as possible about classification; it is a distinct advantage to a person who develops and handles fingerprint evidence. Study of manuals and books dealing with the science of classification is strongly recommended.

9

FINGERPRINT PATTERNS ARE COMPLEX YET SIMPLE

One unfamiliar with fingerprint classification, but knowing that no two fingerprints of two different fingers have ever been found to be identical, would get the impression that classification would be like learning the characters of the Chinese alphabet, and that it would be extremely difficult, or almost impossible, to accurately classify so many fingerprints all different or to develop a system whereby any pattern could definitely and quickly be placed in one particular class of patterns.

A fingerprint may be examined a few seconds and placed in one of three groups of patterns, namely (1) arches, (2) loops, and (3) whorls. Arches are subdivided into two types, plain and tented; loops into right slant or left slant, more specifically radial or ulnar loops, depending on which hand they are found; and whorls are subclassified into four whorl types as shown below, making in all *eight* types of patterns. Accordingly, all prints may be placed in one of the three following groups and eight types (Fig. 7):

ARCH	LOOP	WHORL
1. Plain arch	1. Ulnar loop	1. Plain whorl
2. Tented arch	2. Radial loop	2. Double loop whorl
		3. Central pocket loop whorl
		4. Accidental whorl

After fingerprints are grouped and typed as indicated above, they are further described as to certain details of structure according to very specific rules. Clarification or extension of the classification makes it more complete and descriptive of the fingers.

Since classification is not the point of this handbook, the above brief descriptions of patterns are mentioned for enlightenment rather than as factors to be dealt with in the mechanics or processing of fingerprints.

10

IDENTICAL AND SIMILAR FINGERPRINTS

It was stated in Section 4 that no two fingerprint patterns of different people's fingers nor two patterns of different fingers of the same person have ever been found to be identical. It might be added for clarification that many finger patterns are similar. There is much misunderstanding regarding the use of the words identical and similar in respect to finger patterns among persons unfamiliar with fingerprint work.

Identical, as used in fingerprint work, is the strictest term for absolute and complete agreement in all details. The words *same* and *matching* are often used synonymously with *identical*, but with a different meaning and in a much looser sense when pertaining to number, amount, magnitude, value, and the like; identical means *exactly alike in every detail.* To be identical, two fingerprints must have ridges alike, the same number of ridges, the ridges must correspond in every detail, they must be the same kind, in the same position, and with the same relationship one to another in respect to position. The term *identical* is rarely used in fingerprint identification, as the words *same* and *matching* better describe most prints.

Figure 8 shows two sets of thumbprints made by two different persons; the two left-hand patterns were made by one person

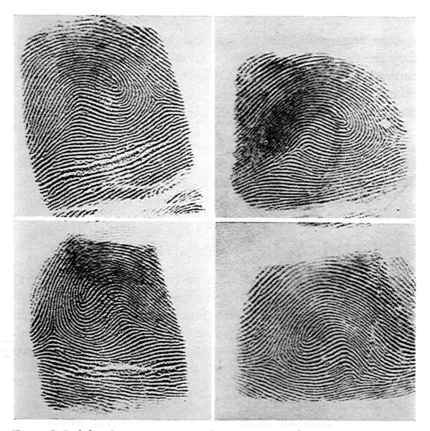

Figure 8. Left-hand impressions are of one person; right two are of another. Pattern types are common, and they illustrate similarity, but they are not identical.

and the right-hand by another. They illustrate the meaning of identical and similar very clearly. The prints are very unusual loop types, and the looping ridges are similar in each man's fingers. Fingerprint examiners will recognize immediately the unusual, yet similar, pattern types. To a casual observer, the prints would appear to be the same, but closer inspection discloses that ridge characteristics are vastly different. No two ridges and no two points or characteristics can be found to correspond identically in both pairs. They are different in every detail—they are similar but not identical.

Confusion of the term identical and similar has often led to erroneous reports in the public press that the fingerprints of identical twins have been found that are identical (Fig. 9). In

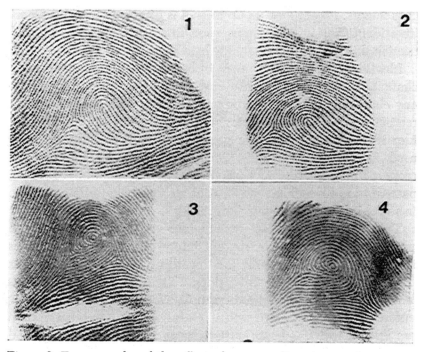

Figure 9. Two examples of the effect of pressure distortion on the appearance of fingerprints. The fingerprints in (1) and (2) were made by the same finger, as were those in (3) and (4). A layman would discard the prints on their appearance alone, but a fingerprint examiner can quickly establish identity by comparison by the individual ridge characteristics.

every such instance, further examination by qualified fingerprint examiners has proven that the allegedly identical prints were in fact only similar and as individualistic as any other person's prints. What often occurs in these cases is that the filing formulas are identical, not the prints themselves.

11

THE SCIENCE OF FINGERPRINT IDENTIFICATION

The science of fingerprint identification and the science of fingerprint classification are closely related but are not the same. *Fingerprint classification* is the filing, searching, and retrieval of fingerprint records and is usually based on all ten of an individual's fingers. *Fingerprint identification* is directed toward the positive identification of an impression made by a specific area of friction skin as having been made by a specific individual.

Identification of fingerprints is based upon distinctive ridge characteristics and their relationship to each other. Essentially, any characteristics that correspond in type, position, and overall relationship to other characteristics in the print can be used for identification purposes. The general and specific pattern types used in classification assist in identification by limiting the scope of inquiry. However, identification cannot be based on pattern type alone, and classification may provide little assistance in searching for fragmentary impressions.

The mechanics of fingerprints involves the techniques and procedures used to recover latent impressions from crime scenes and evidentiary items and the recording of inked impressions for comparison with latent prints. Fingerprint mechanics falls within the scope and duties of almost every investigator and law enforcement officer. Fingerprint classification and identification are limited to trained specialists who also have a knowledge and experience in fingerprint mechanics.

The more legible a fingerprint is, the easier it is to make a comparison and establish positive identification. If either the known or suspected prints are smudges or if for any reason detail is not clear, an identification may be impossible. Many laymen and law enforcement officers are unaware of this fact. To them a fingerprint is a mark made by a finger, whether or not it shows ridge detail. A fingerprint that shows no ridge detail is worthless for positive identification except for whatever other facts it may reveal about the crime.

There are only three possible conclusions that may be made from comparisons of two separate fingerprints: (1) both were made by the same finger, (2) both were not made by the same finger, or (3) there is insufficient clarity or detail in one or both of the prints to make any conclusion. In some instances, a smudged or blurred print may not be sufficient for positive identification but may be a basis for elimination. A smudged print on a murder weapon may lack sufficient ridge characteristics to establish positive identification of the print, but if the pattern type is still discernible, it may be possible to eliminate a suspect. For example, if the latent print is obviously a loop-type pattern and the suspect has all whorls on his fingers, the latent print could not have been made by the suspect even though it is not suitable for identification purposes.

While surface and size are important criteria in deciding what surfaces will be processed for latent prints at crime scenes, an investigator must not become negligent in processing objects for latent prints because of their surface and size, or many suitable impressions may be lost. Brooks (1971) has termed this laxity *the fallacy of surface and size*. As previously mentioned, ridge characteristics and not pattern types are the basis for identification. Therefore, it is possible to recover identifiable latent prints from relatively small areas and establish an identification (Speaks, 1971).

12

CHARACTERISTICS AND POSITION OF CHARACTERISTICS

Two elements enter into proof of identity of fingerprints: (1) characteristics and (2) position of characteristics. A list of many common ridge characteristics, such as bifurcations, ridge endings, and dots, etc., appears in Section 3. Occasionally, fingerprint examiners may refer to ridge characteristics as *Galton details* and *points; the terms are synonymous.*

When a comparison is made of two fingerprints suspected of having been made by the same finger, for example, a latent from a crime scene and a known inked impression, identification depends upon ridge characteristics and the relative position of the characteristics (Fig. 10). Each characteristic must correspond not only in respect to its position on each print but also to its position in relation to all other characteristics in both prints. A clockwise bifurcation in the latent must correspond to a clockwise bifurcation in the inked impression, and an upward thrusting ridge ending two ridge lines away from the bifurcation and toward the core of the pattern must also correspond in both prints. Each characteristic must correspond with each other characteristic in the prints with no *unexplainable* dissimilar characteristics.

Possibilities in position are limitless: Countless thousands of positions exist in every fingerprint. Every characteristic has a par-

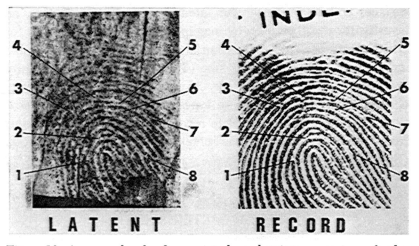

Figure 10. An example of a fingerprint chart showing comparison of ridge characteristics between the latent print and the inked impressions. In this instance, some, but not all, of the characteristics are charted.

ticular position relationship to all others. When proving identity of two patterns, specific characteristics in definite positions are pointed out in one pattern; they are shown to correspond to characteristics and positions in another pattern. Several characteristics are selected; if it can be shown that the same characteristics appear in the same relative positions in both patterns and in the same relationship to each other, the patterns are said to have been made by the same finger.

Many times, to the untrained eye, two different fingerprints may not appear even similar when, in fact, they were made by the same finger. Sometimes a ridge ending in one print may appear as a bifurcation in another print made by the same finger due to excessive inking or foreign material on the fingers, or lack of proper inking may cause a bifurcation to appear as a ridge ending. Excessive pressure and the nature of the receiving surface may superficially alter the apparent relative positions of the characteristics, but their relationship to each other will remain the same. For example, a latent print on a curved surface, such as a doorknob, may not appear identical to a print on a flat fingerprint card due to distortion by pressure and the nature of the receiving surface. It is factors such as these that necessitate a close examination of ridge details and their relative position to each other and not overall appearance and pattern type.

13

NUMBER OF CHARACTERISTICS REQUIRED FOR IDENTIFICATION

There is no valid scientific basis for requiring a minimum number of ridge characteristics which must be present in two fingerprints in order to establish positive identification. The Standardization Committee of the International Association for Identification completed a three-year study in 1973 on the question of establishing minimum standards for ridge characteristics. The report of this committee, adopted by resolution of the association, was that no valid basis exists for such a requirement.

There is no valid scientific basis for requiring a minimum number of ridge characteristics which must be present in two fingerprints in order to establish positive identification. It is necessary to emphasize and reemphasize this statement in order to dispel misconceptions regarding minimum characteristics and the frequently quoted twelve-point standard or rule. Some countries in Europe adopted standards requiring a minimum number of characteristics, but these standards are without a valid scientific basis and were adopted prior to any meaningful experience in dealing with large numbers of fingerprint files. While the origin of the twelve-point standard is somewhat obscure, it probably originated from the writing of the French criminalist, Edmond Locard (Kingston, 1965), and there is no indication of any scientific basis for the standard.

One theory of the origin of the twelve-point standard has been advanced by Kingston and Kirk (1965). They suspected that it was a reaction to the failure of the Bertillon system of identification, which was eventually replaced by fingerprints. Whereas the Bertillon system was based on eleven body measurements, the reasoning may have been to require at least one more characteristic for the system which supplanted the discredited one. This view is a logical explanation of the origin of the standard and, if true, illustrates the lack of a valid scientific basis.

There are only three basic types of ridge characteristics: bifurcations, ridge endings, and dots, and each of these basic types may be considered a point. Other types of characteristics are formed by combinations of one or two of the three basic types. An enclosure is formed by two bifurcations, a spur by a bifurcation and a ridge ending, etc.; therefore, these other characteristics are actually two characteristics.

Several other factors must also be considered in fingerprint identification: rarity of pattern type, frequency of the ridge characteristic for the particular pattern type, and the presence or absence of dissimilar characteristics that cannot be satisfactorily explained. The first two factors serve primarily as an aid in searching for an impression, while the third is essential to positive identification. If the pattern type of a suspect fingerprint is a tented arch, the fingerprint examiner can eliminate all other pattern types in his search for the matching inked impression. In some instances, the type of characteristic may facilitate searching for the matching inked impression. Experienced fingerprint examiners note that certain ridge characteristics appear with greater frequency in one type of pattern than in others; for example, enclosures are more common in whorl-type than in arch- or loop-type patterns. This does not mean that they do not appear in the other pattern types, just that they appear more frequently in whorl pattern types. Therefore, even though the pattern type may not be apparent in a latent, an examiner may search the whorls first when he has three or four adjacent enclosures.

The absence of unexplainable dissimilar characteristics in a fingerprint is essential for positive identification, but sometimes a characteristic may appear dissimilar to the layman and can be satisfactorily explained by a qualified examiner who has the experience of comparing thousands of fingerprints. Apparent dissimilar characteristics which can be adequately explained do not detract from a positive identification.

One argument often advanced in support of the individuality of fingerprints is that no two individuals have ever been found who have identical fingerprints. The counterargument advanced is that no one has ever compared the fingerprints of everyone in the world. Both statements are true, but the weight of evidence supports the first. In the entire history of fingerprint identification, no one has successfully challenged the individuality and uniqueness of fingerprints, despite offers of rewards and repeated attempts. Even attempts to demonstrate that fingerprints made by two different fingers have six matching characteristics have been unsuccessful, because of obvious dissimilar characteristics within the same areas.

Fingerprint identification is based on the statistical probability that the chances of two individuals having the same identical ridge characteristics, in the same relative positions, is so remote as to be impossible. Sir Francis Galton made the first scientific study of ridge characteristics and established by means of statistical probability analyses that the fingerprints of no two individuals are identical (1892). In the years since Galton's studies, the exact methods for statistical design of experiments and for making statistical inferences have advanced considerably. A recent study, applying modern statistical methods, concluded that the probability of two individuals having twelve identical characteristics in the same relative positions is one in ten million million, or 1 in 10,000,000,000,000 (Osterburg, 1974). This study indicates that the probability for even a fewer number of characteristics would still be sufficiently high enough to support positive identification. The burden of proof rests with those who wish to prove otherwise.

There is no valid scientific basis for requiring a minimum number of ridge characteristics which must be present in two fingerprints in order to establish positive identification.

14

POROSCOPY AND EDGEOSCOPY

In fingerprint work, *poroscopy* is the term applied to a specialized study of pore structure found on the papillary ridges of the skin as a means of identification. The skin on the palmar surfaces of the hands and the plantar surfaces of the feet are covered with ridges, as explained in Section 2. Papillary skin contains an average of 2,700 sweat glands per square inch, and each gland opens through a duct onto the ridge surface. An opening at the ridge surface is called a *pore*. It is slightly funnel shaped, and it is continuously active in excreting sweat, which evaporates quickly on exposure to air.

Poroscopy is an extension or refinement of the science of identification by ridge characteristics. Pore structure of papillary skin is as characteristic of the skin as ridges, but because of the microscopic nature of the pores and the fact that they are not commonly reproduced by ordinary physical methods of development, their presence in an impression cannot be depended upon. They are seen in powdered images occasionally, but they are revealed in chemically developed images more often. Pore structure is revealed most satisfactorily by the ninhydrin and silver nitrate latent fingerprint techniques.

In ordinary powder development, powder particles may "fill in" the pores even though they are present in a latent print. In iodine development, the sweat tends to "spread" in a blotterlike fashion, resulting, in time, in loss of the microscopic, pore structure.

The fingerprint in the photograph of Figure 11 is unusual in that the pores are prominent. Figure 11B is an enlarged photograph of the ridges in the center of the pattern. The enlargement shows characteristic irregularity of occurrence, position, and shape.

If a fingertip is pressed backward gently under a strong light

Figure 11. Pores afford a positive means of identification. (A) Prominent pores in a fingerprint pattern. (B) An enlarged section of the core area showing pore structure in detail.

and the friction ridges are observed closely a short time, tiny globules of sweat may be seen as they come to the surface of the ridges or the openings of the pores where they quickly evaporate on exposure to the air. They originate in the sweat glands and shine momentarily on the surface of the ridge before vanishing. The process is continuous. When a person is under an emotional strain, for example, when committing a crime, the tempo of the process may be stepped up. The result of increased activity of sweat glands is sometimes seen on objects which have been handled at crime scenes.

Figure 12 shows an inked-finger impression, which is unusual in that pore structure is conspicuously absent. This does not mean that pores do not exist in this case; their absence is perhaps due to the fact that they are very tiny, or that they were inactive, or both. Ridge and pore characteristics vary greatly with individuals; they are present in all fingers, although they may be inconspicuous in some. Most inked impressions reveal visible traces of pores; some are microscopic or perhaps invisible to the unaided eye, but in most instances, if a finger is properly inked, pore structure is visible in an inked impression. Developing prints with powder so that pores are visible is another matter, as previously discussed.

Most inked impressions reveal the presence of pores somewhat between those shown in Figures 11 and 12. The two impressions are extremes; one shows prominent pore structures and the other shows none.

Pores may be lost by photographic processes. For example, if the finger impression in Figure 11 were photographed with a film of extreme contrast, such as Kodalith®, overexposed, and a print made, the pores would be lost in the process. In the language of the photographer, they would be "blocked out." When pore structure is photographed, care must be taken to avoid its loss by the use of proper negative and paper materials and photographic process.

Careful inspection of the photograph in Figure 12 reveals that the pores have not been blocked out. In the blocking-out process, the ridges spread out and obscure the adjacent areas, in-

Figure 12. Pores may not be visible in some inked impressions; they are present in all papillary skin, although they do not always show in inked or latent impressions.

cluding the pores. Sharp definition is lost between ridges and intervening spaces, or ridges and pores tend to disappear. The photograph is an excellent reproduction of the original inked impression used in this case.

Poroscopy was first practiced by Edmond Locard, who also made what may be the only identification based solely upon pore structure (O'Hara and Osterburg, 1949). Identification by pore structure alone is an extremely difficult and time-consuming task, considering the number of pores that must be searched (2,700 per square inch) and requires inked impressions of superior quality. The best and most practical approach is the use of poroscopy as an adjunct to identification by ridge characteristics when only a few ridge characteristics are available for comparison.

Edgeoscopy is a term applied to the study of the characteristics formed by the sides or edges of papillary ridges as a means of identification. Like poroscopy, edgeoscopy is an extension of identification by ridge characteristics, and the characteristics are microscopic in nature. Papillary ridges are formed during fetal life, first as apertures around the pores and then are joined together into rows forming the ridges. These ridges have irregular edges as individualistic and unique as pore and ridge characteristics.

Both the concept and term edgeoscopy were developed by S. K. Chatterjee (1963) of India, who defined the edge characteristics of papillary ridges as follows:
1. Straight
2. Convex
3. Peak—the edge protrudes and the protrusion has a broad base and pointed top
4. Table—the edge has a protrusion with a narrow base and a broad flat top
5. Pocket—the edge looks like a pocket with a narrow opening. This characteristic is formed by a single pore with one side not completely enclosed by the ridge.
6. Concave
7. Angle
8. Infinite—any characteristics other than those mentioned above

Edgeoscopy is similar to poroscopy in that it may rarely be used as a basis for identification without being considered as an adjunct to ridge formations. The problem of adequate inked impressions for comparison and the difficult task of comparison of so many possible characteristics makes edgeoscopy impractical as the sole means of identification. Considering the difficulties that may be expected in developing techniques and pressure distortion, the possible applications of edgeoscopy are extremely limited. There is no publicized case of an actual identification based on edgeoscopy. However, as previously stated, any characteristic which appears in more than one print made by the same finger may be used to establish identification.

Figure 13 is a fingerprint showing good pore and edge structure in the ridges. The fragmentary ridge depicted in the photograph on the bottom is an enlargement of a portion of one of the ridges in the top print. It can be easily located in the fingerprint by either pore or edge structure, but the task gives some idea of the difficulty of trying to locate the same area if its position on the hands or feet is unknown.

Figure 13. Photograph of an inked fingerprint showing exceptionally clear ridge and pore structure. A portion of a ridge located six ridges to the right of the core has been enlarged to illustrate the characteristics of ridge edges.

15

PALMPRINTS ARE USED TO ESTABLISH IDENTITY

Many investigators have asked whether palmprints can be used to establish identity or as evidence in a case the same as fingerprints. The answer is definitely, yes. Palmprints are not normally recorded and filed for identification purposes, but an increasing number of law enforcement agencies are doing so. Until a practical palmprint classification system was developed (Alexander, 1973), palmprints were normally filed by the person's name, with the fingerprint cards, or by *modus operandi.* It is a good practice to take major case prints from all suspects, victims, and important witnesses in investigations of serious offenses.

The same definitions, procedures, and techniques that apply to fingerprint identification and fingerprint mechanics apply in every respect to palmprints. The evidential value of the latter is equal to fingerprint evidence. With respect to ridge characteristics and pore and ridge edge structure, palmprints afford a means of positive identification in exactly the same manner as fingerprints.

Palmprint evidence is sought just as diligently as fingerprints by investigators at crime scenes. No distinction is made between the two from the standpoint of evidence.

An experienced fingerprint examiner would rather work with palmprints than fingerprints in proving identity. Comparisons are less common, because palmprint evidence is less frequently encountered in investigations, and inked palm impressions are seldom routinely taken.

In the great majority of instances, when objects are picked up or handled, they are touched almost exclusively by the fingers. Palmprints are most frequently discovered on bulky or heavy objects carried or moved or at the point of entry in a burglary. The size or weight of the object necessitates increased contact with hand areas or more than the fingertips provide. The sides or edges of palmprints are commonly found on documentary evidence containing writings of the suspect. These statements may be checked very quickly by making a personal observation. When you, the reader, pick up the next ten to fifteen objects, make a mental note of how many times the palms come into contact with the objects.

In Figure 14, it is noted that the flexion creases are prominent and that there are definite pattern flows by the ridges. All these points are conspicuous and are at times helpful when one is trying to determine what portion of the palm or fingers made ridge patterns found at a crime scene. An experienced examiner can

Figure 14. Papillary skin covers the complete palmar surface of the hands. Palm ridges are often used to establish identity; any area of friction-ridged skin may be used for identification purposes.

determine the approximate area that made an impression with a relatively small partial latent impression.

The thumbprint in Figure 15, when compared with the impression of the same thumb in Figure 14, shows that the thumb must be taken independently when a complete palm is wanted. The sides or edges of the palms should also be taken.

If the palmprint in Figure 14 is turned upside down and examined at a spot under the ring finger, a ridge formation which approximates a loop is seen. It has all the essential fundamentals of a loop-type pattern. A delta on either the right- or left-hand side may be selected to make the pattern a right- or left-slant loop. A partial latent palmprint made by only this area could be mistaken for a fingerprint rather than a partial palmprint. Experienced examiners do not overlook such a possibility and are, therefore, exacting in their comparisons.

Figure 15. (A) When a palmprint is taken, the thumb is printed separately to obtain a complete pattern. Some palm areas reveal patterns that look very much like fingerprints. (B) If the palmprint in Figure 14 is examined, this loop pattern is found below the ring finger.

If identifiable fingerprint evidence is found at a crime scene, the investigator may be able to check the evidence against the known prints of a suspect in the fingerprint files of the local law enforcement agency and prove or disprove identity. If the evidence is verified, the investigation is simplified—the suspect may be identified as a result of the evidence prior to his apprehension. Such a shortcut is not always possible with palmprints. Unless the local law enforcement agency was farsighted enough to maintain palmprints as part of their files, comparison and verification must await apprehension of the suspect.

16

PATTERN AREAS, FLEXION, AND TENSION CREASES OF THE PALMS

The papillary ridges of the palms form definite patterns, and the palm may be marked off into distinctive pattern areas or *zones*. The purpose of designating pattern areas on the palms may be for classification or simply for describing identifying ridge structure. The greater the understanding of the general pattern flow and configuration of the different pattern areas of the hand, the easier it is for an examiner to recognize which area of the hand made a specific latent impression, thereby expediting the comparison work.

Certain terms are common to all palmprints and are used to denote direction rather than position. An understanding of these terms aids in understanding the terminology of the pattern areas.

Distal—farthest from the center or point of attachment; terminal

Medial—at or near the center

Proximal—situated nearest the point of attachment

Radial—near the radius, the smaller of the two bones of the forearm, on the same side as the thumb

Ulnar—near the ulna, the larger of the two bones of the forearm, on the side opposite the thumb

Figure 16 is a photograph of two palmprints with the pattern areas marked off for explanation. Both palmprints are impressions of the same palm; one has been photographically reversed to provide a mirror image of the other. The pattern flow and configuration of each area is readily apparent. The Roman numerals in the figure represent the *interdigital spaces* located between the delta formations at the base of the fingers. The pattern areas or zones are named as follows:

A. Palmar zone—the area at the base of the fingers.

B. Thenar zone—the large cushion area of the palm at the base of the thumb. Latent impressions of this area are commonly found on objects requiring grasping by the entire hand to properly handle, for example, hammers, rifle stocks, and pipes used as weapons, etc.

C. Hypothenar zone—the large cushion area of the palm at the base of the little finger. Latent impressions of this area may commonly be found on questioned documents bearing the handwriting of the suspect.

D. Carpal delta zone—the area of the palm containing a delta

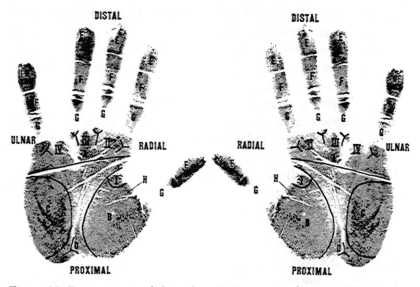

Figure 16. Pattern areas of the palms. Pattern areas designated by the letters are described in text.

formation nearest the wrist. Latent impressions of this area are not commonly found at crime scenes but may appear on window sills and counter tops when a suspect has required support for climbing.

E. Fingerprint pattern area—the area on the ball of the fingertips. This is the primary surface of the hand used for grasping objects and accounts for the most common type of papillary ridge impressions found at crime scenes.

F. Medial phalangeal zone—the second or middle joint of the finger.

G. Proximal phalangeal zone—the area or finger joint located adjacent to the palm.

H. Pattern vistige.

Flexion and tension creases on the palm assist in identification primarily as a means of providing a quick reference point to begin a comparison of ridge characteristics. Flexion creases represent the sites of attachment of the skin to underlying structures and enable the skin to fold during grasping and movement by the hand. Figure 17 is a photograph of a palmprint of a left hand, and the flexion creases have been marked off. They are named as follows:

1. Distal interphalangeal flexion creases
2. Medial interphalangeal flexion creases
3. Proximal interphalangeal flexion creases, more commonly referred to as metacarpophalangeal creases
4. Radial longitudinal flexion crease
5. Distal interphalangeal flexion creases
6. Proximal interphalangeal flexion creases or metacarpophalangeal creases
7. Proximal transverse flexion crease
8. Distal transverse flexion crease
9. Ring creases: These are not flexion creases but may also appear with prominence on the hand due to prolonged wearing of finger rings.

Flexion creases are prominent features of the palm, even more obvious to the casual observer than the ridge formations. Other creases also appear on the palm and phalanges, usually in

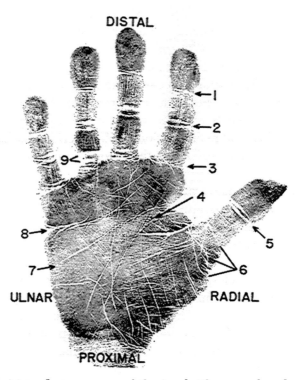

Figure 17. Major flexion creases of the hand. These numbered creases are described in the text.

crisscrossing patterns or at right angles to the ridges. These secondary creases are known as tension creases and are not normally found on the hands at birth. Similar to flexion creases, tension creases may assist as reference points when comparing two impressions. Many examiners have noted an increased frequency in the number of tension creases in the prints of women; however, this is a generality which cannot be used to establish sex by means of finger- or palmprints alone. There is no scientific method of positively establishing sex, race, or criminality solely by friction ridge impressions.

17
FOOTPRINTS

The soles of the feet, like fingers and palms, are covered with papillary ridges and pores. Only one member of the foot usually reveals a classifiable pattern similar to a fingerprint when an inked impression is taken of the foot; that is the great toe. Its pattern is much like a plain inked impression of a finger except for the absence of a flexion crease. Complete arch, loop, and whorl patterns appear on all the toes, but due to their position and the relatively small areas touching the surface stepped or walked upon, the other toes do not leave complete impressions of their pattern formations—only partial impressions of the tips of these toes. Therefore, any system of classification based on all ten toes would present obtacles and prove impractical.

There have been several footprint classification systems devised and based on the ridge patterns on the ball of the foot. The FBI developed a system for classifying footprints as a special file for those persons who have suffered the loss of fingers. The United States Air Force has maintained footprints in the files of their flight personnel as a means for establishing identity of deceased personnel in aircraft accidents. The flight boot normally protects the foot from complete destruction, thereby enabling identification of a victim when it is otherwise impossible (Fig. 18).

Figure 19 is a photograph of a set of footprints with the pattern areas of each foot marked off and indicated by letters. Whereas direction is indicated in palmprints by the bones of the forearm, in footprints, the bones of the lower leg are used to indicate direction. The tibial side of a footprint is the inner side, named for the *tibia,* the inner and larger of the two bones of the lower leg. The fibular side of a footprint is the outside portion, from the *fibula,* the outside and smaller of the two bones of the lower leg. The terms *distal* and *proximal* have the same

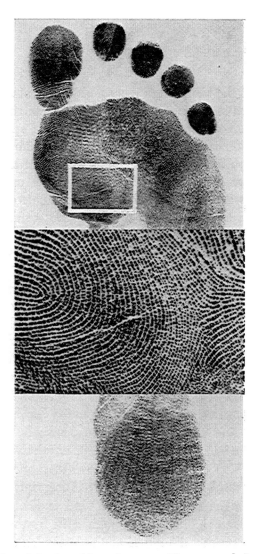

Figure 18. Soles of the feet, like palms, are ridge covered. Inset is area out-lined by rectangle.

meaning as for palmprints. The pattern areas of the feet are as follows:

A. Ball pattern zone

B. Plantar pattern zone

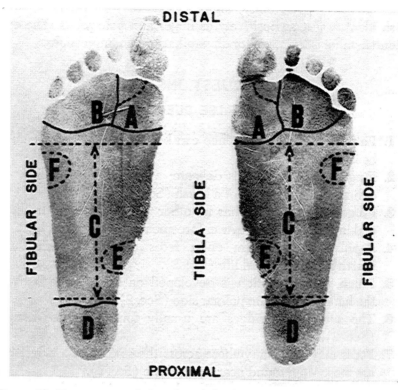

Figure 19. Pattern areas of the soles of the feet. Pattern areas are designated by letters and are described in text.

C. Tread area or medial pattern zone
D. Calcar pattern zone
E. Rare tibial pattern zone
F. Rare fibular pattern zone

The interdigital spaces between the deltas at the base of the toes may be designated with Roman numerals in the same manner as with palmprints, beginning with the delta at the base of the great toe.

Flexion and tension creases also appear in footprints and, as for palmprints, may assist in identification by providing reference points to begin comparisons of ridge details. Footprint evidence is rarely found at crime scenes, but investigators must be alert for every possibility, for footprints may be used to establish identity just as positively as finger and palmprints. The evidential value is the same for all papillary ridge impressions.

QUESTIONS

TRUE-FALSE QUESTIONS

1. Latent fingerprint evidence can be developed, but it cannot be intensified (Sec. 1).
2. Fingerprint evidence is delicate; a powdered print may be obliterated by a stroke of a brush (Sec. 1).
3. Fingerprint evidence has no other application than in criminal investigations by law enforcement agencies (Sec. 1).
4. Papillary ridges form on a fetus during the third and fourth months of fetal life (Sec. 2).
5. Much greater friction is developed on skin on the back of the hand than on the palmar side (Sec. 2).
6. The surfaces of ridges are usually found in cross section (Sec. 2).
7. Pores may occur anywhere across the surface of a ridge, but are most often found near the midline (Sec. 2).
8. A permanent scar may result when the epidermis but not the dermis layer of skin is damaged (Sec. 2).
9. Fingerprint patterns serve the purposes of the investigator, but friction ridges do not (Sec. 3).
10. There is common agreement among authorities of the exact definitions and types of ridge characteristics (Sec. 3).
11. A trifurcation is one of the three basic types of ridge characteristics (Sec. 3).
12. Fingerprint patterns and characteristics of two fingers of the same individual are on rare occasions found to be identical (Secs. 4 and 10).
13. Fingerprints may be used in criminal investigations only to establish guilt (Sec. 4).
14. Fingerprint patterns increase in size between childhood and maturity (Sec. 6).

15. Occupational damage to ridge formations is usually temporary, and the damage may be corrected in time if given an opportunity (Sec. 6).

16. The Henry system of fingerprint classification is based on all ten of an individual's fingers (Sec. 7).

17. A knowledge of fingerprint classification is not particularly useful unless a person's duties also include classifying fingerprints (Secs. 7 and 8).

18. The terms *identical* and *similar* may be used interchangeably (Sec. 10).

19. Positive identification of fingerprints may be made by pattern type alone (Sec. 11).

20. The more legible a fingerprint, the easier it is to make a comparison and establish positive identification (Sec. 11).

21. An obvious dissimilar ridge characteristic appearing in a latent but not in an inked impression does not interfere with positive identification (Sec. 13).

22. There is no valid scientific basis for requiring a minimum number of ridge characteristics which must be present in two fingerprints in order to establish positive identification (Sec. 13).

23. Some European countries have adopted minimum standards regarding a minimum number of ridge characteristics, based on a scientific analysis of ridge characteristics and their frequency of distribution within fingerprint pattern areas (Sec. 13).

24. Powder development of latent prints usually fills or covers the pores even though they may be present in the print (Sec. 14).

25. The result of increased activity of sweat glands is sometimes seen on objects handled by suspects at crime scenes (Sec. 14).

26. Pore structure in developed latents may be lost to view in photographic prints through improper photographic processes (Sec. 14).

27. Darker areas obscure lighter areas in the blocking-out process in photographic processes (Sec. 14).

28. The evidential value of palmprints is not equal to fingerprint evidence (Sec. 15).
29. Impressions of the hypothenar pattern zone of the palm are not commonly found on questioned documents (Sec. 16).
30. Creases in palmprints and footprints are of little or no assistance when making comparisons of friction ridge characteristics (Secs. 16 and 17).

COMPLETION QUESTIONS

31. The ridges on the fingers, palms and soles of the feet are commonly referred to as .... or .... ridges (Sec. 2).
32. The three basic types of ridge characteristics are ...., ..., and .... (Sec. 3).
33. The papillary system consists of ...., ..., ..., and .... (Sec. 2).
34. .... are the basis of fingerprint identification (Sec. 3).
35. A ridge that splits or forks into two ridges is called a ...... (Sec. 3).
36. Ridge formations in life are changed only by ...., ..., ..., ... or other similar causes—or in rare instances, ... (Sec. 6).
37. The .... of fingerprint classification is the basis of the present system used in the United States (Sec. 7).
38. Identical, as used in fingerprint work, is the strictest term for .... and .... agreement in all details (Sec. 10).
39. Two elements that enter into proof of identity of fingerprints are .... and .... (Sec. 12).
40. .... and the nature of the .... may superficially alter the relative positions of ridge characteristics (Sec. 12).
41. The presence or absence of .... dissimilar characteristics is essential for positive identification of fingerprints (Sec. 13).

42. Fingerprint identification is based on the ....
that the chances of two individuals having the same identical ridge characteristics in the same relative positions is so
remote as to be impossible (Sec. 13).

43. In fingerprint work .... is the term applied to a specialized study of sweat gland openings found on the papillary ridges of the skin as a means of identification (Sec. 14).

44. In ordinary powder development, powder particles may fill
in the .... even though they may be present in a latent
print (Sec. 14).

45. .... is the term applied to a study of the characteristics formed by the sides of papillary ridges as a means of
identification (Sec. 14).

46. It is always good practice to take major case prints in investigations of serious offenses from all ...., ..., and
.... (Sec. 15).

47. .... evidence is sought just as diligently as fingerprints
by investigators at crime scenes (Sec. 15).

48. The large cushion area of a palm at the base of the little
finger is referred to as the .... pattern zone (Sec. 16).

49. Papillary ridges may be found on the ...., ...,
and .... (Sec. 17).

50. The tibial side of a footprint is named for the tibia, which
is the .... and .... of the two bones of the lower
leg (Sec. 17).

REFERENCES

Alexander, Harold L. V.: *Classifying Palmprints.* Springfield, Thomas, 1973.

"Amnesia victim identified," *FBI Law Enforcement Bulletin.* vol. 19 (Oct.
1950), p. 16.

Bateson, V.: "Personal identification by means of finger-print impressions,"
British Medical Journal. vol. 1 (1906), p. 1029.

Battley, Harry: "All about fingerprints," *The Police Journal.* vol. 9 (1936),
p. 202.

Beuys, Werner: "The value of fingerprints, apart from the identification of
criminals," *Die Polizei.* vol. 57 (Sept., 1966), p. 41.

Brooks, Andrew J., Jr.: "The fallacy of surface and size," *Fingerprint and
Identification Magazine.* vol. 53 (Nov., 1971), p. 3.

Burks, J. W.: "Alteration of finger prints by dermabrasion," *Fingerprint and Identification Magazine.* vol. 39 (Feb., 1958), p. 3.

"The case for legible footprints," *Hospital.* vol. 40 (Aug., 1966), p. 45.

Chatterjee, S. K.: "Edgeoscopy," *Fingerprint and Identification Magazine.* vol. 44 (Sept., 1962), p. 3.

————: "Edgeoscopy," *International Criminal Police Review.* vol. 18 (May, 1963), p. 139.

Cherrill, F. R.: "Finger prints and disease," *Nature.* vol. 166 (1950), p. 581.

"Concluding Report of the IAI Standardization Committee," *Identification News.* vol. 24 (Aug., 1974), p. 5.

Cummins, Harold: "The use of foot-prints and finger-prints as identity records in the maternity," *New Orleans Medical and Surgical Journal.* vol. 81 (1929), p. 493.

————: "Uniqueness of the individual," *American Journal of Physical Anthropology.* vol. 4 (June, 1946), p. 191.

————: "Fingerprints: Normal and abnormal patterns," *Fingerprint and Identification Magazine.* vol. 49 (Nov., 1967), p. 3.

David, T. J., A. B. Ajdukiewicz, and A. E. Reed: "Effects of diseases on fingerprints," *Identification News.* vol. 21 (Mar., 1971), p. 4.

"Debunking the debunkers," *Identification News.* vol. 15-16 (Dec., 1965-Jan., 1966), p. 10.

Dillon, D. J.: "The identification of impressions of nonfriction-ridge-bearing skin," *Journal of Forensic Sciences.* vol. 8 (1963), p. 576.

Eriksson, S., and T. Romanus: "The qualitative value of finger patterns," *International Criminal Police Review.* vol. 14 (Dec., 1959), p. 295.

"FBI and footprints confirm identities of twins," *FBI Law Enforcement Bulletin.* vol. 40 (Mar., 1959), p. 6.

Ferguson, B.: "Identification of dermal ridge characteristics," *The Police Journal.* vol. 39 (1966), p. 386.

"Finger print identification," *American Law Review.* vol. 52 (Nov., 1918), p. 920.

"Fingerprint mutilation," *FBI Law Enforcement Bulletin.* vol. 26 (June, 1957), p. 19.

"Fingerprinting in criminal investigation," *Royal Canadian Mounted Police Gazette.* vol. 30 (June, 1968), p. 8.

"Fingerprinting: It's not just for criminals," *Identification News.* vol. 15 (May, 1965), p. 11.

"Finger prints as defensive evidence," *Law Notes.* vol. 26 (Apr., 1922), p. 3.

"Fingerprints: The infallible means of personal identification," *FBI Law Enforcement Bulletin.* vol. 33 (July, 1964), p. 3.

Galton, Francis: *The Patterns in Thumb and Finger Marks.* London, Kegan, Paul, French, Trubner & Co., 1891.

————: *Finger Prints.* New York, Macmillan, 1892.

Gibbs, R. C.: "Finger and palm print alterations due to keratosis," *Fingerprint and Identification Magazine,* vol. 47 (July, 1965), p. 3.

Gupta, S. R.: "Statistical survey of ridge characteristics," *International Criminal Police Review.* vol. 23 (1968), p. 130.

Henry, Edward R.: *Classification and Uses of Finger Prints.* 8th ed. London, H.M.S.O., 1937.

Hirsch, W.: "Biological aspects of finger prints, palms and soles," *Fingerprint and Identification Magazine.* vol. 46 (Aug., 1964), p. 3.

Hoover, J. E.: "Hoover responds to 'Some fingerprints lie,'" *Identification News.* vol. 19 (Sept., 1969), p. 11.

"IAI committee confirms identification of print in the Kent case," *Fingerprint and Identification Magazine.* vol. 53 (Oct., 1971), p. 11.

"Ichtyosis prevents fingerprinting," *Royal Canadian Mounted Police Gazette.* vol. 22 (Sept., 1960), p. 11.

"Inky records; protection in accident, amnesia, and kidnaping," *Literary Digest.* vol. 121 (June, 1936), p. 7.

"Is infant foot printing a luxury or necessity?" *Fingerprint and Identification Magazine.* vol. 45 (June, 1964), p. 2.

King, D. P.: "Palm and foot prints: Their legal aspects," *Fingerprint and Identification Magazine.* vol. 44 (Dec., 1962), p. 13.

Kingston, C. R.: *Probabilistic Analysis of Partial Fingerprint Patterns.* Doctor of Criminology Thesis, University of California, Berkeley. Xerox Corporation, Ann Arbor, MI, 1965.

Kingston, C. R., and P. L. Kirk: "Historical development and evaluation of the '12 point rule' in fingerprint identification," *International Criminal Police Review.* vol. 20 (1965), p. 62.

Laufer, B.: "Concerning the history of finger-prints," *Science.* vol. 45 (1917), p. 504.

Lauritic, E.: "Some fingerprints lie," *Identification News.* vol. 19 (Sept., 1969), p. 3.

Locard, E.: "Les pores et l'identification des criminals," *Biologica.* vol. 2 (1912), p. 357.

Mairs, G. T.: "Identification of individuals by means of finger prints, palm prints and sole prints." *Scientific Monthly.* vol. 7 (1918), p. 299.

Miller, J. R.: "Dermal ridge patterns: technique for their study in human fetuses," *Journal of Pediatrics.* vol. 73 (Oct., 1968), p. 614.

Moenssens, Andre A.: "Finger printing is no punishment," *Fingerprint and Identification Magazine.* vol. 43 (Feb., 1962), p. 11.

————: "Poroscopy—Identification by pore structure," *Fingerprint and Identification Magazine.* vol. 52 (July, 1970), p. 3.

Morfopoulos, V. C.: "The anatomy of evidence," *Identification News.* vol. 20 (Dec., 1970), p. 10.

"No two finger prints alike," *Scientific American.* vol. 105 (Aug., 1911), p. 166.

O'Hara, Charles E. and James W. Osterburg: *An Introduction to Criminalistics.* New York, Macmillan, 1949.

O'Neill, M. E.: "Fingerprints in criminal investigations," *Journal of Criminal Law, Criminology and Police Science.* vol. 30 (1940), p. 929.

Osborn, A. S.: "Proof of finger-prints," *Journal of Criminal Law, Criminology and Police Science.* vol. 26 (1935), p. 587.

Osterburg, J. W.: "An inquiry into the nature of proof—The identity of fingerprints," *Journal of Forensic Sciences.* vol. 9 (1964), p. 413.

————: "Fingerprint probability calculations based on the number of individual characteristics present," *Identification News.* vol. 24 (Oct., 1974), p. 3.

Prado, A. B.: "Metodo para o estudo das impressoes digito-palmares," *Revista de Identificacao e Ciencias Conexas* (Brazil). vol. 16 (1960), p. 139.

"Prisoner attempts finger print scarring," *Fingerprint and Identification Magazine.* vol. 46 (May, 1965), p. 11.

Polson, C. J.: "Finger prints and finger printing: An historical study," *Journal of Criminal Law, Criminology and Police Science.* vol. 41 (1950-1951), Part I. p. 495, Part II. p. 690.

Puri, D. K. S.: "Footprints," *International Criminal Police Review.* vol. 20 (1965), p. 106.

"The question of print removal by surgical planing," *FBI Law Enforcement Bulletin.* vol. 27 (Mar., 1958), p. 18.

"Report of the Standardization Committee of the International Association for Identification," *Identification News.* vol. 23 (Aug., 1973), p. 13.

Ribeiro, L.: "Diseases affecting workmen's finger prints and their treatment," *Medico-Legal Review.* vol. 6 (1938), p. 376.

"Second Interim Report of the Standardization Committee of the International Association for Identification," *Identification News.* vol. 22 (Nov., 1972), p. 11.

Singh, P.: "Pressure distortions in fingerprinting," *The Police Journal.* vol. 36 (1963), p. 79.

Speaks, H. A.: "Expert finds many details in small area of arch pattern," *Fingerprint and Identification Magazine.* vol. 41 (Apr., 1960), p. 3.

————: "Expert finds many details in small area of arch pattern," *Fingerprint and Identification Magazine.* vol. 53 (July, 1971), p. 12.

Straub, R.: "Foot prints as evidence," *Law Notes.* vol. 27 (1924), p. 206.

Trotter, C. L.: "Footprinting of infants," *Fingerprint and Identification Magazine.* vol. 49 (July, 1967), p. 5.

Woj, C.; "The development and use of the fingerprint in commercial transactions," *Identification News.* vol. 24 (Oct., 1974), p. 13.

Chapter II

Taking Finger-, Palm-, and Footprints

18

THE IMPORTANCE OF LEGIBLE FINGERPRINTS

FINGERPRINT CLASSIFIERS often remark that if the person who took a set of fingerprints was responsible for their correct classification, print quality would improve spectacularly. The value of an inked impression is directly dependent upon legibility of ridge detail, and legibility, in turn, depends upon impression quality. Correct classification of a pattern in the great majority of cases depends upon one particular ridge or a specific point on that ridge. Accordingly, one can readily appreciate that each individual ridge in an inked impression should be as distinct and legible as possible. If the ridge characteristics necessary for correct classification are blurred or smudged, it follows that the classification may be questionable. Clear and strong inked impressions are extremely important for correct classification, proper filing, and searching, and they are essential for comparison with latent fingerprint evidence developed at crime scenes.

The act of taking good, clean impressions is not difficult; it is a matter of knowing what constitutes a fingerprint or what the essentials of a pattern are, the exercise of a reasonable amount of diligence in taking the impressions, having the simple equipment necessary for taking inked impressions, and most important of all, keeping those few tools clean and in a workmanlike condition. Proper care of equipment and diligence in taking inked impressions cannot be stressed too much or too often.

Blurred, indistinct or illegible inked impressions which are faulty by reason of skin condition or occupational damage to the skin constitute only a small percentage of all prints taken, as will be seen by examining Figures 24 and 25 (Secs. 27 and 28). There are several times as many impressions in every fingerprint file which reflect faulty workmanship as there are prints which are imperfect as the result of bad skin condition, damaged fingers, or other faults credited to the fingers. Faulty workmanship becomes conspicuous when a comparison is made between rolled and plain impressions of the same fingers on a fingerprint card; one may be more legible than the other, not necessarily by reason of the type of impression but because of improper taking. If one impression is good and the other bad, the fault lays with the operator, not the finger or the condition of the skin.

Whenever latent fingerprint evidence is obtained, it usually is not good at best; it cannot be likened favorably with good inked impressions by any stretch of the imagination. Latents are made under what may be termed *normal* handling conditions. In actual fingerprint investigations, smudged latents outnumber clear impressions, superimposed patterns are as common as single impressions, and partially blurred patterns occur much more frequently than clear and distinct latents. The investigator has no choice; he takes what he finds as he finds it, and he endeavors to improve the evidence by the most practical means.

Known prints, those on file in the identification bureau or prints taken expressly for purposes of comparison, are used for comparison with latent prints, and it is only logical that all prints which are taken under favorable conditions, either for identification or comparison, be the best possible. Good workmanship should be reflected by fingerprints each time they are taken; no one knows at what time the same prints may become critical in connection with an investigation; they are always critical from the standpoint of classification.

19

ELIMINATION OF FINGERPRINT EVIDENCE

If fingerprint evidence is developed at a crime scene, it becomes necessary to eliminate prints of all persons not involved in the offense who have legitimate access to the premises by reason of employment, residence, or any other reason. Prints of such persons are compared with those found at the scene to either exclude them from complicity in the crime or, if the latent should be found to belong to one of those persons, to eliminate the prints from further consideration as evidence. It is also important to eliminate every officer or other person who worked at the scene in any capacity. If an investigation is conducted properly, a lot of time, which would otherwise have to be spent making comparisons, is saved. Those persons who have no connection with an investigation should not be permitted to complicate it.

The purpose in eliminating prints of persons known to have been at the crime scene is to identify the latents, to learn whether the latents are foreign to the scene, and to verify the statements of victims and witnesses. If they cannot be identified as belonging to an innocent party, their weight as evidence is enhanced, and the investigator may reasonably assume that the prints belong to the person who committed the offense. Eliminations simply narrow the search for the suspect. Often prints are made in such a position or location or under such circumstances that they could only have been made by the person who committed the crime.

Elimination prints of victims and witnesses identified with latent impressions recovered from a crime scene may also assist in collaborating or disproving their statements regarding the incident. Their statements may, unwittingly or intentionally, contain erroneous information that hinders the investigation or subsequent legal proceedings. There is an old German adage, "Er lügt wie Augenzeuge" (He lies like an eyewitness). Memory is not reliable, especially regarding events experienced or observed by an individual under emotional stress or excitement, and observations and descriptions of incidents are often colored with the individual's own prejudices and biases. Erroneous information in statements may be due to any one or a combination of a variety of reasons: faulty memory, partial involvement in the commission of the offense, fear of disclosure of unrelated personal information, not wanting to admit handling of evidentiary items, or numerous other reasons.

The most important time and place to get fingerprints for elimination is *at the scene* and *while the investigation is underway*. Taking elimination prints is part of the investigation. If their taking is delayed until the following day, that phase of the investigation is delayed just that long, and employees and others may have to be absent from their work for the additional time necessary to get their prints. Elimination prints taken at the scene during the investigation speed up the investigative processes immeasurably. Time is vital; it is uneconomical from an investigative viewpoint to unnecessarily postpone an important part in an investigation.

Occasionally, victims and witnesses may object to having their prints taken for elimination purposes, some even reacting violently to the idea. Most objections can easily be overcome by properly explaining the reason elimination prints are necessary, by taking the prints in an area removed from public view, and by using inkless recording techniques (*see* Sec. 32).

When taking prints for elimination, the investigator should consider the possibility of an *inside job*. Very often crimes are planned and carried out by persons who are thoroughly familiar with the premises and routines and who have legitimate access to the premises. An investigator cannot jump to a conclusion that prints are of no value because they happen to belong to an employee. The situation simply becomes more complicated or involved, and investigative techniques have to be adapted to the circumstances. Also, insiders whose prints are found under questionable circumstances may have ready alibis for their prints. When they do, the ingenuity and resourcefulness of the investigator are taxed, and solution of the crime may be made more difficult. It is not the purpose of this handbook to outline a plan of procedure for any particular type of investigation; the point is to alert the investigator to what may be encountered in using fingerprint evidence.

Another group of persons to keep in mind in making eliminations are recently discharged employees and persons who have indirect ways of knowing the premises. Every person who has direct or indirect connection with the scene of an incident, including police officers, is a subject of elimination prints.

20

THE FINGERPRINT CARD

The size of fingerprint cards has been standardized at 8-by-8 inches, because that size has been found to be adequate for receiving five rolled impressions across the card, and the size is convenient for handling and filing.

The card is white, lightweight cardboard with a semiglazed surface. Fingerprint cards are handled countless times in con-

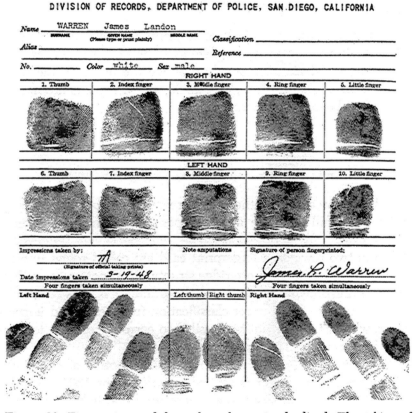

Figure 20. Fingerprint card forms have been standardized. The taking of each impression is an important operation in itself; correct classification may be impossible if one of the rolled impressions is not legible.

stant searching, and they may be kept in a file for a great many years. Therefore, the texture of the card and strength of the paper must be such that it will withstand frequent handling without tearing or becoming frayed on the edges or corners. The fingerprint classification is ordinarily written in the upper right-hand corner of the card in a space provided for that purpose.

Individual spaces are provided for each of the ten fingers, impressions are taken of the fingers of the right hand from left to right across the card in the upper of two rows of spaces, and impressions of the left hand are taken underneath in the same sequence, that is from thumb to little finger and from left to right.

Figure 20 shows a typical set of prints without the classification; the impressions are complete as to points required for classification, the flexion creases show above the baseline, the plain impressions are taken at a slight angle, and the prints are not superimposed over the signature.

21

TWO KINDS OF INKED IMPRESSIONS

Inked impressions of the fingers recorded on standard fingerprint cards fall into one of two types, *rolled* and *plain*, sometimes called *flat impressions*. The ten individual impressions taken in two rows on a fingerprint card are called *rolled impressions*. Since they show more ridge structure and pattern area than plain impressions, they are more important. It is possible to obtain a complete and correct classification from ten rolled impressions, whereas it may not be possible to correctly classify ten fingers from as many flat impressions.

Rolled impressions are made by a rolling motion of each individual finger; the finger is rotated a half-turn or 180°. This degree of rotation actually reveals more than one half of the total skin area around a finger. The finger is manipulated as though it were a cylinder, and it is rolled expressly for the purpose of obtaining all of the pattern area essential to correct classification. The pattern area is not always complete on the palmar surface of a finger; points necessary for classification may be found on the side of a finger and, in some instances, close to the nail. Sometimes, it is possible to arrive at the correct classification from ten plain impressions, but since this is not always possible, it is necessary to obtain one complete set of rolled impressions of each set of fingers to make allowances for any possible shortage of pattern area in any finger. Rolled impressions may be smudged because of the shape of a finger or because of movement of the flesh during the rolling operation. Movement of the flesh or skin results in slight smudging of the ridges, but ordinarily, it is not enough to appreciably interfere with legibility of the pattern or classification.

When a rolled impression is correctly taken, the fissure or flexion creases of the finger show in the inked impression in the space on a fingerprint card (*see* Fig. 20, Sec. 19). The pattern area is found nearer the fissure than the tip of the finger. The fingertip is of no consequence in classification but may be of extreme importance in identifying latent fingerprints. On occasions, fingertip impressions may be found as latent images at crime scenes, and they are commonly found on questioned documents. When latent fingertip impressions are found, special prints must be taken of the fingers for purposes of comparison inasmuch as fingertips do not show in ordinary inked impressions. Like palmprints, fingertips present additional problems from the viewpoint of requiring special inked impressions.

A fingerprint classifier may be able to look at a finger and determine the type of pattern and decide whether or not it is necessary to roll the finger from "nail-to-nail." This procedure is not recommended unless the operator is thoroughly familiar with all types of patterns and fingerprint classification. Such shortcuts may later prove to be a disadvantage when it is necessary to compare partial latents from a crime scene with the prints on the fingerprint card. Another way to arrive at the type of pattern on a finger and to know whether the finger is properly inked is by examining the impression made by the finger on the inking plate. The pattern shows plainly in the ink if the film is of the right consistency and especially if the plate is backed with white. The inking plate serves as a useful guide by which the operator can determine whether or not a finger is properly inked.

Plain impressions are taken of four fingers of a hand simultaneously on the bottom of the fingerprint card, the impressions of the left four fingers on the left side of the card and the right four on the right. The thumbs are taken separately to the right and left of the midline of the card in a position on the card corresponding to their position on the hands.

Plain impressions are sometimes made at a slight angle to the vertical to bring the short little finger up into a position where it will show on the fingerprint card and, if possible, far enough up to show the fissure. If the plain impressions are taken in a straightforward position on the card, the little finger, being shorter than the others, may make an incomplete impression on the bottom of the card. If all four fingers are moved up, the longer fingers will appear well up on the card and perhaps cover the signature or obscure portions of the rolled impressions.

Plain impressions serve as a double check or verification of position and sequence of rolled impressions. This check prevents an incorrect classification of the prints in instances where the operator has rolled the prints out of sequence or reversed the rows for the hands. Also, if the ridge detail is not clear in the rolled impressions because of movement or for any other reason, the plain impressions afford a second chance for finding clear ridge detail necessary for correct classification.

With plain impressions, inasmuch as they are taken for purposes of checking position of rolled impressions, no particular attempt is made to obtain complete pattern areas, and they may or may not show in their entirety. Ordinarily, plain impressions show more distinct and legible ridge detail because there is no movement of the fingers in taking them.

A person who classifies fingerprints normally does a lot of checking back and forth between the plain and rolled impressions on a card. Since there are two impressions of each finger, one or the other is, or may be, more distinct and legible, and the clearer of the two impressions is used when making close decisions concerning the rules of classification.

22
TAKING FINGERPRINTS MEANS JUST THAT

Taking fingerprints is not a difficult task, but it does require a modicum of initiative; it is a matter of doing exactly what the term implies. Absolute control of the subject's hand is necessary —the sole function of the subject is merely to supply the fingers and stand in a relaxed position. The officer taking the prints may be referred to as the *fingerprint recorder* (Moenssens, 1971), and this title accurately describes the officer's function—recording finger and palm impressions.

All fingerprint recorders must remember that they are *taking* the prints; subjects do not give their prints, nor should they be permitted to take their own. A few persons obligingly volunteer to take their own prints; they are overly anxious to assist or to get it over with, but assistance and haste usually turn out to be handicaps. Some persons remark, "Oh, I've been fingerprinted several times, I know all about it; they have my prints in Washington and on my driver's license." If not restrained, they will proceed to give a demonstration, and the result will be anything but satisfactory.

Equipment for taking good impressions is so simple, and easily obtained and cared for that it offers no excuse for botching the taking of prints. The taking of each print should be considered as a single and complete operation in itself, and each print should be made with particular care; it is like firing a pistol—to obtain a perfect score, each shot must be a bull's-eye.

Knowledge of what constitutes a fingerprint is extremely important. The fingerprint recorder should know what comprises a single, legible, classifiable pattern, and he or she must know when a pattern is complete. Knowledge of the points required for proper classification is an aid to the taking of good impressions. Points which are often missed in rolled impressions and which are essential to correct classification, are the *deltas*. If fingerprint recorders are taught to look for the deltas in patterns which contain deltas, which is about 95 percent of all patterns, and to make sure that they are included in the rolled impressions, the patterns should be classifiable. If recorders are delta conscious and make a special effort to obtain clear and legible deltas, there need not be any worry about the quality of the rest of the pattern. If the deltas are clear and distinct, the remainder of the pattern is very apt to be of good quality.

Instructions in taking prints together with a few pointers on patterns and deltas give fingerprint recorders confidence and produce good inked impressions.

23

HOW TO TAKE FINGERPRINTS

The equipment for taking fingerprints is simple and consists of a device to hold the card, a means to apply a suitable coat of ink to the fingers, and an appropriate ink. Ink is applied in the vast majority of cases by fingerprint ink rolled on a glass plate. The first and most important step in taking a set of fingerprints is to clean the inking plate thoroughly. The film of ink on a plate must be fresh—good impressions cannot be made with a film of ink that is dry or hard.

After the plate is cleaned, a dab of ink about the size of a match head is deposited on the edge of the plate, another in the center, and another on the opposite edge. The roller is then touched to the first dab, and a film of ink is rolled the length of the plate. The roller must be passed over the plate until the ink film has the desired smooth, even, uniform thickness. To prevent buildup of ink where the dabs of ink were deposited and are heaviest on the roller, the roller should be lifted after two or three passes and allowed to spin in the air. This action permits a different portion of the roller to contact the heavier areas of ink. It is advantageous to place a strip of plain white paper under the glass plate (Fig. 21). This gives a rapid evaluation of the thickness of the ink film and also a check of the adequacy of the inking of the fingers. The final ink film along the front edge of the plate should be rolled out smoothly and evenly.

The first step in obtaining a set of fingerprints is to have the subject sign the card. It is recommended that the identity of the person, if known, is established and that all essential data required on the card is completed prior to taking the prints. This action is particularly important when taking the prints of a large number of persons. One can readily imagine the embarrassment and possible repercussions if, when taking the prints of a group of subjects, the operator were to accidentally take a person's prints on the wrong card. Each card should be completed when the prints are being taken in the presence of the recorder taking the prints.

It is assumed that the average person who is fingerprinted does not know as much about the mechanics of taking prints as the person taking the impressions. Therefore, a few simple instructions to the subject are in order at the outset. Subjects who are trying to help are usually more of a hindrance, and they should be told to look away while their prints are being taken and that all pressure and movement required will be made by the recorder. The subject should be told to relax his wrist and fingers and not to attempt to assist in any manner.

Figure 21. If the inking plate is set on a white background, patterns may be examined as fingers are inked to determine whether or not inking is effective.

When the plate is ready and the card has been properly filled out and placed in the cardholder, the subject is asked to stand in front of the cardholder, facing the cardholder and at a distance of about the length of the forearm. The inking plate and the cardholder should be side by side with the cardholder nearest the operator. It is more convenient to reach across the card and holder to the inking plate than across the inking plate to the card while taking inked impressions.

The fingers should be inked in the same order in which the impressions are taken, and the film of ink on the plate should be sufficiently heavy so that contact of the skin with the ink makes a contrasting and legible impression on the fingerprint card. It should never be necessary to roll a finger back and forth two or more times in an attempt to cover the member thoroughly with ink. If the recorder thinks not enough ink adheres in one roll, he may ink the plate more heavily or roll the finger in another spot on the plate. The finger should be cleaned prior to reinking to prevent buildup of ink on portions of the finger.

Occasionally, even the most experienced technician gets too much ink on the plate. This situation usually occurs during cold weather when extra pressure is required to get the ink out of the tube, and too much ink is squeezed by mistake. If there is too much ink on the plate, the excess ink may be easily removed by taking the roller and rolling it on a newspaper or paper towel, then run the roller over the plate several times and back again to the paper. This procedure is repeated until a sufficient amount of ink has been removed from the plate.

The fingers should be rolled on the card in the same sequence that the spaces appear on the card, starting with the right thumb and ending with the left little finger. Rolled impressions are taken from "nail-to-nail" or three quarters of the way around a finger. The hand should be turned in such a manner that the finger and forearm rotate approximately 180 degrees in making the rolled impressions, and movement should be from a strained to a relaxed position.

If you, the reader, hold your arms in front of you with the backs of the hands touching each other, you will find that this is a strained and somewhat awkward position. As you turn your hands over so that they are palm to palm, you will find that they now are in a comfortable position. The fingers should be rolled by starting in the awkward position and ending with them in the comfortable position, or rolled away from the center of the subject's body.

The foregoing does not apply to the thumbs. If you hold both hands in front of you again, palms up and thumbs extended, you will find that there is a feeling of some strain. Notice also that the inside edges of the thumbs are down in the proper position for starting the rolling process. Now hold your hands in front of you with the palms down; you will find that it is a more comfortable position and will notice that the outsides of the thumbs are in a perfect position for completing the roll. Therefore, the thumbs are rolled toward the center of the body.

Various fingerprint instructors generally like to add phrases emphasizing the direction for rolling fingers and thumbs to this portion of their block of instruction. "Thumbs in, fingers out," is one such slogan, and many military instructors use the brass belt buckle as the point of reference.

The fingerprint recorder should firmly grip the finger that is to be printed so that maximum control is assured with minimum discomfort to the subject during inking and printing. The recorder's right thumb and index finger should grip the subject's finger at the first joint, with the recorder's right middle, ring, and little fingers placed over the back of the subject's other fingers to hold them back out of the way. The recorder's left thumb and index finger are used to control the placement of the subject's finger on the card by grasping the tip of the subject's finger.

When a rolled impression is taken in an individual space on a fingerprint card, the flexion crease should appear in the frame slightly above the bottom line of the frame. As long as the flexion crease appears in the rolled impression, the pattern may be considered complete in that direction.

Movement of the finger during rolling while inking and printing should be one smooth, continuous movement. Longitudinal movement of the finger is slippage, which will cause a blurred impression on the card. Hesitation during the rolling movement may cause slippage of the finger or a double impression of portions of the print. If a mistake is made in taking the impressions on a card, it is better to stop and start over again with a new card.

When flat impressions are taken, the operator may show the subject how to hold the hands and fingers, as shown in Figure 22.

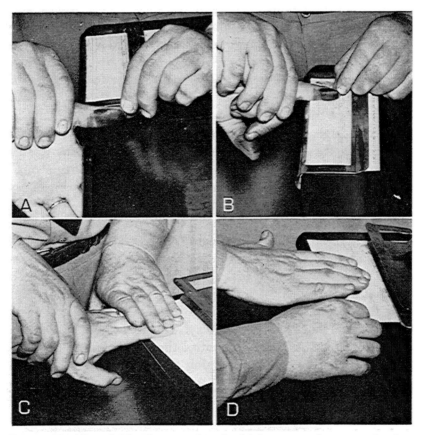

Figure 22. (A and B) The recorder should have complete control when taking fingerprints. Each finger is inked so that the flexion crease shows in the rolled impression. (C) When plain impressions are taken, the subject's hands and fingers are extended; light pressure may be applied on the back of the fingers. (D) The subject should be shown how to hold his hand; a demonstration is more effective than an explanation.

A quick demonstration should be given the subject, saying the hand should be held "this way," and the subject shown with the recorder's hand what to do. A demonstration is more effective than verbal instructions.

The four fingers should remain together and extended for taking plain impressions; this is an exception to the rule of relaxation. The subject holds his fingers straight out and taut for taking the plain impressions. The operator may press on the top of the four fingers to insure good contact throughout, as shown in Figure 22, and, at the same time, the hand may be controlled by grasping either the wrist or the back of the hand as shown.

24
STANCE FOR TAKING PRINTS

Most officers stand on the left side of the person whose prints are being taken for the simple reason that more people are right-handed. They normally work more efficiently and to better advantage toward the right; therefore, most fingerprint stands are made so that the printing is done on the left front corner. Considering that some officers may be left-handed, the fingerprint stand should be so constructed that prints may be taken from either side and not in such a manner that prints may be taken from one side only. The job should be done in the most natural and easiest manner with the least strain and discomfort. The officer recording the prints should always work so that the card-holder is nearer than the inking plate and should not attempt to take the inked impressions by reaching across the inking plate or work at a distance and disadvantage. Rolling the inked impressions should be done in the most advantageous manner or position, which is the position nearest the officer. Inking the fingers and taking rolled impressions are both important, but when it comes to a choice between the two, the latter should receive the most consideration, as it results in the final product.

The position of the officer in respect to the fingerprint stand and the subject is important. They may stand side by side in front of a common table, one on either side of the corner, or the officer may stand at an angle of about 45 degrees. Most officers are observed to stand as last described, which permits ample freedom to both the officer and the subject. This again is a matter of common sense and convenience; the objective is to do the job in the easiest, simplest, and most natural manner to obtain the best possible results.

It is advisable for officers to be unarmed while taking the prints of prisoners. While taking prints, the officer's right side is toward the subject, and the attention of the officer is directed towards the printing operation. If the officer is carrying a sidearm, it is not difficult for a subject to grab the weapon.

25

MAJOR CASE PRINTS

Latent prints recovered from crime scenes are chance or unintentional impressions and, therefore, may be from any area of the hand. Although the thumbs and fingers are the primary members of the hand used for grasping, impressions of other areas of the hands may also be expected to be present in certain situations.

Latent impressions of the palms are commonly found on windowsills at the point of entry in housebreakings and burglaries. On questioned documents bearing handwriting, latent prints of the ulnar side or edge of the palm may be expected to be present where the hand would normally rest during writing. On negotiable instruments, such as checks and money orders, the edge of the palm may be expected to be present under the endorsement and the fingertip impressions of the suspect commonly appear near the center of the document, for it is normally pushed across a counter with the fingertips toward the cashier. These are but a few examples of situations in which latent impressions of different areas of the hands, other than fingerprints, may be expected to be found, but such impressions may be expected in any investigation.

The majority of latent prints recovered from crime scenes are partial or fragmentary impressions lacking complete pattern areas and are, therefore, unclassifiable. Lack of essential requirements for classification does not necessarily mean that the latent cannot be identified or eliminated. Individual ridge characteristics are the basis for positive identification; therefore, partial impressions may often be identified or eliminated if adequate inked impressions are available for comparison.

Major case prints is the term applied to a set of inked impressions recording the complete ridge structure of the hands. Papillary ridges are found on the palmar surfaces of the hands, the tips or ends of the fingers below the nails, and the sides of the fingers and palms. In addition to the rolled and plain impressions on the fingerprint card, major case prints should include palmprints, impressions of the ulnar side of the palms, complete rolled impressions of the fingers, including the medial and proximal phalangeal pattern zones, and fingertip impressions rolled from the center of the finger to the nail and from one side to the other.

It is important to always remember that any area of the hand bearing friction ridges may be used to identify latent prints. The Chicago Police Department had a case involving the murder of a police officer that readily illustrates this point (Brooks, 1975). A latent print was developed on the grip of the murder weapon, an automatic pistol, and the latent was in such a position that it could only have been made by the area between the thumb and index finger of a person holding the weapon in a firing position. This particular area of the hand, the *fulcrum* area, is not normally recorded in inked palmprints because the thumb must be opposing the fingers to fully record the area.

The latent print was identified and the case solved by the ingenuity and resourcefulness of the technician. A satisfactory inked impression of the fulcrum area of the suspect's palm was obtained by having the suspect make a **V** with his thumb and index finger. The area was then inked, and a card was wrapped around a flash gun battery holder and the rounded card was then placed into the V and gently pressed down into the center of the palm.

It would be impractical to take major case prints in all cases, but they should be taken as a matter of routine for both suspect and elimination prints in investigations of serious offenses. It may be possible to limit the major case prints to certain areas of the hands if the investigator can establish the nature of the latents recovered. For example, there is no need to take inked fingertip impressions if no latent fingertip impressions are recovered. However, if there is any doubt, it is always better to take a complete set of major case prints.

26

TAKING PALMPRINTS AND FOOTPRINTS

The palmprint in Figure 14 (*see* Sec. 15) was obtained by inking the palm and fingers with a roller as shown in Figure 23. A thin film of ink was rolled out on the inking plate with particular care being taken to avoid edge marks of the roller. If a heavy film of ink is picked up by the roller, edge marks show not only on the palm but on the inked impression on the paper as well. Uneven spreading of the ink on the palm detracts from the appearance of the impression, and it may give some of the ridges the appearance of being heavier than others. Taking palmprints is chiefly a matter of careful preparation of the palm with an even film of ink, with particular care being taken to avoid heavy inking. The palm may be inked and reinked until a film of the desired consistency is prepared for making a cleancut impression of the palm on paper. The ink film should be *built up* on the ridge surfaces.

After the hand is inked, an impression on paper may be made by simply pressing the open hand firmly down on a large card on a flat surface such as a table top. This procedure does not provide the best impressions of the palm, as portions at the base of the fingers and in the center of the palm are not always recorded. When taking major case prints, the palm should be rotated

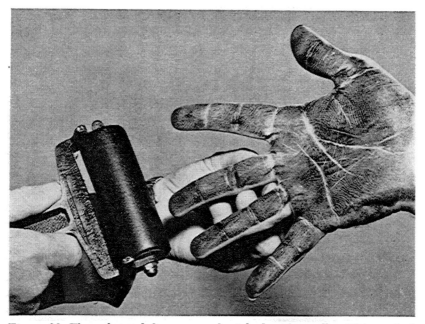

Figure 23. The palm and fingers may be inked with a roller. This method is advantageous when particular pattern areas are wanted.

towards the ulnar side of the hand to record the impression of that edge of the palm.

The most complete inked impressions of the palmar surfaces of the hand may be obtained by rolling the fingers and palm over a cylindrical object to which a card is attached. A rolling pin or a quart wine bottle serves the purpose admirably. A card of the same quality as that used for fingerprint cards is the most desirable form for recording palm impressions; however, if such cards are not available, any good-quality plain white bond paper may be used. The card is rolled around the cylinder and attached securely with an easily removable tape.

Many technicians prefer to roll the hand over the cylinder in a forward motion from the fingers toward the wrist. The fingers, or fingertips, are pressed on the top edge of the card, and the rest of the hand follows through in a continuous forward motion until a complete impression is recorded on the card. Other technicians prefer to roll the hand in a backward motion from the wrist toward the fingers. This latter method requires less cooperation from the subject, as there is a pulling-away effect, since the rolling is a backward motion. Also, the technician has greater control over the position of the print on the card and hand movement by the subject. By firmly grasping the subject's wrist, the technician can effectively prevent any lateral movement of the subject's hand while also controlling the speed of the rolling movement. In all cases, the thumb has to be printed separately because of its position on the hand.

Taking a palm impression on a cylinder requires more patience, skill, and cooperation from the subject than palmprints on a flat surface, but rolled palmprints provide the best-quality impressions. As an expediency, some fingerprint recorders use rigid, nonmoving, convex cardholders for palmprints or have the subject grasp the card while it is wrapped around a cylinder. Palm impressions taken by these expedient methods are foreshortened in both appearance and fact because of the tendency of the hand to bend slightly to accommodate the curvature of the surface of the plate and because the flesh "gives" inward during flexion of the hand around the cylinder.

Departments and agencies that take palmprints on a routine basis may find it advantageous to purchase special palmprinting equipment to expedite the taking of palmprints. One example of the special equipment available for taking palmprints is the *Autopalm Printer Outfit*™ manufactured by Sirchie Finger Print Laboratories, Inc. The outfit consists of a Porelon® roller and a snap-lock cardholder cylinder mounted on a stand that is easily portable and can be set on any table or desk.

Palmprints are usually taken for a specific reason: comparison with latent palmprints recovered from crime scenes or evidentiary items. It is better for the technician who is working with palmprint evidence to take impressions in a manner corresponding with the position and appearance shown by the latent evidence. The latent evidence should be imitated as nearly as possible, concerning curvature and area of the hand by the inked impressions, so that the inked prints are similar in appearance to the latents. In cases where the technician does not have knowledge of the appearance of the latents or if he is unsure, major case prints should be taken.

The procedures for taking footprints are essentially the same as those for taking palmprints, but several differences are necessitated because of the nature of the feet. The foot is inked in the same manner as the hands with an even, thin film of ink covering all papillary ridge surfaces. Plain impressions of the foot may be made by placing the card on the floor and having the subject step on the card, but this requires cooperation from the subject; too much pressure, such as the entire body weight, blurs the prints as does any movement of the foot. The best method for plain impresssions of the foot is for the technician to mount the card on a flat board and press it against the subject's foot while the subject is in a sitting position with his leg and foot elevated and supported.

Rolled impressions of the feet may be taken in the same manner as palmprints, except that the card and cylinder must be larger because of the length of the foot. Plain white legal-size bond paper approximately 8½-by-14 inches provides an adequate form for recording footprints and the necessary identifying data. Cylinders for rolling footprints should be about 5 inches in diameter to accommodate the card and the entire foot impression, while cylinders for palmprints are normally 3 inches in diameter. Cans, such as 3-pound coffee cans and shortening cans, make good cylinders for rolling footprints, providing the surfaces of the can are smooth.

When rolling footprints, the roll should be made from the heel of the foot toward the toes. The roll must be made in one smooth, continuous motion, allowing the cylinder to pass completely over the toes. The toes of the subject should not curl downward or an incomplete impression will result.

Latent footprints are far less commonly found at crime scenes than either finger or palmprints, but a technician must be alert for all types of friction ridge impressions and must be capable of recording inked impressions from all areas of friction ridge bearing skin.

27

ERRORS IN TAKING FINGERPRINTS

When cards in a fingerprint file are examined at random, a surprising number of errors on the part of the persons who take, or record, fingerprints are found. It is obvious that most of the poor-quality prints are faulty, illegible, or incomplete either because the persons who took the impressions did not know they were taking them improperly, or they did not care. The error in the great majority of cases can be traced directly to the person who did the work, the fingerprint recorder. Among the few causes of numerous, imperfectly inked impressions are carelessness, ignorance, lack of skill, and unclean equipment. Perhaps the most common and obvious fault is carelessness, which accounts for more unsuitable prints than any other cause.

Sixteen inked impressions are reproduced in Figure 24. They do not represent all errors or faults in the taking of inked impressions by any means, but they are representative, and all of them point to the recorder. Any one of the prints could have been good with the exercise of reasonable care in its taking. Many of the impressions show multiple errors and are unclassifiable, or a classification would be doubtful. The faults can be picked out easily by a fingerprint classifier and illustrate why all fingerprint recorders should be familiar with the rules of classification. The impressions and the errors in their taking are discussed briefly as follows:

1. The finger was improperly inked and the pattern is, therefore, incomplete. Points necessary to determine the type of pattern are absent. This fingerprint is unclassifiable.

2. The finger was rolled too high in the space; the flexion crease needs to appear only above the baseline. This fingerprint is unclassifiable.

3. The finger was not rolled, and only a plain impression was obtained. The pattern is a whorl, but the print is unclassifiable since neither delta was recorded.

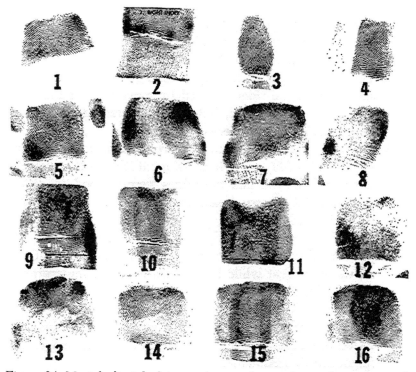

Figure 24. Most faulty inked impressions on fingerprint cards are the result of careless workmanship. Faults depicted above are described in the text.

4. This fingerprint was the result of uneven inking; the dark edgemark of the inked roller is clearly visible near the center of the print. In this case, the fingerprint is classifiable, but the same error in another type of pattern could result in an unclassifiable print.

5. The recorder got almost as much ink on his own fingers as he did the subject's fingers. Marks caused by the recorder's hands demonstrate poor workmanship and control. The fingerprint in this case is classifiable, but such marks from the recorder's hands could destroy an otherwise classifiable print.

6. It appears that the recorder was told to roll the prints and complied implicitly and literally without knowing why

they should be rolled. There was movement of the finger half-way through the roll and improper inking of the finger. The pattern may be classified as a loop, but an accurate ridge count cannot be obtained.

7. The pattern shows improper inking of the finger and smudging of the ridges caused by movement of the flesh. The pattern is a whorl, but the ridge tracing can be determined only by chance.

8. The plate was not sufficiently inked to make a readable fingerprint. The plain impression at the bottom of the same card showed that the ridges were in good condition, yet the print is very weak. This fingerprint is classifiable only with difficulty.

9. The plate was improperly and unevenly inked, the subject's hands were perspiring excessively, and the print also shows movement while being recorded. The fingerprint is classifiable, but the workmanship is poor.

10. It appears that the recorder prepared the subject's finger to take a plain impression but changed his mind and rolled the finger instead, resulting in a double image. The fingerprint is classifiable.

11. The plate was improperly and unevenly inked, resulting in too much ink on the subject's finger. The fingerprint pattern is a loop, but a ridge count cannot be obtained.

12. Improper inking of the plate and lack of cleanliness is seen. The fingerprint is not classifiable.

13. The top portion of the finger was inked excessively, while the pattern area was neglected. If the ink had been spread evenly over the entire pattern area, an excellent print could have been obtained. The fingerprint pattern is a loop, but the ridge count can be only estimated.

14. The plate was unevenly inked, and the finger was inked over an area of the plate where another finger has been inked previously. Note the crisscrossing of the ridges on the left side of the print. The fingerprint is classifiable but only after considerable eyestrain by the classifier.

15. This print looks like a shadowgraph and was caused by a buildup of ink on the inking plate after recording a considerable number of prints. The fingerprint is classifiable but is a good illustration of the necessity of periodically cleaning the inking plate.

16. This fingerprint is an example of a very dirty inking plate. In this instance, the fingerprint is classifiable but only by chance, as the dirt could easily have obscured the pattern area.

To sum up briefly the errors which appear in the sixteen fingerprints shown in Figure 24, there is only one which is prominent in each instance—the carelessness of the recorder taking the impressions. With the exercise of reasonable care, each of the sixteen prints could have been distinct and legible.

The critique of the fingerprints in Figure 24 has been on the basis of classification, but clarity and legibility of all areas of a fingerprint is even more critical when the impressions are taken for purposes of comparison with latent prints. Smudged, blurred, faint, and otherwise unreadable portions of an inked impression may hinder or thwart the identification or elimination of latent prints. It has been stressed repeatedly in previous sections that latent prints may be from any area of the fingers and palms and, therefore, all inked impressions of friction ridges should be clear and distinct.

Many other errors by a recorder show up on fingerprint cards. One of them might be called the unpardonable sin in fingerprint recording: *transposition*—taking an impression in the wrong space on the card. The purpose of the plain impressions at the bottom of a fingerprint card is to serve as a means for checking against this error. It appears that nothing is impossible when it comes to taking fingerprints—this statement can be verified by examining prints in a fingerprint file, which represents the work of many persons. The necessity and importance of taking inked impressions of good quality are even more critical when computerized filing and searching of fingerprint records is achieved.

28

OCCUPATIONAL DAMAGE AND BAD SKIN CONDITION

There are occasions when it is difficult if not impossible to obtain legible impressions of the fingers of some individuals because of occupational damage to the skin or a bad skin condition of either a temporary or permanent nature. Eight impressions that reflect both damage and disfigurement of the ridge structure of the skin are shown in Figure 25, below.

Frequently, it is impossible to correctly classify an impression because the skin is damaged to such an extent that points necessary for classification are obscured, yet the condition is only temporary. If the skin is permitted to recuperate for a time, the ridge structure is restored through natural processes. If the condition is permanent, rules of classification which govern such situations are applied. If the condition is temporary and a classification is based on a permanent disfigurement, the classification may be incorrect. At a later time when taking impressions of

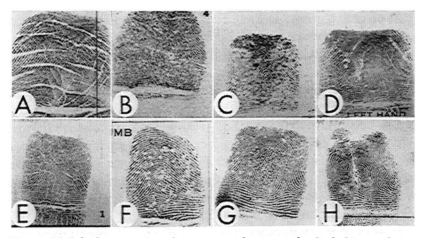

Figure 25. Inked impressions that are poor because of a bad skin condition of occupational damage are in the minority: (A) glazier, (B) plasterer, (C) laborer, (D) battery worker, (E) creasing, (F) spotted print, (G) mottled print, and (H) scar.

fingers which are badly damaged, a notation of whether or not the condition is temporary should be made on the fingerprint card. If it is temporary, a special effort should be made to ink and roll the finger to the best advantage to obtain the correct classification. Special care sometimes produces a legible print; it is a matter of using good judgment each time the problem comes up.

Many occupations result in temporary damage to the ridge structure of skin and even the shape of fingers. Occupations represented in Figure 25A-D above are glazier, plasterer, laborer, and battery worker. There are all degrees of damage to the skin from minor injuries to total obscuration of ridges. Fingerprint records are permanent records, whether they are of good or poor quality, and it is necessary to take impressions when the subject is in custody. It is not expedient to wait until the skin condition is cleared; therefore, it is imperative that the job is done with the utmost care and skill.

Figure 25A is that of a glazier. The "cuts" are temporary, and they do not interfere with classification in this case, but they do remove considerable pattern area which could be very important in some types of patterns. Figure 25B is that of a plasterer, 25C is a laborer's print, and 25D is from the hand of a battery worker. The trade of each has left its mark on the respective fingers. The plasterer's pattern is particularly illegible; if a latent impression of this finger were developed at a crime scene, it would be extremely difficult to compare it with a print of the same finger as shown in the figure. It is the fingerprint technician's job to get the best possible prints under the circumstances.

The four impressions of Figure 25E-H reveal skin conditions and a scar. Figure 25E shows unusual *creasing*, which in no way affects the classification of the print, but the condition would be classed as permanent. Creasing, like fingerprint patterns, is characteristic of individuals, and it affords an additional means of identification; if severe, it may affect the classification.

Figure 25F is *spotted;* it is not known whether the condition is permanent or temporary, but many prints are found which have this appearance. The time the condition lasts depends upon the cause, and it may or may not interfere with classification. Inexperienced operators taking inked fingerprints must take care and closely observe the fingers with a magnifier whenever they spot this condition in a print to ascertain whether or not it actually is a skin condition. Some operators have confused spotting due to perspiration with this skin condition.

Figure 25G reflects a *mottled* skin condition, which is permanent. Ridge detail is present in the area affected, but the ridges are dissociated, lacking any continuous pattern flow. The core of the impression is totally obscured, but the damage does not interfere with classification in this particular instance. Mottled or dissociated ridges are commonly found where the skin has been damaged by burns, but the condition may also be inherited in rare cases and cover large areas of papillary ridges (Cummins, 1970).

Figure 25H shows a conspicuous scar through the midline of the pattern. Classification has not been altered in this particular pattern, but scars may change the type of pattern, the count, the tracing, or they may necessitate giving the pattern an arbitrary classification. It is important to establish the age of the scar, especially if it alters the classification. Brief information concerning a scar may be noted on the fingerprint card as is done in the case of amputations, inasmuch as the pattern type and classification may be changed by the scar.

29

TECHNIQUES FOR TAKING PROBLEM PRINTS

Problems may be encountered in taking inked finger-, palm-, and footprints, which make the task of taking good impressions more difficult but, depending on the skill, resourcefulness, and ingenuity of the technician, not impossible. If the subject is perspiring excessively, has deformed hands or fingers, skin that is too dry or too soft, a bad skin condition due to disease or occupation, or an extremely fine ridge structure, to name a few problems that may be expected, special techniques must be used to obtain good impressions.

If the subject's fingers and hands are so deformed that normal printing operations cannot be accomplished, there are several techniques that may be attempted. Success has been achieved by inking the fingers directly with a small roller, or by rolling out a thin film of ink on a spatula and transferring the ink to the fingers. Small rollers may be made, using rubber rollers from typewriter paperholder bails, which may be purchased from any typewriter-repair shop.

In taking the impression of a deformed finger, it may be necessary to cut a square from another fingerprint card and by holding the square in the palm of the hand, rotate it around the finger. A satisfactory print has been obtained by holding the square embedded in modeling clay. If the deformity of the finger is such that the finger remains permanently flexed or curled inwards toward the palm, it may be necessary to use lifting tape to obtain the impression. The tape is placed over the fingertip and pulled against the fingerprint pattern area with the inked impression then appearing on the tape. Care must be exercised to not permit the tape to touch the finger until it is directly over the area to be printed, or double impressions and smudges will result. White opaque lifting tape with transparent covers should be used for this technique. The print is cut out in approximately the same size of the square on the card and attached to the card. Transparent tape should not be used and affixed directly to the card, as the print would be reversed.

Through certain kinds of occupational work, the skin on the tips of the fingers may become rough and dry. Rubbing the bulbs of the fingers with petroleum jelly or oil often permits them to become sufficiently pliable and soft to enable them to be printed. Ice held against the fingers will sometimes help, if the ridges are fine and small and the skin is soft, as with women, children, and the aged.

Sometimes the subject's ridge structure may be so fine that the ink completely covers the finger, ridges and furrows alike. Even with very light inking, the prints will appear as smudges. Often this obstacle can be successfully overcome by lightly dusting the fingers with black fingerprint powder and a brush. The prints are then lifted with white opaque lifting tape, as previously described.

Excessive perspiration is a problem that is easily surmounted in taking good impressions. There are several approaches to the problem. This problem area was frequently encountered by military law enforcement agencies in Indochina and other tropical areas. Perhaps the best approach is to wash the subject's hands in alcohol and dry them immediately before printing. Another technique is for the technician to keep a cloth on the fingerprint stand and wipe off each finger immediately before printing. Ice held against the fingers sometimes helps.

In extreme cases of deformity, casting may provide the only means of recording impressions of the fingers and hands. Casting techniques are covered in Section 32, but it must be remembered that the features on such casts are reversed; that is, the ridges of the fingers appear as furrows in the cast and the furrows of the finger as ridges.

30

POSTMORTEM FINGERPRINTING

It is a relatively easy task to obtain the prints of a body recently dead, as the members of the body are flexible and relaxed. The situation changes considerably when rigor mortis or rigidity sets in. Fingerprinting deceased persons under some circumstances may be a very difficult task.

There are several satisfactory ways to ink the fingers of a dead body. One method is to use a spatula prepared by inking with a regular ink roller (Figs. 26 and 27). The film of ink is then transferred to the fingers. A spatula is convenient for inking under difficult situations, since it is small and may be rolled around a fingertip with ease. Another method of inking is to use a small postmortem Porelon inker or small rollers as described for use with problem prints.

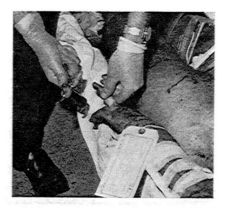

Figure 26. One method of inking the fingers of the deceased for postmortem printing is to apply the ink with the fingerprint ink roller.

In many cases when fingerprinting is attempted on deceased persons, the cords in the wrist, forearm, and fingers are drawn. It is better to take advantage of this condition than to try to overcome it, by bending the wrist still further toward the inner forearm and pressing the fingers one at a time toward the palm or wrist. In this position, they separate and straighten out in such a way that each finger can be printed without interference.

Figure 27. Recording the postmortem fingerprints of the deceased on a strip which is afterwards affixed to a fingerprint card. All known data regarding the deceased would also be entered on the card: physical description, marks, scars, tattoos, etc.

Before starting to take inked impressions of a deceased person's fingers, all materials required should be laid out in readiness so that the items may be readily picked up and used as needed. With respect to the paper upon which the prints are taken, a standard fingerprint card may be cut up into two strips of five spaces and used in a "stripholder" or spoon as shown in Figure 28. The position of the strip is changed each time a new impression is taken. Some spoons are designed to receive a strip folded four times into five squares or spaces.

The ten individual spaces on a card may be cut out individually and one marked for each finger by using the initials of each finger in turn if the spaces are not already marked. Individual cards may be used manually without the aid of a spoon. This technique may require practice or necessitate taking more than one impression of some fingers in case first attempts are not successful or the card slips. If individual cards are used, it is well to have more than ten squares cut and ready in case some of

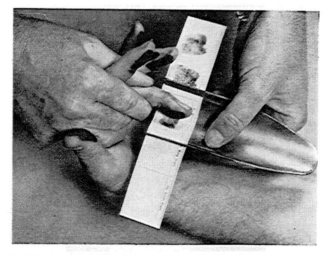

Figure 28. When taking inked impressions of a body after rigor mortis has set in, advantage should be taken of the normally drawn condition of the cords in the wrist and forearm by pressing the hand and fingers still further toward the forearm. In this position, the members may be printed one at a time without difficulty.

them are spoiled or if the pattern area is not complete when the finger is printed.

No matter what system is used, it is very important that the strips or cards are adequately identified, preferably before they are used, so that there is no chance of crossing them up. The use of a spoon and strips should prevent this kind of error.

Each impression should be examined immediately after it is taken to make sure it is complete and clear; if not, the procedure should be repeated until a legible impression is obtained. When a spoon is used, the strip or individual card is placed in the spoon with the top side of the strip toward the handle of the spoon. The end of the spoon used in direct contact should have rounded and smooth corners and be slightly concave in cross section to hold the strips firmly and to accommodate the shape of the finger.

Wrinkles that prevent the taking of classifiable fingerprints may often be eliminated by pulling the skin tight across the pattern area when printing. When this procedure fails, the wrinkles may be removed: Fill a hypodermic syringe with *hot water, glycerin,* or *tissue builder* and insert the needle below the first flexion crease, in the medial phalangeal zone, and up into the tip of the finger, taking care to keep the needle below the surface of the skin. Inject sufficient fluid to round out the pattern area. To prevent seepage of the injected fluid, tie a piece of string tightly around the finger just above the point at which the needle entered the finger. If injection at one point does not produce the results desired, inject the fluid at other points on the finger, such as the sides or tip, until suitable results are obtained. Exercise care so as not to inject too much fluid, or the pressure may cause the skin to break and tear, especially if decomposition has begun.

If the skin of the fingers has started to deteriorate or decay, or if the skin is dehydrated or mummified, or if it is water soaked and wrinkled, the problem becomes more difficult and complex (Fig. 29). Steps may be taken to restore the skin to a near-normal condition, which is possible in most cases. If the

Figure 29. In some cases, the skin may be in such an advanced state of decomposition that the epidermis is extremely fragile and tears away from the fingers at the slightest touch. In the case depicted, the fragile epidermis was removed, mounted between two glass slides, and photographed. The ridge structure is clear, and identification can be established.

skin is dehydrated and hard, it may be satisfactorily restored to an almost normal condition by soaking in a 3% lye solution (potassium hydroxide) in lukewarm water for a period of time long enough to restore them to near normal. After this, the fingers may be washed in distilled water to remove the lye solution. The fingers may have to be severed to accomplish restoration and printing by this method.

Often when the skin is shriveled and wrinkled due to long exposure to water, the skin is so loose that an incision of the epidermis circumscribing the finger in the medial phalangeal zone enables removal of the skin. The skin can be placed over the finger of the technician wearing gloves and inked and printed as if it were his own.

A technician should never jump to the conclusion that a body is too decomposed to obtain prints as long as either the epidermis or dermis remains (Fig. 30). Frequently, burned and charred bodies appear too badly damaged to obtain good prints, but contraction of the flexion muscles of the hand in such cases generally protects the fingerprint pattern areas, because the hands form a fist. Whenever there is any doubt as to how to proceed, it would be a good practice to contact the Identification Division of the Federal Bureau of Investigation for advice.

As a matter of routine in investigations of serious offenses, it is a good practice to take major case prints from all deceased persons connected with the case. This practice would preclude the possibility of unidentified latent prints from the crime scene by insuring the availability of comparison prints, even after the body has been removed for burial.

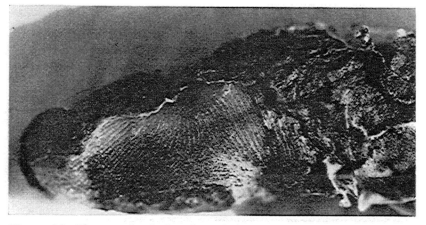

Figure 30. Photograph of the charred finger of a burning victim. The charred and brittle epidermis has broken away from the finger, revealing the underlying dermis. The ridge details of the dermis may be used to establish identity.

31

INK METHODS FOR TAKING FINGERPRINTS

Those persons whose prints must be taken in connection with an investigation may be handled in one of two ways. They may be requested to report to the Identification Bureau at their earliest convenience where their prints are taken in the regular manner, or the investigator may obtain their prints at the scene of the crime while the investigation is under way. As far as obtaining good prints is concerned, high-quality prints can be obtained in either place. The first procedure is not the choice for several reasons: It inconveniences those whose prints must be taken perhaps to the extent that they do not show up at the bureau or they may wait several days before reporting; it delays the investigation unduly; it is not businesslike; and it does not reflect efficiency or progressiveness on the part of the police agency or its personnel. Elimination prints may be taken at the scene in a matter of minutes; thereby, the job is done where and when it should be, saving time for all concerned and expediting the investigative processes.

WITH INKING PLATE, INK, AND ROLLER

Good prints can be obtained for elimination or any other purpose by using standard fingerprinting equipment, a glass plate, a roller and ink, and a cardholder on a fingerprinting stand. The majority of fingerprinting kits now available on the market have inking materials included with the cardholder attached to the carrying case. However, the standard inking method is most practical in its place in identification bureaus and police detention facilities. The time required in preparing the inking plate may be put to better advantage at crime scenes in collecting evidence and expediting the investigation.

Regular commercial fingerprint ink formulated for fingerprint work should be used for taking inked impressions. Such ink produces a dense black impression and dries quickly on paper. Fingerprint impressions should not be taken with printer's ink, stamp pad ink, ordinary writing ink, or other colored inks, as they are too light, too thin, or do not dry quickly. Another disadvantage that must be noted in using stamp pads is the weave pattern of the pad, which is usually apparent in an impression.

PORELON PAD

Porelon pads are special inking pads that require no ink supply or roller. The pad is a microreticulated thermoplastic resin impregnated with a special permanent and nonfading ink. The pad contains a two-year supply of fingerprint ink, enough for 50,000 fingerprints, and the inked impression dries in seconds on any paper. The pad is in a steel case and comes in both pocket- and desk-size models. When taking inked impressions, the fingers can be rolled or impressed on the same spot on the pad over and over again. The pad requires no replenishing of the ink supply, but it should be wiped off occasionally with a cleansing tissue to remove any finger moisture, dirt, or dust. The cover of the pad should be closed when not in use to prevent drying of the ink supply.

Porelon pads are available from all major fingerprint supply companies. The cost of the pads is extremely reasonable, considering their usefulness and durability. The pocket model may be easily carried by investigators and is a means of obtaining good-quality prints on any type of paper expeditiously.

SPECIAL INKING METHODS

The following methods of taking impressions are limited to specific instances where direct photographic enlargement or direct projection is desired. These methods are not used in identification work but may be used for making instructional materials for training programs.

Forndran (1964) described a method of taking finger impressions in which the finger is coated with pigment by a cotton swab, and the impression is made directly onto a specially prepared 35-mm slide. The resulting impression may then be used for making direct projections or as negatives for photographic enlargements. The color of the photographic enlargements of this method are reversed; the ridges appear white and the paper black. MacDonell (1965) devised a variation of this method using regular fingerprint ink and translucent (frosted) lifting tape on 35-mm glass slides, thereby eliminating the need for special pigments or specially prepared slides. The translucent tape is placed on the glass slide, and the inked finger is rolled onto the tape surface. Points, type lines, and ridge characteristics, etc., can be marked out, as the frosted, matte-finish surface of the tape is conducive to writing with either pen or pencil.

Kodak Ektagraphic Write-on® Slides provide about the same medium for direct projection of prints as the method described by MacDonell; however, the translucent material of both present disadvantages. The projected images lack good contrast, and photographic enlargements are not of good quality. Clear transparent lifting tape provides the best means for making photographic enlargements with sharp definition and excellent contrast. Regular fingerprint ink may be used with the impression made on the adhesive side of the tape and the tape then placed on a glass slide, or the impression may be made on the glass slide and covered with the tape.

To make 35-mm slides for direct projection as training aids, with the points marked off, Kodak Ektagraphic Write-on Slides and a suitable opaque medium provide good results. Regular fingerprint ink is not sufficiently opaque, and the projected image does not have adequate contrast between the ridges and the background. Excellent-quality slides have been made by this method using a thin film of enamel paint and artist's oil paint as the inking medium. The Kodak Ektagraphic Write-on Slides may be obtained in boxes of 100 slides.

32

INKLESS FINGERPRINT TECHNIQUES

A number of inkless methods of recording fingerprints whereby excellent results may be obtained are given in the following pages. The value of each method lies in its applicability under a special set of circumstances, the requirements of the agency concerned, and the frequency of use. Many of the methods described produce results equally as good as the regular inking method, and some are makeshift but worth knowing. Makeshift methods should be considered as field expediencies when the material for the other methods is not available. Successful results may be obtained with these methods, but commercially prepared methods specifically designed for fingerprint use produce consistently better results. As in all fields, "You get exactly what you pay for." The best way to insure good results is to use the proper equipment designed for the job.

Fingerprints taken at identification bureaus and detention facilities are more economically taken by standard inking methods. Inkless fingerprint methods are almost always applicable when obtaining elimination prints from victims and witnesses at crime scenes. Greater cooperation can be expected when the inconvenience is minimized and the persons printed can quickly return to their normal daily routines. The use of inkless methods may help to alleviate the objections of many persons to getting ink on their hands when being fingerprinted. Such objections are particularly encountered with store and office employees.

Some of the methods described are applicable only to taking problem fingerprints when all other methods have failed. Most of the methods may be used by banking institutions, department stores, and other businesses to identify persons cashing checks. This practice is becoming more common in the business community and serves as both a preventive and enforcement measure.

FAUROT INKLESS METHOD

Faurot, Inc. of New York City has long offered on the market an inkless method of taking fingerprints. The method is based on a chemical reaction between a chemical in the inkless pad and a specially prepared sensitized paper. When a finger is pressed on the Faurot pad and an impression made on a special card, a permanent print develops instantly. The sensitized paper may be ordered to the specifications of the customer, and the paper remains active indefinitely. The pad lasts for thousands of prints.

NATIONAL IDENTIFICATION BUREAU, INC.

The National Identification Bureau, Inc., Hickory, Pennsylvania, offers inkless fingerprint equipment to law enforcement agencies and provides the *Personal-Seal System* of fingerprint identification for businesses as a means of protection against forged and fraudulent checks. The method consists of a 2-by-3-inch sensitized pad and strips of a specially prepared paper. The finger is pressed onto the sensitizing pad and the impression made on the special paper. The paper strip may then be placed onto a regular fingerprint card or any other desired form. A clear contrasting black on white print is obtained. One section needs to be redone but it is not necessary to retake the entire card; that particular finger can be taken again and the square cut out and placed over the imperfect one.

SIGNATURE GUARDIAN SYSTEMS, INC.

Signature Guardian Systems, Inc., Las Vegas, Nevada, offers an inkless method that is available in a variety of pad sizes and has the advantage that the pads may be recharged. The method is similar to the inkless methods previously described and consists of a sensitizing pad and a specially prepared paper. This system is used by the Canal Zone Police. The company will reproduce any form desired. The sensitizing pads are available in three sizes: SP 100®, 2⁵⁄₁₆-by-2¾ inches; SP 200®, 2¾-by-4¼ inches; and SP 300®, 4¼-by-7¼ inches. Two sizes of pad rechargers are available: PR 100®, ⅛ ounce and PR 200®, 1 ounce.

VERIPRINT 10

The Veriprint Systems Corporation, Encino, California, offers inkless methods of fingerprinting for business, industrial security, and law enforcement. The systems range from Veriprint 1®, a single digit fingerprinter, to Veriprint 10®, a ten finger-palm printer, to Vericomp®, an electro-optical fingerprint comparison and verification system for security control. The Veriprint 10 has two inkless pressureproof pads that have a firm surface for metering the right amount of coating to the skin for clear prints.

No specially prepared paper is required, and standard forms may be used. After the fingers are pressed onto the pads and the impression taken on the card, the card is placed in a tray and inserted into the developer chamber of the Veriprint 10. The actuator is depressed to release the developer, and in seconds, the completed fingerprint card is removed from the tray. The impressions dry instantly and do not smudge or smear. The Veriprint 10 is portable and can be used either in the office or in the field.

LEAD OLEATE PASTE FORMULA

Lead oleate is a paste for taking fingerprints and is particularly useful in that it can be prepared locally and requires no special equipment or paper. Prints may be taken without leaving visible traces of the paste on the fingers, and the paste may be wiped off the hands with a paper towel. It does not discolor or stain the hands.

A disinfectant (phenol) is added to the formula for sanitary purposes, and a small quantity of oil of wintergreen is included for scenting. If prepared as a thin paste, it may be used on an ink pad; otherwise, it is used in a jar or open-top contained as a thick, heavy paste. If an inkpad is used, the pad should have a closely woven surface.

The paste is very simple to use; the fingers are pressed onto the ink pad or the paste in a jar, and invisible impressions are made on paper in the same manner as in recording regular impressions. The invisible impressions are subjected to an aqueous solution of sodium sulfide by a cotton swab or a pencil sponge. Impressions may also be developed by means of a tube containing a pledget of cotton saturated with ammonium sulfide.

When invisible impressions of the fingers made with the paste are subjected to the fumes of ammonium sulfide or the sodium sulfide solution, a chemical reaction between the lead oleate paste and the sulfides causes the ridges to become dark brown— they develop by exposure to vapors of ammonium sulfide. This method is very effective, but it is also objectionable because of the disagreeable (rotten egg) odor of sulfides. The impressions developed with the paste and sulfides are not permanent; they fade gradually depending upon exposure to light and air.

The formula for the paste is as follows:

Lead oleate plaster, USP	200 parts
Ferric chloride	1 part
Oil of wintergreen	1 part
Oleic acid	QS (to make)

A 1 percent disinfectant such as phenol is added for sanitary purposes. The lead oleate plaster and ferric chloride are thoroughly mixed with sufficient oleic acid to form a smooth paste for the purpose for which it is to be used.

The developing agent is made as follows: one or two pills of flaked sodium sulfide, 60%, are dissolved in 1 ounce of water and used on a cotton swab or in a pencil sponge.

DUSTING METHOD

Taking record impressions by means of regular brush and powder techniques is a makeshift method that produces less than satisfactory prints that are easily destroyed by handling. Many investigators like to take prints by this method to impress subjects with how prints may be recovered as evidentiary items. The results may be disappointing for either purpose.

The impressions should be covered with a transparent tape to protect them from damage, as further handling may remove the powder. One variation of this method which enhances the prints is to apply a thin film of glycerine to the fingers and then make the impressions. The impressions are then developed with powder (Cherrill, 1954).

PHOTOGRAPHY

Photographic recording of friction ridge patterns on fingers is a method normally reserved for problem prints that cannot be recorded by any other method. In this method, a pane of clear glass is placed over the upturned hand of the subject and just enough pressure is applied to flatten out the skin tissue and bring the friction ridges into sharp relief on one plane. The fingers are then photographed individually, using oblique lighting placed on either side of the finger. Careful manipulation of the light source produces sufficient contrast in the core and delta areas to be recorded on film. By reversing the negative in printing, a photograph showing the print in proper relation to the other fingers may be obtained, and the photograph may be mounted on a sheet of paper attached to the fingerprint card (Truby, 1962).

THE PHOTOPAPER METHOD

This method was developed by the Dallas County Sheriff's Office, Dallas, Texas, as a method for printing deceased persons (Cron, 1974). However, the method may also be used for taking problem prints. The method may be used in light as exposing the photographic paper does not affect the results. The procedure is quite simple: Lightly coat the finger with a small amount of Kodak Ektamatic A10 Activator®, covering all the ridges, and then take the impressions on a piece of Ilfoprint Contact Paper S4-1P Single Weight 4 Extra Hard Glossy®, cut to size. For postmortem printing, apply a coat of formaldehyde, let it set for ten to twenty minutes and dry with a swab or towel before applying the activator. After a good, clear print has been obtained, it may be photographed or fixed by being placed in a hypo bath and dried.

PHOTOGRAPHIC FILM METHOD

Arthur (1972) developed a method that permits the direct photographic enlargement of finger impressions and is applicable when fine detail is required. The method is suitable for problem prints involving fine ridge structure and involves taking impressions on regular photographic film, using a developing solution as the inking medium. For taking problem prints, strips of 35-mm photographic film cut in lengths of 8 inches provide contact prints which may be attached directly to a standard fingerprint card. The unprocessed film may be cut and used in regular light and the prints may be marked if desired by using a felt pen dipped in the developing solution. After the impressions are taken on the film, the film is then fixed in ordinary photographer's hypo and dried.

The developing solution is applied to the fingers by saturating a piece of blotting paper with the solution and using the paper as a pad. A few practice prints may be necessary to insure the right amount of developing solution is soaked into the paper. The formula for the developing solution is as follows: Fill two beakers with 50 ml distilled water each; into one beaker add 5 g of sodium hydroxide and 25 g of sodium sulfide and dissolve by heating to 86° F; then dissolve 2 g soluble starch in the second beaker and add the starch solution slowly to the first and allow the mixture to cool slowly while stirring vigorously. When cool, the developing solution may be used to saturate the pad.

LIFTING METHOD

This method was developed by Oscar H. Baker (Corr, 1959) as a postmortem fingerprinting method using ink and either fingerprint lifting tape or rubber fingerprint lifters. The method is also applicable to taking prints in cases where, due to injury or disease, the subject's fingers remain in a permanent flexed position and cannot be extended. A variation of this method has been used by the U.S. Army Criminal Investigation Laboratory for over fifteen years. The method is quite simple and produces quality impressions. The fingers are lightly dusted with black fingerprint powder, and a fingerprint brush, a very stiff brush, may be used to remove the excess powder between the ridges. Impressions may then be cut out of the lifting material and affixed to the fingerprint card. Clear lifting tape may be used, but clear tape should not be affixed directly to the card, as the impression would be reversed—clear tape must be placed on a transparent cover and then affixed to the card. White opaque lifting tape with transparent covers is the best material to use. This tape precludes any possibility of reversing the impression when placing it on the card.

CASTING METHODS

There are a variety of casting materials available for casting finger impressions: liquid latex, dental casting compounds, Duplicast® (a brand of silicone rubber), agar, moulage, and clay are a few of the many substances that may be used. After the finger has been cast, the impression may be recorded by photographing with oblique lighting—the ridges in the photograph appear light and the furrows dark as the ridges cast shadows. The impression may also be recorded by using the cast of the finger as a mold. Silicone rubber is poured into the cast, and after hardening, the silicone rubber cast may be dusted and the impression lifted as described in Section 10. The silicone rubber cast may also be inked and the impressions rolled directly onto a fingerprint card, but ink has a tendency to fill in fine ridge structure and "buildup" on the cast.

THE ELECTRONIC FINGERPRINTING METHOD

The electronic method of inkless fingerprinting was developed by the National Police Agency of Tokyo, Japan (Kimura, 1965), and does not appear to have gained much acceptance outside of that country. There are several disadvantages to this method: Only parts of the fingers are shown, and the method imposes a considerable burden in that the equipment, paper, and chemicals must be specially purchased. Basically, the method uses a specially prepared recording paper sensitized with an electrostatic charge, and the fingers are rolled directly onto the paper. Where the ridges touch the paper, the electrostatic charge is lost, as the human body is an excellent conductor of electricity. The paper is then processed in essentially the same manner as all xerographic processes.

33
COPYING OF FINGERPRINT CARDS

Identification officers are frequently called upon to supply copies of fingerprint cards to outside law enforcement agencies. The best practice when the officer knows that cards must automatically be provided to other agencies is to take several sets of impressions at the time the subject is printed. It is common practice for local agencies to take at least three sets of prints: one for the local agency, one for the state identification bureau, and one forwarded to the Federal Bureau of Investigation for a records check.

There are many methods available for copying fingerprint cards. Agencies with xerographic copying machines available often use this method for copying fingerprint records. However, copies obtained by this method are not always of the best quality; therefore, the copy should be checked with a fingerprint magnifier to insure quality. One effective, fast, and economical method of making reproductions of such *line* material as fingerprints is by a photographic process called *reflex printing* or *reflex copying*. No special equipment is required other than a contact printed large enough to accommodate a fingerprint card (which may be made locally) and regular photographic darkroom facilities for tray developing.

No photographic film is required in this method; all steps are accomplished with a contact printer and reflex paper, such as Kodagraph Fine-Line Contact® paper. A reflex paper negative is made from the subject matter by placing the paper between the surface to be copied and the light source, with the emulsion side toward the subject matter. Exposure is made through the reflex sheet, and timing is determined by tests. The paper negative is developed, fixed, washed briefly, squeegeed, and dried. A positive reprint is then made by placing the paper negative on the contact printer emulsion side up, and a second sheet of reflex paper is laid on the negative emulsion side down, emulsion side to emulsion side. After a second exposure, the reflex paper is developed, fixed, washed, and dried. The result is a facsimile of the original fingerprint card.

The paper negative may be used after it has been squeegeed without drying, but better handling and results are obtained if dried. Developing, fixing, and washing are done in the normal manner for any photographic paper.

"Even at their best the contact reflex copiers do not give as sharp an image as a good copy camera . . ." (Scott, 1955). Positive identification of fingerprints is dependent upon individual ridge characteristics; therefore, it is essential that reproductions of fingerprint records are as clear and sharp as possible. If the agency has a good copy camera as part of its photographic facilities, quality reproductions are no problem. A good film for photographic copying of fingerprint cards is Kodak Contrast Process Ortho Film®. If a copy camera is not available, a simple copying outfit can be constructed for the 4 × 5 Speed and Crown Graphic® cameras commonly found in most law enforcement agencies (*see* Sec. 46).

QUESTIONS

TRUE-FALSE QUESTIONS

1. The value of an inked impression is independent of legibility of ridge detail (Sec. 18). FALSE

2. Correct classification of a fingerprint pattern very often depends upon one particular ridge and even a point on that ridge (Sec. 18). TRUE

3. Blurred, indistinct, and illegible inked impressions which are faulty by reason of skin condition or occupational damage constitute a large percentage of all prints taken (Sec. 18). FALSE

4. Knowledge of what constitutes a fingerprint pattern is a valuable aid to the taking of good impressions (Sec. 18). TRUE

5. In actual fingerprint investigations, smudged latents outnumber clear impressions (Sec. 18). TRUE

F 6. Good workmanship, as reflected in inked impressions, is not critical from the standpoint of classification (Sec. 18). FALSE

F 7. If a latent fingerprint is developed at a crime scene, it is unnecessary to eliminate the prints of those persons who can account for their presence at the scene, if their presence is legitimate (Sec. 19). FALSE

T 8. Elimination prints narrow the search for the suspect (Sec. 19). TRUE

T 9. Oftentimes, prints are made in such positions and locations and under such circumstances that they could only have been made by the person who committed the crime (Sec. 19). TRUE

T 10. Elimination prints of victims and witness may sometimes be used to collaborate or disprove their statements regarding an incident (Sec. 19). TRUE

11. The most opportune time and place to take elimination prints is at the scene while the investigation is underway (Sec. 19). TRUE

12. Delay in obtaining fingerprints for elimination purposes is of no consequence (Sec. 19). FALSE

13. If the prints of an insider are found at a crime scene, they are of no value as evidence (Sec. 19). FALSE

14. Plain impressions show more ridge structure than rolled impressions; therefore, they are more important (Sec. 21). FALSE

15. In the making of an inked impression, 180 degrees of rotation actually shows more than one half of the total skin area around a finger (Sec. 21). TRUE

16. The pattern area of a fingerprint is always complete on the palmar surface of a finger (Sec. 21). FALSE

17. The pattern area of a finger is found nearer the tip than the flexion crease of a finger (Sec. 21). FALSE

18. When plain impressions are taken, a particular attempt should be made to obtain the complete pattern area (Sec. 21). FALSE

19. A fingerprint classifier may be able to look at a finger and determine the type of pattern and decide whether or not it is necessary to roll the finger from "nail-to-nail" (Sec. 21). TRUE

20. Plain impressions ordinarily show more distinct and legible ridge detail than do rolled impressions (Sec. 21). TRUE

21. Rolled impressions serve as a double check or verification of position of plain impressions (Sec. 21). FALSE

22. A person who classifies fingerprints seldom uses the flat impressions for purposes of arriving at the correct classification (Sec. 21). FALSE

23. It is good practice to permit a subject to "take" his own impressions if he is familiar with the procedure (Sec. 22). FALSE

24. Knowledge of what constitutes a fingerprint is unimportant to the taking of good impressions (Sec. 22). FALSE

25. Deltas are present in not more than 65 percent of all fingerprint patterns (Sec. 22). FALSE

26. When rolled impressions are taken, the subject should be

told to hold his fingers out rigidly one at a time and to assist as much as possible (Sec. 23). FALSE

27. The thumb may be rolled equally well either way, inasmuch as the palmar surface faces downward midway on a 180 degree roll (Sec. 23). FALSE

28. A palm impression made by rolling the palm over a cylinder may appear to be, and in fact be slightly foreshortened (Sec. 26). TRUE

29. Mottled skin is a temporary condition which is overcome in time (Sec. 28). FALSE

30. When taking fingerprints, the recording officer should stand and work so that the inking plate is nearer than the cardholder (Sec. 24). FALSE

31. More faulty prints can be traced to skin conditions or occupational damage than to carelessness on the part of the person who takes the prints (Sec. 27). FALSE

32. Occupational damage may result in either temporary or permanent damage to the skin (Sec. 28). TRUE

33. If the subject's hands are so deformed that normal printing operations cannot be accomplished there is no possibility of obtaining good impressions (Sec. 29). FALSE

34. A technician should never jump to the conclusion that a body is too decomposed to obtain prints so long as the epidermis or dermis remains (Sec. 30). TRUE

35. The Porelon pad is a special inking pad which requires no ink supply or roller (Sec. 31). TRUE

COMPLETION QUESTIONS

36. Impressions recorded on a standard fingerprint card fall into one or the other of two types which are rolled... and plain. impressions (Sec. 21).

37. When a rolled impression is correctly taken, the fissure... or flexion creases shows in the inked impression just above the bottom line of the space (Sec. 21).

38. One way to determine whether the finger is properly inked is by examining the impression made by the finger on the inking.. plate (Sec. 21).

39. When taking fingerprints, absolute control of the subject's hand is necessary (Sec. 22).
40. Points often missed in rolling impressions and essential to correct classification are the deltas ... (Sec. 22).
41. The first and most important step in taking a set of finger-prints is to clean ... the inking .. plate ... thoroughly (Sec. 23).
42. If the fingerprint card and inking plate are side by side, the recording officer should reach across the .card ... to work on the inking. plate (Sec. 23).
43. When taking rolled impressions of the fingers, the finger and forearm should be rotated in such a way that movement is from a strained . to a relaxed . position (Sec. 23).
44. Three occupations which may cause damage to the skin which in turn makes classification difficult if not impossible are Laborer ..., plasterer ., and battery worker (Sec. 28).
45. Two of the most common faults which result in poor-quality impressions are carelessness and lack of skill ... (Sec. 27).
46. When the fingers are rough and dry, rubbing the bulbs of the fingers with petroleum. jelly .... or .oil .... often permits them to become sufficiently pliable and soft to enable them to be printed (Sec. 29).
47. In extreme cases of deformity, casting .. may provide the only means of recording impressions of the fingers and hands (Sec. 29).
48. No matter what system is used in postmortem fingerprinting, it is very important that the strips or cards be adequately identified .. (Sec. 30).
49. When taking postmortem fingerprints, each impression should be examined immediately after it is taken (Sec. 30).
50. Major ... case ... points ... is the term applied to a set of inked impressions recording the complete ridge structure of the hands (Sec. 25).

REFERENCES

Arthur, A. M.: "A new method for taking fingerprints using photographic film," *American Journal of Physical Anthropology.* vol. 36 (1972), p. 441.

Balshy, J. C.: "Tanning human skin to produce legible prints for identification," *Fingerprint and Identification Magazine.* vol. 54 (Feb., 1953), p. 12.

Bernardi, A., and P. Tarditi: "Rilievi papillari nel cadavere ai fini della identificazione personale," *Rivista Di Polizia.* vol. 17 (1964), p. 337.

Brooks, A. J.: Inked Finger and Palmprints. Personal communication. August 5, 1975.

Califania, A. L.; "Fingerprinting the deceased," *Law and Order.* vol. 17 (Dec., 1969), p. 46.

———: "Some random thoughts about post mortem identification," *Fingerprint and Identification Magazine.* vol. 55 (Dec., 1973), p. 11.

Castellanos, I.: "New techniques of skin impressions," *Identification News.* vol. 20 (Jan., 1970), p. 13.

Cherrill, Frederick R.: *The Finger Print System at Scotland Yard.* London, H.M.S.O., 1954.

"Clear fingerprints needed of unknown dead," *FBI Law Enforcement Bulletin.* vol. 34 (Jan., 1965).

"Common mistakes in taking inked fingerprints," *FBI Law Enforcement Bulletin.* vol. 26 (May, 1957).

Cooke, T. D.: "Unusual techniques in post mortem finger printing," *Fingerprint and Identification Magazine.* vol. 40 (Aug., 1958), p. 3.

Cordy, R. E.: "A novel corpse identification method," *Fingerprint and Identification Magazine.* vol. 49 (July, 1967), p. 3.

Corr, J. J.: "Post mortem fingerprinting," *Military Police Journal.* vol. 10 (Dec., 1959), p. 16.

———: "Post mortem printing under difficult conditions," *Fingerprint and Identification Magazine.* vol. 41 (Feb., 1960), p. 4.

Cowan, M. E.: "Preparation of fingers for post mortem printing following extreme deterioration," *Fingerprint and Identification Magazine.* vol. 41 (July, 1959), p. 3.

Cron, J. G.: "The photo-paper method of printing the deceased," *Fingerprint and Identification Magazine.* vol. 56 (Aug., 1974), p. 11.

Cummins, H.: "Comments on odd Jamaican patterns," *Fingerprint and Identification Magazine.* vol. 52 (Aug., 1970), p. 12.

Dalstrom, G.: "A simplified method of recording infant palm and heel prints," *Fingerprint and Identification Magazine.* vol. 40 (June, 1959), p. 3.

Davis, C. A.: "Method of obtaining finger prints for identification by histologie section," *Journal of Criminal Law, Criminology and Police Science.* vol. 48 (1957), p. 468.

"Delivery room nurses learn how to footprint the newborn," *Hospitals.* vol. 39 (Nov., 1965), p. 65.

"Digital amputation in post mortem cases," *Fingerprint and Identification Magazine.* vol. 46 (Apr., 1965), p. 3.

Estery, T.: "New method solves fingerprint record problems," *Law and Order.* vol. 10 (Dec., 1962).

"Fingerprint work in major public disasters," *FBI Law Enforcement Bulletin.* vol. 27 (Sept., 1958), p. 17.

"Fingerprints of deceased persons," *FBI Law Enforcement Bulletin.* vol. 22 (Jan., 1953), p. 23.

Forndran, W. E.: "New method for recording friction skin patterns," *Fingerprint and Identification Magazine.* vol. 46 (Sept., 1964), p. 3.

Fowler, D. C.: "Further thoughts on casting finger prints," *Fingerprint and Identification Magazine.* vol. 39 (Feb., 1958), p. 6.

Ginnelly, T. J., and J. Nemec: "Fingerprinting the deceased and injured," *Fingerprint and Identification Magazine.* vol. 54 (June, 1973), p. 3.

Harrick, N. J.: "Het maken van fingerafdrukken met behulp van totale reflexie," *Tijdschrift Voor De Politie.* vol. 26 (1964), p. 50.

Heine, D.: "Abnahme von Vergleichs-fingerabdrucken gagen den Willen des Betroffenen," *Kriminalistik.* vol. 19 (1965), p. 305.

Hobart, V. B.: "Precision recording (optical) of fingerprints," *Law and Order.* vol. 8 (Dec., 1960).

"Importance of good rolled prints," *Fingerprint and Identification Magazine.* vol. 49 (Sept., 1967), p. 12.

"Inner surface print names river's victim," *Fingerprint and Identification Magazine.* vol. 39 (Mar., 1958), p. 4.

"An interesting post mortem technique," *Fingerprint and Identification Magazine.* vol. 42 (May, 1961), p. 6.

Jordan, H.: "Verfahren zur daktyloskopischen Bearbeitung der mumifizierten Leichenhand," *Archiv fur Kriminologie.* vol. 138 (1966), p. 153.

Jordan, H., and A. Simon: "Die fingerabdrucknahme von faulnisveranderten Leichen," *Archiv fur Kriminologie.* vol. 144 (1969), p. 41.

Kimura, Y.: "The electronic finger printing method," *Fingerprint and Identification Magazine.* vol. 46 (Jan., 1965), p. 3.

King, D. P.: "Post mortem fingerprinting," *Police.* vol. 7 (Sept.-Oct., 1962), p. 21.

King, R. J.: "Importance of good rolled prints," *Fingerprint and Identification Magazine.* vol. 49 (Sept., 1967), p. 12.

Koch, D.: "Zur Technik der Leichen-daktyloskopie," *Archiv fur Kriminologie.* vol. 138 (1966), p. 148.

Konopka, W.: "Fingerprinting mummified tissue," *Fingerprint and Identification Magazine.* vol. 55 (June, 1974), p. 3.

Liebenberg, I. J.: "Obtaining a print from a mummified finger," *Journal of Criminal Law, Criminology and Police Science.* vol. 41 (1950), p. 224.

MacDonell, H. L.: "Direct projection of rolled impressions," *Identification News.* vol. 15 (Oct.-Nov., 1965), p. 13.

Mansfield, E. R.: "The importance of taking good finger impressions," *Fingerprint and Identification Magazine.* vol. 53 (Jan., 1972), p. 3.

Margarida, A. G.: "La reseña necrodactilar," *Guardia Civil.* vol. 25 (1968), no. 289, p. 12.

McKeehan, H. E.: "The restoration of desiccated cadaveric fingers for the purpose of identification," *Journal of the Forensic Science Society.* vol. 10 (1970), p. 115.

Mercer, J. T.: "Tanning of murder victim's fingers results in his identification," *Fingerprint and Identification Magazine.* vol. 42 (Jan., 1961), p. 3.

―――: "Obtaining finger prints from mummified fingers," *Fingerprint and Identification Magazine.* vol. 47 (Feb., 1966), p. 3.

Moenssens, Andre A.: *Fingerprint Techniques.* New York, Chilton, 1971.

Moore, R. L.: *The Influence of Ink on the Quality of Fingerprint Impressions, NBSIR 74-627,* National Bureau of Standards. Washington, D.C., U.S. Govt. Print Office, 1974.

Myers, H. J.: "Digital amputation and the law," *Fingerprint and Identification Magazine.* vol. 43 (Dec., 1961), p. 3.

Norkus, P. M.: "Record palm and major case prints," *The Detective.* vol. 6 (Spring, 1976), p. 24.

Ollivier, H., and F. Vuillet: "Considérations pratiques à propos du relève sur le cadavre de certaines empreintes digitales alterées," *Annales De Medecine Legale.* vol. 45 (1965), p. 468.

Padron, F.: "Necrodactylography," *Fingerprint and Identification Magazine.* vol. 45 (Dec., 1963), p. 3.

―――: "Difficulties in recording finger prints," *Fingerprint and Identification Magazine.* vol. 48 (Jan., 1967), p. 3.

"Post mortem prints identified through latents," *Fingerprint and Identification Magazine.* vol. 43 (Nov., 1961), p. 6.

"Problems involved in preparation of fingerprint cards," *FBI Law Enforcement Bulletin.* vol. 29 (Sept., 1960), p. 18.

"Proper preparation and use of arrest fingerprint cards," *FBI Law Enforcement Bulletin.* vol. 26 (July, 1957), p. 16.

"Proper preparation and use of civil fingerprint cards," *FBI Law Enforcement Bulletin.* vol. 26 (Oct., 1957), p. 18.

Pullen, W.: "Is het mogelijk het dactyloscopische inktprocede te vervangen," *Tijdschrift Voor De Politie.* vol. 26 (1964), p. 54.

Richardson, L., and L. Kade: "Readable fingerprints from mummified or putrefied specimens," *Identification News.* vol. 23 (Jan., 1973), p. 3.

Scott, C. C.: *Photographic Evidence.* St. Paul, MN, West Publishing Co., 1955, vol. 2, p. 216.

"Shark and sea victim identified by fingerprints," *FBI Law Enforcement Bulletin.* vol. 19 (Aug., 1950), p. 21.

Simon, A., and H. Jordan: "Die daktyloskopie von brandleichen mit silikongummipaste," *Archiv fur Kriminologie.* vol. 141 (1968), p. 28.

Sullivan, T. F.: "Entire hand skin peels off like a glove: Victim named," *Fingerprint and Identification Magazine.* vol. 52 (Dec., 1970), p. 12.

Thomson, M. W.: "The fingerprinting of cadavers," *Fingerprint and Identification Magazine.* vol. 53 (Aug., 1971), p. 14.

"3,500-year old fingerprints," *Science Digest.* vol. 31 (Jan., 1952), p. 60.

Trotter, C. L.: "Organized plans needed to identify disaster victims," *FBI Law Enforcement Bulletin.* vol. 29 (May, 1960), p. 13.

Truby, C. L.: "Advice on recording fingerprints that are difficult to ink and record," *Military Police Journal.* vol. 12 (June, 1962), p. 12.

"Ways of obtaining good fingerprints, insuring legibility," *FBI Law Enforcement Bulletin.* vol. 30 (July, 1961), p. 20.

Wier, B. R.: "How liquid latex identified Willie Williams," *Fingerprint and Identication Magazine.* vol. 40 (Nov., 1958), p. 3.

Wilson, R.: "Fingerprint identification of a burned body," *Identification News.* vol. 25 (Feb., 1975), p. 3.

Woodward, F. V.: "Mass identification—by photography and fingerprints," *The Police Journal.* vol. 35 (1962), p. 91.

Zeldenrust, J.: "Identificatie van slachtoffers bij rampen," *Tijdschrift Voor De Politie.* vol. 25 (1963), p. 241.

Chapter III

Latent Fingerprints and Crime Scene Procedures

VALUE OF FINGERPRINT EVIDENCE

L AW ENFORCEMENT OFFICERS and the general public associate
fingerprint evidence with criminal investigations and the apprehension of criminals more than any other category of physical evidence (Fig. 31). In fact, fingerprint evidence is applicable to almost all investigations; fingerprints are specific in that
they prove the presence at a crime scene of the person who made
the impressions and establish that a person once had contact with
an evidentiary item.

Unfortunately, fingerprint evidence and physical evidence in
general are not sought after by investigators as diligently as they
should be. The Science and Technology Task Force Report
(President's Commission, 1967) describes a Los Angeles case
study of 626 burglaries in which a fingerprint technician was re-

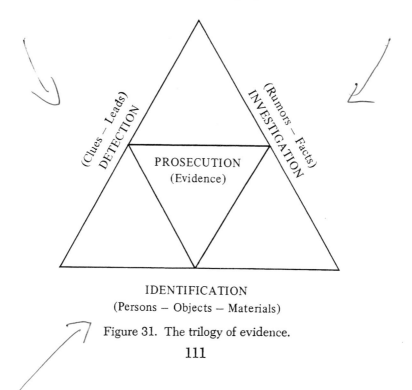

IDENTIFICATION
(Persons — Objects — Materials)

Figure 31. The trilogy of evidence.

111

quested in only slightly more than 40 percent of all cases. No information was available as to how many of the requests a technician actually responded, but actual fingerprint evidence was produced in only 5 percent of the total cases.

Peterson (1974) reports one study which revealed that, in one city, evidence was more frequently collected in offenses where a suspect was already in custody, and in many cities, officers made an extra effort when they had a suspect against whom they could compare latent prints. Another study cited by Peterson revealed that of 749 cases examined in a medium-sized western city, 88 percent were judged to have physical evidence at the scene, but fingerprints rated second in frequency of occurrence. The foregoing information is disturbing in that it indicates not that fingerprint evidence cannot be recovered, but that law enforcement officers are not properly processing crime scenes and seeking fingerprint evidence as diligently as they should.

One fingerprint may establish the presence of the accused at a crime scene, and when presented as evidence in a case, it establishes beyond a reasonable doubt the fact that the accused was at the scene, and it opens the way to a successful prosecution. Better yet, as so often happens, when a stolid, sullen uncooperative individual who demands his Constitutional rights is confronted with fingerprint evidence, he is apt to change his attitude and tactics and admit the facts. Some defendants may elect to stand on their Constitutional rights, remain silent, and make it necessary to prove every point and every step in court. Fingerprint evidence is useful in this type of case.

Fingerprint identification is positive. A defendant may successfully convince a court that his fingerprints were placed at a crime scene when he was legitimately there, but he cannot successfully refute the identification of his fingerprints. Moenssens (1972) has pointed out that law enforcement agencies should not be uncooperative with defense attorneys who request to have fingerprint identifications checked by another examiner. Every *qualified* examiner who looks at the prints will come to the same conclusion. Rather than detract from the prosecution's case, such additional examinations should serve to strengthen it.

An investigator should strive to obtain that one good bit of fingerprint evidence in every case wherein it is a factor, and conversely, he should recover all possible fingerprint evidence even though at first it does not look too promising. It is better to have a selection, and when it comes time to use the evidence, he may choose that which he thinks is most useful. It often happens that a number of useful prints are developed, in which case the investigator is free to use what he thinks is the "best evidence," disregarding but not discarding the rest.

Fingerprint evidence is particularly useful in investigations of narcotics and other drug offenses. Not only may fingerprints assist in establishing possession of contraband, but they may also aid in establishing the identity of suppliers. Defendants may recant their confessions or flatly deny possession of prohibited drugs, witnesses may change their testimony, and courts may find an element of doubt in the prosecution's case, but the positive identification of a suspect's latent fingerprints may establish unlawful possession of drugs beyond any reasonable doubt. Fingerprints may strengthen an already fine investigation, and they may even prove to be the difference between acquittal and conviction.

One important aspect of fingerprint evidence that is frequently overlooked by the general public is that while fingerprints assist in the convictions of criminal suspects, they are also valuable evidence in establishing innocence. The identification of a latent print is not in itself proof of guilt nor can it be considered so until all other elements and facts of the case are considered by a court of law. Law enforcement agencies may develop sufficient information and evidence to charge a person with committing a crime, but only a court of law may determine guilt. Many individuals are, however, cleared of any wrongdoing in the investigative stage, and latent fingerprints assist in establishing their innocence. Latent prints found at a crime scene and which are in such a position or location that only the perpetrator of the crime could have made them assist immeasurably in eliminating all other suspects.

Fingerprint evidence may also aid an investigator in establishing ownership of stolen property. Quite often stolen property is found in the possession of a suspect, but a solid case cannot be established against the suspect because the property cannot be positively identified with the true owner. In such cases it is not necessary for the suspect to prove lawful possession, as the police must prove that the property lawfully belongs to another. Latent fingerprints of the lawful owner developed on stolen property places the suspect in the position of accounting for the presence of the prints and, therefore, indirectly proving legal possession.

Fingerprint evidence differs from most other physical evidence. One person and only one person can make a given fingerprint impression. In this sense, fingerprints have both a positive and negative value—positive in establishing the identity of the person who made the impression and negative in that all other persons may be eliminated.

35

LATENT FINGERPRINTS

Latent fingerprints are visualized by the layman as impressions made by the fingers on surfaces or objects which are handled. For all practical purposes, the conception is correct, but the fingerprint technician recognizes and deals with all degrees of latency from total invisibility to prints as good as impressions taken on paper for identification.

The word *latent* mean "hidden" or not visible or apparent, but the word in a strict sense has no such limited application in the experiences of the fingerprint technician. In modern police usage, the term *latent* is applied to all chance or unintentional impressions that are of evidentiary value. Latent fingerprints are divided into two categories, invisible and visible. Invisible prints are made by perspiration and other substances on the skin surface and require the application of a latent fingerprint technique to develop the print so that it may be examined and photographed.

Visible fingerprints may be further divided into two classes:

plastic fingerprints and fingerprints made by contamination of the skin with such substances as blood, paint, ink, or grease, etc. Plastic impressions are molds formed by the friction ridges in soft pliable substances, for example, putty, modeling clay, axle grease, chocolate, butter, or soap, etc.

Regardless of the nature of the latent print, visible or invisible, or whether it is a plastic impression or made by contamination of the fingers, the individual ridge characteristics and their relationship to each other are the features essential for identification. If ridge structure is discernible and legible or can be so made with latent fingerprint techniques, the impression passes for a fingerprint for purposes of the fingerprint technician; otherwise, it is considered a smudge or finger mark. Evidential value of a fingerprint depends directly upon the individual ridge characteristics, which possess a sufficiency of clear detail to make a comparison with known prints possible.

36

PALMAR SWEAT DIFFERS FROM OTHER SKIN SECRETIONS

There is a demonstrable difference between the secretion of the sweat glands on the papillary ridges of the hands and fingers and the secretions of the hairy portion of the body skin—the scalp, face, and neck, etc.—which contains secretions of the sebaceous glands. Figure 32 depicts two pairs of fingerprints developed by brush and powder, showing the difference between palmar sweat and sebum, the secretion of sebaceous glands, insofar as its reaction to powder.

The two impressions in Figure 32A were made by two fingers of a hand after it had been thoroughly washed and dried before it had made contact with any other skin surface or object. It is seen that the print is "spotty"; the pore structure is revealed as a result of glandular activity. The powder adheres strongly in places and it leaves other places blank.

After Figure 32A was made, the hand was washed, dried, and

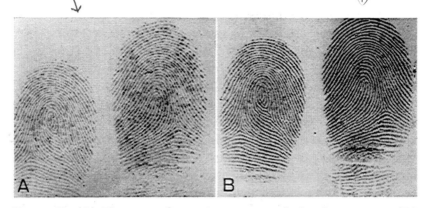

Figure 32. (A) These two fingerprints were made by finger sweat. (B) These fingerprints were made after rubbing the fingers on the neck below the ear. Oils from the sebaceous glands produce better impressions from the standpoint of development when using powders or fuming techniques.

rubbed on the neck below the ear and the Figure 32B impressions were made. Result of powdering is a very even distribution of the powder particles over the ridges; pores are absent; and the ridges are complete, continuous, and strong. The latent impressions were made on the same surface under identical conditions and within a few moments of each other. The same powder was used to develop both sets of prints.

Sweat glands, properly called *eccrine glands*, are found on almost all surface skin areas of the body with their greatest density on the palmar surfaces of the hands and the plantar surfaces of the feet. Sebaceous glands are associated with the hair follicles. Sebum, the secretion of sebaceous glands, contributes oils and fatty substances to the film of perspiration on the skin; hence, the better adhesion of powder particles. Although there is a significant demonstrable difference between sweat and sebum, this knowledge is not of any great practical value to the fingerprint technician, as the choice of latent fingerprint techniques used depends more upon the nature of the surface to be examined.

Modern instrumental chemical analyses have revealed that sweat is approximately 99.0 to 99.5 percent water, with the remaining 0.5 to 1.0 percent being solids. About one half of the solids are organic substances and one-half inorganic salts. The predominant inorganic salt is sodium chloride (ordinary salt). The organic substances include a variety of acids and nitrogenous compounds, the most important of which, for fingerprint technicians, are amino acids.

A complete description of the chemical composition of palmar sweat and sebum is essential for anyone wishing to conduct research programs for new, improved latent fingerprint techniques, but it does not have any significant practical value for the technician recovering fingerprint evidence. A technician should have a rudimentary knowledge of the techniques he uses and the substances they react with, but when dealing with fingerprint evidence, it is the positive identification of a print that is of paramount importance, not the chemical processes of the techniques used. When testifying in courts as to the identification of fingerprints, *a technician should not, regardless of his background and training, be drawn into a description of the chemical reaction between latent techniques and chemical substances in the latent print residue.* Such approaches by a defense attorney are aimed at confusing the jury and clouding the issue. Neither the chemical substances involved nor the nature of their processes have any direct effect upon identification of friction ridge characteristics.

37

FACTORS AFFECTING LATENT FINGERPRINTS

Even with proper handling and application of the appropriate latent fingerprint technique, not all attempts to recover latent fingerprints are successful. Failure to recover latent fingerprints does not in itself necessarily mean that the prints were wiped off. The absence of latent fingerprints on an evidentiary item may be due to numerous factors, each depending on conditions existing before, during, and after the finger touched or handled the surface examined. Generally, the fingerprint technician does not have any prior knowledge of these factors when he processes the evidence for latent prints. However, an understanding of the factors affecting latent prints aids the technician in explaining to laymen the fragile and transitory nature of latent fingerprints and why latent prints cannot always be recovered.

A latent fingerprint is a chance or accidental impression of the friction ridges of the skin. It is a reversed reproduction transferred onto a receiving surface by a transferring medium. The transferring medium or method of transfer determines the type of latent impression—invisible print, plastic impression, etc. The factors affecting a latent fingerprint may be grouped into three stages in the formation of a latent print: pretransfer conditions (subject factors), transfer conditions (transposal factors), and post-transfer conditions (environmental factors). All these factors are relative, and rarely are conditions identical in two separate cases. Knowledge of the factors assist in understanding the fragile and elusive nature of latent impressions and are presented for this purpose rather than as an aid in recovering latent prints or for identification. More often than not, the factors are cumulative in effect and the isolation of any one factor as the direct cause for the lack of latents is impossible.

SUBJECT FACTORS

Subject factors apply to the subject making the latent impressions and are the most variable of all factors affecting latent impressions, as they vary not only between individuals but from day-to-day for the same individual. The observations are general in nature and do not purport to apply in every individual case. *It is not possible to determine the age, sex, or race of an individual solely from their fingerprints.*

AGE. Senile atrophy of the skin starts shortly after the age of forty. The epidermis becomes thinner at the expense of the lower strata; the papillae of the dermis flatten and lose their elastic fibers; and numerous creases appear in the friction ridge skin areas. Certain diseases associated with aging may affect the friction ridges. Deterioration of the skin produced by age is not in itself necessarily the cause of a disease; simply, the longer one lives, the greater the chance of meeting with a disease-producing set of circumstances.

The response to thermal sweating is slower for older persons, and it is also slower to return to a normal rate. The rate of insensible sweating is also lower than in younger persons. After the age of forty, the sebaceous glands are reduced in number of active glands, and the glands show certain qualitative changes. Individuals over twenty-five years of age appear to secrete lower concentrations of amino acids than younger subjects (Edwards et al., 1966). These briefly described characteristics of the effects of aging tend to indicate that there is a diminished probability of success in recovering latent impressions of very old individuals.

SEX. Several factors based on sexual differences may affect latent fingerprints. Statistically, in young adults, the friction ridges of women are significantly finer (or narrower) than those of men (Cummins and Midlo, 1943). Fine ridges may also be found in the very young and the very old, and manual labor has a tendency to strengthen ridges; therefore, no attempt should ever be made to identify a latent print as a woman's solely on fine ridges. The effect of fine ridge structure on latent impressions is obvious; less skin surface touching the receiving surface leaves less latent print residue to react with latent fingerprint techniques and is accordingly, spotty in appearance.

Women tend to perspire at a lower rate than men, although they have greater densities of heat-activated sweat glands per square centimeter, and the concentration of sodium chloride is lower for women. Anyone who has examined a number of fingerprints soon notes that there is a significantly greater number of creases in the fingerprint pattern areas of women. Creases may be found in the fingerprints of men, especially with increasing age, but are common in those of women. It is not uncommon to find fingerprints of women that cannot be properly classified because of creases and fine ridge structure.

STIMULI. There are three types of sweating: thermal, emotional, and gustatory sweating. Each is induced by a different type of stimuli. Thermal sweating is stimulated by warmth, exertion, nausea, fever, and drugs. Its effect on latent fingerprints depends on the rate and duration of sweating and the acclimatization of the subject. Excessive thermal sweating adversely affects latent prints as there is too much moisture of the fingers, and the latent appears as a blurred image. Emotional sweating is stimulated by anxiety, tension, or pain—conditions most likely to be present for a subject when committing a crime. Emotional sweating could possibly account for the majority of latent prints recovered from crime scenes. Gustatory sweating is induced by eating spicy foods and has little application to latents at crime scenes.

OCCUPATION. Occupational effects on the skin condition of subjects has been discussed in Section 28. However, occupation may also affect the subject, concerning his rate and duration of perspiration. During the hot summer months, persons who work in cold storage and other relatively cold areas have little opportunity to acclimatize to warm weather. Such persons may sweat profusely when outside of their occupational environment. Conversely, during the cold winter months, persons who work in a hot and humid occupational environment do not perspire as readily as those acclimated to the lower temperatures.

MEDICAL CONDITION. The medical condition of the subject may affect both the physical condition of the skin and sweat gland activity. Examples of diseases which may affect friction ridges are: dermatitis venenata, tinea, verrucae, scabies, pompholyx, keratoderma palmare et plantare, erythema multiforme, syphilis, dermatitis repens, carcinoma, melanoma, arsenical keratoderma, and gonorrheal keratoderma. Certain diseases and the medical treatment for some diseases may also affect the rate, duration and chemical composition of sweat.

TRANSPOSAL FACTORS

The most significant transposal factor having an effect on latent fingerprints is the nature of the receiving surface. Very rough surfaces may retain the deposits of latent print residue, but the nature of the surface may make distinguishing of ridge characteristics impossible. Extremely soft substances may be so sticky that much of it adheres to the fingers, thereby destroying any plastic impressions that the ridges may have made in the substance. Contaminants on the hands may be so heavy that too much material is deposited and the ridge impressions obscured, or in some cases heavy concentrations of contaminants on the receiving surface may also preclude the possibility of latent fingerprints; well-oiled firearms is one such example. Extremely porous surfaces and substances with a high coarse-fiber content may also prove to be a poor receiving surface for latent prints.

Transposal factors also include the manner in which the friction ridges come into contact with the receiving surface. Certain objects may be handled in only one manner, while others are constructed in such a way that direct grasping is impossible. The amount of pressure may also be a factor in that too great a pressure may destory ridge details, and prolonged contact of the fingers with the receiving surface may blur the latent impression because of the increased deposit of sweat.

ENVIRONMENTAL FACTORS

Environmental factors may be defined as those conditions and situations to which a latent fingerprint is exposed after its deposit on a receiving surface. Temperature, humidity, and handling are the three primary factors within this group which may adversely affect a latent fingerprint. Time may also be considered a factor and is an important consideration both from the investigative viewpoint and for the successful recovery of latent prints. However, time is not in itself a factor affecting latent prints; quite simply, the longer the period between deposit of the latent until it is processed, the greater its exposure to temperature, humidity, and handling.

TEMPERATURE AND HUMIDITY. Although temperature and humidity may be measured independently, their effect upon latent fingerprints is interdependent with each other. Bluhm and Lougheed (1968) found that the ideal temperature-humidity condition for preserving latent fingerprints on a nonporous surface is 40° F and 55 percent relative humidity. Latent prints on nonporous surfaces deteriorate faster at temperatures exceeding

70° F and corresponding relative humidity of 25 percent or less than latent prints at lower temperatures. Excessively high temperatures with corresponding low relative humidity tend to dry out a latent print through evaporation of the moisture content.

Exposure of latent impressions to adverse temperatures and humidity conditions may indicate a lower probability of successfully recovering good latent prints but does not necessarily mean that all such impressions cannot be successfully recovered. High concentrations of sebum and other chemical substances may prolong the life of a latent under such conditions.

Another situation in which temperature and humidity may adversely affect latent prints is the temperature of the object on which the latent is located in relation to the surrounding air. If an object is taken from a cool environment and placed in a warm environment, for example, a pistol found in a driveway is brought into the house for examination, the object tends to "sweat" as condensation forms on it. Such sweating of an object tends to wash away any latent print residue. Evidentiary objects found outside in unprotected areas must be protected from the weather. Dust, dew, and rain may obscure or completely eradicate latent fingerprints. Latents may also be destroyed by strong sunlight or heat.

Improper and excessive handling of evidentiary items probably destroys more latent fingerprints than any other factor. Fingerprint evidence must be carefully protected even after latent prints have been developed. Tests conducted at the United States Army Criminal Investigation Laboratory, Fort Gordon, Georgia, indicate that latent impressions are more easily damaged after they have been developed with powder than before processing. The most critical period in preserving fingerprint evidence is during removal from the crime scene to the laboratory or identification bureau. The investigator must take all appropriate measures to protect all surfaces bearing latent impressions while transporting the evidence.

38

HOW LONG DO LATENT FINGERPRINTS LAST?

In the mechanics of fingerprints, the life of latents is considered as that time in which the impressions may be processed or developed to a point of usefulness from an investigative standpoint and for evidentiary purposes.

All the factors cited in Section 37 and their cumulative effects determine the life of a latent impression. Latent prints ordinarily remain for several days in a condition in which they may be readily processed, but as time passes from the instant of impression, their acceptance of powder diminishes until a point is reached when insufficient powder adheres to reveal enough detail to make an identifiable fingerprint. The first twenty-four or thirty-six hours appears to make no appreciable change in receptivity to powder for latents on nonporous surfaces. Prints may be developed by powders to a better advantage an hour or two or several hours after they are made, than if they are powdered immediately after being made.

For good acceptance of powder, latents should be free of visible particles of moisture, which are usually present in latents immediately after they are made. Better ridge detail is revealed after the excess moisture has evaporated. Excessive moisture in a fresh print holds an excessive amount of powder. Conversely, there are times when the latent print is dried out and is not receptive to powders. In such instances, the investigator may blow onto the surface while he is applying the powder, as his breath adds the necessary moisture to the latent print residue. When using the breath technique, the object examined must not be too cool or the investigator's breath forms moisture over the entire surface and the powder paints the surface, thereby obscuring any latent prints.

If latent impressions are subject to ideal environmental conditions, they may last indefinitely. In one case, the Pittsburgh Police Department was able to develop and lift good latent prints from a metal box that had been in storage for eight years ("Latent Prints, 8 Years Old, Help Solve Bizarre Murder," 1963). Good latent prints have also been developed by the ninhydrin technique on records that have been sealed for thirty years (Svenssen and Wendel, 1965). These are unusual instances where the evidentiary items were not subjected to adverse conditions and cannot be expected to be normally found—as fresh prints represent one extreme, these cases represent the other. In actual practice, if nonporous surfaces are not processed within a few days, there is a reduced chance of obtaining good latents. However, two aspects must be stressed: Latents may last for quite lengthy periods on porous surfaces, such as paper, and be recovered with appropriate chemical techniques, and an attempt should always be made to develop latent impressions, regardless of the time lapsed since the time of the offense. The factors af-

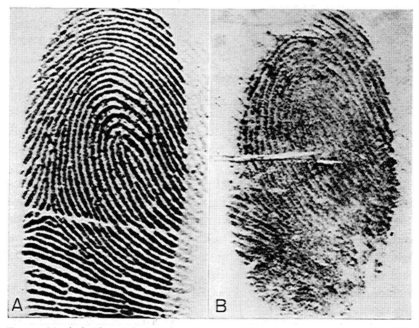

Figure 33. (A) Plain inked impression was taken for comparison with (B) five-month-old latent developed on glazed surface. Latent was "dated" by scar showing in the inked impression, which was known to have been made five months previously.

fecting the life of latent prints are so numerous and varied that it is not possible to determine the likelihood of their presence unless a thorough examination has been made (Fig. 33).

39
LATENT FINGERPRINT TECHNIQUES

A latent fingerprint technique is any method, process, procedure or technique used to intensify or enhance latent fingerprint impressions for identification purposes. Techniques may vary from observation under a strong light to the application of radioactive chemical compounds. Chapters V through VIII cover latent fingerprint techniques and their preparation and use. Some of the techniques have been used to connect offenders with crime scenes, others are relatively new, while still others are novel and have little or no practical value. Some are experimental, and their practical value has yet to be established. As many techniques as possible are listed in order to acquaint and familiarize the reader with all possible techniques for recovering latent impressions.

No single latent fingerprint technique should ever be adopted to the complete exclusion of all others. Each has its time and place applicable to particular situations and circumstances. For example, the normal procedure for developing latent impressions on paper is application of the iodine technique, then ninhydrin, and finally silver nitrate, in that order. However, in one specific case, only the iodine technique could be used because the evidence was counterfeit currency supplied by an informer and had to be returned by the informer to the suspect without any traces of processing. In this case, the iodine technique was used, the latents photographed, the iodine cleared, and the counterfeit currency returned without the suspect's knowledge, thereby aiding not only in the apprehension of the counterfeiters but also their distributors.

"Regardless of the technique used, it should be remembered that the ultimate value of any technique is entirely dependent upon the skill of the person using it. A paintbrush and face powder in the hands of a skilled technician could give better results than the most sophisticated equipment in the hands of a novice" (Brooks, 1972). This statement needs no elaboration. Experience is essential in fingerprint work, not only for proper use and application of techniques but also to determine which technique to use. It is easy to state in general terms that powders should be the first choice of techniques for nonporous surfaces, such as a glass window pane, but other considerations may also make this a wrong choice. One example is a glass pane from the kitchen window of a cafe, where there is a thin film of grease over the glass, or a pane from a dirty warehouse. In the first instance, powder paints the surface; in the latter it does not adhere to the dirt and may even remove it.

For the person beginning fingerprint training and who does not have ready access to training facilities, one way to gain experience in developing latent impressions is to process everyday items around the office or home. Both intentional and chance impressions should be developed on a variety of surfaces. Such practice and experience aids immeasurably when one is called upon to develop latents in an actual case.

40

PRESERVATION OF FINGERPRINT EVIDENCE

It is extremely important that latent fingerprints and all physical evidence are fully protected until they are collected and preserved by the investigator or crime scene technician. The first police officer to arrive at the scene must take adequate precautions to preserve the integrity of the evidence, to safeguard it against loss, mutilation, destruction, alteration, rearrangement, concealment, or unauthorized removal.

The intentional loss or destruction of evidence is always a possibility, but the greatest threat to the preservation of physical evidence is from the carelessness and ignorance of unauthorized persons entering the crime scene. The more serious the nature of the crime committed, the greater the likelihood of crowds of curious sightseers in and around the crime scene. Neighbors, relatives, employees, and others, no matter how remotely connected with the victim or scene, may demand entry to the scene for a variety of reasons. Professionals of the news media may also inadvertently destroy valuable evidence when, in their enthusiasm to collect the news, they wander through the crime scene with their equipment. All noninvestigative personnel must be kept out of the crime scene area. The problem of the officer in protecting the scene may prove a considerable task but one which must be accomplished if the investigation is to proceed in a competent and professional manner.

Protection of the crime scene depends upon the location, size, and area of the crime scene; the type of evidence found; and the progress of the investigation. If the entire scene is located within one or two rooms of a building, the scene may be secured merely by sealing the entrances. Large areas located outdoors may be secured by roping off the area, erecting barriers, and establishing fixed or roving patrols around the area. Crime scenes located outdoors in unsheltered areas also present the additional necessity of protecting evidence from the weather. The security measures that must be taken to protect physical evidence at crime scenes are neither complicated nor elaborate—they are largely a matter of common sense.

A cardinal rule to observe at crime scenes is to avoid touching or moving any evidence until it has been properly photographed, sketched, its position measured, and all pertinent data recorded. Once an item is handled, it can never be restored to its exact, original position. Every detail and aspect of the crime scene must be photographed and recorded *before* making any search for latent prints and other physical evidence. The purpose of these initial procedures is to depict and describe the scene as it appeared when the police first arrived at the scene.

41

USE OF A STRONG LIGHT IN FINGERPRINT WORK

Light, particularly strong illumination, is one of the most useful and valuable tools a fingerprint technician has at his disposal, both for locating and reproducing fingerprint evidence. In nearly every case where fingerprint evidence is sought, the search for latents, development, or intensification, or all three are accomplished with the aid of illumination. Fingerprint evidence must be examined to best advantage and this can be done only under good light conditions.

The reflector in Figure 34, which holds a No. 1 photoflood, is very useful for examining a surface. The unit is held opposite the observer in such a position that light is reflected toward the eyes from the surface being examined. Correct positions for the light and eyes must be found by trial and error or by experimentation; it varies with different surfaces, but a position can be found where a latent print is seen to best advantage. A print may be invisible with the light in one position, and it may show very plainly with the light in another position.

In Figure 34, a set of four prints is visible to the observer, although it is invisible from the point of view of the camera that took the picture. The prints are undeveloped in a green surface, and they are sufficiently strong as viewed by the reflected light to be photographed without development. This condition exists frequently in fingerprint searches.

It is important to remember that the surface bearing the la-

Figure 34. Latent fingerprints on some surfaces may be revealed by reflected light. A strong light source is a valuable aid in a search for fingerprint evidence.

tent fingerprints should not be overheated by the light. If latent fingerprints are not destroyed by excessive heat, they may deteriorate to a point where they cannot be developed or photographed. Heat causes rapid deterioration of latent fingerprints.

42

POINTS TO REMEMBER IN A FINGERPRINT SEARCH

THE OBJECT OF ATTACK

It is extremely important in every investigation and search for physical evidence to quickly determine the *object of attack*, so that the investigator will know where to concentrate his efforts. It enables him to devise a method of procedure for recovery of evidence. In burglary and theft cases, the object of attack is the property stolen.

It is important to determine the object of attack as it is the point of entry. It may reveal whether the crime was planned or committed on the spur of the moment and about how long the intruder was on the premises—both of which are important in investigations.

The object of attack usually is apparent immediately, or at least it may be ascertained quickly. It may be money in the cash register, clothing or valuables in a residence, narcotics or drugs in a pharmacy or doctor's office, or coin boxes in vending machines. The object of attack has much to do with an intelligent search for latent fingerprint evidence. However, never accept the obvious at face value, as it may have been planned as a cover for the real motive. For example, a simple burglary in a plant engaged in national defense activities could be easily a cover for the real motive of espionage, or a person killed during a robbery could be the victim of premeditated murder.

CONDUCT THE SEARCH INTELLIGENTLY, SYSTEMATICALLY, AND THOROUGHLY

The search for latent fingerprint evidence should be intelligent, systematic, and thorough. There are no substitutes for careful attention to detail and thoroughness when searching for evidence. The logical place to start a search for fingerprint evidence is the point of entry or the starting place. An examination of the entire scene should be made for the purpose of determining how, where, and when to search. Then return to the starting point and proceed with the search. For the sake of uniformity, a clockwise search is recommended to insure that every item of evidence which may have a bearing upon the investigation is found.

Open or large areas may be divided into smaller areas and searched either clockwise or lengthwise and crosswise in a grid pattern. The investigator should never be satisfied to search a scene only one time, as evidence may be overlooked. Generally, the initial search should serve to locate evidence and a second search to collect it. Subsequent searches insure that the crime scene has yielded all available evidence.

The point of entry used by the suspect, if forced, should reveal evidence of the intruder's hands, and it may disclose whether or not he wore protective devices or gloves to avoid leaving fingerprints. The burglar in making a forced entry operates in an unnatural or abnormal manner, and he is certain to leave some evidence of his operations, regardless of whether the evidence is useful from the standpoint of fingerprints. The amount of time and force consumed in the operation, the difficulties encountered in gaining entry, as well as the condition of the surfaces adjacent to the point of entry, must all be taken into consideration.

USE A STRONG LIGHT

Perhaps one of the most productive methods of locating latent fingerprints on exposed surfaces is by using a strong light. The light is used at varying angles; if prints are present, they will usually be found. This is not a positive rule—it works in most cases, but there are occasions when it fails. Good fingerprint evidence which is invisible is often developed with the aid of a light. It is always worth a trial as a preliminary step, and it is particularly adaptable to flat and top surfaces. The light should be in a reflector and shielded as shown in Figure 28. The use of light is critical with respect to the angle of observation, and it necessitates considerable experimentation.

A FLASHLIGHT IS A VALUABLE PIECE OF EQUIPMENT

An ordinary flashlight is commonly used as a light source in searching for latent prints. It is good within its limitations, but is not as effective as a stronger light source. The beam of a flashlight is limited and weak, but it is convenient, and it is a necessity in a fingerprint kit. It usually is very easy to determine whether a surface, especially a top surface, has been touched recently: A strong light causes dust particles to luminesce and become visible. Where dust has been disturbed, fingerprints or fingermarks are likely to be found. The use of a light speeds up the search, but it is not conclusive in itself, for all surfaces should be processed for latent prints regardless of the results of observation under a light source.

LOOK FOR THE UNUSUAL, THE ABNORMAL

An investigator sometimes can reconstruct the crime by observing and studying clues left by the perpetrator. If the investigator can visualize the suspect's movements, the search is made easier. Use of powers of observation are helpful in this respect.

Familiarity with movements and actions of the blind once aided a U.S. Army Criminal Investigation Department (CID) agent in searching for latent fingerprints. The crime had taken place during the hours of darkness in a room on the third floor of a building; the only entrance was through the door. The lights had not been turned on, as this would have alerted a guard posted outside the building. Before processing the scene for latent prints, the agent turned out the lights and noted that the only light source was through one window. Knowing from past experiences that partially blind persons naturally move toward light, he surmised that the suspect, after entering the room, walked toward the window with outstretched hands groping for any objects in his path. The first object he examined was a table between the door and the window, and he found two clear, distinct hand prints on the table top. The suspect was identified by these latent prints (Kirby, 1972).

All objects or articles of furniture and fixtures showing any signs of having been disturbed or touched, laying between the point of entry and the object of attack, or having any connection with the actions of the intruder should be examined for latent prints.

Particular attention should be given to objects known to have been handled by the suspect. No object should be touched with bare hands before the investigator has an opportunity to examine it. When it is necessary to handle an object during an investigation, it should be handled in a manner that does not obliterate or mar existing fingerprints. It is possible to handle objects at points where prints cannot possibly be made. Pieces of glass may be handled by the edges and a gun held by the grips, if they are checked.

It is important to take a firm grip of an object to avoid dropping it or permitting it to slip from the hands. A slip in the hands may destroy existing prints or make unintentional new ones.

PAPER FOLDS

One of the most convenient methods of handling objects is by paper folds. Most objects permit handling with paper folds in such a way and in such places that they can be held in perfect safety without marring fingerprint evidence.

Paper folds are particularly adaptable to flat objects, such as papers, glass, sides of boxes, etc. Any sheet of paper can be safely handled so as not to jeopardize fingerprint evidence by the use of two small folded pieces of paper. It is a rare crime scene in which pieces of paper are unobtainable. Paper is one of the most common articles in all places at all times. Of course, no paper should be used which may have any connection with the crime. The investigator should go out of his way to avoid that possibility. Pieces of torn paper as wide or wider than the palm of the hand are satisfactory; they may be folded once to permit slipping them over edges. Paper folds are as useful as gloves.

It is not intended in this section to convey the idea that paper folds may be carelessly pressed against surfaces bearing latent prints. It is better to use two hands on opposite sides of an object so the folds of paper press against edges or corners. This way, no fingerprint evidence on any surface is jeopardized.

43

COLLECTION AND IDENTIFICATION
OF FINGERPRINT EVIDENCE

The search of the crime scene, as described in Section 42, must be accomplished in a careful and systematic manner. All evidence must also be collected in a careful and systematic manner to preserve any latent characteristics and to prevent destruction or contamination. Care should be exercised, when collecting, to insure that evidence is preserved, as far as possible, in the same condition as when it was originally found. If the investigator touches a piece of evidence in a manner that leaves his own fingerprints on the item, he should indicate this fact in his notes, inform the fingerprint technician or crime laboratory, and forward a set of his own fingerprints for elimination.

Occasions may arise where it may be necessary to damage, partially destroy, or otherwise decrease the effectiveness of an item in order to collect important evidence. For instance, it may be necessary to cut out a section of a wall to collect and preserve a handprint in blood. The question invariably arises in deciding whether or not an object is evidence. The investigator must resolve this question by evaluating the object, circumstances, and conditions at the scene, supporting his decision with good judgment, common sense, and past experiences. If a doubt exists, then the object is secured and processed as evidence. Subsequent evaluation determines the worth of such evidence to the investigator.

To facilitate the preservation and handling of evidence, latent impressions developed by brush and powder should be photographed as soon as possible at the crime scene. After the latent print has been photographically recorded, it may be lifted if it is on a fixed object or an object which cannot be removed from the crime scene (*see* Sec. 112). If the latent impression is on a small object that can be easily removed to the agency's evidence retaining area, the powdered impressions should simply be taped over with transparent lifting tape and left in their original place.

Papers and paper products may be collected by simply placing the items in envelopes for handling. If the papers are folded, they should be left in that condition, and new or additional folds should not be made. Self-seal polyethylene bags provide adequate containers for objects that must be collected and removed from the crime scene. Large objects may be placed in cardboard boxes for handling.

Always note exactly where latent prints are found at the crime scene and the location of the prints in respect to the object. The angle and position at which they are found on objects and fixtures tells how an object was held or the position of the hand when the fingerprint was made. An example of this is a case in which a latent impression on the slide of an automatic pistol was in a normal position for operating the slide.

Facts concerning latent prints should be noted briefly and concisely in an officer's report, either by words or by simple sketches, or preferably by both. All this data written down at the time of development of the evidence becomes critical and important weeks or months later when the evidence is to be used in court and when scores of cases have been handled in the meantime and the details of each have been dimmed in the mind of the investigator.

Each latent impression developed at a crime scene and each object collected as evidence must be marked so that the investigator can identify a specific latent or object obtained in connection with a specific investigation. This is accomplished by the investigator who initially collects or develops the latent, marking it for identification. As a minimum, the marking should include the date, time, investigator's name or initials, original location, and the agency's case number, if available. If the object cannot be marked directly, a tag with the necessary information may be affixed to the object. Latents should be marked prior to photographing, so that the identifying data appears in the photograph.

44

SPECIAL LABORATORY CONSIDERATIONS

No crime scene search for latent fingerprints should ever be so thoughtless that other types of physical evidence are overlooked, destroyed, or diminished in evidentiary value in any way. It is the duty of the investigator to meticulously collect, preserve, and forward to the crime laboratory for analyses all available physical evidence. The importance of all types of physical evidence cannot be overemphasized, as physical evidence is one of the most important phases in determining the who, what, when, where, why, and how aspects in a criminal investigation. The responsibility for obtaining physical evidence falls primarily upon the investigator at the scene, and the investigator must always observe the cardinal rule for handling physical evidence—**avoid contamination.**

BLOOD AND BODY FLUIDS

In any investigation, but particularly in crimes of violence, bloodstained evidence, if properly handled, may be of great value to the investigator. Examinations of the bloodstains by the serology section of the crime laboratory may establish whether or not the blood is of human origin and may establish the blood group type, subgroup, and RH factors. Through comparisons, it may then be established whether the blood was from the victim or suspect. Such information may assist the investigator in pinpointing the exact location of the crime scene, identify the weapon used, eliminate suspects, and prove or disprove a suspect's alibi.

Other body fluids, in addition to blood, are often found at crime scenes. These fluids include semen, saliva, urine, perspiration, pus, milk, nasal mucus, and tears. If the body fluids are from a *secretor,* an individual whose body fluids, as well as blood, may be grouped, the fluids may assist in establishing the identity of the individual the same as blood.

Contamination is the greatest threat to bloodstain and other body fluid evidence. When a serologist examines bloodstains, a control sample is taken from another area on the same surface to insure that possible contaminants on the same surface are not interfering with any reactions. Application of latent fingerprint techniques to any object bearing bloodstains or stains of other body fluids may destroy the evidence beyond recovery insofar as identification and typing of the stains. In turn, this could negate the value of any fingerprint evidence recovered. For example, a bloody handprint of the suspect in a murder case may be found in the suspect's own car, but if the print is damaged to the extent that it cannot be determined that the blood is the same blood group type as the victim, or even that it is human blood, the impression would have little value. The suspect could offer a variety of explanations, none of which could be proved or disproved if adequate examinations cannot be made.

Evidence involving bloodstains and other body fluids should not be examined for latent fingerprints until *after* it has been examined by a serologist. Evidence of this nature is generally examined to better advantage at the crime laboratory, where the serologist and fingerprint technician may jointly examine the evidence and insure that neither hinders the examinations of the other. If a serologist or experienced crime scene technician is available at the crime scene, then the evidence may be processed at the scene; however, not all agencies have the manpower resources for this procedure. If there is any doubt as to the proper procedure for this type of evidence, the crime laboratory should be contacted for advice.

HAIR AND FIBER EVIDENCE

Hairs and fibers are seldom conclusive as evidence but, in conjunction with other details, have proven to be important and essential aids to the investigator. The origin and texture of hairs and fibers found at the crime scene or upon the body, clothing, or hat of a suspect or victim, may be exceedingly important evidence, particularly in homicides and sex crimes.

Laboratory examination of hairs from a crime scene may establish whether the hair is of animal or human origin, and, if human, the race of the person; the area of the body that it came from; how the hair was removed, naturally or forcibly; how the hair had been treated, bleached, dyed, waved, and whether the hair was cut with a dull or sharp instrument; recency of cutting; or whether it was crushed or burned.

Fabrics, tapes, ropes, and similar end-products may be subjected to fiber examination. Fibers may be identified according to type, color, and matching characteristics, based on laboratory microscopic, microchemical, and melting-point examinations. The most difficult task for the investigator is to initially locate hair and fiber evidence at the crime scene. The search must be thorough, detailed, and exacting. Hair and fiber evidence recovered by the investigator should be placed in containers, such as small envelopes, and the container marked with all the essential identifying data. Of paramount importance is the basic rule for physical evidence: **avoid contamination.**

Imagine the chagrin of the investigator who collects hairs at the crime scene only to find out that they are from his own fingerprint brush or that the color of evidentiary hairs cannot be accurately determined because the hair was contaminated by chemical latent fingerprint techniques. All hair and fiber evidence must be properly collected and preserved *before* processing the scene or object for latent fingerprint impressions.

QUESTIONED DOCUMENTS

In the broadest definition of the term, questioned documents are any materials bearing handwriting, handprinting, print, typewriting, or any kind of drawing or mark whose genuineness is questioned. Questioned documents may arise in a variety of investigations, the most common of which is forgery but may also include suicide notes or extortion letters, etc. Suspected indented writings also come within the purview of questioned document examiners. There are many factors to be considered by questioned documents examiners when examining such documents. Many of the latent fingerprint techniques applicable to materials bearing questioned writings may damage the material, writings, or inks to such an extent that any subsequent examination by the questioned document examiner may not be possible.

The average person generally looks only at the form of the letters in questioned writing, but the questioned documents examiner must examine all features, many microscopically. The exact shading of a pen stroke may determine if it is a beginning or ending stroke or which line crosses another. Such details may be easily destroyed.

The best procedure to follow for questioned documents is to submit them to the documents examiner before processing for latent fingerprints. The questioned documents examiner may handle the materials with gloves or enclose them within a transparent document protector, if the evidence is to be examined for latent prints later. After the examination, the documents examiner may select certain portions of the writings to preserve photographically. Photographic reproductions of the writings must be at the direction of the questioned documents examiner to insure adequate and workable photographs.

FIREARMS AND TOOLMARKS

When considering firearm evidence, the majority of people think only of whether or not a particular bullet was fired from a specific weapon and whether or not the fingerprints of the suspect are on the weapon. Both of these aspects are important considerations in criminal investigations, but firearms evidence also includes other items than the weapon and bullet. Cartridges found at a scene may be matched with a particular weapon by ejection and extraction markings or sometimes by chamber markings. Powder pattern determinations are used to establish the distance at which the weapon was fired and, in some instances, to determine whether or not an individual has fired a weapon recently.

The greatest threat to the preservation and evaluation of firearms evidence is the same as that for all physical evidence—contamination. Excessive and careless application of fingerprint powders to a weapon may severely hinder determinations of whether or not the weapon has been fired recently, particularly if the powder enters the barrel and chamber. Certain chemical latent fingerprint techniques used to develop latent prints on brass cartridges may destroy extractor, ejector, and firing-pin markings. Firearm powder patterns may also be destroyed by inappropriate application of latent fingerprint techniques.

No two tools are alike in every detail; they do not leave identical impressions. Toolmark evidence may be used to establish whether a given tool found at a crime scene made a mark that is material to the crime, to determine whether a door or window was opened from the inside or the outside, and to link a person who uses or possesses a given tool to the crime scene. Toolmarks are microscopic in nature and can be easily destroyed or obscured by careless application of latent fingerprint techniques.

The approach to processing all physical evidence is basically one of common sense. The search for one type of evidence cannot completely disregard all other types. In some cases, a decision will have to be made of which is more important, as the paucity of material may preclude examinations for more than one type of evidence, or the nature of the examinations may prevent additional examinations. The most important step for an investigator to follow is to always avoid contamination of physical evidence and, if in doubt as how to proceed, contact the crime laboratory for advice.

45

PACKAGING FINGERPRINT EVIDENCE

Many local law enforcement agencies that do not have fingerprint or evidence technicians available for processing evidence must forward their evidence to a regional or state crime laboratory for examination, particularly when other types of physical evidence are involved. Whenever feasible, evidence should be carried by hand to the laboratory, preferably by the investigator conducting the investigation. This procedure insures that all pertinent facts regarding the evidence are related to the laboratory examiners who will examine the evidence. If evidence cannot be hand carried to the laboratory, it must be forwarded either through postal channels or by express freight. Shipping evidence to the laboratory presents the problem of properly packaging the evidence in a manner to preserve the evidentiary value of each item.

All evidence shipped to the crime laboratory should be double wrapped with the invoice and request for laboratory examination securely taped to the outside of the inner sealed package. This method permits the laboratory to determine the nature of the case and assign the evidence to the appropriate laboratory personnel without gaining access to the evidence, thereby insuring that the first person to open the sealed evidence is the laboratory technician who will perform the examinations.

The fragile nature of latent fingerprints has been repeatedly stressed, and this must be a primary consideration in packaging and wrapping latent fingerprint evidence for shipment. Certain types of materials bearing possible latent impressions present no problems. Paper and paper products may be placed in an envelope or document protector for shipment. Latent impressions on nonporous surfaces, particularly on bulky or fragile items, present problems that may tax the ingenuity and resourcefulness of the investigator. Such items must be packaged in a manner that the surfaces cannot rub or touch the sides of the container or packaging material.

Latent fingerprint bearing objects shipped through the mails are particularly sensitive to damage, because of the possible exposure to temperature extremes during shipment. When packages are taken from a warm post office building during the winter months and exposed to cold temperatures in trucks or planes, moisture inside the package may condensate on the object. If anything is touching or rubbing against the object, the combined conditions of temperature, moisture, and rubbing may destroy any latent impressions.

There are many methods by which objects may be secured within a package to minimize contact between the surfaces of the object and the package. One method is to secure the object to a flat piece of wood or cardboard with string or wire and then secure the piece of wood to one side of the evidence container. Another is to place cardboard inserts around the object within the evidence container in such a fashion as to prevent movement or slippage of the object and minimum contact with the sides or inserts. Flat objects may often be secured by sandwiching the edges between two pieces of cardboard and taping the cardboard together. The approaches to the problem of packaging may be as varied as the different types of objects that may be encountered. The only true measure of whether or not any packaging method is adequate is in the result achieved.

Every investigator preparing and packaging evidence for submission to a crime laboratory must exercise common sense and take all proper precautions for the type of evidence involved. Adequate packaging may be time consuming, but the results of the laboratory examination may make all efforts worth the expenditure in time.

46

FINGERPRINT PHOTOGRAPHY

Photography is an important and essential phase of all investigative activity at a crime scene. Photographs serve as supplements to an investigator's notes and sketches and provide a pictorial record of crime scenes and evidentiary objects. Evidentiary photographs become of particular importance when the actual scene or object is changed by time or destruction.

Photography is applicable to almost every phase of fingerprint work. Photographs taken at the scene should be used to depict the location and position of latent fingerprints in relation to the object on which they are located and with respect to the overall scene. Latent fingerprints should always be photographed prior to any attempt to lift the impressions or remove the object bearing the prints as a precautionary measure in the event of accidental damage or destruction of the latent prints.

In addition to recording all essential data pertaining to the latent impressions in the investigator's case notes, each photograph should be numbered or marked in such a manner that it can be easily identified at a later date. This may be easily accomplished by marking a tag with a number corresponding to the appropriate entry in the investigator's notes and with the date, time, and investigator's name or initials. Such procedures may provide a means for the successful rebuttal of any future claims regarding the authenticity of the photographs.

Photography is also used in fingerprint work to record inked impressions and to prepare enlargements for charts used for demonstration purposes in courts. Photography is neither an adjunct nor supplement to the mechanics of fingerprints; it is intrinsic to nearly all phases of fingerprint work. Every person involved in the collection and identification of fingerprint evidence should be proficient in fingerprint photography.

FUNDAMENTALS

A photographic film exposure consists of four basic variables: subject light, camera lens aperture setting, camera shutter speed setting, and the speed of the selected film. Every good lens has an adjustable diaphragm that controls the amount of light transmitted through the lens. By increasing the aperture size of the lens (diameter of the diaphragm) one f-stop, for example from $f/11$ to $f/8$, the amount of light transmitted through the lens is doubled. Conversely, by decreasing the aperture size one f-stop, for example from $f/11$ to $f/16$, the amount of light transmitted through the lens is decreased by one-half.

The camera shutter speed setting also controls the amount of light transmitted through the lens. Each time the setting of the shutter is advanced to the next smaller fraction, for example from $1/50$ to $1/100$ second, the amount of time the shutter remains open and the amount of light reaching the film is reduced by one-half. Accordingly, if all other variables remain constant, increasing the aperture from $f/11$ to $f/16$ and decreasing the shutter speed from $1/50$ to $1/25$ second would provide the same film exposure as the original setting.

Film emulsion speeds are related to each other in the same manner as f-stops and shutter speeds. A film which has an ASA film speed rating of 100 is twice as fast as one with a rating of

50. Therefore, subject light remaining constant, if the proper exposure settings for a film rated at ASA 100 is determined to be $f/11$ at ¹⁄₁₀₀ second, changing to a film with an ASA rating of 50 requires changing the exposure settings to either $f/8$ at ¹⁄₁₀₀ second or $f/11$ at ¹⁄₅₀ second.

Depth of field is also an important consideration when determining correct exposure settings. Depth of field is the distance from the nearest point of acceptably sharp focus to the farthest point of acceptably sharp focus of a subject being photographed. Depth of field increases as the lens aperture setting is increased; therefore, a lens aperture setting of $f/22$ provides greater depth of field than a setting of $f/8$. All fingerprint cameras are fixed-focus cameras designed to photograph subjects on flat surfaces on the same plane as the front aperture or nose of the camera. Therefore, when photographing latent fingerprints on a curved surface, depth of field must be considered when computing exposure settings. Generally speaking, those portions of the subject more than ⅛ inch away from the front aperture place are out of focus at lens aperture settings of $f/11$ and below. When photographing latent prints on a curved surface with a fingerprint camera, an advisable lens aperture setting would be the smallest opening attainable for the camera, for example $f/22$, to insure the greatest depth of field possible.

Greater depth of field does not necessarily correspond with a clear sharp photograph, because the resolving power of a lens decreases with smaller f-stops. "Ultimate sharpness with most process lenses is obtainable at an opening one or two stops away from wide open" (Kodak, 1971). If the largest lens aperture opening for a particular fingerprint camera is $f/3.5$ or $f/4.5$, settings of $f/5.6$ and $f/8$ would provide the sharpest images. As a general rule of thumb, when photographing subjects on a flat surface with the fingerprint camera either of the midrange f-stops, $f/8$ or $f/11$, provide adequate results.

THE FINGERPRINT CAMERA IN USE

Before using a fingerprint camera, a preoperational check must be made to insure that it is functioning properly. This is particularly true in regard to the light and power sources, both of which must be functioning at peak performance; otherwise, the exposure settings will not be accurate. Burned-out, loose, or weak bulbs and weak batteries not detected before making exposures at the scene could result in irretrievable loss of fingerprint evidence. During the preoperational check, the camera shutter action and the lens and the front aperture or nose of the camera should be checked for cleanliness.

The latent fingerprint is positioned in the center of the front aperture for adequate distribution of light over the subject, and the identification card or tag pertaining to the latent is placed near the subject. To insure correct positioning of the subject, the ground-glass focusing panel at the camera back of nearly all fingerprint cameras may be used to view the subject exactly as it will appear on the film. When using the ground-glass panel for viewing, the shutter must be set on time, and the lens aperture should be set at the largest opening attainable, $f/3.5$ or $f/4.5$.

After correctly positioning the subject, the appropriate exposure settings may then be made and the film loaded into the camera. When making the exposure, the camera should be held steady with the hand or forearm, because any movement of the camera may result in a blurred image.

There is a variety of photographic films available for use with fingerprint cameras, ranging from Polaroid-type films providing both a photographic print and a negative, to film packs and roll-and-cut film. The selection of film type depends upon the requirements of each agency and the photographic experience and skill of the personnel involved. When selecting the type of film to be used for general purpose fingerprint photography, consideration should be given to high-contrast films, such as Kodak Contrast Process Panchromatic® (CPP) and Kodak Contrast Process Orthochromatic® (CPO).

As mentioned previously, a photographic film exposure consists of four basic variables: subject light, camera lens aperture setting, camera shutter speed setting, and the speed of the selected film. Early models of fingerprint cameras had fixed apertures and, providing the light and power sources were functioning properly, the exposure variables were limited to camera shutter speed and speed of the film. The most commonly used film type with the early models is Kodak Tri-X®. Commonly used shutter speeds using Tri-X film with these early models is "snapshot" for black latents on white or light backgrounds and 1 second for gray prints on a black or dark background.

The new models of fingerprint cameras offer the advantage of lens aperture settings, a wide selection of camera shutter speeds, a variety of light and power sources, and accommodation of film sizes up to 4-by-5 inches. Fingerprint cameras with a 4-by-5-inch film-size format enable the selection of a greater variety of film types and provide for photographing larger areas when required, such as necessitated by palmprints and simultaneous impressions.

Exposure settings for specific categories of latent fingerprints may vary between camera models due to their different types of light sources. The best method of establishing basic exposure settings for a particular camera is to take trial exposures of various latent prints on different backgrounds and to mark the data on a card which is affixed to the camera or placed within the camera case. Figure 35 gives three tables that may be used as a guide

A. Film Emulsion Values

Film type	Kodak CPO and Polaroid Type 55P/N®	Kodak CPP and Polaroid Type 51*®	Kodak Tri-X and Polaroid Type 52®	Polaroid Type 57® and Type 107®
ASA film speed rating	50	80	400	3000
Total value number	9	10	12	15

B. Shutter Speed Values

Seconds	1 (1.0)	1/2 (0.5)	1/4 (0.25)	1/10 (0.1)	1/25 (0.04)	1/50 (0.02)	1/100 (0.01)	1/200 (0.005)
Value Number	0	1	2	3	4	5	6	7

C. Lens Aperture Values

f-stop	2.8	4	5.6	8	11	16	22
Value number	3	4	5	6	7	8	9

Figure 35.

when computing exposure settings required for various categories of latent fingerprints. The data in the tables is based upon exposure settings applicable for use with the Sirchie SFP-3 Fingerprint Camera®, which uses four GE13® lamps as the light source. The data should also be applicable for use with the Faurot®, Watson-Holmes®, Criminal Research Products®, and other Sirchie fingerprint cameras using similar light sources.

Figure 35A lists various types of film, the approximate film speed rating for each, and a total exposure value number for each. The total exposure value number provides the basis for computing the lens aperture settings and the camera shutter speed settings applicable to 95 percent of the work performed with the fingerprint camera. All data are based on properly functioning light and power sources.

Figure 35B lists value numbers for each shutter speed setting and 35C the value numbers for each lens aperture setting. After selecting the film type, exposure settings may be determined by selecting any combination of shutter speed values and lens aperture values, which add up to the total exposure value number of the selected film. For example, if the film type selected is Kodak Contrast Process Panchromatic (CPP), which has an ASA rating of 80 and a total exposure value number of 10, any pair of shutter speed and lens aperture value numbers which add up to a total of 10 will provide a standard setting. Therefore, a shutter speed setting of ½ second (value 1) and a lens aperture setting of $f/22$ (value 9) provide the required exposure setting.

Figures 35B and 35C may also be used to compute various exposure settings after any standard exposure setting has been established for a particular camera and film type. Any pair of value numbers listed which adds up to the same total value provides identical exposures. For example, a shutter speed setting of ½ second and a lens aperture setting of $f/11$ (1 + 7) has a total value of 8 and provides an exposure identical to ⅟₅₀ second at $f/2.8$ (5 + 3) if all other variables remain constant.

The total exposure value numbers listed for various film types in Figure 35A are applicable when photographing latent fingerprints developed on a white or light background with any of the following fingerprint powders: black, brown, dragon blood, red, green, blue, or asphaltum. The values also apply to latent prints developed on a black or dark background with silver, aluminum bronze, gold metallic, and copper metallic powders. The values may also be used to photograph clear latent prints developed on light backgrounds with iodine fuming, ninhydrin, and silver nitrate techniques.

The total exposure value numbers of Figure 35A must be decreased by 2 for the following types of latent fingerprints developed on a black or dark background: white, gray, gold bronze, and dragon blood. Accordingly, the total exposure value number for films with an ASA rating of 50 would be decreased from 9 to 7, and for those with an ASA rating of 3000, the value would be decreased from 15 to 13.

FINGERPRINT PHOTOGRAPHY WITH PRESS CAMERAS

Due to budget limitations and infrequent usage, many small police departments cannot purchase fingerprint cameras. These agencies may attempt to build their photographic capabilities around one general-purpose camera model and one film-size format. The present trend in law enforcement photography appears to be toward greater use of roll film, particularly in the 120 film-size format. Almost any camera can be adapted to fingerprint work by the use of fixed-focus frames, special bellows extensions, or sometimes merely with special techniques applicable to the particular camera make and model.

The fingerprint photography techniques discussed in this subsection pertain to the Crown®, Super®, and Speed Graphic® press cameras. These cameras have, through years of use, proven to be excellent cameras for both general purpose and specialized crime scene photography. The Graphic press cameras are no longer manufactured, but these cameras are still available for purchase and may commonly be found in the photographic equipment inventory of most law enforcement agencies.

When photographing latent fingerprints found on curved surfaces, a Graphic press camera with double bellows extension may be preferable to a fingerprint camera. The double bellows extension provides for one-to-one image size in the negative and the 4-by-5-inch film size provides for covering a large area. The camera is easily focused with the ground-glass focusing plate, but a fixed-focus frame may also be used, such as the Faurot Foto Focuser® or the Sirchie Latent Focus Adapter®.

Graphic press cameras are easily adjusted to the double-bellows extension setting. The following procedure, applicable for the Speed Graphic, may be used to initially establish the double-bellows extension setting and the camera bed and carriage track should be marked showing the front standard assembly position for future reference. (1) Open the camera bed by pushing the bed release button, and pull the bed down until it locks in the open position. (2) Flip the infinity stops on the bed carriage tracks down to clear passage for the front standard assembly. (3) Unlock the front standard assembly, and move the assembly forward until the leading edge is even with the end of the carriage tracks. (4) Turn the focusing knob until the leading edge of the tracks is even with the camera bed. (5) Open the ground-glass focusing panel at the camera back; set the lens aperture at the largest opening and the shutter speed at time exposure. (6) With the camera securely mounted on a tripod or fixed in a stationary position, place a ruler 10 inches away from the lens. (7) Using a second ruler, measure the image on the ground glass and adjust the lens with the focusing knob until a clear one-to-one image is obtained. (8) Mark the position of the front standard assembly on the camera bed for future reference.

For a Graphic press camera with a 127-mm lens, the lens-to-film distance is 10 inches and the lens-to-subject distance is 10 inches. For cameras with 135-mm lens, the distance for both is 10.6 inches. However, for each camera, it is best to determine the exact adjustment settings as described above and mark the camera as indicated.

It is always advisable to use a light meter to determine exposure settings, but whenever using the double-bellows extension, an increased exposure of 4 (two f-stops) is required to compensate for the amount of light lost. Thus, an exposure setting indicated by the light meter as being $f/16$ at $\frac{1}{100}$ second would become $f/16$ at $\frac{1}{25}$ second.

An inexpensive and easy-to-build copy stand can be constructed for use with the Graphic press cameras. A copy stand may be used for photographing latent fingerprints on flat surfaces, such as fingerprint lifts and documents. With the camera at single-bellows extension, the stand may also be used for copying fingerprint cards and overall views of documents. Some care must be exercised in the construction of the stand, since the plane of the film and the plane of the subject must be identical. Any deviation causes distortion of the copy image, and since there is a very shallow depth of field, the image may be out of focus on one side. The copy easel should have a piece of flawless glass mounted over the object to secure it and smooth out any wrinkles. The glass can be held in place by means of large rubber bands, which can be placed around the ends of the easel and glass.

Figure 36 is a diagram of a copy stand which may be constructed. The box on which the camera is mounted can be moved

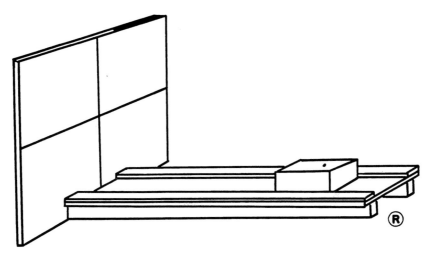

Figure 36. A horizontal copy stand for Graflex-type cameras. This copy stand can be easily constructed and set on top of a desk or table. The camera is mounted on the box which slides back and forward, and the image if focused on the ground-glass viewing panel on the camera back.

forward or backward as required. Strips of window screen molding may be attached to the top of the box to form a recessed well for the camera body to prevent movement, or a camera bracket screw may be passed through the top of the box.

SPECIAL PHOTOGRAPHIC TECHNIQUES

When photographing plastic fingerprint impressions, it is necessary to use side or cross lighting in order to record friction ridge details impressed into a substance. When using fingerprint cameras, side lighting may be obtained simply by unscrewing the lamps on one side of the camera. When using Graphic press cameras, a photoflash is preferred, since the heat from photoflood lamps may melt the substance containing the print.

Latent fingerprints developed by the ninhydrin chemical technique are not always dark and clear in all areas. Frequently, many areas on such a latent appear faint, while other areas are much more dense and legible. To obtain maximum contrast while attempting to retain as great a range of density of tones as possible for ninhydrin-developed latents, it is advisable to use Kodak Tri-X film and a Kodak Wratten No. 58® (medium green) filter. This filter has a filter factor of 8, indicating the exposure must be increased eightfold (three f-stops). Therefore, an exposure setting of $f/16$ at $\frac{1}{25}$ second would become $f/16$ at $\frac{1}{2}$ second.

When latent fingerprints have been developed on a dark background with light-colored powders, it is usually desirable to reverse the color of the photographs so that the latent prints appear dark against a light background. This process is called color reversal. The easiest and quickest method of obtaining a color reversal photograph is with the fingerprint camera. Place the original negative on a light box or simply tape it to a clean windowpane and secure a sheet of tracing paper with tape to the opposite side of the glass. Remove the lamps of the camera or disconnect the power source. Determine the correct exposure settings by measuring the amount of light passing through the negative. Then simply place the camera over the negative and photograph it. The second negative will be a color reversal of the first.

A second method for making a color reversal photograph is one similar to making a photographic contact print. This method is more time consuming, and the entire operation must be accomplished in a darkroom. To avoid operating in total darkness, it is advisable to use an orthochromatic film for the second negative, so that a red safelight may be used. Place the sheet of unexposed film in a sheet film holder with the emulsion-side up and then load the negative into the same holder directly over the unexposed film, but with the emulsion-side down. Then insert the safety slide to protect the film against accidental exposure to light. This is of particular importance during the exposure phase of the operation when more than one color reversal photograph is to be prepared.

The next step is to prepare the light source to be used for exposing the film. A photographic enlarger provides an excellent light source, as the exposure can be timed and the amount of light regulated. To make the exposure, the aperture of the enlarger should be set at the smallest opening possible. The time of the exposure depends upon the density of the negative, the amount of light, and the speed of the film selected. If the film selected is Kodak CPO and the amount of light at the film surface is two footcandles, an exposure of ½ second would be a good reference point to begin exposures. Several exposures may be required before an acceptable photograph is obtained. The safety slide should not be removed from the holder until the exposure is to be made, and then it should be reinserted in the holder.

QUESTIONS

TRUE-FALSE QUESTIONS

1. More than one fingerprint is necessary to place a suspect at a crime scene (Sec. 34). FALSE
2. Fingerprint evidence and physical evidence in general is not sought after by investigators as diligently as it should be (Sec. 34). TRUE
3. Every qualified examiner who examines a specific fingerprint should arrive at the same conclusion regarding identity (Sec. 34). TRUE

4. Fingerprints are of little use in establishing innocence in all cases (Sec. 34). FALSE

5. In modern police usage, the term *latent* is applied to all chance or unintentional fingerprint impressions that are of evidentiary value (Sec. 35). TRUE

6. Plastic impressions are molds formed by the friction ridges in soft substances (Sec. 35). TRUE

7. There is a demonstrable difference between the secretion of the sweat glands on the palms and fingers and the secretions of the hairy portions of the skin (Sec. 36). TRUE

8. A thorough knowledge of the chemical composition of latent fingerprint residue is of significant practical value to a fingerprint technician (Sec. 36). FALSE

9. Failure to recover latent fingerprints from an item means that the prints have been wiped off intentionally (Sec. 37). FALSE

10. It is possible to determine the age, sex, and race of an individual solely by means of fingerprints (Sec. 37). FALSE

11. Extremes in temperature and humidity may have an adverse effect on latent fingerprints (Sec. 37). TRUE

12. Latent fingerprints on either a porous or nonporous surface last indefinitely and can always be recovered with the appropriate latent fingerprint technique (Sec. 38). FALSE

13. No latent fingerprint technique should ever be adopted to the complete exclusion of all others (Sec. 39). TRUE

14. The ultimate value of any latent fingerprint technique is entirely dependent upon the skill of the person using it (Sec. 39). TRUE

15. It is extremely important that latent fingerprints and all physical evidence be fully protected until it is collected and preserved by the investigator or crime scene technician (Sec. 40). TRUE

16. The greatest threat to the preservation of physical evidence is from intentional loss or destruction (Sec. 40). FALSE

17. A cardinal rule to observe at crime scenes is to avoid touching or moving any evidence until it has been properly photo-

graphed, sketched, its position measured, and all pertinent data recorded (Sec. 40). TRUE

18. During a crime scene search, it is not as important to determine the point of attack as it is the point of entry (Sec. 42). FALSE

19. A clockwise search of a crime scene is recommended (Sec. 42). TRUE

20. All objects or articles of furniture which show any signs of having been disturbed or touched should be examined for latent fingerprints (Sec. 42). TRUE

21. No crime scene search for latent fingerprints should ever be so thoughtless that other types of physical evidence are overlooked, destroyed, or diminished in evidentiary value in any way (Sec. 44). TRUE

22. Evidence involving bloodstains and other body fluids should be processed for latent fingerprints before it is examined by a serologist (Sec. 44). FALSE

23. Hairs and fibers are seldom conclusive as evidence and, therefore, are of little assistance to the investigator (Sec. 44). FALSE

24. The best procedure to follow for questioned documents is to submit them to the documents examiner before processing for latent fingerprints (Sec. 44). TRUE

25. The basic rule regarding all types of physical evidence is to avoid contamination (Sec. 44). TRUE

26. The fragile nature of latent fingerprints must be a consideration when packaging the evidence for shipment (Sec. 45). TRUE

27. Photographs serve as supplements to an investigator's notes and sketches and provide a pictorial record of crime scenes and evidentiary objects (Sec. 46). TRUE

28. In addition to recording all essential data pertaining to the latent impressions in the investigator's case notes, each photograph should be numbered or marked for identification purposes (Sec. 46). TRUE

29. When photographing latent fingerprints on a curved surface, depth of field is an important consideration (Sec. 46). TRUE

30. Graphic press cameras can be easily adapted for photograph-

Explain hair and ~~fingerprint~~ fiber evidence and its relationships to crime scenes.

✗ Take out section about civil trials.

ing latent fingerprints by means of the double-bellows extension (Sec. 46). TRUE

COMPLETION QUESTIONS

31. Fingerprint evidence differs from most other physical evidence in that one person and only one person can make a given fingerprint impression (Sec. 34).

32. Visible fingerprints may be divided into two classes, plastic fingerprints and fingerprints made by contamination of the skin (Sec. 35).

33. There are three stages in the formation of a latent fingerprint: pretransfer conditions (subject factors), transfer conditions (transposal factors) and post-transfer conditions (environmental factors) (Sec. 37).

34. Light, particularly strong illumination, is one of the most useful and valuable tools a fingerprint technician has at his disposal (Sec. 41).

35. In burglary and theft cases, the object of attack is the property stolen (Sec. 42).

36. The search for latent fingerprint evidence should be intelligent, systematic, and thorough (Sec. 42).

37. Photography is an important and essential phase of all investigative activity at a crime scene (Sec. 46).

38. Photography is applicable to almost every phase of fingerprint work (Sec. 46).

39. Photography is used in fingerprint work to record inked impressions and to prepare enlargements for charts used for demonstration purposes in court (Sec. 46).

40. A photographic film exposure consists of four basic variables (Sec. 46).

41. Every good lens has an adjustable diaphragm that controls the amount of light transmitted through the lens (Sec. 46).

42. By decreasing the aperture size one f-stop the amount of light transmitted through the lens is decreased by one half (Sec. 46).

43. A film which has an ASA film speed rating of 100 is twice as fast as one with a rating of 50 (Sec. 46).

44. DEPTH. OF. FIELD.. is the distance from the nearest point of acceptably sharp focus of a subject being photographed (Sec. 46).

45. All fingerprint cameras are .FIXED.. focus cameras designed to photograph subjects on a . FLAT... surface (Sec. 46).

46. Early models of fingerprint cameras had .FIXED... apertures (Sec. 46).

47. When using the Graphic press type cameras, the .DOUBLE.. bellows extension provides for one-to-one image size in the negative (Sec. 46).

48. It is always advisable to use a LIGHT... METER.. to determine exposure settings (Sec. 46).

49. When photographing plastic fingerprint impressions it is necessary to use SIDE.... or CROSS... lighting in order to record friction ridge details impressed into a substance (Sec. 46).

50. A method for making color reversal photographs is one similar to making a photographic .CONTACT. print (Sec. 46).

REFERENCES

Angst, E.: "Unterschungen zur Bestimmong des Alters von Daktyloskopischen," *Kriminalistik.* vol. 15 (1961), no. 2, p. 1.

Billinghurst, A. C.: "Some elementary aspects of fingerprinting photography," *The Police Journal.* vol. 39 (1966), p. 89.

Bloch, P. B., and D. R. Weidman: *Managing Criminal Investigations,* Washington, D.C., Law Enforcement Assistance Administration, 1975.

Bluhm, R. J., and W. J. Lougheed: "Results of time, temperature and humidity on latent fingerprints," *Identification News.* vol. 18 (3 parts); (July, 1968), p. 14; (Aug., 1968), p. 5; (Sept., 1968), p. 15.

Bohne, G.: "Ein neues Verfahren zur Reproduktion von Fingerspuren auf ebenen Glasflachen, besonders bei starken Vergrosserung," *Archiv fur Kriminologie.* vol. 102 (1938), p. 147.

Brooks, A. J.: "Techniques for finding latent prints," *Fingerprint and Identification Magazine.* vol. 54 (Nov., 1972), p. 3.

————: "Errata and addenda to techniques for finding latent prints," *Fingerprint and Identification Magazine.* vol. 56 (Feb., 1975), p. 11.

Buhrke, B. J.: "Evaluation—Latent prints," *Identification News.* vol. 20 (Oct., 1970), p. 4.

Califana, A. L.: "Methods for reversal of color of latent fingerprint negatives," *Law and Order.* vol. 19 (1971), no. 2, p. 26.

Connor, C. M.: "Methods for the development of latent fingerprints," *Journal of the Association of Official Analytical Chemists.* vol. 55 (1972), p. 827.

Cummins, Harold, and Charles Midlo: *Finger Prints, Palms and Soles.* Philadelphia, Blakiston, 1943.

Edwards, C. J.: "Some observations on the detection of fingerprints using ninhydrin," *Journal of the Forensic Science Society.* vol. 6 (1966), p. 183.

Engeset, E.: "Hvor ofte etterlater forbryteren sitt fingeravtykk paa gjeringsstedet?" *Nordisk Kriminalltenisk Tidskrift.* vol. 32 (1962), no. 8, p. 160.

Glick, D. P.: "Developing latent finger prints," *Scientific American.* vol. 155 (Aug., 1936), p. 113.

Godsell, J.: "Fingerprint techniques," *Journal of the Forensic Science Society.* vol. 3 (1963), p. 79.

Gundesen, B.: "Fingerprint photography," *The Australian Police Journal.* vol. 21 (1967), p. 236.

Hardinge, D. D.: "Fingerprint preservation on motor vehicles by use of an auxiliary wheel," *Journal of the Forensic Science Society.* vol. 8 (1968), p. 59.

Harper, W. W.: "Latent fingerprints at high temperatures," *Journal of Criminal Law, Criminology and Police Science.* vol. 29 (1938), p. 580.

Heathcote, A. E.: "If you can see it, you can photograph it," *The Police Journal.* vol. 36 (1963), p. 171.

Hoon, L. C.: "We shoot latents without tears," *Fingerprint and Identification Magazine.* vol. 43 (Aug., 1961), p. 11.

Jennrich, H. L.: "Painting with a flashlight," *Identification News.* vol. 18 (Apr., 1968), p. 3.

Johnson, P. L.: "Life of latents," *Identification News.* vol. 23 (Apr., 1973), p. 10.

Kirby, F. J.: Crime Scene Processing. Personal communication. Aug. 8, 1972.

Kodak: *Small Lens Openings Destroy Image Sharpness.* Rochester, N.Y., Eastman Kodak Pamphlet Q-104, 1971.

Latent Fingerprints, Lesson plan, Feb., 1967. Fort Gordon, Georgia U.S. Army Military Police School.

"Latent prints, 8 years old, help solve bizarre murder," *FBI Law Enforcement Bulletin.* vol. 32 (Dec., 1963), p. 13.

"Latent prints on phonograph record," *Fingerprint and Identification Magazine.* vol. 48 (Mar., 1967), p. 6.

Lieber, Z.: "There's always a chance," *International Criminal Police Review.* vol. 16 (June-July, 1961), p. 168.

Mason, D. H., and C. E. Carlson: "Fingerprints in putty," *Law and Order.* vol. 8 (Sept., 1960).

Moenssens, A. A.: "Testifying as a fingerprint witness," Identification News. vol. 22 (Aug.-Sept., 1972), p. 5.

Molony, B. C.: "Factors to consider in a crime scene fingerprint system," *Identification News.* vol. 22 (Apr., 1972), p. 11.

Murphy, C. J.: "New techniques in fingerprint photography," *Identification News.* vol. 24 (Jan., 1974), p. 7.

Norkus, P. M.: *Fingerprints.* Lesson plan, Fort Gordon, Georgia, U.S. Army Military Police School, 1974.

O'Neill, M. E.: "The development of latent finger-prints on paper," *Journal of Criminal Law, Criminology and Police Science.* vol. 28 (1937), p. 432.

————: "Fingerprints in criminal investigations," *Journal of Criminal Law, Criminology and Police Science.* vol. 29 (1940), p. 929.

"Packaging of fingerprint evidence for transmittal to laboratory," *Military Police Journal.* vol. 13 (May, 1964), p. 14.

Pascual, M. V.: "Soportes aptos no aptos para recibir impresiones de crestas papilares," *Guardia Civil.* vol. 19 (1962), p. 32.

Payton, G. T.: "Training patrolmen to dust for latent prints," *Police.* vol. 8 (Mar.-Apr., 1964), p. 41.

"Periphography," *Identification News.* vol. 19 (July, 1969), p. 4.

Peterson, J. L.: *The Utilization of Criminalistics Services by the Police. An Analysis of the Physical Evidence Recovery Process.* Washington, D.C., Law Enforcement Assistance Administration, 1974.

"Plastic fingerprints," *Chemical and Engineering News.* vol. 36 (Nov. 17, 1958), p. 38.

President's Commission of Law Enforcement and Administration of Criminal Justice: *Task Force Report: Science and Technology.* Washington, DC, Government Printing Office, 1967.

Samen, C. C.: "Evidence collection," *Identification News.* vol. 21 (Jan., 1971), p. 6.

Sams, C.: "The role of the fingerprint officer," *Journal of the Forensic Science Society.* vol. 10 (1970), p. 219.

"Seasonal effects of humidity in the chemical development of latent fingerprints," *FBI Law Enforcement Bulletin.* vol. 8 (Nov., 1939), p. 21.

Svensson, Arne, and Otto Wendel: *Techniques of Crime Scene Investigation.* New York, American Elsevier, 1965.

Trotter, C. L.: *Crime Scene Latent Fingerprints,* Proceedings of the Forty-

Fourth Annual Conference of the International Association for Identification, Pittsburgh, PA, July 7-9, 1959, p. 108.

"Try, try again," *FBI Law Enforcement Bulletin.* (June, 1966), p. 23.

"Useful hint for latent print photography," *Fingerprint and Identification Magazine.* vol. 43 (Apr., 1962), p. 23.

Woodward, F. V.: "Fingerprint photography," *The Police Journal.* vol. 36 (1963), no. 10, p. 49.

Chapter IV

Fingerprint Equipment

47

THE FINGERPRINT KIT

A FINGERPRINT KIT, like a first aid kit, reflects as many ideas as there are persons using the kits. The components of the kit, also like a first aid kit, must also reflect the nature of the incident it is intended to be used for, whether major or minor. There are simple and complex kits, and there is a wide choice of accessories and equipment available for kits. Fingerprint kits assigned to patrol vehicles and investigators for incidents of a minor nature may be simple kits containing only the minimum amount of equipment. However, for major crimes, more complex kits should be assigned to investigators and evidence technicians who possess the training and skill to use such kits.

Many metropolitan police agencies maintain and operate mobile crime laboratories and evidence-collection vans staffed by highly qualified personnel. The majority of local law enforcement agencies lack both the fiscal and manpower resources to support such mobile units and must select kits applicable to their local needs. Except for very small departments, a wise selection would be one simple fingerprint kit for general use and one well-equipped professional investigation kit for use in all major crimes. Ordinarily, a person answering a call to a crime scene knows in advance what kind of call it is, whether burglary, robbery, or homicide, and through experience knows the appropriate equipment to cope with the problems involved. The more important the crime, the greater the necessity to take as much equipment as may be required to properly accomplish the tasks required to fully search the scene. Conditions at the crime scene cannot always be controlled in such a manner to protect physical evidence for a prolonged period, and valuable evidence may be irretrievably lost if the investigator arrives at the crime scene with too little equipment.

Most commercial fingerprint kits are well designed, compact, durable, and of excellent quality. Major manufacturers of fingerprint equipment and supplies have designed their equipment based upon years of extensive research and practical field experience. Whenever a law enforcement agency is considering purchase of fingerprint kits, descriptive literature should be requested from each manufacturer. Some manufacturers may, upon request, provide technical sales representatives to assist in evaluating the needs of the agency and suggest the appropriate kits for those needs.

As a skilled surgeon may perform a successful major surgical operation with the crudest instruments and under the most adverse of conditions, so may a skilled fingerprint technician achieve maximum results with minimal equipment. A few well-chosen items accomplish the fingerprint job that has to be done at a great majority of crime scenes—it is not so much the amount and variety of equipment carried to a crime scene that is important, it is the resourcefulness with which it is used.

If the job requires equipment beyond that carried in an average kit, the technician should be able to devise methods of accomplishing the job without loss of evidence, preferably by transporting it to the laboratory where it will receive the best possible attention. In most cases, a better job can be accomplished at the laboratory where suitable equipment is available and the worker is not performing against time before a group of onlookers. The purpose of crime scene kits is to collect evidence for later evaluation, not to solve all cases immediately at the scene.

Some items included in commercial fingerprint kits are essential and are used in almost every case, while other items may be used infrequently or rarely. It is not advisable to remove and discard an item from a kit merely because it does not receive constant usage. Circumstances may well develop in an extremely important case where a discarded item is required. When kits are assigned to several persons, it is particularly unwise for one person to arrange and stock the kit according to his own choices and prejudices. The equipment and techniques one person may find adequate may not prove successful to another person with differing training and skills.

KEEP THE KIT CLEAN, ORDERLY, AND WELL SUPPLIED

The kit and all its contents should be checked and replenished periodically and the kit and equipment cleaned regularly. These simple preventive maintenance tasks are best accomplished on a routine schedule by personnel assigned the duty by the supervising officer. Not only can a better job be accomplished with a clean, well-kept kit, but the period of serviceability for the kit is extended by proper preventive maintenance. In hot, humid climates, a light coat of oil may be applied to the carrying case and all metal parts to prevent rust and deterioration. The contents of the kit must also be kept in their proper places, so that if another technician uses the kit, valuable time is not lost looking for an item. In many respects, the pride and professionalism of the individuals who use the kit are reflected by the condition and appearance of the kit.

A quick check should be made of the kit and its contents each time it is picked up to go on a job to see that everything is in order. This check is particularly important in respect to fingerprint powders and lifting materials, which are the most commonly used items. Even with scheduled maintenance checks, these items may become depleted through usage.

KEEP THE POWDERS DRY AND LOOSE

Never permit powder to become compacted into a solid mass. Some powders may have a tendency to become compressed or to roll up in tiny balls. Most commercial powders are satisfactory, as they tend to remain loose and workable, but all powders should be kept tightly sealed when not in use to prevent them from absorbing moisture in the air. Moisture is the greatest enemy of fingerprint powders and is the cause of the powder forming tiny balls. The extent of this problem is directly related to the frequency of use of the powder. Naturally, if the powder is used daily, the problem of moisture is diminished, because the powder is used before it can be adversely affected.

The St. Paul Police Crime Laboratory developed one solution to the problem of moisture affecting fingerprint powders (Hanggi and Alfultis, 1969). Their method calls for the use of silica gel capsules in special jars, with the silica gel absorbing the moisture. Another method that may be used for magnetic powders that become lumpy due to moisture is to grind the powder using a mortar and pestle. However, if at any time there is any doubt as to the suitability of a powder, the best procedure is to discard the powder and replace it. The successful recovery of latent fingerprints at crime scenes is far more important than any possible economy achieved by using unsatisfactory powders.

48

SEVENTEEN ITEMS THAT MAKE UP A SERVICEABLE FINGERPRINT KIT

The fingerprint kit components described in this section meet the requirements for most situations encountered by the average investigator or patrolman. Naturally, fingerprint kits intended for use by evidence technicians at crime scenes may be more complex and contain a greater variety of items, but only because the nature and extent of the evidence is more complex and requires more comprehensive examinations. The following articles may make up a fingerprint kit (Figs. 37 and 38):

1. A *carrying case:* A medium-sized carrying case similar to the small case depicted in Figure 34 is adequate for the average kit. These cases and their contents are available from all manufacturers and suppliers of fingerprint equipment.
2. A *fingerprint card holder* may be attached to the lid of the case where it is available for immediate use.
3. An *inking device:* A plate and roller, a Porelon pad, inkless devices, or other materials to take comparison prints at the crime scene should be added.
4. *Fingerprint powders:* At least two contrasting powders, black and gray or white. More black powder is generally used than any other color; therefore, if an extra supply of any color is carried, it should be black powder. Fluorescent powders, usually advised for multicolored back-

grounds, need not be included in basic kits because of the requirement for ultraviolet light (UV) equipment. Dragon blood powder is a good substitute for fluorescent powders, as that powder photographs light on a dark background and dark on a light background. Black and silver magnetic powders may also be included in the kit.

5. A two-cell *flashlight*, preferably a focusing light, for searching for latents primarily, but also for many other purposes in fingerprint work, either day or night is needed.

6. A *rule* or roll tape measure: A folding-type extension rule or a 25-foot tape measure may be used for overall measurements for the crime scene sketch. Pressure-sensitive evidence rule tapes which may be cut into desired lengths and marked with identifying data are ideal for placing near latents on an object for both identification and pho-

Figure 37. A serviceable fingerprint kit may be designed and stocked by individual investigators to meet their own requirements.

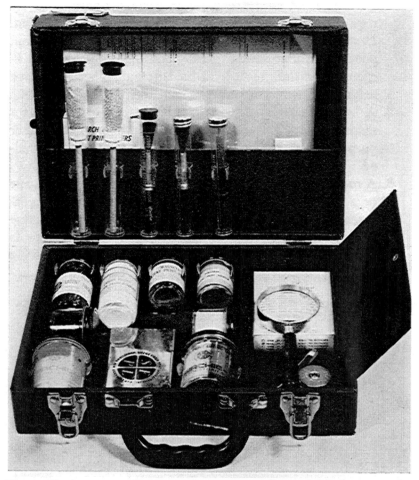

Figure 38. A compact fingerprint kit commercially available from a major manufacturer of fingerprint equipment.

tographic purposes. All rules should be clearly marked for easy reading.

7. *Evidence bags,* self-seal type, and *evidence identification tapes or tags.* Extra-strength polyethylene bags for transporting evidence with the tag or tape affixed to the bags for identification purposes, in addition to marking the object for identification, are necessary.

8. *Scissors* or small-sized shears: A scalpel with detachable blade may also be used.

9. *Marking devices:* Pencils, black and white evidence markers, ball-point pens, and an evidence scriber with either a carbide or diamond tip for identification marking of evidentiary items are included.

10. *Brushes,* perhaps six, three of a small size with hair less than 1¼ inches long and three larger sizes. Many technicians prefer fiberglass brushes in lieu of the larger hair brushes. It is not necessary to carry brushes for every bottle of powder; if brushes are handled properly, they may be used for more than one color powder. A magnetic powder applicator should be carried if magnetic powders are included in the kit.

11. *Fingerprint cards* and *plain bond paper* must be carried for recording inked comparison prints and, if necessary, major case prints.

12. *Latent fingerprint lifting materials:* An adequate supply of lifting tape should be carried at all times. Frosted lifting tape is preferable to clear tape, because identifying data may be easily marked on the tape and it is easier to photograph, as there is less reflection of light. A supply of black and white rubber lifters should also be included, as these lifters are excellent for lifting latent prints from curved surfaces. The disadvantage of rubber lifts is that the prints are reversed and must be photographed and the comparison made with reversed photographs.

13. *Lifting tape covers and backing:* A supply of white index cards should be carried for placing tape lifts of prints developed with black powder. A supply of black paper, such as exposed photographic paper, should also be carried for lifts of prints developed with light-colored powders. Transparent and frosted lifting tape covers are supplied by manufacturers and are preferred by many examiners.

14. A pair of *forceps* about 6 inches long, either wood or plastic should be included.

15. A *magnifying glass:* A small-sized hand magnifier or reading glass is useful.
16. Sheets of *graph paper* for accurately sketching locations of latent prints and indicating measurements and exact positions of objects are useful.
17. *Postmortem fingerprinting equipment:* Inker, spoon, hypodermic syringe, bottle of tissue-builder solvent, and bottle of finger-tissue cleaner.

49

FINGERPRINT BRUSHES

Many kinds, sizes, and shapes of brushes may be used in fingerprint work. They fall into one of four classes or types—hair, feather, fiberglass, and magnetic powder applicators (magnetic wands or brushes). Figure 39 shows various types of hair and feather brushes; fiberglass brushes and magnetic powder applicators are not included. The illustration is not intended to con-

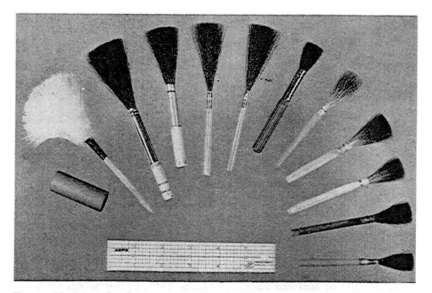

Figure 39. Many kinds, sizes, and shapes of brushes are used in fingerprint work: Softness is the most important consideration.

vey the idea that the brushes shown are the only kinds of brushes, even within the two classes, that are useful in fingerprint work: They are only a representative sample.

If hair brushes are used, the hair should be very soft and pliable. In no case should the brush contain stiff bristles. Bristles in a brush reveal themselves by conspicuous streaking in a powdered image. Hair brushes are more durable and cheaper than feather brushes, and they may be purchased in a variety of shapes and sizes. Feather brushes or dusters are daintier and fluffier than hair brushes and perhaps not as convenient or durable; they have to be handled with greater care.

Fiberglass brushes have gained wide acceptance in recent years, and many investigators prefer these brushes over either hair or feather brushes. The fiberglass brush costs more than either of the other two brushes but lasts much longer, and the brush may be cleaned periodically by gently washing with a dishwashing detergent and thoroughly rinsing and drying. Some technicians have used the same fiberglass brushes for years and claim the bristles retain their same soft quality as when first purchased.

Magnetic powder applicators, commonly called *magnetic wands* or *brushes,* are simply magnetized steel rods enclosed in a sheath similar in size to an old-fashioned fountain pen. When the rod is fully inserted in the sheath, magnetic powders may be picked-up with the tip of the sheath and applied to a surface for latent prints in the same manner as a regular brush. The powders actually form a bristleless brush. Pulling the rod to an extended position releases the powder from the tip of the sheath. The advantage of magnetic powders is that only the powder touches the surface and the latent print; there are no bristles to streak the print as may occur with hair brushes. Magnetic powders are particularly suitable for latent prints on plastic and nonferrous items, and excellent-quality latent prints have been recovered from the grooved areas of phonograph records with these powders. Magnetic powders are not, however, applicable to many items and should not be considered to the exclusion of regular brush and powder techniques.

As for sizes of brushes to be carried in a kit, there should be at least two, if hair brushes are used exclusively. Larger brushes can be used for larger areas and the smaller ones on concentrated work, or individual latents. If fiberglass brushes are used, the same brush may be used for either larger or smaller areas.

If colored powders are used, fine pale gold lining, for example, it is well to use a special brush for such special powders, although it is not necessary to use different brushes for two different kinds of the same-colored powder, except in the case of fluorescent powders. Every effort should be made to keep from contaminating powders.

The total number of brushes in a kit depends upon the types of brushes used and the different types and colors of powders carried. An extra brush or two for particular jobs occasionally produces better workmanship, but there is no necessity to carry a large collection of brushes. Each brush should be cleaned before it is returned to the kit by tapping or shaking to remove all excess powder. Each brush should be placed within an individual container inside the kit; if they are all carried in a case together, it is not clear for which powders they are intended. When necessary, hair brushes may be cleaned very effectively by washing in carbon tetrachloride.

50

FINGERPRINT POWDERS AND PHOSPHORS

Fingerprint powders obviously are one of the most important and indispensable items in fingerprint work. A majority of all latent fingerprints recovered at crime scenes are developed by the use of powders. Long experience has shown that it is as unnecessary to carry fifteen varieties or colors of powders as it is to have six lead pencils of varying degrees of hardness for purposes of notetaking. It would not be a mis-statement to say that a skillful fingerprint technician could take two powders, one a black powder and the other a light-colored powder, and together with the skillful use of photography, satisfactorily accomplish 99 percent of all fingerprint tasks where powder development is applicable.

Powders may be purchased ready-mixed or they may be prepared according to formulas. Most departments prefer to purchase powders, as a little powder goes a long way. Particularly, if only a small quantity is used, it is as economical to buy the prepared powders as it is to buy the necessary grinding equipment, sieves, and bulk ingredients for preparing fingerprint powders in small quantities. A further consideration is quality control. Commercially prepared powders are of consistently excellent quality prepared under exacting standards, while the quality of locally prepared powders may depend greatly on the skill, comprehensiveness, and equipment of the person preparing the powder. The adage that you get exactly what you pay for particularly applies to fingerprint powders. Part of the price for commercial powders is the assurance of quality.

A group of synthetic and natural chemical compounds known as *phosphors* may be used as fingerprint powders. These powders are not intended for general use, but are useful when developing latent fingerprints on multicolored surfaces. They not only form a group of light-colored powders, either to the eye or under ultraviolet light, but they are also suitable for mixing with dark-colored pigments to produce a dark-colored powder which, when activated by UV light, may be photographed as a light-colored powder.

Characteristics, technical aspects, and techniques of fingerprint powders are discussed in Chapter V. The selection or choice of specific powders is dependent entirely upon the experience and judgment of the individual technician. One person may find a particular type of powder suitable for a specific task, while another may prefer another type of powder, but both may achieve the same results.

51

FINGERPRINT MAGNIFYING GLASSES

A fingerprint magnifying glass is indispensable for classifying and comparing prints if accuracy is to be achieved and unnecessary eye strain avoided. Magnifiers of the type shown in Figure 40 are most commonly used. It is an older model Bausch & Lomb glass. All models of this type are sturdily built heavy-duty magnifying glasses with an adjustable eyepiece adapted for

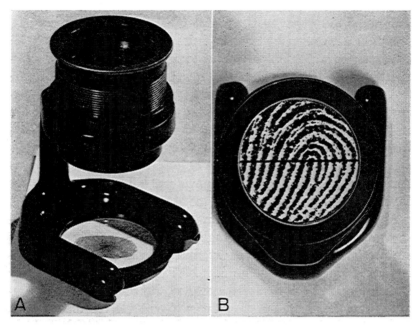

Figure 40. (A) Bausch & Lomb fingerprint glass with Henry disc. (B) The view through the eyepiece shows the core of a fingerprint pattern.

focusing for different individuals' eyes. Magnifying glasses of this type have special removable reticules positioned at the base of the magnifier. These reticules are used for special types of work such as single fingerprint classification. The most common reticules in use today are the Henry or Battley discs or a combination Henry-Battley half-circle disc. The discs are interchangable and easily removed from the magnifier. The discs may be rotated so that the engraved images on their surfaces may be turned in any desired direction.

The disc shown in Figure 40 is a Henry disc; it has a single line ruled across the diameter or the disc for ridge-counting in the Henry system of classification. In ridge counting, the line on the disc is placed over the print in such a way that it passes through the core and the delta. Ridges crossing the line between those points are counted in classification. In such a manner, the ridge count of a loop-type pattern is determined (Fig. 41).

Figure 41. Fingerprint magnifying glasses are designed for classification work. However, the glasses may also be used for comparing latent and inked impressions.

Extreme magnification is neither required nor desirable for the examination of fingerprints. Almost all fingerprint magnifiers have a magnifying power of 4.5 times. This degree of magnification is sufficient for determining ridge characteristics and provides sufficient field of view to determine the relative position of the characteristics, one to another.

Good illumination should be provided for all types of fingerprint work as it is eyestraining at best. If the technician is able to work in a relaxed and unstrained manner, the work will not

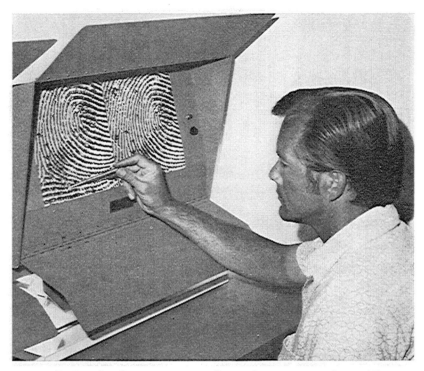

Figure 42. Regular fingerprint magnifiers enlarge a print about 4.5 times. In some cases, particularly when instructing students in classification work, greater enlargements using a comparator, such as the one depicted, are desirable.

be so tiring. Too much light can be as harmful as too little. Generally, the intensity of illumination within the fingerprint work area should be 50 to 100 footcandles. Strong illumination is used when searching for latent prints on an object but not for general duties, such as comparison work.

Another very useful and convenient type of magnifier is a folding-type glass having a magnifying power of 5. This type of glass is basically a linen tester but is suitable for fingerprint work and may be conveniently carried in a fingerprint kit. Although it is not used generally in classifying, it is very convenient for field work. Magnifiers of this type are available from all the major fingerprint equipment and supply manufacturers.

52

FINGERPRINT LIFTING MATERIALS

Fingerprint lifting materials and techniques will be more fully covered in Chapter IX. This section lists some of the lifting materials that should be included in fingerprint kits. There are basically two requirements that apply when selecting adequate lifting materials—these requirements actually apply to the selection of any fingerprint technique, equipment, or material— and these requirements are *results* and *practicality*. There are many lifting techniques which produce excellent results but are impracticable for use in the field at crime scenes. The most successful technique available is of little use either in the field or in the crime laboratory if the results are outweighed by elaborate requirements for preparation or application.

There is a wide variety of practical fingerprint lifting materials available for use by an investigator and which require minimal training and experience to use successfully: black and white rubber lifters, black and white opaque lifting tape, and transparent and frosted lifting tape with black, white, and clear covers. Generally, the choice of color for a rubber lifter or cover for tapes and tabs depends upon the color of the latent print. White rubber lifters and covers for latents developed with dark powders and black for those developed with light powders. However, it is possible to use transparent lifting tape or tabs with clear covers with any color of powder if the lift is to be used as a negative for photographic enlargement of the print.

Black and white rubber lifters may be purchased in sizes ranging from 2-by-2 inches to 4-by-10 inches. The lifters may be cut into smaller sizes as needed. All rubber lifters have clear transparent plastic covers. Rubber lifters produce a reversed image of the impression lifted and must, therefore, be photographically reversed for comparison purposes. Rubber lifters are ideal for latent prints on curved surfaces, such as the steering wheels of automobiles.

Black and white opaque lifting tapes also have the disadvantage that the latent impressions are reversed and must be reversed by means of photographs. These tapes provide a good contrasting background for latent prints and may be mounted on any transparent cover or sheet.

Transparent and frosted lifting tapes and tabs are perhaps the most ideal lifting materials that can be carried in a fingerprint kit. These listing materials offer several advantages: direct comparison of the latent with record inked impressions and the choice of numerous types of covers. The tapes and tabs may be mounted directly on backing sheets, which are preprinted forms providing spaces for entering all essential identifying data regarding the latent print. Transparent lifting tapes and tabs may also be placed on almost any type of backing, regular 3-by-5-inch index cards, rigid vinyl black or white covers, photographic paper, or regular bond paper. The roles of tape may be purchased in two widths, 1½-inch or 2-inch rolls, which are 30 feet in length. The tabs may be 1½-by-1½ inches, 2-by-4 inches or 4-by-4 inches in size.

Fingerprint lifting tapes are specifically designed for fingerprint work. The tapes are pressure wound to eliminate "fisheyes" and streaks. Transparent tapes commonly found in retail stores for general usage are not suitable for fingerprint work and should not be used except as a last resource when regular tape is not available.

Sheets of transparent evidence-collection lifters designed for lifting footwear prints and trace evidence may sometimes be used to lift palmprints and areas containing multiple fingerprint impressions. These sheets are usually 6-by-12 inches in size.

At least one package each of black and white rubber lifters and, as a minimum, one roll of transparent or frosted lifting tape should be carried in a fingerprint kit. The types of covers or backing material is the choice of the technician. Generally, white backing material, cards or paper, may be obtained easily at or near the scene, but adequate black backing material is not easily found, and a good supply should be carried in the kit.

53
THE FINGERPRINT CAMERA

The fingerprint camera is a specially designed copying camera; it is a complete self-contained unit for making full size, exact one-to-one reproductions of subjects on a plane surface within an area commensurate with the size of film used. The description *self-contained* is appropriate, as the camera has everything necessary to take a photograph, including a lighting system, built-in. The lighting system includes both the light and power sources. All fingerprint cameras utilize either batteries or a power pack as power sources for portability, but many models are also adapted for use with regular 110 to 120 volt alternating current.

Fingerprint cameras have been developed specifically for law enforcement work and particularly for photographing fingerprints. Because of their completeness and portability, they may be adapted to additional uses such as photographing questioned writings, toolmarks, jewelry, printed matter, and other subjects requiring little depth of field.

Over the years, there have been almost twenty different models of fingerprint cameras released by various manufacturers. Many of the models have been discontinued but may still be found in use by various agencies; occasionally, some may be found for sale in surplus and used-camera retail stores. Handled with proper care and with the performance of regularly scheduled preventive maintenance, a fingerprint camera may last almost indefinitely.

All fingerprint cameras are fixed-focus cameras requiring a minimum of photographic training and experience to operate. The early models of fingerprint cameras had nonadjustable apertures, and the choice of shutter speeds was limited to time and bulb settings. To accommodate the greater variety of film speeds offered by modern photographic films, all models of fingerprint cameras manufactured today have adjustable apertures and variable shutters.

The light source for the majority of fingerprint cameras is four frosted bulbs mounted within the nose of the camera. Whenever oblique or side lighting is desired, the bulbs on one side may be removed. Several newer models use an electronic flash mounted within the nose of the camera.

Film sizes for the various models of fingerprint cameras vary from 2¼-by-3¼ inches to 4-by-5 inches, and many models also accommodate Polaroid type films. There are several advantages to the 4-by-5-inch film-size format: (1) partial palmprints and simultaneous impressions may be photographed in one film exposure, (2) a Polaroid film adapter may be used to take test exposures before exposing cut film or film packs, and (3) most police photographic facilities are designed for processing 4-by-5-inch film.

Fingerprint photographic techniques are discussed in Section 46. Operational procedures for each model of fingerprint camera may be found in the technical information booklets each manufacturer provides with purchase of the camera. Listed below are limited descriptions of fingerprint cameras that are and have been available from various manufacturers.

FAUROT

The Faurot® fingerprint camera has lens aperture settings from $f/4.5$ to $f/22$; an adjustable shutter with time, bulb, and ½₅ to ¹⁄₁₅₀ second settings; and uses 2¼-by-3¼-inch film. The lighting system consists of four bulbs as a light source and uses standard flashlight batteries as the power source.

FOLMER-GRAFLEX

The Folmer® fingerprint camera was manufactured by the former Graflex, Inc., of Rochester, New York, and was one of the earliest fingerprint cameras (Fig 43). The military designation of this camera was PH-503/PF. The camera had a fixed $f/6.3$ lens aperture and time and bulbs shutter settings. Film size

Figure 43. Officer using a Folmer-Graflex fingerprint camera. (A) The aperture of the camera may be used to frame the subject matter. (B) Slightly rounded surfaces may be photographed by opening the aperture compartment and positioning the object as shown.

for the camera was 2¼-by-3¼ inches. Although the camera has not been manufactured for a considerable number of years, it may be found still in use in many agencies.

CRIMINAL RESEARCH PRODUCTS, INC.

This company offers three models of fingerprint cameras, all accommodating 4-by-5-inch film. Two models permit the use of Polaroid in addition to 4-by-5-inch film. All three cameras have lens apertures adjustable from $f/8$ to $f/32$ and adjustable shutters with time, bulb, and ¼₅ to ¼₅₀ second settings. The lighting system for all three cameras consists of four frosted bulbs as a light source and uses regular flashlight batteries as the power source.

POLAROID CORPORATION

THE POLAROID CU-5 CLOSE-UP CAMERA®. This unique camera may be purchased with a number of combinations of camera bodies, lenses, ratio multipliers, and framing attachments (Fig. 44). Either a 3¼-by-4¼-inch film pack camera body or a 4-by-5-inch-film camera body may be selected. For fingerprint photography, a 3-inch lens with aperture settings from $f/4.5$ to $f/45$

Figure 44. The Polaroid CU-5 Close-up camera.

and shutter speed settings of time, bulb, and 1 to ⅟₁₂₅ second, for 1 : 1, 2 : 1, and 3 : 1 magnification ratios is provided. The light source is a built-in electronic flash ring light, which encompasses the lens. A polarizing filter may be used to eliminate or reduce reflections from reflective surfaces. Two power packs are available for use with this camera. The AC power pack connects to household AC circuits, and the portable power pack, which is battery operated, provides about 1,000 flashes.

THE POLAROID MP-4 MULTIPURPOSE CAMERA®. This camera is not suitable for field or crime scene use, as it was designed for use in the photography studio or laboratory. The camera provides a versatile photographic recording system, enabling the photographer to photograph fingerprint evidence in almost every type of situation that may be encountered in a police laboratory. The camera head and column rotate 360 degrees and can be locked in any position, permitting pictures to be taken in any direction or at any angle. The lighting is fully adjustable with removable lamp heads to permit lighting of any subject, flat copy or three-dimensional. Either 3¼-by-4¼-inch or 4-by-5-inch film may be used.

SIRCHIE FINGER PRINT LABORATORIES, INC.

Sirchie Laboratories has offered a variety of different models of fingerprint cameras. One early model was the KE-3(1)® manufactured for the U.S. Army and still used by that agency (Fig. 45). This camera used 2¼-by-3¼-inch film, and adjustable lens aperture from $f/6.3$ to $f/11$, shutter speeds of time and bulb, and the standard lighting system of four bulbs and batteries.

The Sirchie Model A®, Model B®, Model C®, and 120 roll-film fingerprint cameras all had adjustable lens apertures from $f/4.5$ to $f/22$ and adjustable shutter speeds of time, bulb, and ½₅ to ½₅₀ second. The lighting system for these cameras was the standard four bulbs and flashlight batteries, but regular household current could also be used. Film sizes for the cameras were 2¼-by-3¼ inches for model A, 4-by-5 inches for model B, and 3¼-by-4¼ inches for model C. This line of fingerprint cameras has been discontinued by the manufacturer.

The new series of Sirchie fingerprint cameras all have adjustable lens apertures and variable speed shutters. All but two of

Figure 45. The military KE-3(1) fingerprint camera.

the cameras use the standard lighting system of four bulbs and batteries as a power source. The SFP-34® and the SFP-45® models both have electronic flash units and may be operated on either batteries or regular household current. The electronic flash units are mounted on the cameras in an oblique manner to eliminate many of the problems related to ring flash units. The SFP-4®, SFP-5®, and SFP-45 models accommodate 4-by-5-inch films, and Polaroid-type films may also be used with the SFP-5 and SFP-45 models. The SFP-3® and SFP-34 models use 3¼-by-4¼-inch Polaroid-type films exclusively.

Sirchie also manufactures an evidence camera with a built-in ultraviolet light source, the model SUV-10®, which may be used to photograph latent fingerprints developed with ultraviolet powders. This camera has an adjustable lens aperture and variable speed shutter and accommodates 4-by-5-inch film.

BURKE & JAMES

Burke & James manufactures the Watson-Holmes® fingerprint camera. Technical data for the camera is similar to that for the Faurot fingerprint camera.

54

EQUIPMENT FOR TAKING FINGER- AND PALMPRINTS

Sections 31 and 32 briefly discuss the equipment required for taking inked or record fingerprint impressions. The equipment is so simple that it is not necessary to elaborate further on their description. One item of equipment essential for taking adequate impressions within a police department or identification bureau is the fingerprint stand.

The plate or pad upon which the fingers are inked preparatory to taking impressions and the surface holding the card should both be on the same level, and they should be at a height above the floor that permits the average subject's hand and forearm to assume a natural horizontal position in front of the elbow. In order to obtain fully rolled impressions, the finger must rotate approximately 180 degrees. Free and unhampered rotation of the hand and forearm is impossible if the hand or forearm is elevated or lowered to an unnatural, cramped, or strained position.

The average table or office desk is approximately 31 inches in height; the inking surface on a fingerprint stand should be ap-

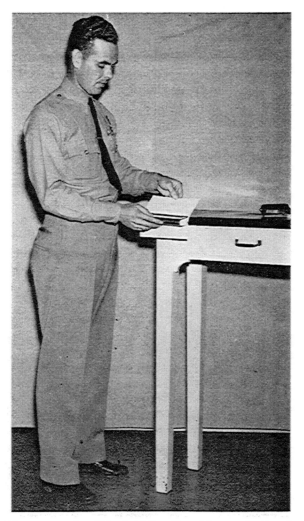

Figure 46. The corner of a 43-inch-high table with a projecting top provides an ideal surface on which to take the prints of an average adult. (The officer depicted is James A. Roberts, who contributed Sec. 132 of this volume. The photograph appeared in the first edition of this book.)

proximately 12 inches above the top of an ordinary desk, thereby making the printing surface approximately 43 inches from the floor for the average person (Fig. 46). A person who is very short or a juvenile finds that height a bit too high, and a person 6 feet or more tall may have to stoop slightly. The objective is to strike an average suitable for the majority of persons.

The juvenile or short person may be accommodated by having near at hand a stool or platform upon which to stand while being printed. Nothing much can be done for the tall person, except to ask him to stoop for the occasion. If strain or unnatural pressure on the fingers is avoided, impressions are more uniform. If the table on which the impressions are inked and rolled projects 1 or 2 inches in front of the table proper, the fingers will swing freely, and they will not interfere with the printing process nor catch on any upright supports for the table.

The stand in Figure 46 is constructed with an inking plate in the center of the top, and any corner may be used for taking prints. Ideally, the stand should be long enough to also hold all equipment necessary for taking palmprints and major case prints whenever the need arises.

55

LIGHTBOXES

A lightbox with a viewing surface of at least 8-by-10 inches is a desirable item of equipment for a police crime laboratory or evidence processing facility (Fig. 47). A lightbox is extremely useful when processing transparent objects, such as pieces of glass or plastic bags, for latent fingerprints. It is also useful as a means for providing backlighting when photographing latent prints on transparent objects. The lightbox may also be used when evaluating and masking out photographic negatives for making court charts and when examining latent prints on transparent lifters.

An x-ray viewer commonly used by medical personnel makes an excellent lightbox for fingerprint work. If preferred, it is a simple task to construct a lightbox. Essentially all that is re-

Figure 47. A lightbox is extremely useful when examining transparent objects for latent prints. In the photograph above, an examiner is processing a plastic bag with magnetic powder, using a medical x-ray viewer.

quired is a small box containing a light source and with a translucent top cover of glass or plastic.

56

ULTRAVIOLET LIGHT SOURCES

A handbook on fingerprint mechanics would be incomplete without at least a brief discussion of the uses of ultraviolet light in searching for and recovering latent fingerprints. The applications of ultraviolet light in fingerprint work is discussed in Section 77. The purpose of this section is to briefly explain the nature of ultraviolet light as a means of acquainting the reader with the various types of ultraviolet light sources available.

Within the electromagnetic spectrum, visible light is a very small band with a range in wavelengths from about 4,000 angstroms to about 7,700 angstroms (Å), which is 400 nanometers to 770 nanometers (nm). To the human eye, these wavelengths correspond from extreme violet to extreme red. Ultraviolet light has wavelengths of approximately 200 nm to 400 nm and is, therefore, shorter in wavelength than visible light. Within the ultraviolet band of the spectrum, there are two major subdivisions: short-wave ultraviolet light, 200 nm to 280 nm; and long-wave ultraviolet light, 320 nm to 380 nm.

Luminescence is described as the emission of radiant energy, usually visible light, from a substance under the influence of an activation or exciting agent, usually ultraviolet light. The short wavelengths of ultraviolet light are transformed into the longer wavelengths of visible light. Luminescence is distinguished from incandescence in that the former includes all kinds of light radiation except those caused by temperature. *Thermoluminescence* is associated with heat, and when a substance emits visible light by temperature, it is said to be incandescent.

The term *fluorescence* refers to the property of a substance that causes it to emit light of a constant intensity when continuously exposed to a uniform source of radiant energy of the proper wavelength. Fluorescence actually is the transformation of light by matter; certain substances, when illuminated, radiate an unpolarized light of a different and usually greater wavelength. Fluorescence exists only as long as the exciting agent is present and active.

If the emission of light by a substance continues after the exciting agent is removed or stopped, the resulting phenomenon is called *phosphorescence*. Fluorescence and phosphorescence are identical physically, except that the emission of visible light continues even after the agent that caused the excitation is withdrawn. Phosphorescent afterglow may last for hours depending upon the substance, and the substance can be activated again and again by renewed exposure to ultraviolet light.

Some substances fluoresce only under short-wave ultraviolet light, others only under long-wave, and still others under both. Almost all commercial ultraviolet fingerprint powders fluoresce under long-wave ultraviolet light. This is an important advantage in that lamps producing long-wave ultraviolet light, commonly called *blacklights,* do not damage the eyes. Short-wave ultraviolet light can harm the skin and eyes unless adequate safety precautions are taken. Approved safety glasses should always be worn when working with short-wave ultraviolet radiation.

There are many different models of ultraviolet light sources currently available. Long-wave ultraviolet lamps may be easily obtained as regular Edison-base blacklight bulbs, and blacklight filter bulbs for any fluorescent light fixture are available in almost every city. Ultraviolet light sources may be purchased from every major manufacturer of fingerprint equipment, scientific equipment supply companies, and lapidary supply stores. A desirable ultraviolet light source for a crime laboratory is the Model C-5 Chromato-Vue Cabinet®, manufactured by Ultra-Violet Products, Inc., San Gabriel, California. This cabinet provides an adequate and safe means for processing and viewing evidence with either short- or long-wave ultraviolet light.

57

A STRONG LIGHT SOURCE

Experienced fingerprint technicians know that one of the most effective devices for discovering, developing, and photographing latent fingerprint evidence is a strong light. A flashlight is an important piece of equipment in a fingerprint kit, but there are occasions both in the field and in the laboratory when a stronger light is necessary.

A strong light reveals fingerprints that may not be discovered under ordinary room lighting or daylight. Figure 34 shows a strong light being used in detecting latent images on a green metal box; the prints are invisible without the aid of the light, yet when the light is reflected off the latents at the proper angle, the images are revealed with amazing contrast.

Reflectors similar to the one shown are obtainable in photographic stores. Many sizes and types of light and reflectors are used in fingerprint work. Two important considerations are that the light must be strong, and the light beam must be controlled. The reflector shown in Figure 48 is light aluminum. It is 5 inches in diameter and about 5½ inches deep. It will accommodate light globes up to 150 watts, but it is more effective if equipped with a No. 1 photoflood lamp. A 150-watt indoor-outdoor flood-light bulb mounted in a portable weatherproof nylon holder also makes an excellent light for fingerprint work.

A strong light source in a reflector has unlimited uses when searching for physical evidence either at crime scenes or in the laboratory. One of the most valuable uses is in connection with latent fingerprint and footwear impressions in dust; they are revealed with striking clarity and detail when lighted from the side. A strong light is also useful when searching for trace evidence, such as hairs and fibers. Effectiveness of strong controlled side lighting under the circumstances indicated is surprising.

Figure 48. Next to brushes and powder, an investigator's most valuable piece of equipment is a strong light source when searching for latent prints.

58

MORTAR AND PESTLE

A mortar and pestle are indispensable for those who wish to prepare their own fingerprint powders or are interested in experimentation with fingerprint powders and formulas. An ordinary glass mortar and pestle containing a quantity of lead sulfide is shown in Figure 49. Metallic lumps have been ground into a powder which will pass through a 100-mesh sieve without difficulty. Many compounds can be ground into a fine powder very quickly in a mortar. One can learn much about powders by experimenting with them in this manner.

A mortar and pestle are also practical items for the technician

Figure 49. Coarse lumpy chemical compounds, such as lead sulfide, may be ground to a powder suitable for fingerprint work in a short time by using a mortar and pestle.

who wishes to maintain the serviceability of powders for as long as possible. Powders, particularly magnetic powders, may become caked or lumped into solid masses due to exposure to moisture. Such powders may be baked for about thirty minutes in an oven at a temperature of 120° F to remove all moisture and then pulverized in a mortar and passed through a sieve.

Mortar-and-pestle sets are obtainable from drug and chemical supply houses in various sizes. A convenient size for grinding small quantities of powder for limited use is a mortar 3 inches in diameter or larger. The mortar in Figure 49 measures 4 inches in inside diameter. Glass sets are also convenient.

59

FUMING CABINETS

A fuming cabinet is a useful item of equipment in a police crime laboratory. It is simple, easily operated, and effective for processing objects suspected of bearing fresh latent fingerprints with any of several latent fingerprint fuming techniques. Basically, a fuming cabinet is an environmental control chamber in which an object is exposed to a high concentration of fumes from a particular substance. Fuming cabinets are specifically designed to achieve optimum results when using fuming techniques to recover latent prints. The cabinets should always be used in a well-ventilated area, preferably a chemical exhaust hood, to remove all excess fumes. All latent fingerprint fuming techniques represent a health hazard, and fuming cabinets cannot be considered an item of safety equipment, as there is no provision for the safe removal of excess fumes.

Sirchie Laboratories manufactures an electric fuming cabinet of vinyl-coated aluminum construction with a crystal glass front and rear panels (Fig. 50). This cabinet may be used for the application of all latent fingerprint fuming techniques, except hydrogen fluoride, which etches glass. Fuming cabinets may also be easily constructed with a minimum expenditure of time and materials. A simple and efficient electrically heated iodine

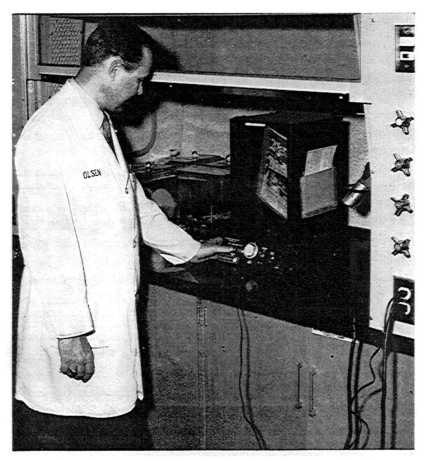

Figure 50. A fuming cabinet commercially available from a major manufacturer of fingerprint equipment. This fuming cabinet is advantageous in that the heat to vaporized crystals can be regulated.

fuming cabinet is shown in Figure 51. The top and front are hinged glass doors, which allow for easy loading of the cabinet and quick removal of items when fingerprints are developed. The sides are glass; it is possible to inspect both sides of an item carefully while it is being processed.

The frame of the cabinet is constructed of wood; the fumes of iodine and other techniques are highly corrosive to metal.

Items are hung by wooden or plastic clothespins on dowel rods which drop into notches in wooden strips across the inside front and back of the top of the cabinet. Tension on the clothespins is provided by rubber bands, which are easily renewed. The life of rubber bands is short: Elasticity is quickly lost on exposure to iodine vapors. Ordinary wooden or plastic clothespins may be used on the dowel rods by simply removing the metal springs and replacing them with rubber bands. The pins may be shortened if necessary.

The lamp socket is fastened to the floor of the cabinet near the back so that it does not interfere with items suspended from the dowel rods. Wiring enters through a hole in the floor under the fixture. A toggle switch on the back side of the cabinet controls the current. The fixture and wiring are protected against iodine vapors by a coating of hot paraffin applied with a brush. Holes in the fixture are plugged with cotton and sealed over with paraffin. A string is tied around the joint between the lamp and the socket before paraffin is applied to keep the wax from filling the socket. It is important that any exposed metal parts are coated with paraffin to avoid unnecessary corrosion. Changing lamps is no problem; the paraffin coating does not interfere with removal of the lamp. When a globe is renewed, it should be sealed in the same manner as the original.

The lamp is an ordinary 40-watt electric globe; a smaller lamp does not generate sufficient heat to vaporize the iodine crystals rapidly enough to encourage development. A 40-watt lamp permits good control of the iodine vapors and vaporization is not too rapid. Heat from the lamp tends to circulate vapors in the cabinet. Plastic is the most suitable material for the cap which holds the crystals in position on top of the lamp. The sole purpose of the cap is to hold the iodine crystals on top of and in contact with the glass of the lamp to speed vaporization.

Several modifications must be made to the fuming cabinet if it is to be used for application of the hydrogen fluoride technique. The electrical fixture should be removed and the cabinet

Figure 51. An iodine fuming cabinet which can be easily constructed. The iodine crystals are vaporized by heat from the light bulb.

made as airtight as possible. As hydrogen fluoride etches glass, the side panels should be constructed with clear plastic. A dowel with plastic fan blades affixed should be inserted through a hole in the floor of the cabinet to circulate the fumes.

60

IODINE FUMING PIPE

The principle and operation of the iodine fuming pipe are simple. Publicity on the pipe has perhaps exceeded its favor and utility. The pipe must be kept in a manner which prevents the drying agent from deliquesing and the iodine vapors from escaping.

A fuming pipe is easily assembled (Fig. 52). A short piece of rubber tubing about 1 foot long (A) is attached to the small end of a calcium chloride drying tube (B). A pledget of glass wool (C) is tucked into the lower end of the bulb, and a small quantity of iodine crystals (D) is dropped onto the glass wool. A second pledget of glass wool (E) large enough to fill the remaining half of the bulb is tucked in on top of the iodine crystals forming an *iodine-glass wool sandwich*. The remaining cylindrical portion of the tube (F) is filled with anhydrous (dry) calcium chloride. Another pledget of glass wool may be used to hold the drying agent in position, or a small calcium chloride drying tube or a small funnel in a one hole cork may be used in the end of the first tube in place of the glass wool. A second drying tube (H) concentrates vapors.

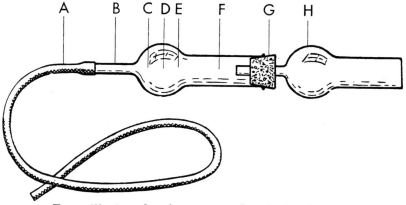

Figure 52. An iodine fuming pipe, described in the text.

When the tube is used, the bulb containing the iodine sandwich is held in the palm of the hand. Heat from the palm causes the iodine crystals to vaporize more rapidly than they would at room temperature. As the iodine vapors are blown through the calcium chloride, breath moisture is absorbed, and dry vapors are emitted from the tube's end.

While blowing in the rubber tube, the opposite end of the fuming pipe is moved slowly over the suspected area at close range, about ½ inch. When and if latent prints show, the area is given more concentrated treatment to intensify the developing images. When operating the fuming pipe, the mouth tube should always be blown through; *never inhale*. Iodine fumes may be extremely harmful to the lungs and membranes of the throat.

61

CHEMICAL EXHAUST HOODS

Many chemical substances and powders used in latent fingerprint techniques constitute potential or definite health or safety hazards. Many of these substances and the maximum exposure limit for each is prescribed by the Occupational Safety and Health Administration. Nearly all chemical substances that may be used by fingerprint technicians, except benzidine and its salts, may be safely handled and used within a chemical exhaust hood. Such hoods must have sufficient ventilating properties; that is, there must be at least 100 feet/min. capture velocity at the open face of the hood.

An adequate chemical exhaust hood must be considered an essential piece of equipment for all latent fingerprint processing facilities. All fuming cabinets should be placed within the hoods for safe removal of fumes; all flammable chemical techniques and fingerprint powders should be used only within the hood. There are many commercial chemical exhaust hoods available ranging considerably in size, features, and price. Each agency must determine the particular model that meets its needs, based upon frequency of use, types of techniques used, and budget limitations.

62

GLOVEBOXES

Gloveboxes are required only when using the benzidine free base and benzidine blood spray techniques. Of all the latent fingerprint techniques used by fingerprint technicians, the most hazardous to health are those involving benzidine. Benzidine has been identified as a carcinogenic substance which may be absorbed through the skin and may cause cancer of the bladder. Exposure times as short as 131 days have been demonstrated to be associated with the subsequent development of cancer, although the usual latent period is generally accepted to be fifteen to twenty-five years. The use of benzidine has been prohibited

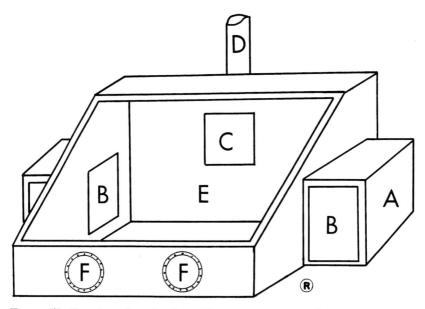

Figure 53. Drawing of a glovebox. This equipment may be constructed locally and is essential when using hazardous chemicals, such as benzidine. Components of the glovebox are as follows: (A) air lock, (B) self-closing door, (C) filter, (D) vent to final filter and fan, (E) glass cover for viewing window, and (F) glove ports. Gloves must be secured in front side of box.

by the United Kingdom and other European nations, and all United States Army Criminal Investigation Laboratories have abandoned use of the substance.

The *Federal Register* (Jan. 29, 1974) established guidelines for specific safeguards that must be made when employees are exposed to concentrations of benzidine of 0.1 percent or more. The concentration used in latent fingerprint techniques is at least ten times that amount. A glovebox is one of the safeguards prescribed. Figure 53 is a drawing of a glovebox. The gloves should be of neoprene or butyl rubber securely attached to the box. All waste must be sealed in an impervious bag, i.e., Mylar®, Tedlar®, or an equivalent, and incinerated. After processing, each item contaminated with benzidine should be sealed in a suitable container and the container clearly marked so as to prevent accidental opening without adequate safeguards. If latent prints are developed on the items, they should be handled with neoprene or butyl rubber gloves while being photographed and then sealed in a container.

63

HUMIDITY CABINETS

Research conducted by the Chicago Laboratory of the U.S. Postal Service established that optimum development of ninhydrin-treated latent prints is obtained when the items processed are subjected to a post-processing environment of 65 to 80 percent relative humidity (Lesk, 1971). Experience has shown that the developing time for ninhydrin-developed latent prints in such an environment may vary from twenty minutes to twenty-four hours. Some technicians prefer to use an ordinary steam iron to develop ninhydrin prints on paper, but the results are not always as desirable as those obtained with a humidity cabinet.

Fuming cabinets may be used as humidity cabinets for small quantities of evidence. A small glass container of water may be secured over the lamp in the cabinet, and the heat of the lamp will evaporate sufficient moisture. Agencies routinely processing large quantities of items with ninhydrin require larger cabinets. The sources of moisture may be either a hotplate set at its low-

Relative Humidity from Dry and Wet Bulb Thermometer Readings								
t - t' t	2.0	2.5	3.0	3.5	4.0	4.5	5.0	5.5
68	83	78	74	70	66	–	–	–
69	83	78	74	70	66	–	–	–
70	83	79	75	71	67	–	–	–
71	83	80	76	72	68	–	--	–
72	83	80	76	72	68	65	–	–
73	84	80	76	72	69	65	–	–
74	84	80	76	72	69	65	–	–
75	84	80	77	73	69	66	–	–
76	84	80	77	73	69	66	–	–
77	84	81	77	74	70	67	–	–
78	84	81	77	74	70	67	--	–
79	85	81	78	74	71	67	–	–
80	85	82	78	75	71	68	65	–
81	85	82	78	75	71	68	65	–
82	85	82	78	75	72	69	65	–
83	85	82	78	75	72	69	65	–
84	86	82	79	76	72	69	66	–
85	86	82	79	76	72	69	66	–
86	86	83	79	76	73	70	67	–
87	86	83	79	76	73	70	67	–
88	86	83	80	77	73	70	67	65
89	86	83	80	77	73	71	68	65
90	86	83	80	77	74	71	68	65

Figure 54. Relative humidity table.

est setting and a pan of water or a home vaporizer. Care must be taken to prevent excessive moisture from coming in direct contact with the items being processed, as such moisture may destroy any latent prints. Condensation may form on glass and metal sides of a cabinet; therefore, items should not be placed near the sides.

Regardless of the size and type of construction of a humidity cabinet, it is necessary to have a means for determining the relative humidity of the atmosphere within the cabinet in order to regulate the amount of moisture present. The simplest and most inexpensive method is to place two thermometers within the cabinet, dry and wet bulb thermometers. The dry bulb thermometer is an ordinary thermometer used to determine the ambient air temperature within the cabinet. The wet bulb thermometer is an ordinary thermometer with a piece of tight-fitting muslin cloth covering the bulb. The muslin cloth is wetted with distilled water and evaporation of the water cools the thermometer. The amount of cooling depends upon the quantity of water vapor present in the air.

Figure 54 is a table from which relative humidity may be computed from dry and wet bulb readings. Listed are approximate relative humidity values for a selected cross section of readings; all temperature readings are in degrees Fahrenheit. Figures in the far left vertical column are dry bulb readings *(t)*. Figures in the top horizontal line are the difference between the dry and wet bulb readings *(t − t')*. To determine relative humidity, subtract the wet bulb reading *(t')* from the dry bulb reading, and then locate the difference *(t − t')* in the top horizontal line. Read down this column at a point across from the dry bulb reading to obtain relative humidity. For example, when the dry bulb reading is 82° F and the wet bulb reading is 78° F, the relative humidity is 72 percent.

64

CLEAN EQUIPMENT

Clean equipment and proper preventive maintenance is of paramount importance to ensure the proper functioning of equipment at all times and to obtain maximum use from all equipment. Dirt and moisture have an adverse effect on the serviceability of equipment, particularly metallic components, which should be lightly oiled periodically. The time to clean equipment is as soon as possible after use. It is also advisable to schedule weekly maintenance sessions to ensure adequate preventive maintenance and cleaning of all equipment.

The inking plate, cardholder, and roller on fingerprint stands should be cleaned daily, regardless of whether or not they are used. If the inking plate is not cleaned, the ink film becomes dry, hard, and useless. If the roller is inked and not used, the film of ink on its surface will become dry and hard.

Many noninflammable solvents, such as those used in dry cleaning, are useful for cleaning fingerprint equipment. Cloths, rags, and paper towels may be used for cleaning inking equipment, but the latter may leave lint or paper fibers, especially on the roller, which in turn contaminates the ink film and mars the inked impressions on the fingerprint card. Blank or clear spots in an inked impression may be caused by lint or dust in the film of ink on the inking plate. When the plate and roller are not in use, they should be covered to keep the ink from drying and to prevent dust from settling on them. Dust is always in the air, and an uncovered film of ink is a natural trap.

Fuming cabinets should always be cleaned immediately after use, as the fuming reagents are highly corrosive to metal parts. During scheduled preventive maintenance checks, all kits should be checked for adequate supply of materials and kits containing iodine fuming equipment for corrosion. All flashlight and camera batteries should be checked for power and leakage.

Cleanliness and preventive maintenance are as much a part of good fingerprint work as classification or knowledge of latent fingerprint techniques. Good work performance frequently depends on properly functioning equipment, and the condition of the equipment people use usually reflects their attitudes toward their profession.

65
LIST OF MANUFACTURERS OF FINGERPRINT EQUIPMENT

The following concerns are manufacturers of fingerprint equipment. Their literature and catalogs are informative, and they keep abreast of developments in the field of fingerprints. Their equipment and supplies are based upon extensive research and field experience.

George F. Cake Corp.
1200 Fifth Street
Berkeley, CA 94710

Criminalistics, Inc.
P.O. Box 363
Opa-Locka, FL 33054

Criminal Research Products, Inc.
Conshohocken, PA 19428

Faurot, Inc.
299 Broadway
New York, NY 10007

Fingerprint Equipment Laboratory, Inc.
5526 North Elston Avenue
Chicago, IL 60630

Lightning Powder Company
P.O. Box 5157
San Mateo, CA 94402

MacDonell Associates, Inc.
P.O. Box 1111
Corning, NY 14830

F. Morton Pitt Company
1444 South San Gabriel Boulevard
San Gabriel, CA 91776

Sirchie Finger Print Laboratories, Inc.
Moorestown, NJ 08057

U.S. Fingerprint Products
R.R. 20
Kansas City, MO 64165

Manufacturers producing a limited or specialized line of fingerprint equipment or supplies are not included in the above list. Many manufacturers within this latter group are listed in the sections of this book pertaining to their particular products.

QUESTIONS

TRUE-FALSE QUESTIONS

1. All commercial fingerprint kits are well designed, compact, durable, and of excellent quality (Sec. 47). ~~TRUE~~ FALSE

2. The purpose of crime scene kits is to collect evidence for later evaluation (Sec. 47). TRUE

3. It is necessary to carry and use a different brush for every color powder in a fingerprint kit (Sec. 52). FALSE

4. Phosphors are sometimes used as fingerprint powders (Sec. 50). TRUE

5. Long experience has shown that it is necessary to carry a wide variety, perhaps as many as fifteen fingerprint powders (Sec. 50). FALSE

6. Commercially prepared fingerprint powders are of consistently excellent quality (Sec. 50). TRUE

7. The line on a Henry disc used in classifying fingerprints is ruled on the top side of the disc and the line is used for ridge counting (Sec. 50). TRUE

8. Extreme magnification is required for the proper examination of fingerprints (Sec. 51). FALSE

9. It is possible to lift latent developed with any color powder with clear lifting tape or tabs with clear covers (Sec. 52). TRUE

10. The fingerprint camera is a copy camera adopted for use in fingerprint photography (Sec. 53). TRUE

11. Fingerprint cameras may be described as self-contained units (Sec. 53). TRUE

12. Fingerprint cameras do not have a very long period of serviceability (Sec. 53). FALSE

13. To accommodate the greater variety of film speeds offered by modern photographic films, fingerprint cameras today have adjustable apertures and variable shutters (Sec. 53). TRUE

14. The average table or office desk is of sufficient height for taking inked fingerprint impressions (Sec. 54). FALSE

15. A lightbox is used in a laboratory only for evaluating and masking out photographic negatives (Sec. 55). FALSE

16. Angstrom (Å) and nanometers (nm) are interchangeable terms; they have the same meaning (Sec. 56). FALSE

17. Visible light is but a small part of the complete radiation spectrum (Sec. 56). TRUE

18. Luminescence is not distinguished from incandescence (Sec. 56). FALSE

19. Fluorescence and phosphorescence are identical physically (Sec. 56). FALSE

20. A strong light source reveals fingerprints which may not be visible under ordinary room lighting or daylight (Sec. 57). TRUE

21. Few, if any, latent fingerprint fuming techniques may be considered a health hazard (Sec. 59). FALSE

22. The lamp in a fuming cabinet is for the purpose of viewing the items being processed (Sec. 59). FALSE

23. The lamp in a fuming cabinet is an ordinary 100-watt electric globe (Sec. 59). FALSE

24. Several modifications must be made to a fuming cabinet if hydrogen fluoride is to be used (Sec. 59). TRUE

25. Iodine fumes may be extremely harmful to the lungs and membranes of the throat (Sec. 60). TRUE

26. Benzidine has been identified as a carcinogenic substance (Sec. 62). TRUE

27. A glovebox is one of the safeguards prescribed as a protective measure when using the hydrogen fluoride technique (Sec. 62). FALSE

28. Humidity cabinets are used to provide a postprocessing environment for ninhydrin-treated latent prints (Sec. 63). TRUE

29. An ordinary steam iron may be used to develop ninhydrin treated latent fingerprints (Sec. 63). TRUE

30. If equipment is kept clean at all times, it is not necessary to schedule periodic preventive maintenance (Sec. 64). FALSE

COMPLETION QUESTIONS

164 X 31. Name ten articles of equipment suitable for a well-equipped fingerprint kit (Sec. 48).

32. There are four classes of fingerprint brushes, HAIR....., FEATHER..., FIBERGLASS, and MAGNETIC POWDER... (Sec. 49).
APPLICATOR

33. A fingerprint MAGNIFYING GLASS is indispensable for classifying and comparing prints if accuracy is to be achieved and unnecessary eye strain avoided (Sec. 51).

34. Extreme magnification is neither REQUIRED nor DESIRABLE for the examination of fingerprints (Sec. 51).

35. The two basic requirements for any fingerprint technique, equipment or material are RESULTS and PRACTICALITY (Sec. 52).

36. The fingerprint camera is a specially designed COPYING camera developed specifically for LAW ENFORCEMENT work (Sec. 53).

37. All fingerprint cameras are fixed-focus cameras requiring a minimum of PHOTOGRAPHIC TRAINING and EXPERIENCE to operate (Sec. 53).

38. An x-ray viewer commonly used by medical personnel makes an excellent LIGHT BOX for fingerprint work (Sec. 55).

39. Within the ultraviolet band of the spectrum, the two major subdivisions are SHORT WAVE and LONG WAVE ultraviolet light (Sec. 56).

40. Fluorescence exists only so long as the exciting agent is PRESENT and ACTIVE (Sec. 56).

41. Phosphorescent afterglow may last for hours depending upon the SUBSTANCE (Sec. 56).

42. One of the most effective devices for discovering, developing and photographing latent fingerprint evidence is a .... STRONG LIGHT (Sec. 57).

43. A convenient mortar size for grinding small quantities of powder for limited use is one THREE inches in diameter or larger (Sec. 58).

44. Fuming cabinets are specifically designed to achieve OPTIMUM results when using fuming techniques to recover latent prints (Sec. 59).

45. The substance placed in iodine fuming pipes to absorb breath moisture is CALCIUM CHLORIDE (Sec. 60).

46. Of all the latent fingerprint techniques used by fingerprint

technicians, the most hazardous to health are those involving
BENZIDINE (Sec. 62).

47. Optimum development of ninhydrin-treated latent prints is
obtained when the items processed are subjected to a postprocessing environment of . 65 . . . . to . . 80 . . . . percent relative humidity (Sec. 63).

48. . DIRT . . . and MOISTURE. have an adverse effect on the serviceability of equipment (Sec. 64).

49. Blank or clear spots in an inked impression may be caused
by . LINT . . . or DUST . . . . in the film of ink on the inking
plate (Sec. 64).

50. At least . TWO . . . contrasting powders should be included in
a fingerprint kit (Sec. 48).

REFERENCES

37 Fed. Reg. 22139 (1974).

Berry, A. N.: "Fingerprint lift reproduction equipment," *Police Journal.* vol.
45 (1972), p. 61.

"California designs compact print outfit," *Fingerprint and Identification
Magazine.* vol. 39 (Feb., 1958), p. 16.

Chamberlin, J. H.: "New style print comparator now available," *Fingerprint
and Identification Magazine.* vol. 40 (Nov., 1958), p. 15.

"Establishment of local fingerprint identification bureaus," *FBI Law Enforcement Bulletin.* vol. 27 (Dec., 1958), p. 17.

"Finger print identification devices," *Scientific American.* vol. 147 (Sept.,
1932), p. 177.

Hanggi, C. A., and H. M. Alfultis: "Improved technique in the development
and lifting of latent fingerprints," *Identification News.* vol. 19 (June,
1969), p. 5.

Lesk, J. J.: "Development of latent fingerprints by the ninhydrin method,"
Fingerprint and Identification Magazine. vol. 54 (July, 1972), p. 13.

Londesborough, J. E.: "The beam focus finger print camera," *Journal of the
Forensic Science Society.* vol. 4 (1965), p. 181.

"Miniature ink rollers aid printing of crippled hands," *Fingerprint and
Identification Magazine.* vol. 45 (Feb., 1964), p. 15.

Neilson, M.: "A camera designed for fingerprint photography," *The Australian Police Journal.* vol. 21 (1967), p. 93.

"New pad revolutionizes recording of prints," *Fingerprint and Identification
Magazine.* vol. 45 (Aug., 1963), p. 11.

"New spoon for printing crippled fingers," *Fingerprint and Identification
Magazine.* vol. 45 (May, 1964), p. 7.

"New table eases fingerprinting," *Military Police Journal.* vol. 12 (June, 1962), p. 11.

Nitz, E.: "Neues Daktyloskopisches Vergleichsgerat," *Kriminalistik.* vol. 20 (1966), p. 254.

Ostler, R. D.: "A fingerprint camera," *The Police Journal.* vol. 35 (1962), p. 122.

Sowter, G. H.: "A twin comparison fingerprint viewer," *The Police Journal.* vol. 39 (1966), p. 241.

Wild, A.: "Identification equipment used in Switzerland," *International Criminal Police Review.* vol. 22 (Mar., 1967), p. 72.

Chapter V

Latent Fingerprint Powder Techniques

66

WHY POWDER LATENT FINGERPRINTS?

THERE ARE THREE sound reasons for powdering latent fingerprints: (1) to make the images visible; (2) to develop contrast for photographic purposes; and (3) to develop powdered
images for lifting and preserving.

If latent fingerprints are visible, it may be unnecessary and
sometimes unwise to attempt powder development: Such attempts may result in destruction of the latent evidence. The visibility of latent prints is often a result of light refraction, particularly on metal surfaces, and such latents can be easily lost by
processing with powder. If possible, latent prints should always
be photographed before processing with any latent fingerprint
technique.

When an investigator starts out to develop a latent print, there
must be a definite objective in mind. Procedure depends upon
the objective, upon the nature of the surface upon which the
latent is found, and how it can best be handled. If latents are
powdered primarily for color contrast for photographic reasons,
a powder which contrasts strongly with the surface is used. If
the primary objective is to transform the latent into a powdered
reproduction for purposes of lifting, powder color is of secondary importance, as the lift may be placed on any desired
color of background material. When lifting is the primary objective, the powder may be selected for its tenacity or applicability according to the nature of the surface on which the latent is
located, without regard to contrast.

It appears to be unorthodox procedure to develop a latent
with powder the same color as the surface upon which the latent
is found, but if the investigator wishes to obtain the best results, and after making tests, knows that a particular powder
gives better results, it is sensible to proceed in such a manner.
This technique may be successful in many situations where the
primary objective is to lift the latent impression. Each investi-

209

gator must decide how the evidence can be handled to the best advantage, based on his own experience and training and, after determining the primary objective for developing the latents, proceed accordingly.

67

LOOK FOR LATENT PRINTS BEFORE POWDERING

There are two ways to discover latent fingerprint evidence: by *blind development* and by a *visual search*. It is possible in many cases to locate latent fingerprints on objects or surfaces at a crime scene or in the laboratory before any form of development is attempted. This is not always true, but it is true so often that it should be standard procedure to make a thorough visual examination for latent fingerprint evidence in every instance before development of any kind is attempted. If latent prints can be found by a visual search, the whole procedure is simplified. There is something about "seeing" latent fingerprint evidence before attempting development which inspires a feeling of confidence. The technician feels that the evidence is not going to be lost; if anything, it will be improved.

Blind development is like pinning the tail on a paper donkey —One knows generally where the donkey is, but much guesswork enters into attaching the tail correctly. If latent evidence can be seen first, even though faintly, a lot of exploratory work is spared, and evidence secured under such circumstances is more apt to be of superior quality. If evidence can be seen, it can be photographed to advantage and usually improved—it should never be lost if it is seen first.

There are situations where a visual search would be fruitless, and blind development is the only alternative; for example, on some painted surfaces. Very often when a technician is processing a surface where some latents are visible, other unseen latents pop up unexpectedly.

Looking before powdering applies not only to powder techniques but to all forms of development as well, and in all situations. There should be no exceptions to the visual search rule.

68

WHEN IN DOUBT, MAKE TEST PRINTS

Frequently, an investigator is uncertain of the use of a certain powder, whether it is the right medium for developing a latent image on a questionable surface. Images may be visible, and they may be the only positive evidence that can be used to identify the perpetrator of a crime: They are too valuable for experimentation. The investigator cannot take any chances on obscuring the evidence. An investigator must know that when a latent is developed with powder, the evidence is going to wind up in a condition equally as good or better than when it was found.

There is a way to predetermine the result of the attempt, and that is by making test prints on the same or similar surface at a point where they do not interfere with the latent evidence. If the test prints prove satisfactory, the same results may be expected of the latent evidence. Testing gives technicians confidence in their techniques, and it supports their judgment, especially when the element of uncertainty may result in destruction of otherwise valuable evidence. If test printing fails, the procedure certainly cannot be relied upon to succeed with the latent image, and a different approach may be attempted until a procedure is chosen which meets with success or it is decided the situation is impossible. Test printing very often saves evidence, whereas depending on luck or blind development may result in loss.

A point to keep in mind when making a test print is to destroy the test image immediately after it has served its purpose. When test prints are made, particular care should be taken to make them where they do not interfere with latent evidence associated with the crime. A surface similar to the suspected surface can be found at the crime scene for making tests, or a small area of the suspected surface may be explored "blindly," wiped clean, and used for testing.

69

FINGERPRINT POWDERS

The first edition of this book included one chapter devoted completely to fingerprint powders, their formulas, and preparation. Much of this material has been deleted from this edition; today higher-quality and more economical powders than those generally prepared by individual technicians may be readily purchased from major manufacturers of fingerprint supplies.

Figure 55, a photomicrograph of a commercial fingerprint powder, illustrates the advantages of quality control in commercial powders. Viewed at a magnification of ×400 with transmitted light, the individual particles of powder appear as the small disc-shaped objects with white centers. Each individual powder particle is about the same size, and all are only several thousandths of a millimeter in diameter. Consistent quality, as indicated by the uniform size of the particles, is difficult for individuals preparing their own powders to achieve.

Almost any powdered substance, even cigarette ashes, may be used by experienced fingerprint technicians to develop latent fingerprints with a reasonable degree of success. However, the ability to successfully use a particular substance in one instance does not in itself indicate whether or not that substance is a good fingerprint powder. No single powder has universal application, but a good fingerprint powder must provide satisfactory results under all conditions of a similar nature. When a fingerprint technician selects a specific powder for use on a particular surface, there must be a reasonable degree of predictability of the results that may be obtained with that powder.

Powders have been used to develop latent fingerprints on nonporous surfaces since the beginning of this century, and over the years, almost every possible substance has been tried as a fingerprint powder. Some substances, such as talc, chalk, and charcoal, were used by early technicians and produced reasonably good images of latent prints. Such powders, however, lacked holding power, producing images so fragile as to be almost useless.

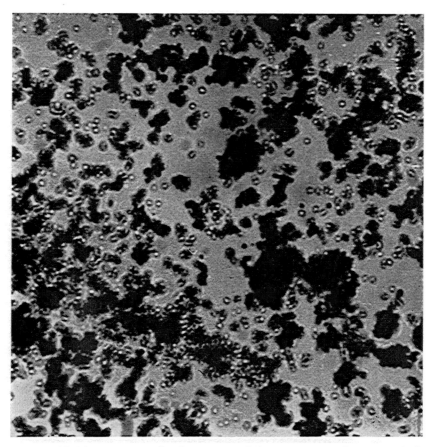

Figure 55. Photomicrograph of commercial fingerprint powder. Magnified 400 times. The individual particles of powder are disc shaped, and the black areas are heavy deposits of the powder.

The moisture and oil content of latent fingerprint residue is an important factor in the adhesion of fingerprint powders to a latent print, but it would be an inaccurate description of the mechanism of adhesion to merely state that the moisture in the latent print absorbs the powder. If absorption alone accounted for the adhesion of powder to a latent impression, then charcoal would prove to be a better fingerprint powder than aluminum powder, which is not the case. One study of the physical aspects of fingerprints indicates that the shape of the individual particles of powder is fundamental to adhesion; the force of adhesion is proportional to the area of contact between the powder particle and the latent print residue (Thomas, 1975).

Many substances used for a considerable time to develop latent prints and which make good fingerprint powders should not be used except under controlled conditions within a laboratory because of their toxic nature. Lead oxides, antimony, and mercury compounds are examples of such powders.

There are six general classes or groups of fingerprint powders as determined by either their method of application or method of response: (1) standard fingerprint powders comprising a long list of chemical elements, substances, and compounds, all of which have long been used as developing agents; (2) fluorescent and phosphorescent powders which respond to ultraviolet light; (3) specially prepared metallic powders, which are applied by a magnetic applicator; (4) thermoplastic powders originally designed for use in copying machines, but which are also used in the fused-print technique; (5) fine lead dust, 200 to 400 mesh, used for x-ray fingerprint techniques; and (6) specific metallic elements used in metal-evaporation techniques.

The cost of commercial fingerprint powders, especially those used with specialized techniques, may at first glance appear high, several dollars for a few ounces, but considering the quality, they are well worth the price. One 2 ounce jar of powder can

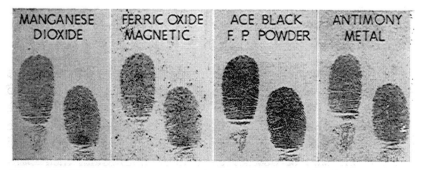

Figure 56. The above images were developed on paper by the powders indicated over each set of impressions. Note that the best image was obtained with a commercial powder.

last for a considerable time if the powder is properly used. Considering the value that latent fingerprint evidence may have in an investigation, it is only logical to use the best equipment and supplies available (Fig. 56).

70

USING FINGERPRINT BRUSHES .

Only brushes with very soft hair should be selected for fingerprint work. The hair should be as soft as the hair of a camera lens brush—the softer the better. The brush should be free from powder from previous jobs or powders of a different color than that intended for the job at hand. The hairs should be dry, soft, and loose, not clustered, damp, or stiff. Each new job should be started with fresh, clean powder. The brush may be cleaned by holding the handle between the palms of the hands and spinning it by a rolling motion; the hairs separate and foreign substances are expelled.

If the powder in a jar has a tendency to pack into a solid mass, it may be loosened by tapping a bottom corner of the jar lightly on a table top and turning it at the same time or until the powder is loose and fluffy, so that when the brush is dipped into the bottle, the powder is picked up by the hair of the brush. Bottles used for fingerprint powders should have a mouth large enough to accommodate the type of brush carried in the kit, that is except feather brushes, or saltshaker caps may be used on the bottles. The latter method is useful only if the surface being examined is a top surface; otherwise, the powder will have to be applied with a brush.

A common mistake made by beginners is the excessive use of powder. More latent prints are lost because of excessive powder and insufficient brushing than any other causes. When a quantity of powder is picked up with the brush, the excess powder should be removed by tapping the brush with a finger while holding it over the powder container. If a large top surface is being examined, the excess powder may be dropped over the suspected area. The powder should be applied evenly and smoothly to the surface with very light, short, and quick strokes of the brush, using only the tips of the bristles.

The powder is spread over the surface with the brush until recognized ridges begin to appear. The ridges may not be conspicuous; they have to be developed and strengthened with great care. Development should be concentrated and carefully controlled as soon as any ridges appear until peak development is reached. Once the contour or pattern flow of the ridges is visible, the brush strokes should conform to the direction of flow. This enables the pattern to be brushed without destroying the ridge impressions. After the latent print has become visible, all excess powder adhering between the ridges is gently brushed away. This step is extremely important, because the excess powder may destroy the clarity of the ridge detail and render the latent print useless for identification.

In some cases, it is not possible to remove the excess powder with a brush. This is particularly true of oily latent prints developed on glass or metal surfaces. When this situation occurs, it is sometimes possible to remove the excess powder with lifting tape. In many instances, the latent print is not removed entirely by the lifting tape, and the print remaining on the object is sufficiently clean and distinct to permit identification. If the latent is not clear after using the lifting tape, it is sometimes possible to redevelop the latent with brush and powder.

As experience is gained in brush and powder techniques, it is soon noted that some prints do not develop as readily as others. This is particularly true of older impressions. This situation may sometimes be overcome by gently blowing on the surface while dusting for latents; the breath adds moisture to the latent print residue (Fig. 57). However, if the surface is cold, too much moisture condensates on the surface and the powder "paints" the surface as it adheres to this excess moisture. If breath is used on a cold surface, the excess moisture is visible under a strong light, and brushing should begin only after the excess moisture has disappeared.

Very old latents cannot be developed by normal brushing strokes such as those used in developing relative fresh prints;

Figure 57. Gently blowing on a surface while dusting for latent prints some-times adds moisture to the latent print residue, thereby enabling the pow-der to adhere to the ridge structure of the latent. This procedure is known as the breath technique.

they do not "hold" powder; their adhesive properties are di-minished. One method of developing an old latent with powder is to cover it with a fairly thick film of powder. When the image is evenly covered, the powder may be tamped or compressed with the side of the brush; the film of powder prevents the hairs of the brush from making direct contact with the image. The brush must be very soft and the compressing action very gentle. If this technique fails to recover the latent print, and if the surface ex-amined is not combustible, flame techniques may be used as a last resort.

Generally speaking, it may be stated that powder techniques should be the first choice when examining nonporous surfaces, such as glass and metal, for latent prints. However, it must be recognized that this generality cannot be applied in all situa-tions. If the latent impressions appear in a film of dust, oil, or grease, powder may destroy rather than enhance the images. Plas-tic impressions in soft substances adhering to nonporous surfaces, such as paint, respond better to photographic and lifting techniques. Latent impressions made by dried blood and other body fluids should be developed with chemical techniques. These are only a few of the many different types of situations that may be encountered. No individual or group should attempt to prescribe specific techniques as "official procedures" to be applied for particular types of surfaces, as it is not possible to enumerate every situation that may be encountered. The appropriate technique depends upon the situation immediately at hand and the experience and judgment of the technician performing the work.

Brushes may become contaminated with oils and grease from surfaces examined, and moisture may cause powder to cake between the hair bristles. Brushes may be easily cleaned by gently washing the brush in a solution of water and ordinary liquid dishwashing detergent. During washing, the bristles are gently rotated between the thumb and index finger, thereby spreading out the bristles to remove all foreign materials. After washing, the brush must be rinsed to remove all trace of the detergent and thoroughly dried before use. Even fiberglass brushes, which are designed to retain powder, should be periodically cleaned in the manner described to remove foreign substances that may have been picked up from a processed surface.

71

PHOTOGRAPHING LATENTS BEFORE POWDER DEVELOPMENT

If a latent print is plainly visible to the eye, even though it may be seen only with the assistance of a strong light, it is good procedure to photograph the image before it is powdered or a lift is attempted. It is important to photographically record the latent impression *before* each stage of an examination that may result in damage or loss of the latent. When developing latent impressions with powder, the two most critical stages are the application of the powder with a brush and lifting the impression.

Sometimes the only way to satisfactorily recover latent print evidence is to lift it, because the print may be in a position or location where photography is impossible. However, an investigator should not be too quick to conclude that it is impossible to photograph a particular latent because of either its position or location. With the application of a little ingenuity, many latents which at first appear to be impossible to photograph may be successfully photographed by varying or modifying photographic techniques. Some photographic situations present problems in respect to latent evidence, which requires much planning and maneuvering, and they are time consuming, particularly if the prints are in awkward or near-impossible positions.

It is very difficult under some circumstances to photograph latent prints and at the same time be sure the result is satisfactory. Such conditions exist even in the laboratory, and sometimes it is necessary to take more than one picture. Even the best photographer is fooled at times by lighting conditions and film response in different situations, especially when it comes to photographing fingerprint evidence. In difficult situations, the Polaroid adapter is extremely helpful, as a Polaroid photograph provides a means for immediate evaluation of the photograph.

Small, portable objects bearing fingerprint evidence, such as bottles and drinking glasses, etc., should be taken to the laboratory where working conditions are more satisfactory and facilities adequate. Many latents and much valuable evidence is recovered by lifting which would otherwise be passed up because of difficulties involved in photographing or transporting. Evidence that cannot be satisfactorily lifted may be secured by photography. Lifts are the answer to many fingerprint problems, and photography is the answer to many more. A good axiom to follow is, if in doubt, photograph first.

72

THE EFFECT OF BRUSHING POWDER ON PAPER

Normally, latent prints on paper and other porous items should be developed by fuming and chemical techniques rather than with powder. Powder, at best, develops only relatively fresh prints, because porous items have a tendency to absorb latent print residue. However, under certain circumstances, an investigator may determine that powder development of latents on paper is necessary. The best results in such cases is obtained with magnetic powders (Sec. 74).

The use of a brush in developing a latent fingerprint on paper usually results in damage to the image. Brushing disturbs the fibers of the paper to the extent that ridge detail may be destroyed in the developed image. One method that may be used as an alternative to brushing is to simply slide a quantity of powder across the suspected area without attempting to brush the powder. A maximum amount of powder adheres to a latent on paper without brushing. A disadvantage of this method is that often the excess powder cannot be removed, while the advantage of magnetic powders is that only the powder touches the surface, and excess powder may be removed by simply passing the application over the surface.

A good illustration of the effect of brushing powder on paper is an experiment which may be made by the reader. Place your own latent prints on three pieces of paper: one a fibrous paper, one semiglazed, and the other a glazed paper. Then process each piece of paper with brush and powder. The result on the fibrous paper is striking to the eye, and it is alarming when viewed under a magnifier. Powder adhering to the paper generally obscures the ridge structure of the latent prints. The effect is not as pronounced with the semiglazed and glazed papers, but it is still present. Try the same experiment using papers with latents twelve, twenty-four, and seventy-two hours old. Few prints develop with powder when the prints on paper are over twenty-four hours old and rarely when in excess of seventy-two hours.

Although processing papers with brush and powder usually prevents further processing with chemical techniques, it is possible in some cases. For example, a piece of paper may have been erroneously processed with magnetic powder by another investigator, and it is determined that the evidence should be further processed with ninhydrin. The paper may be treated with ninhydrin and, where the ninhydrin-developed prints appear, the powder may be removed by gently erasing with an art gum eraser. The erasing action must be very gentle to minimize disturbance of the paper fibers. This technique does not work if the paper is very fibrous and the powder is deeply embedded in the fibers.

73

POWDER TECHNIQUES FOR LARGE AREAS

In certain cases, the circumstances regarding latent print evidence may present a rather awesome situation to the beginner, not only because of the number of latent prints that may possibly be recovered but also due to the size of the area to be examined. Except for their size, large areas, such as sales counters, store windows, large doors, automobiles, and walls, etc., present no special problems and may be examined in the same manner as smaller objects. The procedure for examining all objects is essentially the same—visual search and blind development.

Upon arrival at the crime scene, the fingerprint technician should obtain as much information as possible about the incident from officers at the scene. Frequently, the movements of the suspects at the scene may be established through statements of witnesses or other evidence. This is a commonsense approach to narrow the limits of the search for latent prints, as there is no need to search areas the suspect did not enter. Another approach is to concentrate efforts on those areas where the suspect would have to touch objects in order to commit the crime, such as in the case of a car theft, the door, steering wheel, and rearview mirror, etc. In all cases, the points of entry, attack, and exit must be examined thoroughly.

Over the years, several techniques have been developed to facilitate the processing of large areas with powder. Two such techniques are the use of atomizers and aerosol spray cans. Few fingerprint technicians stick with either technique after experimenting with them. They are not effective devices for developing prints under conditions normally encountered in fingerprint investigations. The idea and principle of atomizers and aerosol sprays are theoretically sound, but in actual practice, they leave much to be desired. When powder is blown onto a latent by a blast of air, there is no physical contact that might destroy or mar ridge detail with the impression. The blast of air charged with powder is not in itself strong enough to develop the kind of an image necessary for photographing or lifting. For best results, the latent has to be enhanced by regular brushing techniques.

Atomizers and particularly aerosol spray powders have a tendency to paint a surface as the air forces the powder into surface depressions, pores, or scratches, which may not normally fill with powder if processed by regular brushing techniques. This effect is particularly pronounced with aerosol sprays and may be due to the nature of the propellants. One of the most disagreeable features of atomizers and aerosol spray powders is the excessive blowing of fingerprint powders in the air and the unnecessary scattering of objectionable powder. Powdering should always be controlled as much as possible. Control is difficult when using atomizers or sprays. Such techniques are not conducive to cleanliness and generally contaminate large portions of surrounding areas. Another disadvantage, when these techniques are used within enclosed areas without adequate ventilation, is that considerable amounts of the airborne powder particles may enter the respiratory system of the investigator.

A variation of the aerosol technique was developed by a team of Japanese technicians who call their technique the *wet method* (Nariyuki et al., 1972). This technique consists of spraying the surface to be examined with a liquid solution and then brushing in the regular manner after the solution has dried. The solution is prepared by mixing 10 g of a specially prepared powder in 100 ml of a solution of 15% methyl ether, 80% acetone, and 5% ethyl alcohol. The formula for the powder is 30% deoilnated aluminum powder, 50% mica powder (300-mesh), and 20% hignum powder (Nariyuki, 1973).

Perhaps the greatest disadvantage of all spraying techniques is their tendency to paint the entire surface with powder. The greater the force of air carrying the powder or solution, the greater the tendency of the powder to stick to the surface. Powders sprayed onto a surface also enter all scratches and depressions on that surface and cannot be brushed away.

One technique that may be successful in expeditiously searching extremely large areas for latent prints with powder is the use of cotton wads (Brooks, 1972). Large wads of cotton are used to pick up powder, and the powder is applied on the surface being examined with a patting motion much like the use of a powder puff. Wide-mouth containers may be used or the powder simply dumped onto a large paper, such as a newspaper, for charging the cotton wads. Once ridge structure is located, regular fingerprint brushes are used to develop latents to their maximum clarity and contrast.

The Federal Bureau of Investigation recommends application of powder with a brush in all instances, inasmuch as the amount of powder applied can be controlled with greater ease ("Development of Latent Impressions with Powders," 1950). Large camel's hair and feather brushes are very effective for powdering large areas, and a skilled technician using a fiberglass brush can satisfactorily examine a considerable area within a reasonable period of time. In fingerprint work, no shortcuts should ever be adopted unless the results are at least equally as good as the original technique. The standard brush-and-powder technique remains the best technique for developing latent fingerprints on nonporous surfaces uncontaminated by grease, oil, or dust.

74

MAGNETIC FINGERPRINT POWDER TECHNIQUES

Regular fingerprint powders cannot normally be used with any degree of success on certain types of surfaces, such as leather, which are either extremely porous or rough. Regular powders have a tendency to paint such surfaces, thereby obscuring the ridge details of any latent prints. Regular powders are also not particularly successful on certain other types of surfaces, plastic bags, for example, as brushing tends to remove any latent print residue. Magnetic powders were developed to eliminate the disadvantages commonly associated with ordinary powder brushing techniques (MacDonell, 1961). Magnetic powders are specially prepared powders containing ferromagnetic elements, which are not in themselves magnetized but may be applied by a magnetic applicator or wand.

The magnetic applicator is simply a magnetized steel rod encased within a nonmagnetic sheath. The rod is movable within the sheath: When the rod is fully inserted, powder may be picked up with the tip of the sheath, and when it is fully retracted, the powder is dropped from the sheath. The powder is applied to a surface by moving the applicator tip loaded with powder over the surface, being careful that only the powder and not the applicator touches the surface. After brushing, the powder on the applicator is returned to the container, and the applicator is passed over the surface again to remove all excess powder which does not adhere to the print residue. The powder may be used over and over again. When not in use, containers of magnetic powders should be tightly sealed to prevent moisture from caking the powder into a solid mass.

The advantage of magnetic powders is that only the powder touches the latent print, thereby eliminating the possible damage that may result from regular brushes. However, magnetic powders should be considered a special technique to be used for particular types of surfaces and not as a total replacement for regular brush and powder techniques. Occasionally, one extra pass of the powder over a latent print removes rather than enhances ridge details.

Generally, magnetic powders should not be used for examining objects made of ferrous metals, as the applicator magnetizes the metal and the powder clings to the surface of the object. However, small objects, such as beverage cans, may be processed with the powder and the object tapped sharply against a table to remove the powder. Paper should not normally be processed with any powder techniques, as chemical techniques are far superior. However, if the use of powder is necessary, magnetic powders yield better results than any other powder technique.

There are several types of surfaces for which magnetic powder is the only technique to provide successful results. Figure 58 is an example of such a surface—the grooved area of a phonograph record. Regular powders generally fill in the grooves, and brushing further compresses the powder in the grooves rather than removing it. As excess magnetic powders may be removed by passing the applicator over the surface, the surface may be cleaned up, and the latent stands out clearly. The same procedure applies to similar rough surfaces and porous items such as leather.

Figure 58. Latent fingerprints developed on a 45-rpm phonograph record using magnetic powder. Regular fingerprint powder would fill in the grooves of the record and obscure the latent print.

Magnetic powders also provide excellent results on extremely smooth surfaces, such as plastic bags and colored glazed paper, which cannot normally be processed with other techniques. When examining plastic bags, it is usually desirable to breathe onto the surface while applying the powder, as the moisture from the breath enhances the latent prints. Another technique particularly applicable when examining plastic bags is to slightly modify the powder formula so that any latents may be enhanced and greater contrast obtained. This may be accomplished by adding regular fingerprint powder of the same color to the magnetic powder; about one-third regular powder to two-thirds magnetic powder, by volume, provides a good mixture (Wilson, 1974).

One aspect of latent prints on plastic bags that an investigator should be aware of is the not uncommon occurrence of reversed color of ridge structure. Some plastics may have a very thin film of an oily substance covering the surfaces, and in such cases, the

Figure 59. Latent fingerprint on a plastic sandwich bag developed with magnetic powder. Plastic bags are a common type of evidence in drug cases.

ridges of the skin may remove the film. Upon processing, the powder adheres to the film on the plastic surface, and the ridge structure of the latent print is clear (Fig. 59). Instances have been noted where plastic bags processed with black magnetic powders have had dark ridge structures in some areas and been clear in others on the same latent fingerprint.

Large areas cannot be searched for latent fingerprints expeditiously with magnetic powders, but this and the other disadvantages should not detract from their usefulness. In some situations, they are the only techniques that may be successfully used. It is a wide precaution to include magnetic powders in a fingerprint kit, in addition to regular powders.

75
THERMOPLASTIC POWDERS

Thermoplastic powdering techniques involve the use of Xerox® toners (Jones, 1967) or dry inks (Micik, 1974). Latent fingerprints developed with such powders, upon exposure to heat, become fused to the surface upon which they are located and remain semipermanent. This technique is commonly referred to as the *fused-print technique.*

Xerox toners were developed by the Xerox Corporation for use in their electrostatic reproduction machines. The reproduction process uses a photographic image projected onto an electrically charged plate, which attracts the powder particles selectively and transfers them to the paper. The powder particles on the paper are then fused by heat to become the printed impression. The toners are extremely fine-particle powders which may be adapted to fingerprint work. One brand of toner commonly available is Nashua Toner®, manufactured by the Nashua Corporation, Office Product Division, Nashua, New Hampshire, and marketed for use in Xerox 813®, 914®, 720®, and 1000® copiers. Another brand is Type 361 Imaging Powder® manufactured by the Duplication Products Division, 3M Center, Saint Paul, Minnesota, for use in the 3M "VQC" II® copier.

Thermoplastic powders must be applied to a surface with an

atomizer. Brushing in the regular manner destroys any latent impressions, as the adhering qualities of the powders are poor, and brushing readily removes the powders. Excess powder on a surface may be blown off with an empty atomizer. On flat surfaces, the powders may be sprinkled on with a common saltshaker, or a fingerprint brush may be dipped into the powder and the powder spread over the surface by lightly tapping the brush. However, the brush should not at any time come into contact with the surface to be examined. An empty atomizer is then used to blow away all excess powder and to spread the powder over the surface.

One disadvantage of thermoplastic powders is that, since brushing destroys latent prints, the excess powder between fingerprint ridges not removed by blowing cannot be easily removed. Sometimes, this difficulty can be overcome after the print has been fused onto the surface. Using a small cotton swab saturated with ordinary lighter fluid and *gently* brushing the fused print in the direction of ridge flow, the excess powder between ridges may often be removed. The brushing must be limited to the areas of excess powder and it must be done gently, or some ridge detail will also be removed.

Heat sources for fusing thermoplastic prints may vary widely. The special 500-watt lamp used in Xerox machines, photoflood lamps, heat lamps, or even hand-held hair driers may be used. Once the latent print is fused onto the surface, it is semipermanent and is not easily destroyed by normal handling. However, rough handling or excessive rubbing on the print destroys ridge detail.

Regular brush and powder techniques produce better results than the use of thermoplastic powders. One argument that has been advanced in favor of thermoplastic over regular powders is that since the latent print is fused to the surface, the exact location and position of the latent print on an evidentiary item may be viewed by the court. The fact that the latent is fused to a surface is not necessarily in itself an advantage over regular powders, as there are methods of fixing latents developed with regular powders onto the surface on which they are recovered (Chap. IX), and it is not necessary to lift them.

76
LEAD SULFIDE TECHNIQUES

Lead sulfide techniques were used by many early fingerprint technicians to develop latent fingerprints on paper. These techniques have little practical value today, as fuming and chemical techniques yield superior results, compared to powder techniques. One important disadvantage is that the use of lead compounds may represent a serious health hazard to technicians employing such techniques over prolonged periods.

The procedure for lead sulfide techniques is to thoroughly brush both sides of the paper to be examined with either lead acetate or lead carbonate. The processed paper is then exposed to hydrogen sulfide or ammonium sulfide fumes, which reduces the lead compound to a metallic powder and shows the ridge structure as dark-brown lines. The fuming process, particularly when using hydrogen sulfide, should be restricted to laboratory chemical hoods for safety.

Papers with latent prints developed by lead sulfide techniques must be handled carefully and the latent prints photographed immediately, as the metallic powder adheres poorly to the developed ridge structure.

77
FLUORESCENT AND PHOSPHORESCENT FINGERPRINT POWDERS

The distinction between fluorescence and phosphorescence was briefly discussed in Section 56, and there is no need to elaborate further on the differences between these two forms of luminescence. Fluorescent and phosphorescent powders are rarely used in the development and photography of latent fingerprints. Cases are uncommon in which latent prints cannot be developed by ordinary powders or photographed without development.

The theory of the use of fluorescent and phosphorescent powders is that a latent print is developed with the powder, and the ridge structure is then caused to fluoresce under activation of an ultraviolet lamp. The resulting bright image is photographed as a light-colored image, while the background surface appears dark. The technique is theoretically useful for latents found on multicolored backgrounds which otherwise would present a photographic problem if the latent were developed with ordinary powders (Fig. 60).

There are many natural and synthetic substances that fluoresce or phosphoresce upon activation by ultraviolet light; however, many are unsuited for fingerprint work as their relative fluorescent brightness is not high enough or their fluorescent color is not photogenic, or both. Synthetics are believed to be superior to natural fluorescent and phosphorescent substances in that synthetics have an advantage in color variety, brilliancy, and consistency of behavior over natural pigments.

Technicians may, if they so desire, prepare their own fluorescent and phosphorescent powders but, as previously discussed in the case of ordinary powders in Section 69, this practice is not

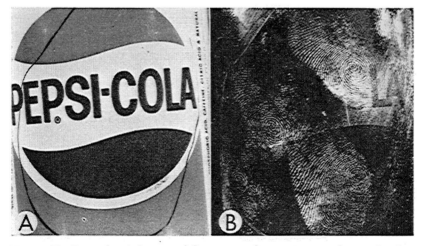

Figure 60. Example of the use of fluorescent fingerprint powder to develop latent prints on a multicolored surface. If either a dark or light regular fingerprint powder had been used, part of each latent print would have been obscured by a background of the same general color.

desirable from the viewpoint of either quality or economy. All major manufacturers of fingerprint supplies offer fluorescent powders in addition to their selection of regular fingerprint powders.

78

DYESTUFFS AS FINGERPRINT POWDERS

Dyes and pigments possess the property of selective light absorption and, therefore, appear colored. Pigments are commonly found in fingerprint powders as lampblack and lead and ferric oxides, etc. Both pigments and dyes contain chromophore groups in their molecules, which are responsible for the color, but dyes also contain auxochrome groups which enable the dye to become attached to fibers. Dyes are substances that attach to fibers and resist removal from fibers by water, soap, and other detergents, while pigments may or may not possess these properties. A dye (Dyestuff) is a chemical substance used in solution for dyeing textiles, as chemical indicators or biological stains.

The theory of the use of dyestuffs in a dry powder form as a fingerprint powder is that the powder adheres to the latent print residue and the solution for the dye, to produce the color, is affected by exposure of the latent print to acid fumes, steam, or both. Dyestuffs were recommended by several early fingerprint authorities, particularly for developing latent prints on paper. However, dyestuffs do not make adequate fingerprint powders and, as previously mentioned, powders are not the best technique for developing latent fingerprints on paper.

Perhaps the earliest reference to the use of dyestuffs as fingerprint powders was made by Stockis (1906) who recommended the use of lycopodium powder with 10% Sudan III, an azo dye. Lycopodium powder is obtained from the spores of a genus of club mosses. Mitchell (1920) recommended the use of a thiazine dye, methylene blue, and Thomas (1937) suggested the use of several dyes manufactured by Imperial Chemical Industries, Ltd., as powders and then fixing the impressions by exposure to acetic acid fumes and to steam.

Over the years many dyes have been tried as fingerprint powders, methyl orange, Sudan IV, Sudan black, Congo red, methyl yellow, and fluorescein, to name a few. Dyestuffs are not accepted as fingerprint powders today, because experience has shown that superior results can be obtained with regular powders.

79
PREPARING FINGERPRINT POWDERS

Commercial fingerprint powders available from all major manufacturers of fingerprint supplies are more economical and of consistently higher quality than those generally prepared by individual technicians. Although commercial powders are recommended for use by all agencies, individuals may, for one reason or another, wish to prepare their own powders for specific cases. It is a simple matter to prepare fingerprint powders; it is a three-step process: (1) combining ingredients according to a formula; (2) grinding the mixture in a mortar; and (3) sifting the ground powder through a sieve to remove grit, foreign particles, and to obtain a soft, even, and workable texture.

MORTAR AND PESTLE

A small-sized glass mortar with a 3- or 4-inch inside diameter is adequate for grinding small amounts, 1 ounce or 2 ounces of powder.

SCREEN SCALE SIEVE

A 5-inch sieve with a 100-mesh brass screen is satisfactory for sifting fingerprint powders. The individual openings of a 100-mesh screen are about 0.149 mm (0.0059 inch) in diameter. This is sufficiently fine for a fingerprint powder but not as fine as most commercially prepared fingerprint powders. Gentle tapping of the sieve causes the powder to sift through the screen, leaving the oversized grains or lumps in the sieve. Particles which do not pass through the sieve may be returned to the mortar for more grinding.

SUBSTANCES USEFUL FOR FINGERPRINT POWDER FORMULAS

The following listed substances may be used in fingerprint powders to obtain the colors indicated. However, it must be recognized that many of the substances listed are potential health hazards. Substances in the following list that are preceeded by an asterisk represent potential health hazards, and caution should be exercised whenever preparing or using powders containing these substances.

Black	*White or Light*	*Gray or Metallic*
Charcoal, animal	Chalk, precipitated	Aluminum fine
Charcoal, wood	Feldspar	lining
° Cobalt oxide	Fuller's earth	° Antimony metal,
° Cupric oxide	Gum arabic	powdered
Ferric oxide,	Kaolin	° Antimony trisulfide,
black magnetic	° Lead carbonate, basic	black powder
° Lampblack	° Phosphors	° Chemist's gray
° Manganese dioxide	Rosin	Graphite, powdered
	Talc	° Lead sulfide
	° Tin, powdered	Zinc powder
	° Titanium dioxide	
Red	*Orange or Yellow*	*Fine Linings*
° Antimony trisulfide	° Lead iodide	Aluminum
° Cuprous oxide	° Lead oxide, yellow	Bronze
Ferric oxide, red	° Mercuric oxide,	° Copper
° Lead oxide, red	yellow	Gold
° Mercuric sulfide, red		

80
FINGERPRINT POWDER FORMULAS

The formulas used in this section call for so many parts of each ingredient rather than for specific weights in grams or ounces. The formulas are given in parts so that they may be easily prepared by anyone without regard to expensive equipment. However, when using the formulas a technician must be consistent; for example, if ounces is used to measure the quantity of one ingredient, the quantities of all other ingredients to be used in that formula must also be measured in ounces.

BLACK FINGERPRINT POWDER FORMULAS
Ferric Oxide Base
10 parts black magnetic ferric oxide
5 parts rosin
5 parts lampblack

Lampblack Base

10 parts lampblack
4 parts rosin
3 parts Fuller's earth

Manganese Dioxide Base

10 parts manganese dioxide
5 parts ferric oxide, black magnetic
5 parts lampblack
3 parts rosin

GOLD FINGERPRINT POWDER FORMULAS
Pale Gold Lining Base

10 parts pale gold lining
5 parts rosin

Pale Gold Lining

Use as is, apply only after making tests.

GRAY FINGERPRINT POWDER FORMULAS
Aluminum Fine Lining

Use as is, apply only after making tests.

Gray Powder

4 parts Chemist's gray
1 part aluminum fine lining

Lead Carbonate Base

7 parts basic lead carbonate
1 part gum arabic
   trace of aluminum fine lining
   lampblack to develop desired gray color

Titanium Dioxide Base

Titanium dioxide and ferric oxide to obtain desired gray.

ORANGE FINGERPRINT POWDER FORMULAS
Red Lead Oxide Base

5 parts red lead oxide
5 parts rosin

5 parts Fuller's earth
15 parts acacia powder

Red Lead Oxide Base

5 parts red lead oxide
10 parts rosin

RED-BROWN FINGERPRINT POWDER FORMULAS
Cuprous Oxide Base

10 parts red cuprous oxide
5 parts basic lead carbonate

Ferric Oxide Base

5 parts red ferric oxide
5 parts rosin

Mercuric Sulfide Base

5 parts red mercuric sulfide
10 parts rosin

WHITE FINGERPRINT POWDER FORMULAS
Titanium Dioxide Base

10 parts titanium dioxide
5 parts basic lead carbonate
5 parts rosin

Lead Carbonate Base

5 parts basic lead carbonate
3 parts titanium dioxide
2 parts gum arabic

Mixed White

5 parts titanium dioxide
5 parts basic lead carbonate
5 parts gum arabic

QUESTIONS
TRUE-FALSE QUESTIONS

1. At times it may be unwise to attempt powder development of latent prints that are visible (Sec. 66).
2. A powder of the same color as the surface upon which a la-

tent print is found should never be used to develop the latent (Sec. 66).

3. It should be routine procedure to make a visual examination for latent fingerprints before any kind of development is attempted (Sec. 67).

4. Very often when a technician is processing a surface where some latents are visible, other unseen latents pop up unexpectedly (Sec. 67).

5. Visual searching before powdering applied not only to powder techniques but to all forms of development as well (Sec. 67).

6. Test printing is, in some cases, a better procedure than blind development (Sec. 68).

7. It is never good procedure for a fingerprint technician to intentionally make his own prints on evidence at a crime scene or in the laboratory (Sec. 68).

8. Fingerprint powders prepared by individual technicians always are of greater quality than commercial powders (Sec. 69).

9. Even cigarette ashes may be used by an experienced fingerprint technician to develop latent fingerprints (Sec. 69).

10. No single powder has universal application (Sec. 69).

11. The moisture content of latent fingerprint residue is not an important factor in the adhesion of fingerprint powders to the latent print (Sec. 69).

12. Commercial fingerprint powders are more economical than those prepared by individuals (Sec. 69).

13. Only brushes with very soft hair should be selected for fingerprint work (Sec. 70).

14. A common mistake by beginners is the insufficient use of powder (Sec. 70).

15. In all cases, it is possible to remove excess fingerprint powder with a brush (Sec. 70).

16. Powder is always used to develop latent fingerprints on nonporous surfaces, such as glass and metal (Sec. 70).

17. Brushes contaminated with oils and grease must be discarded (Sec. 70).

18. It is important to photographically record latent impressions before each stage in an examination that may result in change or loss of the latent (Sec. 71).

19. Sometimes the only way to satisfactorily recover latent print evidence is to lift it (Sec. 71).

20. Powdering should be the first technique to use for developing latent prints on paper and other porous surfaces (Sec. 72).

21. Atomizers and aerosols are more effective than brushes for applying fingerprint powders on a surface (Sec. 73).

22. Regular fingerprint powders are not very effective on rough surfaces, such as leather (Sec. 74).

23. Magnetic powders have an advantage in that the powder may be reused many times (Sec. 74).

24. There are several types of surfaces for which magnetic powder is the only technique to provide successful results (Sec. 74).

25. Thermoplastic powders are applied to a surface by means of an atomizer and then a regular fingerprint brush is used to remove the excess powder (Sec. 75).

26. Fluorescent fingerprint powders are commonly used in the development and photography of latent fingerprints (Sec. 77).

27. Dyestuffs make excellent fingerprint powders (Sec. 78).

28. A 5-inch sieve with a 200-mesh brass screen is satisfactory for sifting fingerprint powders (Sec. 79).

29. Lead and mercury substances in fingerprint powders represent potential health hazards (Sec. 79).

30. A gray fingerprint powder may be prepared by mixing 4 ounces of Chemist's gray with 1 g of aluminum fine lining (Sec. 80).

COMPLETION QUESTIONS

31. Name three sound reasons for powdering latent fingerprints (Sec. 66).

32. Latent fingerprints are powdered primarily for color contrast when . . . . is the objective (Sec. 66).

33 There are two ways to discover latent fingerprint evidence, by .... and .... (Sec. 67).

34. There should be no exception to the .... search rule (Sec. 67).

35. When in doubt as to the success of an attempt to develop latent prints, make .... (Sec. 68).

36. Some substances used by early fingerprint technicians as fingerprint powders lack ...., and the developed images are so fragile that they are almost useless (Sec. 69).

37. Describe the six general classes or groups of fingerprint powders as determined by either their method of application or method of response (Sec. 69).

38. Once the contour or pattern flow of the ridges is visible, the brush strokes should conform to the .... (Sec. 70).

39. It is sometimes possible to remove excess powder from a latent print with .... (Sec. 70).

40. Generally speaking, it may be stated that powder techniques should be the first choice when examining .... surfaces (Sec. 70).

41. If latent impressions appear in a film of dust, oil, or grease, powder may .... the latents (Sec. 70).

42. If a latent print is plainly visible to the eye, it is good procedure to photograph the image before it is .... or a .... is attempted (Sec. 71).

43. Latent fingerprints that cannot be satisfactorily lifted may be secured by .... (Sec. 71).

44. The best powdering technique to use on porous surfaces, such as paper, is .... powders (Sec. 72).

45. One technique which may be successfully used to expeditiously search extremely large areas for latent prints with powder is the use of .... (Sec. 73).

46. Name three types of surfaces where magnetic powders will produce better results than regular powders (Sec. 74).

47. Thermoplastic powdering techniques are commonly referred to as the ....-........ technique (Sec. 75).

48. Dyes and pigments possess the property of selective ....
.... and, therefore, appear colored (Sec. 78).
49. A .... and .... is used to grind substances when
preparing fingerprint powders (Sec. 79).
50. Preparing fingerprint powders is a ....-step process
(Sec. 79).

REFERENCES

Balshy, J. C.: "Fragile, glass latent prints, handle with care," *Fingerprint
and Identification Magazine.* vol. 55 (Apr., 1974), p. 3.

Beuys, W.: "Die 'Magnet-Burste," *Die Polizei.* vol. 54, no. 2 (1963), p. 1.

Bonora, M. J.: "The Bonora method of spraying for prints," *Law and Order.*
vol. 8 (Dec., 1960).

Brose, H. L., and C. G. Winson: "Phosphorescence and finger-prints," *Nature.* vol. 132 (1933), p. 208.

"Development of latent impressions with powders," *FBI Law Enforcement
Bulletin.* vol. 19 (Apr., 1950), p. 5.

Fagerstrom, D.: "The bristleless brush," *Law and Order.* vol. 9 (Oct.,
1961), p. 11.

"Invisible light makes fingerprints visible," *Scientific American.* vol. 156
(May, 1937), p. 346.

Janakiram, C. J.: "Intensifying latent finger impressions on single-colored
surfaces," *Fingerprint and Identification Magazine.* vol. 50 (Nov.,
1968), p. 11.

Jeffreys, R. A.: "Thermo-plastic prints enhance quality of in-court presentation," *Fingerprint and Identification Magazine.* vol. 54 (Feb., 1973),
p. 3.

Jones, R. G.: "Fused finger prints," *Fingerprint and Identification Magazine.* vol. 48 (May, 1967), p. 11.

Lopez-Gomez, J. L., and J. M. Simon-Gonzales: "La làque en aerosol,
nouveau fixateur des empreintes digitales et palmaires après revelations,"
Annales de Medecine Legale. vol. 47 (1967), p. 892.

MacDonell, H. L.: "Bristleless brush development of latent fingerprints,"
Identification News. vol. 11 (Mar., 1961), p. 7.

Micik, W.: "Dry ink works better than toner," *Fingerprint and Identification
Magazine.* vol. 55 (June, 1974), p. 11.

Mitchell, C. A.: "The detection of finger-prints on documents," *Analyst.* vol.
48 (1920), p. 122.

Nariyuki, H., K. Ueda, S. Hori, and T. Kawanura: "Detection of latent
fingerprints by a new wet method," *Fingerprint and Identification Magazine.* vol. 54 (Oct., 1972), p. 11.

Nariyuki, H.: "Comments on new wet method of detecting latent finger-prints," *Fingerprint and Identification Magazine*. vol. 54 (Feb., 1973), p. 17.

Patterson, D.: "Fluortec—A new fluorescent polymeric finger print pow-der," *Fingerprint and Identification Magazine*. vol. 48 (July, 1966), p. 3.

"Poisoning by fingerprint powder," *The Police Review*. vol. 58 (1949), p. 543.

"Pressurized spray fingerprint powders," *Identification News*. vol. 10 (Feb., 1960), p. 3.

"Put up latent powders in aerosol cans," *Fingerprint and Identification Mag-azine*, vol. 41 (Feb., 1960), p. 11.

Rodger, W. J., and H. Smith: "Mercury absorption by fingerprint officers using 'Grey powder,'" *Journal of the Forensic Science Society*. vol. 7 (1967), p. 86.

Russell, R.: "Identification of a reversed latent print," *Fingerprint and Identification Magazine*. vol. 57 (June, 1976), p. 7.

Smith, K. O.: "Developing latent prints on heroin papers," *Fingerprint and Identification Magazine*. vol. 57 (May, 1976), p. 3.

Stockis, E.: *Annales de la Societe Medecine et Legalerties Belges*, (1906), p. 7. In Mitchell, C. A.: "The detection of finger-prints in documents," *Analyst*. vol. 48 (1920), p. 122.

Thomas, G. L.: "The resistivity of fingerprint material," *Journal of the Forensic Science Society*. vol. 15 (1975), p. 133.

Thomas, H. A.: "The development of latent finger-prints with dyestuffs," *Analyst*. vol. 62 (1937), p. 192.

————: "Dyestuffs for developing latent finger-prints," *Analyst*. vol. 62 (1937), p. 539.

Vandiver, J. V.: "Powder comparison," *Identification News*. vol. 23 (Apr., 1973), p. 9.

Wilson, J. C.: "Developing latent prints on plastic bags," *Identification News*. vol. 24 (Sept., 1974), p. 13.

Chapter VI

Latent Fingerprint Physical Techniques

IODINE DEVELOPMENT OF LATENT FINGERPRINTS

DEVELOPING LATENT fingerprints with iodine vapors is similar to selling brushes; a salesman knows a sale will not follow each demonstration, but if enough demonstrations are made, one of them will result in a sale. The same law of averages prevails with iodine development of fingerprints; the technique is not successful in every instance. The success ratio is low, but if attempts are made when conditions are favorable, some of them will meet with success.

In the search for evidence in criminal investigations, the investigator cannot afford to pass up any opportunity to develop evidence simply because the element of chance is involved. If iodine techniques were to be completely discarded simply because of the element of chance, many latent prints would never be recovered. Iodine fuming should be the first technique of choice for developing latent prints on porous surfaces, such as paper, particularly when searching for fresh prints.

The reaction between iodine vapors and latent print residue is not considered a chemical reaction for the iodine is absorbed by the residue. Iodine vapors discolor most surfaces, but they react strongly with latent print residue. The reaction is reasonably fast, depending on the concentration of iodine vapors and the amount of oily substances in the latent print residue. It is these oily substances which absorb iodine vapors. Oily substances are found on the hands only because of contamination, principally from touching such areas as the face or hair. The image intensity of iodine-developed latent prints depends upon several factors—the condition of the fingers, texture of the paper, and the amount of oily substances deposited.

Pressure and time of contact between the finger and paper is not as important as previously believed; the amount of oily substances on the hands appears to outweigh these factors. Tests conducted at the United States Army Criminal Investigation

243

Laboratory, Fort Gordon, Georgia, demonstrated that identifiable latent prints could be developed with iodine with finger pressures of less than 1 ounce at one second of contact. Of course, greater pressure and longer contact enhanced the resulting image.

Iodine is a sensitive yet fugitive developer. When a paper bearing iodine-developed images is aired, the impressions disappear slowly; in time they fade entirely. This factor is not necessarily a disadvantage, for it is this feature that makes iodine fuming the only technique to use for documents that cannot be damaged in any manner, due to either their high intrinsic or sentimental value.

Iodine-developed latent prints may often be redeveloped with iodine after they have faded. The fingerprints in Figure 61 were made by one finger; they are one and the same impression, they were developed at intervals. The latent print was made over a fold in the paper; the fold or crease in the paper developed in the iodine vapors. Iodine vapors penetrate the sizing on paper surfaces when it is broken and thereby reveal the fault.

Investigators are always faced with the possible loss of evidence simply because of the passage of time. If the evidence is not a total loss, its quality decreases until a point is reached

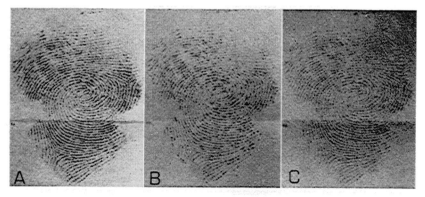

Figure 61. Latent fingerprint on paper developed with iodine vapors. (A) Three days after being made. (B) Same print photographed two weeks later. (C) Same print redeveloped after two months. The paper was left in open air between times.

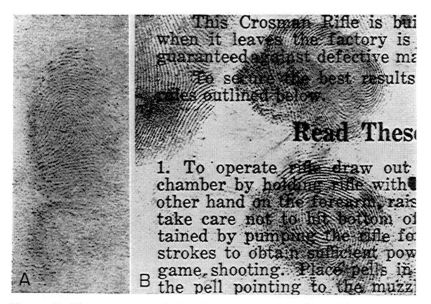

This Crosman Rifle is bui
when it leaves the factory is
guaranteed against defective ma
To secure the best results
ines outlined below.

Read These

1. To operate rifle draw out
chamber by holding rifle with
other hand on the forearm, rais
take care not to lift bottom of
tained by pumping the rifle fo
strokes to obtain sufficient pow
game, shooting. Place pells in
the pell pointing to the muzz

A   B

Figure 62. The manner in which a latent print responds to iodine development depends on the paper. (A) This latent print was developed on a soft-
textured paper. (B) These were developed on a glazed card. All developed
readily and are legible, but those on the card are strong.

where it is no longer possible to develop identifiable impressions.
For iodine development of latent prints, the time element is critical; it is a matter of days or weeks, not months or years. With
iodine development of latent prints, the term *old* implies days
or weeks at the most. Generally speaking, it is difficult to obtain
identifiable latents with iodine on paper after several weeks.

In cases where it is known or suspected that the suspect's
hands were contaminated with oils or grease, iodine fuming
should be attempted, regardless of the time factor. An example
of such a case was a service station robbery where money found
in the suspect's home was examined for latent prints made by
the attendant, who had been making an oil change in a vehicle
at the time of the robbery. Although the money was examined
several weeks after the incident, the latent prints of the attendant were developed with iodine.

Figure 63. Investigator fuming a document with iodine vapors in a fuming cabinet.

Figure 64. Photograph of a test latent impression developed with iodine fuming. After the latent impression was made, the paper was soaked in water for seventy-two hours. After removal from the water, the paper was dried with a stream of hot air from a hair dryer and the print developed with iodine fumes.

THE IODINE FUMING CABINET

Iodine fuming cabinets are simple, easily operated, and effective for processing paper suspected of bearing fresh fingerprint evidence (Fig. 63). Although designed primarily for processing papers, they can be used equally well for light-colored non-metallic objects. Adequate fuming cabinets may be constructed with glass and wood, or the cabinet may be purchased. Sirchie Finger Print Laboratories, Inc., markets a fuming cabinet with an electric heater and temperature control. Heated cabinets develop latent images within a few minutes, as increased heat simply speeds vaporization of the iodine crystals, and of course, the sooner a cabinet is filled with vapors, the sooner the latent develops (Fig. 64).

IODINE FUMING PIPE

The iodine fuming pipe, or tube, is a simple and easily portable device which may be used almost anywhere. A description of how the pipe is prepared for operation was presented in Section 60. To examine a surface for latent prints, the nozzle of the pipe is moved slowly over the suspected area at close range, about ½-inch, while the investigator blows into the rubber tube connected to the opposite end of the pipe. Whenever latent prints begin to show, that area is given more concentrated treatment to intensify the developing images. Investigators using the iodine fuming pipe should always remove the rubber tubing from their mouth before taking a breath. *Always avoid inhaling iodine fumes,* as they may irritate the skin and respiratory tract.

An atomizer may be used in lieu of a fuming pipe if the atomizer does not have metal parts. Iodine vapors are very corrosive to most metals. An advantage of atomizers with glass reservoirs is that vaporization of the iodine crystals may be accelerated by heating the reservoir with a match or cigarette lighter.

COLD IODINE TECHNIQUE

Papers may be processed at room temperature in an unheated fuming cabinet or a self-seal polyethylene bag. At room temperature, development may take from thirty minutes to several hours; however, when using the plastic bag, vaporization of the crystals may be hastened by holding the bottom of the bag with the crystals, firmly in the palm of the hand. Body temperature speeds the vaporization of the crystals. The polyethylene bag is an expedient technique for an investigator in the field, since it does not require extensive preparation. When using this technique, the investigator must be careful to insure that the crystals are at the bottom of the bag and not touching the paper. Iodine crystals in direct contact with paper discolor the area touched and obscure any ridge detail.

NASCENT IODINE TECHNIQUE

Rhodes (1940) states that the French criminalist Edmond Locard recommended a special preparation of iodine, described as nascent iodine, as a very sensitive developer with an advantage of disappearing rapidly, leaving the document essentially unchanged. In this technique, iodine is liberated from potassium iodide by mixing the iodide with manganese dioxide in hydrochloric acid. Considering the chemicals involved and the results achieved, the nascent iodine technique offers little, if any, advantage over other iodine techniques.

POROUS GLASS IODINE FUMING

An iodine fuming powder made from ground, porous glass impregnated with iodine is manufactured and sold under the trademark Driodine® by MacDonell Associates, Inc. (Moenssens, 1971). In this technique, the iodine-impregnated ground glass is poured over the paper being examined and is left on the paper for fifteen to thirty seconds. This method is extremely convenient in both economy and ease of operation. The ground glass may be returned to the container and used again at a later date.

SILICA GEL IODINE FUMING TECHNIQUE

This iodine fuming technique was developed by Ronald Jones of the Kansas Bureau of Investigation (Jones, 1976), and it is a very practical technique that may be used conveniently at a crime scene or in the laboratory. A small cloth bag, usually about 10-by-10 cm, is filled with about 30 to 50 g of silica gel which has been saturated with iodine fumes. A piece of porous tissue paper, such as facial cleansing tissue, is placed over the surface to be examined. The bag of iodine-saturated silica gel is then placed on the tissue, directly over the suspected area, usually for fifteen to thirty seconds, although the actual exposure time varies according to the nature of the surface.

The iodine-saturated silica gel is prepared by first placing a small quantity of iodine crystals, about 3 g, in a glass jar or large test tube. A thin layer of glass wool is then packed over the crystals to prevent the crystals from becoming mixed with the silica gel. The amount of silica gel added depends upon the size of the bag to be used; however, 30 g to 50 g of a 6- to 16-mesh silica gel is sufficient for a 10-by-10 cm bag. The jar is then sealed and the iodine crystals heated. When the silica gel appears glossy black in color, it may then be removed and placed in the cloth bag.

Another method for preparing the iodine-saturated silica gel (Couch, 1977) is to heat the silica gel in an oven at 120° C for thirty to forty-five minutes. The iodine crystals are then mixed with the silica gel, and the mixture placed in the cloth bag. The advantage of the first method of preparation is that the bag may be stored in the same container used for preparation; the remaining iodine crystals will, at room temperatures, serve to replenish iodine lost from the silica gel through usage.

The most suitable material for making the cloth bags is an unbleached muslin. The bag may be constructed entirely of muslin with a conventional drawstring opening, but such bags do not lie flat over a surface. Also, such bags must be handled with forceps or when wearing rubber gloves to prevent staining of the hands. The best method of construction for the bag is to use muslin for one side and a vinyl fabric for the other side, with the vinyl toward the inside of the bag. The bag is sealed with Velcro® tape.

IODINE DUSTING

Iodine crystals may be ground into a fine powder and dusted over the surface of a paper with a fingerprint brush. When the latent prints develop or the paper begins to discolor, the powder is removed. Another method is to simply place the iodine crystals directly onto the paper surface while agitating the paper and after the latent prints develop pour the crystals back into their container. The disadvantages of such techniques are the discoloration of the paper due to direct contact with the iodine crystals and possible obscuring or obliteration of ridge details.

82

FIXING AND INTENSIFYING IODINE-DEVELOPED PRINTS

Much has been said and written about the fugitive nature of iodine-developed fingerprints and methods of intensifying and fixing them. Perhaps the case has been overstated; the fugitive nature of iodine images is not a problem which should cause nervousness on the part of the investigator. Evidence does not have to be handled like a hot potato, and the images are not nearly as fugitive as one is led to believe by reading some printed information on the subject.

If latent prints are developed by iodine fuming in the field, that portion of the paper bearing latent prints may be marked lightly with a pencil and segregated for special attention under more favorable conditions or at least away from the confusion of the crime scene. It is important to locate the evidence and protect it for proper examination in an environment more conducive to good workmanship.

If the evidence is processed in an iodine fuming cabinet, the heating unit may be turned off as soon as full development is reached, and the paper bearing the latent impressions may be left inside indefinitely without noticeable change or undue loss of contrast. It is possible to redevelop iodine images, or the paper may be returned to the cabinet at any time it is feared the images may become too faint or if work on the case is unavoidably delayed.

Temporary intensification of iodine-developed prints may be accomplished in some instances by blowing on the images; carbon dioxide in the breath discolors the image slightly, and it holds temporarily. This method may be helpful if the evidence is to be photographed, but it has a disadvantage: The paper itself may undergo a color change the same as the ridges. Before attempting to intensify iodine images by blowing on them, the paper should be tested at a point where no fingerprint evidence is involved.

Fingerprint powders may also be used to intensify iodine-developed latent prints, but the disadvantages associated with powder development of latent prints on paper also apply in this instance. Magnetic powders prove very successful for intensifying iodine-developed latents, a technique regularly used by technicians at the Polizeiprasidium, Frankfurt, West Germany. An important advantage of this technique is that a dark or black paper may be processed with iodine fumes and then with light-colored magnetic powder to recover latent prints that may not be recovered by other techniques.

It is not always advisable to fix iodine-developed prints even when those prints have been identified as having been made by the suspect. Iodine fuming should always be regarded as only the first stage in a series of techniques to be used to develop latent prints. Iodine fuming should be followed by application of the ninhydrin technique and then the silver nitrate technique, in that sequence and with photographic recording of all prints developed after each stage.

Subsequent processing with the other techniques may reveal additional prints of the suspect or of persons not initially believed to have been connected with the crime. Forged documents are an example of such cases, as the person passing or using the forged document is not always the one who has made the forged writings. Inasmuch as the persons passing a forged document have had the most recent contact with the document, their prints may be considered more apt to be found with iodine fuming, while those of others involved in the forged writing are relatively older and may be considered more likely to be developed with ninhydrin or silver nitrate.

Although fixing iodine-developed latent prints is not generally recommended, there are instances where an investigator wishes to fix such prints. Several methods of fixing iodine-developed prints are, therefore, listed in this section. Photography is not listed as a fixing method, because it is a method for permanently recording the print rather than a fixing method. However, the importance of photography cannot be stressed too greatly. Before applying any latent fingerprint technique of fixing method, all visible prints should be photographically recorded as a precautionary measure against damage or loss of the print.

SEALING THE PAPER

The simplest and easiest method of fixing iodine-developed prints for a limited time is to seal the paper in an airtight place; for example, between two pieces of glass taped at the edges or in a heat-sealed plastic bag. Sealing is not satisfactory for obvious reasons: Much paper evidence is such that it is impossible to seal it, either between sheets of glass or in plastic bags, and the method does not confine the vapors to the developed images; it travels through the paper in time. However, this method does have two important advantages: First, it does not preclude the subsequent use of the ninhydrin and silver nitrate techniques if it should be determined at a later date to use these techniques. Second, this method is very useful when the paper must be restored to its original condition and returned to the owner after trial. In cases involving the theft of old and rare documents of high value, this method may be preferred.

MAGNETIC POWDER FIXING METHOD

Magnetic powders provide a fast and effective method for permanently fixing iodine-developed latent prints. The developed images are brushed with a magnetic powder of contrasting color to the surface upon which the prints are located, the excess powder is removed with the magnetic applicator, and the powdered prints are then lightly sprayed with a clear lacquer. When spraying the lacquer, care must be exercised to insure that the lacquer is lightly and evenly applied. Heavy deposits of the lacquer may run and damage the prints. The disadvantage of this method is that it is permanent and once applied, it cannot be removed without damage to the document.

EARLY CHEMICAL FIXING METHODS

Throughout the years, many chemical methods for fixing iodine-developed prints have been tried. Almost all have proven unsatisfactory and are no longer in use, although references to these methods may still be found in many authoritative texts. These include such methods as calomel (mercurous chloride) and hydrogen sulphide, gallic acid, and silver nitrate, a 10% tannic acid solution, a solution of calcium chloride and potassium bromide, and a solution of gum arabic, alum, and formaldehyde sprayed onto the print (Bridges, 1942).

The chemical fixing method recommended by Bridges (1942), involved the spraying of a solution formed by 20% acetone, 7% gun cotton, 20% absolute alcohol, and 53% ether. Collodion may be substituted for the gun cotton. The spray must be applied to the paper as a very fine mist, as excessive amounts of the solution on the paper cause the ridge details to blur.

Iodine-developed prints may also be fixed onto the surface on which they appear by a solution of palladium chloride, which turns the prints a dark brown. The solution is prepared as follows:

Palladium chloride	1.00 g
Tannic acid	0.25 g
Alum	0.25 g
Hydrochloride acid (10%)	0.50 cc
Distilled water	98.00 cc

After a print has been developed in iodine vapors, it is submerged in the above solution for less than one minute. The paper is then rinsed in a stream of water to remove the palladium chloride and dried. The paper may be dried by ironing or simply air dried. This method is not recommended because its cost is prohibitive, and the solution tends to destroy any inked writings on a document.

STARCH METHODS

The use of starch for fixing iodine-developed prints has been recommended since about 1930 (Moenssens, 1971). Starch reacts with iodine to form a dark-blue complex. The print may be fixed for a considerable time, although it is not permanent. Many methods employing starch have been tried—solutions, pastes, and as a powder—and solutions provide the least desirable results, because an excess of solution on the paper causes the print to run and blur ridge details.

A satisfactory starch solution may be prepared by adding 1 g of starch to 99 cc of distilled water. The starch need not be of reagent or analytical grade; common, everyday laundry starch may be used. If a starch solution is used, the paper should not be submerged in the solution or the solution swabbed onto the paper. The best method of applying the solution is by an aerosol spray mist. Care must be exercised in applying the spray so that only a very fine mist reaches the paper and that the solution is not heavily deposited on the paper.

An excellent method using starch to fix iodine prints is a paste applied directly to the print. The fixed print can be made more permanent by varnishing it with a 3% solution of gum dammar in benzol (O'Neill, 1937). The paste is prepared by thoroughly stirring 1 g of starch in 20 cc of distilled water, then stirring into the paste 2 g of potassium iodine followed by 0.3 g of thymol. The whole mixture is thoroughly mixed together and applied directly over the print with a brush or spatula.

The starch method for fixing iodine-developed prints yielding the best results is the starch powder-steam method (Larsen, 1962). In this method, a finely ground starch powder is applied to the print with a brush, and the excess is blown off. The powdered print is then exposed to a very gentle jet of steam for one or two seconds. Exposure to the jet of steam must be carefully controlled, and the steam must be a very fine mist. Too much moisture from the steam causes the ridge details to blur, and exposure for too long a period causes the print to disappear.

TETRABASE

The tetrabase method of fixing iodine-developed prints was developed and patented by F. Trowell (1975) of England. Iodine prints fixed by this method have remained as long as eight months and more. The solution is prepared by dissolving 0.2 g of tetrabase in 99.8 cc of Freon 113® (1,1,2 trichlorotrifluoroethane) and is applied by dipping the paper into the solution, withdrawing, and allowing it to dry. The solution changes the print to a green blue color. Tetrabase is found in chemical catalogs listed as 4,4′-methylenebis (N,N-dimethylaniline). The disadvantage associated with this method is that Freon 113 causes some ink writings on the paper to run.

83

CLEARING PAPER TREATED WITH IODINE

It is sometimes desirable or necessary to restore papers treated with iodine fumes to their original condition because of their nature or value. Such treatment is exceptional, because most evidential papers in criminal investigations are not cleared and restored, but it is important for the investigator to have knowledge of the processes, in the event it is necessary to clear and restore documents.

Paper processed in iodine vapors may be allowed to clear spontaneously in the air, may be cleared by exposure to ammonia fumes, or may be bleached chemically. Chemical bleaching is the least desirable of the three clearing methods, because the bleaching solutions cause most inks to dissolve and discolor the paper. Some papers, because of their texture, may disintegrate or lose their shape.

The quickest, easiest, and most practical method of removing all traces of iodine from paper is to expose the paper to ammonia fumes. A small amount of ammonium hydroxide may be placed in a glass dish or beaker and held under the stained areas for a minute or so until the iodine discoloration has disappeared. Another method is to simply place the paper and ammonium hydroxide in an iodine fuming cabinet and leave until the paper has been completely cleared. The advantage of clearing paper with either ammonia fumes or spontaneously in the air is that there is no alteration of the document. The paper is restored to its original condition so effectively that it is almost impossible to determine afterwards whether or not the document was ever processed for latent fingerprints.

Chemical bleaching methods should never be used for clearing paper treated with iodine fumes if the ninhydrin and silver nitrate techniques are going to be used later. The easiest chemical bleaching method to prepare and use is a 50% solution of Clorox® and water has almost universal application in fingerprint work, as it may also be used for clearing ninhydrin and silver nitrate stains from papers.

Iodine-developed prints that have been fixed by any of the fixing methods, except the magnetic powder and lacquer method, may be cleared with the ammonia fuming or chemical bleaching clearing methods.

84

CHLORINE AND BROMINE FUMING TECHNIQUES

Chlorine and bromine fuming techniques have no practical value in fingerprint work; both techniques produce results less satisfactory than iodine fuming. Considering the results achieved with these techniques and the toxic nature of the substances involved, the use of these techniques is not recommended, and their use is discouraged. Mention of chlorine and bromine fuming as latent fingerprint techniques, as well as mercuric iodine fuming, may be found in several early references on fingerprint work; therefore, a brief description of the technique is given in this book.

Bromine vapors may be produced by placing a beaker of hydrobromic acid in a fuming cabinet and heating the acid slightly. The bromine vapors produce a faint yellow print of lesser quality than that of iodine-developed prints. A word of caution in the handling of hydrobromic acid is necessary for those not

Figure 65. A fuming cabinet concentrates the fumes within a confined space for complete saturation of the document to be examined. It does not provide a means for the safe exhaust of the fumes. Whenever poisonous chemical fuming techniques are used, a respirator should be worn.

familiar with chemicals. Hydrobromic acid is a dangerous chemical to handle and use; the acid will severely burn the skin, the vapors are poisonous, and the acid reacts violently with water.

Chlorine vapors may be produced within a fuming cabinet by adding a few drops of concentrated hydrochloric acid to a solution of 1 g of calcium hypochlorite in 99 cc of distilled water. The prints developed by chlorine fumes are much fainter than iodine-developed prints.

Mercuric iodine fumes may be produced within a fuming cabinet by heating a mixture of four parts of mercury and five parts of iodine. The fumes produce prints that are initially a dark red but which will soon change to a yellow color (Mitchell, 1920).

The fuming techniques listed in this section represent a great health hazard to the person using them and to anyone in the area of their use. The fumes are highly irritating to the eyes and upper and lower respiratory tract and can cause inflammation of the entire respiratory system. Maximum permissible exposure limits for these substances have been prescribed under Occupational Safety and Health Standards contained in Section 1910 of Title 29 of the *Code of Federal Regulations* (1974) (Fig. 65).

85

BACTERIOLOGICAL TECHNIQUES

Fingerprints have been developed experimentally by growing bacteria cultures on a nutrient agar plate (O'Neill, 1941), but the technique has no practical application as a latent fingerprint technique. In the experimental study cited, the bacteria was a type normally found on the skin. However, a nutrient media was required, as well as a moist warm environment and sufficient time for the bacterial colonies to grow.

The intentional development of latent prints by bacteriological techniques is not practical, but it is conceivable that such prints may be found in warm, moist climates, particularly when considerable time has elapsed between the time of the incident and the processing of the crime scene. No reference to such prints in an actual case can be found, but this does not necessarily preclude the possible existence of such prints. The need to make a thorough visual search at the scene before processing cannot be stressed too greatly.

86
HEAT IS A LATENT FINGERPRINT TECHNIQUE

O'Hara and Osterburg (1949) and Bridges (1942) mention heat as a technique for developing latent fingerprints on documents. The heat is applied to the paper by a common iron, and the heat chars the organic substances in the latent fingerprint residue. As an intentional means of developing latent prints, heat is not a practical technique. Better and more predictable results can be obtained with iodine fuming and the ninhydrin technique.

Although heat cannot be considered a practical latent fingerprint technique, a number of arson cases have been solved as a

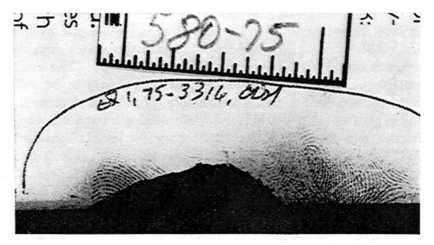

Figure 66. Latent fingerprints on the page of a magazine developed by the heat of a fire. In this case, the prints of an arsonist were developed by the same fire he has perpetrated.

result of latent prints developed by heat. The need for a thorough visual search of all evidence at a crime scene is again illustrated. A good example is an arson case where the fingerprint technician had to look through several hundred pages of charred magazines but found a good heat-developed latent fingerprint made by the suspect (Fig. 66). Such prints may become of paramount importance when processing of the evidence by regular latent fingerprint techniques is precluded by excessive charring of the evidence or when the evidence is damaged by the substances used to extinguish the fire.

87

FLAME TECHNIQUES

Flame techniques for developing latent fingerprints have long been recognized for their successful results with relatively older latent prints which do not respond adequately to ordinary brush and powder techniques (Corr, 1957). The heat apparently softens the dried impressions and makes them receptive to the fine-grain soot.

The flame technique was first used on an experimental basis in 1904 (Heindl, 1957), but the technique was developed by the United States Army Criminal Investigation Laboratories through research conducted by Oscar H. Baker (Corr, 1957). The most suitable materials for flame techniques were found to be soft resinous pine and its products, camphor, pine tar, and nitrocellulose plastics (Fig. 67). When a white residue is required, magnesium and titanium tetrachloride may be used (Vandiver, 1973), but these materials are not as successful with older prints as resinous pine (Fig. 68).

Before describing the method of application of the flame technique, a brief description of the mechanism of soot formation is desirable. Natural fires are diffusion flames consisting of three distinct zones. The innermost zone is gases or volatilized fuel that has not yet fired. The second or middle zone is composed of minute particles of incandescent carbon produced in

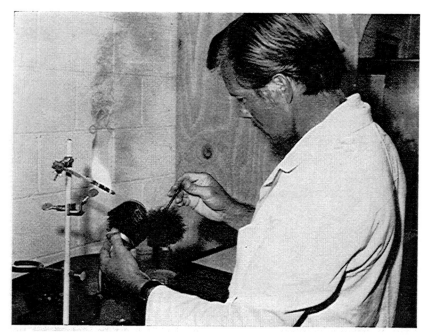

Figure 67. Fingerprint examiner brushing a can with a feather duster after processing the can with the flame technique using resinous pine.

the thermal decomposition of some of the hydrocarbons in the fuel. It is this zone that gives the flame its distinctive yellow white luminous appearance. The third or outer zone has a faint bluish color, and it is composed of the particles of complete combustion. The formation of soot occurs when there is an excess amount of fuel (the high hydrocarbon content of pine) being vaporized by thermal conduction and an insufficient supply of oxygen for complete combustion. The supply of air to natural fires is rarely sufficient for complete combustion of the fuel supply.

Normally, flame techniques are used only after attempts to develop latent prints with regular brush and powder techniques have proven unsuccessful or when the latent prints have been established to be unresponsive to powder techniques by examination of a like item. Some technicians prefer flame techniques

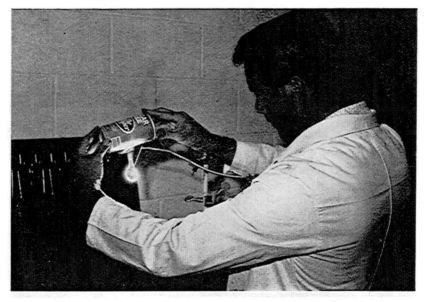

Figure 68. Fingerprint examiner processing a can with the flame technique using a magnesium strip. The magnesium leaves a white deposit on the can.

over regular powder techniques for all glass and metallic objects, but there is no indication that it is in any way superior to powder techniques for ordinary latent prints.

The procedure for using the flame technique is relatively simple, although practice is necessary to fully perfect the method of application. The burning substance is simply passed under the surface being examined until an even deposit of soot is accumulated. The deposit of soot should not be too heavy nor should the flame touch the surface of the object. Too much soot or too much heat causes excessive soot to adhere to the surface and obscures the ridge details of latent prints. After a satisfactory deposit of soot has been placed onto the surface of the object, the surface is then brushed with a feather duster or fiberglass brush to remove excess soot (Fig. 67).

A miner's carbide lamp of the type commonly used by sharpshooters and marksmanship teams to blacken rifle sights makes a handy device when using the flame technique. These lamps

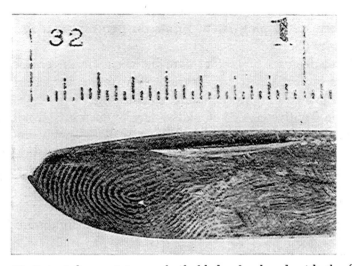

Figure 69. Latent fingerprint on a knife blade, developed with the flame technique.

have a compartment for the calcium carbide below a water reservoir, and as water is released onto the calcium carbide, acetylene is released. The amount of acetylene released depends upon the flow of water, which is regulated by a valve on the top of the lamp. The advantage of this lamp is that it is economical to use and is easy to start and stop as required. The supply of calcium carbide must be kept in a moisture proof container.

During investigations of arson cases, it would be a wise precaution to dust all evidentiary items covered with soot with a feather duster or fiberglass brush. Instances of latent prints being recovered from scenes of fires by such techniques have been reported (Fig. 69) (Eboli, 1954). As stated previously in preceding sections, the need to thoroughly search and examine *all* evidence at a crime scene cannot be stressed too greatly.

QUESTIONS

TRUE-FALSE QUESTIONS

1. Iodine fuming always results in the successful recovery of latent prints (Sec. 81).

2. Iodine fuming should always be the first technique used when developing latent prints on porous surfaces, such as paper (Sec. 81).

3. Pressure and time of contact between the finger and paper are important factors determining whether or not an identifiable latent impression is made (Sec. 81).

4. The fugitive nature of iodine-developed prints is not necessarily a disadvantage (Sec. 81).

5. Iodine crystals must always be heated to produce fumes and cannot be used as a fuming technique at ordinary room temperature (Sec. 81).

6. Temporary intensification of iodine-developed prints may be accomplished in some instances by blowing on the images (Sec. 82).

7. Fingerprint powders should not be used to intensify or fix iodine-developed prints (Sec. 82).

8. Due to their fugitive nature, it is always advisable to fix iodine-developed prints (Sec. 82).

9. Once the latent prints of a suspect have been identified, it is not advisable to further process the evidence with additional latent fingerprint techniques (Sec. 82).

10. Magnetic powders provide a fast and effective method for permanently fixing iodine-developed prints (Sec. 82).

11. Starch methods of fixing iodine-developed prints change the prints from a blue to yellowish color (Sec. 82).

12. The quickest, easiest, and most practical method of removing all traces of iodine from paper is to expose the paper to ammonia fumes (Sec. 83).

13. The chemical bleaching solution of Clorox and water has limited application in fingerprint work (Sec. 83).

14. Chlorine, bromine, and mercuric iodine must be considered dangerous chemicals in fingerprint work (Sec. 84).

15. The flame technique is an excellent technique for developing relatively fresh latent fingerprints (Sec. 87).

COMPLETION QUESTIONS

16. In the search for evidence in criminal investigations, the investigator cannot afford to pass up any opportunity to de-

velop evidence simply because the element of .... is involved (Sec. 81).

17. Generally speaking, it is difficult to obtain identifiable latents with iodine on paper after .... weeks (Sec. 81).

18. Name the five iodine fuming techniques (Sec. 81).

19. Iodine fuming should always be regarded as the .... in a series of techniques to be used to develop latent prints (Sec. 82).

20. Name four methods of fixing iodine-developed prints (Sec. 82).

21. The starch method for fixing iodine-developed prints yielding the best results is the ....-........ method (Sec. 82).

22. It is sometimes desirable or necessary to restore papers which have been treated with iodine fumes to their original condition because of their .... or .... (Sec. 83).

23. Name three methods of clearing papers treated with iodine fumes (Sec. 83).

24. The chlorine and bromine fuming techniques have .... in fingerprint work (Sec. 84).

25. Fingerprints have been developed .... by growing bacteria cultures (Sec. 85).

26. Although heat cannot be considered a practical latent fingerprint technique, a number of .... cases have been solved as a result of latent prints developed by heat (Sec. 86).

27. In the flame technique, the heat apparently .... the dried impressions and makes them .... to the fine-grain soot (Sec. 87).

28. The most suitable materials for flame techniques were found to be .... and its products (Sec. 87).

29. Normally, flame techniques are used only after attempts to develop latent prints with regular .... have proven unsuccessful (Sec. 87).

30. When using the flame technique, too much .... or too much .... causes excessive soot to adhere to the surface and obscure the ridge details of latent prints (Sec. 87).

REFERENCES

Austin, J.: "Breath fixation of iodine-fumed fingerprints," *Scientific Criminal Investigation Bulletin.* vol. 2 (Mar., 1959), p. 33.

Bridges, Burtis C.: *Practical Fingerprinting.* New York, Funk and Wagnalls, 1942.

Boone, A. R.: "New aids for criminology: finger prints raised with iodine," *Scientific American.* vol. 155 (Nov., 1936), p. 274.

Corr, J. J.: "Flame method for the development of latent fingerprints," *Kriminalistik.* vol. 10 (1956), p. 429.

————: "Hot prints: the use of flame in the development of latent prints," *Military Police Journal.* vol. 6 (Jan., 1957), p. 7.

Couch, S. H.: "Latent fingerprint processing: iodine-silverplate transfer method," *Identification News.* vol. 27 (Jan., 1977), p. 9.

Eboli, E.: "The smoking of latent prints on metal and glass, and their resistance to high temperature," *International Criminal Police Review.* vol. 9 (Nov., 1954).

Foley, J. F.: "Development of latent fingerprints—iodine silver transfer method," *Identification News.* vol. 22 (Mar., 1972), p. 14.

Heindl, R.: "Antwort," *Archiv fur Kriminologie.* vol. 119 (1957), p. 3.

————: "Nochmals eine unmassgebliche Bemerkung zur Jodine-Silver-Methode," *Archiv fur Kriminologie.* vol. 119 (1957), p. 30.

Jones, R.: Personal communication. December 27, 1976.

Larsen, J. K.: "The starch powder-steam method of fixing iodine fumed latent prints," *Fingerprint and Identification Magazine.* vol. 44 (July, 1962), p. 3.

MacDonell, H. L.: "Iodine fuming—New apparatus," *Police.* vol. 3 (Mar.-Apr., 1959), p. 12.

Mitchell, C. A.: "The detection of finger prints on documents," *Analyst.* vol. 45 (1920), p. 122.

Moenssens, A. A.: *Fingerprint Techniques.* New York, Chilton, 1971.

"More about fixing iodine fumed prints," *Fingerprint and Identification Magazine.* vol. 44 (Oct., 1962), p. 15.

"A new detection of latent fingerprints by use of chlorine-iodide starch reagent," *Reports of the National Research Institute of Police Science* (Japan). vol. 20 (1967), no. 2, p. 6.

O'Hara, Charles E. and James W. Osterburg: *An Introduction to Criminalistics.* New York, Macmillan, 1949.

Olsen, R. D.: "The oils of latent fingerprints," *Fingerprint and Identification Magazine.* vol. 56 (Jan., 1975), p. 3.

O'Neill, M. E.: "The development of latent fingerprints on paper," *Journal of Criminal Law, Criminology and Police Science.* vol. 28 (1937), p. 432.

————: "Bacterial fingerprints," *Journal of Criminal Law, Criminology and Police Science.* vol. 32 (1941), p. 482.

Rhodes, H. T. F.: *Forensic Chemistry.* New York, Chemical Pub. Co., 1940.

"A simple iodine fuming gun," *FBI Law Enforcement Bulletin.* vol. 22 (June, 1953), p. 12.

"The starch powder-steam method of fixing iodine fumes latent prints," *Fingerprint and Identification Magazine.* vol. 44 (July, 1962), p. 3.

Teeples, E.: "Make your own iodine fuming gun," *Law and Order.* vol. 9 (Mar., 1961).

Trowell, F.: "A method for fixing latent fingerprints developed with iodine," *Journal of the Forensic Science Society.* vol. 15 (1975), p. 189.

Trubey, C. L., and H. O. Medlin: "How to use the flame process," *Military Police Journal.* vol. 27 (Jan., 1968), p. 5.

Vandiver, J. V.: "Comments on smoke technique," *Identification News.* vol. 23 (June, 1973), p. 12.

Chapter VII

Latent Fingerprint Chemical Techniques

THE CHEMICAL COMPOSITION OF LATENT FINGERPRINT RESIDUE

A BRIEF DISCUSSION of the various chemical substances that may be found in latent fingerprint residue is useful as a means of explaining how and why chemical techniques develop latent fingerprints. Each latent fingerprint chemical technique is dependent upon the presence of specific chemical substances in the latent print residue for successful results. Knowledge of these substances and the reactions involved assists an investigator in understanding both the potentials and limitations of each technique.

It is not necessary for an investigator to have knowledge of the exact chemical composition of latent print residue or the chemical processes involved in the techniques to achieve successful results. When determining which technique to use in a particular instance, many factors may govern the selection, but the chemical composition of the latent print is not normally one of these factors. Only when it can be positively established, usually through prior examination by a forensic chemist, that specific substances are present is the chemical composition a determining factor in selecting the appropriate technique. In the majority of instances, the nature of the surface to be examined and the proper sequence in applying chemical techniques is the governing factor.

Contaminants may become an important factor in selecting the appropriate latent fingerprint technique to use, when the contaminant can be positively identified. Examples of contaminants which may affect the choice of techniques are body fluids: blood, saliva, nasal secretions, semen, vaginal fluid, and feces. When latent prints made by these contaminants are suspected on porous surfaces, such as paper, successful results may generally be best obtained with the ninhydrin technique. However, evidentiary items suspected of bearing latent prints with such contaminants should never be processed with any technique, except visual, until after the evidence has been examined by a serologist (*see* Sec. 44).

Chemical substances normally found in human perspiration may be expected to be present in varying concentrations in almost all latent prints, while contaminants may or may not be present. Latent prints made primarily by perspiration on the fingers generally contain varying amounts of oils and fats, as these substances are normally found on the hands due to contact between the hands and other parts of the body, principally the face.

The primary source of oils and fats found in perspiration is sebum, a secretion of the sebaceous glands. The sebaceous glands are usually, but not necessarily, associated with hair follicles and are not found on the palmar surfaces of the hands or the plantar surfaces of the feet. The smallest sebaceous glands are those of the scalp and the largest, and most active in secreting sebum, are those of the mons veneris, scrotum, nose, and external ear. Sebum is present on the hands and fingers primarily due to contact of the hands with the other body sites with high concentrations of sebaceous glands. Small amounts of sebum may also be found on the palms and fingers as perspiration flows from the forearm and dorsal surfaces of the hands onto the palmar surfaces.

The iodine fuming and osmium tetroxide techniques are very successful in developing latent prints that have high deposits of oils and fats. If the proper sequence is followed in applying latent techniques, the presence of oils and fats in latent print residue need not be a consideration in selecting the appropriate technique. The ninhydrin technique cannot be used before the iodine or osmium tetroxide techniques, because oils and fats are soluble in the solvents used in the ninhydrin technique, acetone and ether, etc., which destroy or blur the latent image insofar as techniques reacting with oils and fats are concerned.

Sweat glands (eccrine glands) are found on almost all surface skin areas of the body with the greatest density on the palmar surfaces of the hands and the plantar surfaces of the feet, where the average number is 2,700 per square inch. Medical and biochemical research has established an extensive number of chemical substances in perspiration, but only a limited number of these substances have any practical significance insofar as latent fingerprint techniques now in use are concerned.

Approximately 99.0 to 99.5 percent of perspiration is water, with 0.5 to 1.0 percent being solids. About one-half of the solids are organic substances and about one-half inorganic salts. The salts predominant in perspiration are sodium chloride and potassium chloride, with the ratio of sodium to potassium being about 9 : 1. The concentration of sodium chloride in perspiration is subject to the following factors: rate and duration of sweating, skin and environmental temperatures, and the individual's activity, salt intake, and acclimatization.

The inorganic salts of perspiration present in latent print residue are the substances that react chemically with silver nitrate in solution, forming silver chloride, which darkens upon exposure to light.

Twenty-one amino acids present in perspiration have been identified, but isolation of individual amino acids is not of any particular significance. All alpha-amino acids present in latent print residue react with ninhydrin, producing a latent image ranging in color from pink to violet red. Amino acids are soluble in water; therefore, the ninhydrin technique is not as successful as iodine fuming on documents that have been wet.

The chemical composition of perspiration is extensive, but a detailed examination of all the substances that may be found is of interest only to researchers wishing to develop new or improved latent fingerprint techniques. An investigator employing latent fingerprint techniques needs only a practical understanding of the chemical substances reacting with established and accepted techniques. Fingerprint identification is concerned with the positive identification or elimination of individual fingerprints and not the exact chemical processes involved in the techniques used to visualize latent prints.

89

CHEMICAL FORMULAS

Chemical solutions used in latent fingerprint work are not difficult to prepare, and the formulas for these solutions may be regarded simply as recipes. The formulas merely list the necessary ingredients and their proportions. The formulas are easy to follow and have proven, through practical experience, to be the best suited for latent fingerprint work. In some instances, such as the ninhydrin technique, there may be some disagreement between various agencies and authorities in the field as to the exact formula for a technique. In such instances, the disagreements are noted.

The standard formula for any latent fingerprint chemical technique may vary slightly from one law enforcement agency to another. Slight variations in concentration are not of any great significance. However, once a standard formula is adopted by any agency, it is a wise policy for all personnel of that agency to adhere as closely as possible to that standard formula to insure and maintain consistent quality of all solutions used. If all solutions prepared within an agency are of the same quality, the results obtained with the solutions are more predictable, and each investigator may be reasonably certain that any failure to develop latent prints is not due to an improperly prepared chemical solution.

Exact measurements and proportions when preparing chemical solutions are desirable for consistent quality, but successful results in developing latent fingerprints are not dependent upon unequivocal accuracy. There is a considerable margin for error in preparing chemical solutions for latent fingerprint techniques without adversely affecting the successful development of latent prints. For example, an investigator may wish to prepare a 3% solution of silver nitrate, but if the result is a 2% or 4% solution, the probability of successful development of latent prints is not significantly altered.

It is not necessary for anyone using latent fingerprint techniques to have prior training in chemistry, nor is it essential for them to be familiar with chemical terms and procedures. However, familiarity with basic chemical terms undeniably aids in understanding and preparing the chemical solutions used in latent fingerprint techniques. An analogy may be made to photography; a photographer may take adequate photographs without any understanding of the basic principles and terms of photography, but the greater the knowledge of photographic principles, the greater the expertise in taking photographs.

In a solution of one substance in another, the dissolved substance is called the *solute*. The substance in which the solute is dissolved is called the *solvent*. The most common solvent is water. In a solution of silver nitrate and water, silver nitrate is the solute and water is the solvent. These terms are necessary to provide a basis for discussing the concentrations of solutions.

The concentration of a solution may be dilute, concentrated, or saturated. At specific temperatures, there is a limit to the amount of solute that dissolves in a given quantity of solvent. A saturated solution is one in which the solvent has dissolved all the solute that the solution will hold at a certain temperature. Therefore, all saturated solutions listed in this book will also have a reference to temperature.

The concentrations of most chemical solutions used in latent fingerprint work are expressed in terms of percentages. There are several methods of expressing percentage concentration: weight percent (w/w), volume percent (v/v), and weight-volume percent (w/v). Weight-volume percentage composition is the most frequently used method of expressing concentrations in fingerprint work and it is simply the number of grams of solute per 100 milliliters of solution. This term is defined by the equation

$$\text{weight-volume percent} = \frac{\text{weight of solute, g} \times 100}{\text{volume of solution, ml}}$$

The denominator refers to the solution and not to the solvent alone. For example, a 3% silver nitrate solution is one prepared by dissolving 3 g of silver nitrate in water and diluting to 100 ml. However, because exact percentages of solutions used in latent fingerprint work are not critical, and for the practical expeditious preparation of solutions, the denominator may be regarded as the solvent. Therefore, a 3% silver nitrate solution would be one prepared by dissolving 3 g of silver nitrate in 100 ml of water.

In Section 36, it was stated that neither the chemical substances involved nor the nature of their processes have any direct effect upon identification of friction ridge characteristics. This cannot be stressed too greatly. In sciences such as chemistry, analyses may depend greatly upon the exact concentration and proportion of reagents. However, in latent fingerprint work, the chemicals used merely visualize the prints for comparison purposes. They do not alter the types of ridge characteristics present or change their relative positions. A weak solution may produce very faint latent print images lacking in desirable contrast with the surface upon which the prints are located, but as long as the ridge characteristics are discernible, an identification may be affected.

90

THE NINHYDRIN TECHNIQUE

Ninhydrin is the most consistently successful technique available today for developing latent fingerprints on documents and porous surfaces of a similar nature. Although ninhydrin is of relatively recent origin as a latent fingerprint technique, it has gained wide acceptance and is the most commonly used chemical technique for developing latent prints.

Because the ninhydrin technique has proven to be so successful, there is a tendency for many investigators to use this technique for documentary evidence to the complete exclusion of all other techniques. No single technique for recovering latent prints has universal application under all circumstances. Many factors other than the nature of the surface to be examined must also be considered when determining the appropriate technique to use on a specific item of evidence. The value of the document, preservation of ink writings or indented markings, and presence of body fluids and other stains are a few of the factors that may be considered. Ninhydrin is a valuable technique that an investigator may use in searching for latent prints, but it is not the only tool at his disposal. Its use must be governed on a case-by-case basis, depending upon the circumstances existing in each case.

Normally, the correct procedure for developing latent fingerprints on documents is to use ninhydrin as the second stage in a series of techniques—*after* the iodine technique and *before* the silver nitrate technique. Ninhydrin must be applied after the iodine technique, because the solvents used in ninhydrin solutions dissolve the oils and fatty substances essential for iodine absorption by the latent print residue. It is necessary to use the ninhydrin technique before silver nitrate, because darkening of the silver nitrate upon exposure to light tends to blot out the ninhydrin-developed latent prints and because aqueous silver nitrate solutions tend to blur ninhydrin-developed latent images. The amino acids which react to ninhydrin, and ninhydrin itself, are water soluble.

Amino acids containing a free amino group in the alpha-position give a blue violet color when treated with ninhydrin. This reaction also takes place with proteins, polypeptides, and peptides, which contain a free carboxyl and alpha-amino acid group. Most body fluids, milk, saliva, blood, nasal mucus, urine, feces, cyst contents, semen, vaginal fluid, and sweat, react with the ninhydrin technique.

Ninhydrin crystals have the appearance of a white powder and are available in 5-, 10-, and 25-g bottles from all major chemical supply companies. Synonyms for ninhydrin are ninhydrin hydrate; 1,2,3-triketo-hydrindene; 1,2,3-triketo-hydrindene hydrate; triketo-hydrindene hydrate; 1,2,3-indan-trione monohydrate; 1,2,3-indan-trione, 2-hydrate; 2,2-dihydroxy-1,3-indan-dione. The crystals are irritating to the nasal and respiratory passages, but are not toxic unless taken internally.

Two Swedish scientists, Oden and Hofsten (1954), were the first to advocate the use of ninhydrin as a means for developing latent fingerprints, and Oden subsequently patented the process as a latent fingerprint technique (Brownlie and Patterson, 1962). The validity of the patent has been questioned, because it had been recognized for over forty years prior to the patent application that ninhydrin reacted with the amino acids of sweat. Early researchers using the reagent cautioned against touching anything that was to be treated with the reagent (Conway, 1965). However, the question of whether or not a patent should have been granted for a process already widely known, although not specifically as a latent fingerprint technique, is now moot because the sixteen-year patent monopoly has presumably lapsed (Silliman, 1975).

A large amount of literature exists pertaining to the ninhydrin technique (Figs. 70 and 71), and there is considerable disagreement on the recommended concentrations, the type of solvent to be used, and the correct postprocessing treatment after application of ninhydrin. There is general recognition that, regardless of the concentration, type of solvent used, and postprocessing treatment, some latent prints require a longer time to develop than others; in some instances, even months. The precise cause of this phenomenon is not known, but it is likely that it is due to the type and amount of amino acids present in the latent print residue.

It is also widely recognized that once a document has been treated with ninhydrin, the crystals deposited on the document continue to react and develop the prints of persons handling the document after processing. All items processed with ninhydrin should be handled with forceps or when wearing gloves, and for routine handling, the items should be placed within plastic document protectors.

The concentrations recommended for ninhydrin solutions have varied from the 0.2% solution initially suggested by Oden and Hofsten to 1.5% solution used by the Los Angeles County Sheriff's Department (Speaks, 1964). Solutions of 0.4% and less require a longer reaction time for the latent images to fully develop (Moenssens, 1971), and it has been noted, in one study,

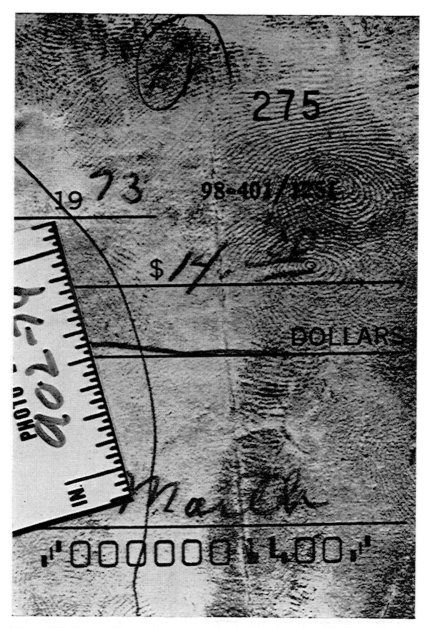

Figure 70. Latent fingerprints on a check, developed with the ninhydrin technique.

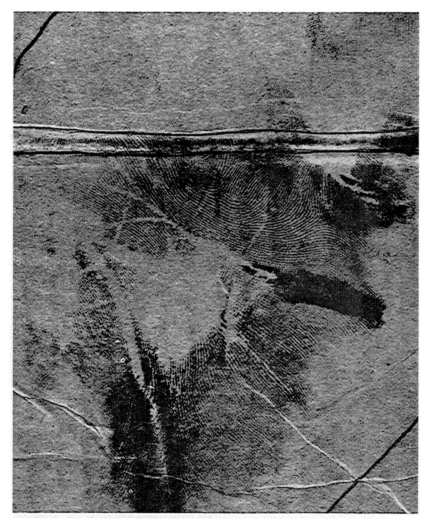

Figure 71. Latent palmprint on a cardboard box, developed with the ninhydrin technique.

that concentrations of 1.0% and more produce a dark-blue discoloration of the background (Shulenberger, 1963).

Tests conducted by the Latent Fingerprint Division of the U.S. Army Criminal Investigation Laboratory, Fort Gordon, Georgia, indicated that best results may normally be obtained when using concentrations between 0.6% and 1.0%. This test also indicated that concentrations in excess of 1.0% tend to result in a heavy deposit of ninhydrin crystals on the surfaces of papers treated with the reagent. These crystals irritate the nasal passages of examiners during their examination of latent prints developed on the papers.

While each individual has his own favorite concentration based on his own experiences, determination of the appropriate concentration for ninhydrin solutions should include consideration of the nature of the evidence to be examined. Normally, concentrations between 0.6% and 1.0% are satisfactory for routine processing of all paper products and porous surfaces. However, the concentration should be reduced to 0.4% or less when examining coated papers having a very smooth or slick appearance to reduce overall discoloration of the evidence (Mooney, 1973). An example of items requiring a reduced concentration, to reduce overall discoloration, is medical prescription boxes, such as morphine syrette containers, which have a specially treated surface to resist moisture.

Figure 72 lists the various amounts of ninhydrin per volume of solution required for different concentrations of ninhydrin. Since ninhydrin crystals may be purchased in 5-, 10-, and 25-g bottles, preparation of the solutions may be expedited in some instances by approximating the desired concentration and dispensing with the necessity of weighing out exact amounts of ninhydrin. For example, 1 gallon of a 0.5% solution may be prepared by mixing 18.92 g of ninhydrin with 1 gallon of solvent. However, simply mixing the contents of two 10-g bottles of ninhydrin with 1 gallon of solvent does not significantly increase the concentration.

Figure 72 may be used for all solvents employed in ninhydrin solutions except ethyl ether. Ethyl ether is commonly sold by weight rather than liquid measurements and is available in 1- and 5-pound cans. Figure 73 lists the various amounts of ninhydrin per pound of ethyl ether required for different concentrations.

The type of solvent recommended for ninhydrin solutions is

FORMULAS FOR DIFFERENT CONCENTRATIONS OF
NINHYDRIN SOLUTIONS
(Weight of ninhydrin in grams per volume of solution)

Volume of Solution	Percentage Concentration						
	0.2	0.4	0.5	0.6	0.75	1.0	1.5
100 ml	0.2 g	0.4 g	0.5 g	0.6 g	0.75 g	1.0 g	1.5 g
1 pint (473.167 ml) ...	0.94 g	1.88 g	2.35 g	2.82 g	3.52 g	4.73 g	7.08 g
1 quart (946.333 ml) ...	1.89 g	3.78 g	4.73 g	5.67 g	7.09 g	9.46 g	14.19 g
1 l (1,000 ml) ..	2.0 g	4.0 g	5.0 g	6.0 g	7.5 g	10.0 g	15.0 g
1 gallon (3,785.3 ml) ...	7.57 g	15.14 g	18.92 g	22.71 g	28.38 g	37.85 g	56.77 g

Figure 72

almost as varied as the recommended concentrations; acetone, ethyl ether, petroleum ether, methyl alcohol, ethyl alcohol, ethyl acetate, ethylene glycol, and trichlorotrifluoroethane (Freon 113). Selection of the appropriate solvent to use depends upon two factors: whether or not inked writings must be protected and the safety hazards associated with a particular solvent.

When a document bearing questioned writings is to be processed for latent fingerprints, the document should always be examined by the questioned document examiner *before* any chem-

FORMULAS FOR DIFFERENT CONCENTRATIONS OF
NINHYDRIN SOLUTIONS
(Weight of ninhydrin in grams per weight of ethyl ether)

Weight of Ethyl Ether	Percentage Concentration							
	0.2	0.4	0.5	0.6	0.75	0.88	1.0	1.5
1 pound (453.5924 g) ...	0.90 g	1.81 g	2.26 g	2.71 g	3.39 g	3.98 g	4.53 g	6.79 g
2 pounds (907.1848 g) ...	1.81 g	3.62 g	4.53 g	5.44 g	6.80 g	7.98 g	9.07 g	13.60 g
3 pounds (1,360.7772 g) .	2.72 g	5.44 g	6.80 g	8.16 g	10.20 g	11.96 g	13.60 g	20.40 g
4 pounds (1,814.3696 g) .	3.62 g	7.25 g	9.07 g	10.88 g	13.60 g	15.96 g	18.14 g	27.21 g
5 pounds (2,267.9620 g) .	4.53 g	9.06 g	11.33 g	13.60 g	17.00 g	20.00 g	22.67 g	34.00 g

Figure 73

icals are applied to the document. During his examination, the questioned document examiner should select the appropriate writing to be preserved by photographic recording. In addition to these selected writings, it is also a good practice to make a photograph of the overall writings as a protective measure in the event that chemical processing for latent prints damages or destroys the writings.

It is the practice of some agencies to mask out questioned writings, such as signatures on checks, by clamping pieces of glass directly over and under the questioned writings and lightly spraying the areas to be examined. This practice may result in the loss of important latent fingerprints and is not necessary if adequate photographs of the writings have been made and the questioned document examiners have completed their examination of the evidence.

Of all the solvents used for ninhydrin solutions, acetone, methyl alcohol, and ethyl alcohol result in the greatest damage to inks. These solvents should not normally be used in cases where questioned writings are important or on magazines, cigarette cartons, and similar items with a large amount of colored inks. However, in those cases where preservation of inked writings is not important, the problem of running or bleeding inks may be overcome by dipping the item in the solution and washing away the dissolved inks. This procedure may be used to prevent the smeared inks from obscuring the ridge details of any latent prints developed.

Ethyl ether, petroleum ether, and Freon 113 cause the least damage to inks of all the solvents that may be used for ninhydrin solutions, but some inks, particularly the colored inks used in magazines, dissolve and run. Early references to the ethyl ether solvent (Mooney, 1966) recommended dissolving the ninhydrin crystals in 20 ml of methyl alcohol and then adding this solution to 980 ml of ethyl ether; however, it is now recognized that the methyl alcohol causes some bleeding of inks. It is recommended that the crystals be mixed directly with the ethyl ether using a magnetic stirrer (Mooney, 1973).

Preparation of the ninhydrin-petroleum ether solution was established by Crown (1963), who recommended mixing the ninhydrin crystals with 40 ml of methyl alcohol and then mixing this solution with 960 ml of petroleum ether. The entire solution is then poured into a separator funnel and allowed to stand for five to ten minutes. Two layers of solution are formed: a small quantity of a deep-yellow liquid on the bottom and a much larger quantity of a pale-yellow liquid on the top. The deep-yellow liquid layer on the bottom is drawn off and discarded. The top pale-yellow layer is the portion used for developing latent prints.

When determining the type of solvent to be used for ninhydrin solutions, consideration must be given to the safety hazards associated with each solvent and the equipment, if any, available to minimize these hazards. The greatest hazard is the flammability of most of the solvents. Acetone, ethyl ether, petroleum ether, methyl alcohol, ethyl alcohol, and ethyl acetate are all highly flammable substances with flash points ranging from −49° F for ethyl ether to 55° F for ethyl alcohol (*Fire Protection Guide*, 1967).

Ethyl ether is the most dangerous of all the solvents that may be used for ninhydrin solutions. Ethyl ether fumes have been known to sink to floor level and travel for considerable distances to a point where they have been ignited by a spark or open flame with a resulting flash burn back to the point of origin. Explosions of ethyl ether fumes may result in severe burns to all parts of the body, and clothing saturated with the fumes will burn. Ethyl ether fumes may also form highly explosive peroxides which may explode spontaneously upon exposure to sunlight. This substance should not be used except within an explosion-proof chemical exhaust hood.

Freon 113 (trichlorotrifluoroethane), which is practically non-flammable and which does not cause most inks to run, is probably the best solvent for ninhydrin solutions for general use. Morris and Goode (1974) recommend the following formula for preparing a ninhydrin solution with this solvent: A stock solution is prepared by mixing 25 g of ninhydrin in 50 ml of glacial acetic acid and 100 ml of absolute ethyl alcohol; a working solution is then prepared by mixing 30 ml of the stock solution with 1 l of Freon 113, stirring, allowing to stand for thirty minutes and filtering if necessary. Morris and Goode also state that the addition of acetic acid to any ninhydrin solution results in better-quality prints. The primary disadvantage of Freon 113 is its cost in relation to the other solvents that may be used.

Acetone is one of the less expensive and most commonly used solvents for ninhydrin solutions. However, there are several disadvantages associated with the use of this solvent. Acetone causes most inks to run, it has a flash point of 0° F, and long exposures to acetone fumes may irritate the mucous membranes and cause headaches, fainting, and general poisoning.

The method of applying ninhydrin solutions may vary from spraying a fine mist, to swabbing the surface with cotton swabs dipped into the solution, or simply dipping the documents into the solution (Figs. 74, 75, and 76). Swabbing provides the least

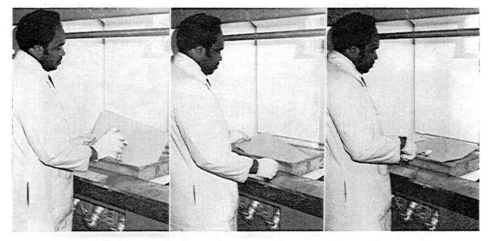

Figure 74. (left) A ninhydrin solution may be sprayed onto the item being examined for latent prints. The spray should be a fine mist and the paper evenly covered and saturated.

Figure 75. (center) A ninhydrin solution may be applied to items by dipping the entire item into the ninhydrin solution. Full coverage and saturation is assured by this method of application, and it is the best method of applying ninhydrin when a large volume of items must be processed.

Figure 76. (right) A ninhydrin solution may be applied by swabbing. This method is very useful when processing single pieces of evidence or very small areas.

desirable results, because this method of application is the most damaging to inks on the document—the swabbing action tends to smear the inks. Spraying is the most time-consuming method, but it should be the preferred method when it is necessary to mask out inked writings. Spraying is also necessary when processing extremely fragile paper items, such as tissue paper, which may fall apart if dipped into the solution or tear if swabbed. When examining such fragile items, it is advisable to spread them out on a clean surface, such as a piece of cardboard, clamp them into place, and spray lightly.

Recommended postprocessing treatment of documents treated with ninhydrin has always included the application of heat, usually by placing the document within an oven (Fig. 77). Recommended exposures have varied from a few minutes at 176° F (Oden and von Hofsten, 1954) to 284° F (O'Hara, 1970). Although it was recognized that best results were obtained during periods of high relative humidity and that a "slow cure" at room temperatures was preferable (Moenssens, 1971), early references

Figure 77. An oven with a tray of water at the bottom may be used for the postprocessing environment of ninhydrin-treated items.

did not establish specific relative humidity values for postprocessing environments.

A study conducted by the United States Postal Service (Lesk, 1971) established that optimum development of ninhydrin-treated latent prints is obtained in postprocessing environments between 65 and 80 percent relative humidity. In tests conducted by the U.S. Army Criminal Investigation Laboratory, best results were obtained when the ninhydrin-treated documents were placed within environments of 80° F and 80 percent relative humidity (Fig. 78).

The development of latent prints with ninhydrin may be accelerated by using an electric steam iron ("Chemical Development of Latent Impressions," 1973). The iron is passed over, but

Figure 78. A humidity cabinet for the postprocessing environment of ninhydrin-treated items. The cabinet contains an explosion proof hotplate to heat a pan of water and a seven-day continuous recording hydrometer. The hole in the cabinet at the far end is to prevent the excessive buildup of moisture within the cabinet. A hose leading into the pan provides a continuous stream of water at a very low rate of flow.

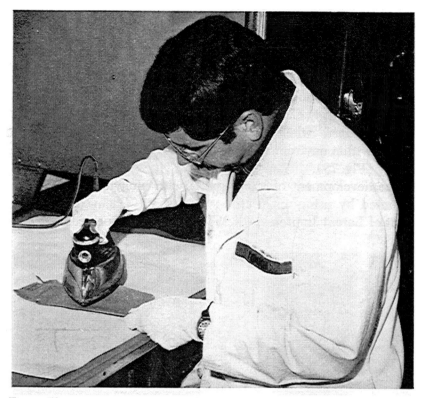

Figure 79. A steam iron may be effectively used to accelerate the development of ninhydrin-treated prints. The iron should not touch the paper surface, but be moved over the surface at a distance of about ½ inch.

not touching, the document until the latent images appear or until it is apparent that no latents will be developed (Fig. 79). Excellent latent images may be obtained with this method; however, the images lack the deep color and contrast of those developed within a humidity cabinet or allowed to cure naturally. The steam iron method should not be used on cardboard or papers with coated surfaces, as the steam has a tendency to condensate on such items, and moisture damages or destroys the latent developed. The steam iron method of postprocessing treatment of ninhydrin-treated documents is extremely useful when processing large volumes of evidence for latent prints.

DRY NINHYDRIN TECHNIQUES

In those cases where it is absolutely imperative that the inked writings on a document are protected from any possible damage and it is questionable as to how the inks will react to the solvents available for use, it is possible to use ninhydrin without solution to develop latent prints on paper. One technique is to cover the paper with a thin layer of ninhydrin crystals; the paper is then placed within a humidity cabinet or a strong paper towel may be placed over it and ironed with a steam iron. When using the steam iron, the paper towel should be subjected to steam for about two to three minutes, but moisture should not form on the towel, as the paper being examined will be stained.

Another dry ninhydrin technique is to saturate a blotter or strong paper towel with a 1% ninhydrin solution. Allow the towel to dry, then place the treated towel over the paper to be examined, and iron with a steam iron. The towel should be moved slightly after each pass with the iron; otherwise, the latent images will appear spotted. Neither of these techniques for dry application of ninhydrin are recommended for general use, as solutions insure saturation of documents and development of all traces of ridge details. If a dry technique is used on a document and no latents are developed, it would be advisable to then apply a ninhydrin solution and reprocess the document.

NINHYDRIN TEST SOLUTION

Occasionally, an investigator may wish to test a ninhydrin solution to determine whether it is reacting with the amino acids of latent prints on treated papers. Stock solutions over two weeks old should always be tested, as such solutions may deteriorate due to exposure or contamination. Sometimes, even a newly prepared solution made with freshly opened bottles of ninhydrin and solvent may not react properly. Frequently, doubts of an investigator on the effectiveness of a ninhydrin solution are more the result of insufficient amino acids in the latent print residue than any loss of effectiveness by the solution.

As the amino acid concentration of latent print residue varies from individual to individual and even within the same individual at different times, it is not a satisfactory practice to test ninhydrin solutions by merely processing intentionally handled papers. One method that may be successfully used is to slightly dampen the fingers with beef broth before making the test prints. A stock solution of beef broth may be prepared by dissolving one beef bouillon cube in 500 ml water. The test impressions are then processed with ninhydrin and give a very dark coloration if the ninhydrin solution is reacting properly.

91

NINHYDRIN CLEARING SOLUTIONS

Normally, evidence processed with ninhydrin should not be cleared, because the clearing solutions may destroy any latent prints that may be developed in the next stage of processing, the silver nitrate technique. In almost all cases, ninhydrin clearing solutions remove the salts of latent fingerprint residue that are essential for the silver nitrate reaction. When it is determined necessary to preserve inked writings that may appear on documents, such documents should not be cleared, because the clearing solutions normally result in greater damage to inks than the ninhydrin solutions.

Although the clearing of ninhydrin stains from documents is not recommended as a general rule, an investigator may determine that clearing is necessary in specific cases: either to remove excessive discoloration before returning a document to its rightful owner or to remove the deposits of ninhydrin crystals from the document to prevent development of prints due to handling after processing.

There are three solutions that may be used for clearing ninhydrin stains from documents. One solution used by the Metropolitan Police Department, Washington, D.C., can be used for clearing iodine, ninhydrin, and silver nitrate stains and is called Formula X (*see* Sec. 93).

Strongly oxidizing bleaching substances, such as calcium hypochlorite and sodium hypochlorite mixed with water make excellent clearing solutions for ninhydrin stains. Clorox, a regular household bleach, provides the simplest and most effective ninhydrin clearing solution and may also be used to clear iodine and silver nitrate stains, but the concentration of Clorox must be increased for silver nitrate. A solution of one part Clorox to two parts water provides an adequate ninhydrin clearing solution.

Ninhydrin stains may also be cleared with a solution of one part of concentrated ammonium hydroxide and two parts of water. On paper items, this solution does not clear as fast as the Clorox solution, but this solution is excellent for cleaning bench tops, trays, and other nonporous surfaces where deposits of ninhydrin may accumulate through use.

Documents and papers should be blotted and dried immediately after application of clearing solutions. An excellent method is to remove excess moisture by placing the document between two large blotters and then drying it with a stream of air. An ordinary pistol-grip, hand-held hair drier makes an excellent device for drying documents.

92

SILVER NITRATE TECHNIQUE

Silver nitrate reacts with the salts of latent print residue—sodium and potassium chloride—to form silver chloride. When the resulting silver chloride is subjected to a developing agent or a strong actinic light such as ultraviolet, it changes color or darkens much the same as a photographic negative or print. The presence of a sufficient quantity of silver chloride results in a legible image, and if the salts are present only in the openings of the pores, as they usually are, the developed image is spotted. The spotty character of silver nitrate developed latent fingerprints is especially noticeable in the photographs of silver nitrate developed latent prints used in this section (Fig. 80).

Salt is present in latent print residue in very small quantities. The amount of salt present is directly proportional to the amount of silver chloride produced by the silver nitrate reaction.

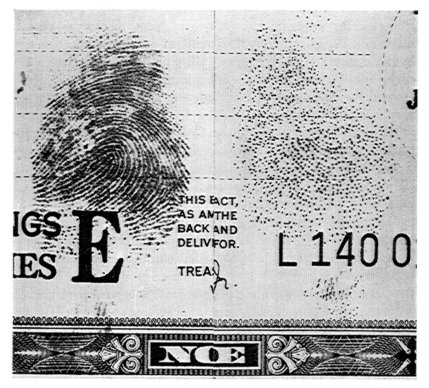

Figure 80. Two examples of silver nitrate developed latent prints. Silver nitrate images are usually spotted, and they show pore structure in a striking manner.

In comparison with the ninhydrin technique, silver nitrate is not as successful with minute quantities. However, the silver nitrate technique should never be neglected or abandoned, because the salts of latent print residue may remain for a considerable time. Silver nitrate is the final stage of the series of chemical techniques that may be used to develop latent prints on papers.

When handling or using silver nitrate solutions or crystals, care should be taken to avoid getting either on the hands or clothing. They may cause burns, or tender skin may be blistered. Silver nitrate stains are particularly difficult to remove from the skin and clothing; they are not at once apparent, and they may appear after several minutes or hours, depending upon light conditions. Skin burns remain for several days under ordinary conditions or until the skin heals.

Silver nitrate is commercially available in sprays, but extreme care must be taken to avoid inhalation of the spray, which must be regarded as a health hazard. Inhalation of silver nitrate spray may cause irreversible damage to the lungs and could result in poisoning due to absorption in the blood.

PREPARATION OF SOLUTIONS

Generally, 3% to 5% silver nitrate solutions are used in fingerprint work. However, due to the increasing cost of silver, many agencies have decreased the concentration to as low as 1% and obtain satisfactory results. A 3% solution of silver nitrate may be prepared by mixing 3 g of silver nitrate with 100 ml of distilled water. Figure 81 lists the amount of silver nitrate per volume of solution for various concentrations.

An aqueous solution is the most commonly used silver nitrate solution. Distilled water is preferable to tap water, because it results in a clear solution. Impurities in tap water may cause a solution to appear milky, although it may or may not affect its usefulness.

Several authorities have recommended slightly acidifying silver nitrate solutions to decompose carbonates and other substances which, if present, might interfere with the silver chloride reaction. The solution may be acidified by adding 1 ml of acetic acid (Rhodes, 1940) or concentrated nitric acid (Moenssens, 1971) per 100 ml of solution.

Although aqueous silver nitrate solutions are adequate for general use, alcoholic solutions may be prepared for special use. Ethyl alcohol may be used as the solvent when it is determined necessary to protect ninhydrin-developed latent prints. Neither ninhydrin nor amino acids are readily soluble in ethyl alcohol, but both are water soluble. The ethyl alcohol solvent is also desirable when examining styrofoam, waxed paper, and cardboard with a waxed finish, as the ethyl alcohol is not repelled by such surfaces. When using ethyl alcohol as a solvent for silver nitrate solutions, *do not add nitric acid.* Stirring a mixture of concen-

FORMULAS FOR VARIOUS CONCENTRATIONS OF SILVER NITRATE SOLUTIONS
(Weight in grams per volume of solvent)

Volume of Solvent	Percentage Concentration									
	1.0	2.0	3.0	4.0	5.0	6.0	7.0	8.0	9.0	10.0
100 ml	1.00 g	2.00 g	3.00 g	4.00 g	5.00 g	6.00 g	7.00 g	8.00 g	9.00 g	10.00 g
1 pint	4.73 g	9.46 g	14.19 g	18.92 g	23.65 g	28.38 g	33.11 g	37.84 g	42.57 g	47.31 g
1 quart	9.46 g	18.92 g	28.38 g	37.84 g	47.30 g	56.76 g	66.22 g	75.68 g	85.14 g	94.63 g
1 l	10.00 g	20.00 g	30.00 g	40.00 g	50.00 g	60.00 g	70.00 g	80.00 g	90.00 g	100.00 g
1 gallon	37.85 g	75.70 g	113.55 g	151.40 g	189.25 g	227.10 g	264.95 g	302.65 g	340.65 g	378.53 g

Figure 81

trated nitric acid and ethyl alcohol may result in a reaction that starts slowly and accelerates to an explosion.

A different alcoholic silver nitrate solution has been developed by the Denver Police Department Crime Laboratory for developing latent fingerprints on dynamite wrappers (Nicoletti, 1974). The solution is prepared by first preparing three separate solutions, each using a different alcohol as solvent, and then mixing the solutions together. Each of the separate solutions develops latent prints on some types of dynamite wrappers, but only the solution of all three mixed together will work for all wrappers.

The solution is prepared by dissolving 6 g of silver nitrate in 10 ml of distilled water and adding to this mixture 100 ml of ethyl alcohol. This procedure is repeated using methyl alcohol and then again using isopropyl alcohol. The three solutions are then mixed together by adding the ethyl alcohol solution to one of the other solutions and then the third. The ethyl alcohol solution and one of the other two must be mixed first for the solution to stay stable—never mix the methyl alcohol and isopropyl alcohol solutions until one has been mixed with the ethyl alcohol solution.

A solution of silver nitrate and osmic acid may be used to develop latent prints on papers, but this solution is not recommended for general usage. The solution cannot be used with good results if the ninhydrin technique has been used on the paper. Since ninhydrin is the most consistently successful technique for developing latent prints on paper, this solution would have little application in general use. However, this is a good technique for developing latent prints on heavy cardboard and heavy craft paper, which usually have a very rough surface and a high content of large, dark fibers. Normally, ninhydrin is not a successful technique for such items, as the dark fibers tend to obscure any ninhydrin-developed latent images.

The solution is prepared by mixing 1 g of osmium tetroxide with 100 ml of distilled water and then mixing 3 g to 5 g of silver nitrate into the solution. The osmium tetroxide reacts with the oils and fatty substances of latent print residue and the silver nitrate with any salts present.

METHODS OF APPLICATION

Silver nitrate solutions may be applied by either dipping or swabbing. Dipping is perhaps the best method of application for small items, such as sheets of paper, while swabbing must be used for large items, such as cardboard boxes. In some instances, the nature of the material to be examined dictates the use of swabbing; for example, red dynamite wrappers should be swabbed rather than dipped. Tissue paper should also be swabbed, as the paper may fall apart when immersed in a solution.

When an item is dipped, it should be immersed in the silver nitrate solution until the surface is completely wet (Fig. 82). It is not necessary that the paper itself is soaked or submerged for an extended period of time; a few seconds is sufficient, as long as the paper surface is wet. Complete saturation of an item is not desirable, especially cardboard, as the greater the amount of solution absorbed, the longer the drying time.

Swabbing may be accomplished by either paint brushes or cotton balls and forceps. The advantage of the cotton balls and forceps is that each piece of cotton may be discarded after use, thereby dispensing with the necessity for cleaning as required for brushes. When very large surfaces are to be examined, medium- to large-sized paint brushes may be used.

If there are oily finger impressions on an item, the silver nitrate-osmic acid solution should be used, but this solution should be applied by dipping rather than swabbing to insure an even deposit of the osmic acid. If the paper itself is greasy, this solution should not be used.

Some authorities suggest that development with silver nitrate solutions be accomplished in a darkened room. This is not necessary if the items are dried right away and all excess solution is removed. However, it is a wise precaution to avoid direct sunlight when applying and drying the solution.

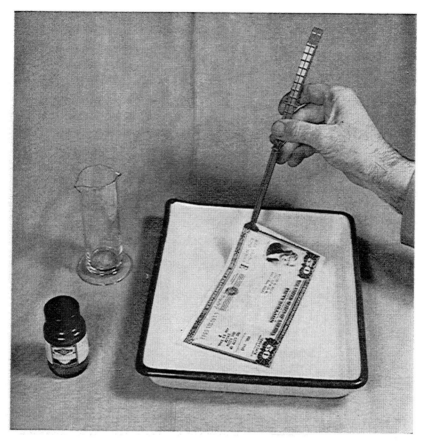

Figure 82. Applying a silver nitrate solution to a document by immersing the document into the solution.

BLOTTING AND DRYING PAPERS

If development is accomplished with a developing chemical solution, blotting is unnecessary; the paper is washed after being removed from the silver nitrate solution to remove the excess silver nitrate solution in the same manner that a photographic paper is washed after being removed from a hypo solution.

When a paper is removed from a silver nitrate solution for the purpose of developing the images by light, the excess solu-

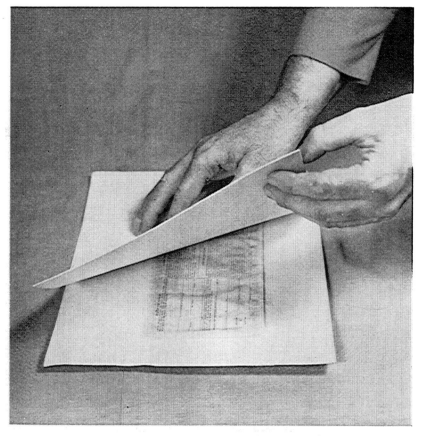

Figure 83. After applying silver nitrate to a document, the excess solution is removed from the document with clean blotters.

tion must be removed by pressing the paper between two blotters or by squeegeeing on a glass plate (Fig. 83). The paper is then thoroughly dried by blowing heated air onto the paper. An ordinary hand-held hair drier may be used quite effectively to achieve complete drying. Aqueous solutions dry at a slower rate than alcoholic solutions, but regardless of the solvent used, the paper should not be exposed to a developing light until the paper is thoroughly dry.

DEVELOPING SILVER NITRATE IMAGES

There are two ways to develop silver nitrate images—chemically or with light. Of the two methods, light is the preferable choice, because chemical development requires an additional immersion in a solution. It must be remembered that some papers cannot be successfully immersed in a solution either because the texture of the paper is such that it will disintegrate or lose its shape when wet or ink writings may dissolve and discolor the paper. Prolonged and repeated soaking may damage any paper to some degree.

A number of light sources are suitable: sunlight, room light, photoflood, or ultraviolet light (Fig. 84). Photofloods and ultraviolet lamps are ordinarily used in the laboratory because of their availability and convenience and the speed with which they do the job. Ultraviolet light is many times faster, and it develops slightly darker images—and it is a cold light. One feature of UV light is that the image may be developed completely while the paper is still wet. If a paper is subjected to the heat of a photoflood, the paper is usually dry by the time images are fully developed.

Photoflood lamps used for development of silver nitrate images should have a 1,000-watt bulb. Iodine cobalt light or other lights with intensity similar to the photoflood lamp are also satisfactory. Large agencies that use the silver nitrate technique on a routine basis may use carbon arc lights for developing.

Silver nitrate developed images appear brown in color, and they develop and darken according to original intensity, kind of paper, light source, exposure time, solution strength, and original contact. In some cases, they become almost black. If exposure to light is continued after full development, the paper itself may discolor to such an extent that the prints may lose contrast, or they may become totally obscured. It is, therefore, necessary to photograph silver nitrate developed images as soon as possible, and care must be taken that the photographic lights do not overexpose the paper.

Figure 84. The images of silver nitrate treated latent prints may be developed with ultraviolet light (as shown above), sunlight, photoflood, or in a photographic paper developer.

Chemical development is accomplished in the same manner a photographic print is developed. After the paper is removed from the silver nitrate solution, it is washed thoroughly and then developed in any good photographic developing solution, such as Kodak Dektol® developer. The images appear almost immediately and develop to full strength in a short time. Chemical development is more convenient than light, and it is perhaps more positive. A chemical developer should be fresh and used in the same dilution as for ordinary contact or projection prints. After

Plate 1-1. Ninhydrin-developed latent print.

Plate 1-2. Silver nitrate developed latent print.

Plate 2-1. Latent print developed by iodine fuming.

Plate 2-2. Osmium tetroxide developed latent print.

fingerprints are developed chemically, the paper is washed and dried.

Many other references to chemical developers may be found in early texts on fingerprint identification, but these are usually more time consuming, as the developing solution must be prepared rather than using commercially prepared developers.

SPECIAL CONSIDERATIONS

Silver nitrate solutions deteriorate, whether used or not, as the result of the action of light; if kept for any length of time, a solution should be kept in a well-stoppered dark-colored bottle or in a dark place. When a solution is prepared and bottled, it should be properly labeled with contents, concentration, and date visible. A silver nitrate solution is good for many months if properly bottled and stored. It deteriorates rapidly when used. If used at once, the solution may be poured into a flat glass, enameled, or plastic tray. It is suggested that different colored trays are used for developing and clearing solutions to avoid crossing them up, as both solutions are colorless and if one is not careful, it is easy to cross up the solutions and pour them back into the wrong bottles. If a document should inadvertently be immersed in the clearing solution first, any latent fingerprints would be destroyed.

Good-quality rag paper, bond paper, money, and bonds may be treated in a silver nitrate solution and cleared, washed, and ironed so effectively that a casual observer does not detect any change in texture or appearance. The quality and texture of paper determine whether or not it can be effectively subjected to silver nitrate solution, cleared, washed, and restored. A paper which cannot undergo such treatment should not be subjected to it. There are so many grades of paper it is impossible to state which can and cannot be immersed. Investigators learn to recognize, through experience, those papers which should not be treated with silver nitrate. If there is a doubt, a test may be made using an identical paper of no evidentiary value or a small corner of the paper to be examined.

Printing and writing must also be considered before using the silver nitrate technique. Whenever it is determined that questioned writings must be protected, such as may be the case with an extortion note, the document should not be treated with silver nitrate. Aqueous solutions and alcoholic solutions in particular tend to damage inks and may, in some cases, completely remove ink writings. In all cases involving questioned writings, the documents should be treated with silver nitrate only after examination by the questioned document examiner, photographic recording of all writings, and mutual agreement between the document examiner and the fingerprint technician.

The silver nitrate technique may be used for several other types of surfaces other than paper. Cow horns, brass cartridge cases, wood, and cloth are examples of such surfaces. A 6% solution of silver nitrate and methyl alcohol has been found to be suitable for cow horns (Watling, 1974) and a 10% acidified aqueous solution for cloth (Moenssens, 1971). Silver nitrate may also provide results when examining papers that have been exposed to excess moisture, whereas ninhydrin, in such cases, will not. Even after papers have been thoroughly soaked, it is sometimes possible to dry the papers and develop good latents with silver nitrate.

93

SILVER NITRATE CLEARING SOLUTIONS

In Section 91, it was suggested that papers treated with ninhydrin should not be cleared unless absolutely necessary, because the clearing solutions normally result in greater damage to inks than the ninhydrin solution itself. In respect to documents treated with silver nitrate the opposite is true. The longer the stains remain on a paper and are exposed to light, the darker they become, until they appear black and obscure any writings and latent prints.

The above holds true for all silver nitrate solutions—regardless of the solvent used. However, stains of solutions of silver nitrate and ethyl alcohol darken at a much slower rate than those of aqueous solutions. The U.S. Army Criminal Investigation

Laboratory, in 1973, treated one half of a latent palmprint with an aqueous solution of silver nitrate and the other half of the same print with an ethyl alcohol solution. After three years, the half treated with the aqueous solution turned completely black, while the half treated with the ethyl alcohol solution still retained a visible print. The paper was not continuously exposed to light the entire three years, but both halves received the same amount of light.

A few words of caution regarding the possible health hazards associated with the mercurial compounds used in some silver nitrate clearing solutions is advisable. Many mercury compounds are of considerable importance in medicine; mercurous chloride, for example, may be used as an internal antiseptic. However, many mercury compounds are also highly poisonous, and others may be poisonous if exposure is prolonged or in high concentrations. Caution should be exercised whenever substances containing mercury are used.

While mercurous chloride is essentially nonpoisonous, mercuric chloride is extremely poisonous. Mercuric nitrate is also a poison, although not as dangerous as mercuric chloride, and it may be absorbed through the skin. During occupational health physical examinations of personnel at one crime laboratory, a high level of mercury was found in the urine of a fingerprint examiner whose only known contact with mercury compounds was mercuric nitrate clearing solutions. Papers treated with such clearing solutions should be handled only with forceps, and rubber gloves should be worn at all times whenever preparing, handling, or using the solution. After clearing, all papers should be washed thoroughly.

When preparing silver nitrate clearing solutions containing mercury compounds, care must be exercised to avoid confusing substances having similar names and composed of the same chemical elements. For example, mercuric chloride must not be confused with mercurous chloride, and mercuric nitrate must not be confused with mercurous nitrate.

All the aforementioned warnings are not intended to discourage anyone from using clearing solutions containing mercury compounds, as these solutions generally yield the best results. However, everyone using potentially dangerous chemical substances should be cognizant of the health and safety hazards associated with each substance used.

MERCURIC NITRATE

A 2% solution of mercuric nitrate provides a very effective clearing solution for removing silver nitrate stains on materials (Fig. 85). The solution should not be used for removing stains on the hands or clothing. A working solution may be prepared by mixing 2 g of mercuric nitrate with 100 ml of distilled wa-

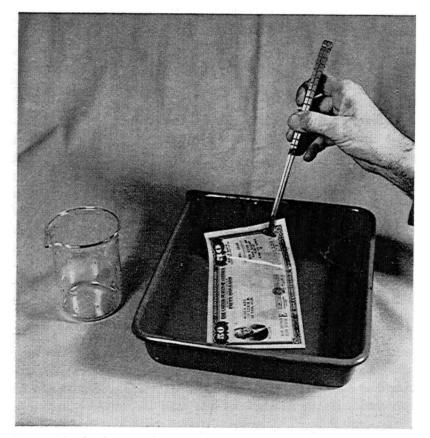

Figure 85. Bleaching a silver nitrate document in a 3% mercuric nitrate solution. Afterward, the document is washed in running water.

ter and adding 2 ml of nitric acid. *Always add acid to water and never water to acid.* If water is added to acid, the acid may boil or spatter onto the skin or in the eyes, causing serious injury. If large amounts of clearing solutions are used on a regular basis by an agency, it may be desirable to prepare 1 l of 20% stock solution, which will make 10 l of a 2% working solution. The stock solution is prepared by dissolving 200 g of mercuric nitrate in 1 l of distilled water and then adding 20 ml of nitric acid. One liter of a 2% working solution may then be prepared by mixing 100 ml of the stock solution with 1 l of distilled water.

MERCURIC CHLORIDE

The preparation of the mercuric chloride clearing solution requires the initial preparation of two separate solutions, which are mixed together to form the final solution. The first solution is prepared by dissolving 5 g of mercuric chloride in 100 ml of distilled water and the second by dissolving 5 g of ammonium chloride in 100 ml of distilled water; the two solutions are then mixed together for the final clearing solution (Moenssens, 1971). The Metropolitan Police Department, Washington, D.C., uses a variation of this solution called Formula X, and it may be used for clearing iodine, ninhydrin, and silver nitrate stains. It is a dangerous solution to use in that mercuric chloride is extremely poisonous.

CLOROX

A solution of the ordinary household bleach Clorox is a satisfactory clearing solution for both ninhydrin and silver nitrate stains. A strong solution is recommended for silver nitrate stains and, if the stains are extremely dark, a full-strength, undiluted solution may be necessary. In cases where the entire document is stained, swabbing may be the preferred method of application to avoid damage to portions of the document bearing questioned writings.

Clorox may be used in some instances to remove silver nitrate stains from clothing by dabbing the stains with the Clorox, rinsing after a few seconds, and then repeating the procedure until the stain is removed. Full-strength Clorox should not be allowed to remain on fabrics too long without rinsing, or the bleach will damage the fabric.

HYPOSODIUM SULFITE

An effective but comparatively slow-acting bleach for removing silver nitrate stains on paper or clothing is a solution of hypo and sodium sulfite. A stained paper should be submerged in the solution until all traces of the stain are removed. The time required may be ten minutes or longer, depending upon the stain. The solution is prepared by mixing 200 g of hypo (sodium thiosulfate) and 140 g of sodium bisulfite in 1 l of distilled water.

REMOVING SILVER NITRATE STAINS FROM THE HANDS

The previously mentioned clearing solutions, particularly those containing mercurial compounds, should not be used to remove silver nitrate stains from the hands or any other area of the body. The best policy for stains on the hands is simply to allow the stains to wear off. However, silver nitrate stains on the hands may be removed by rubbing the stains with a strong acetic acid and then washing with dilute ammonia. *Do not use glacial acetic acid, as this acid causes severe burns on contact with the skin.*

WASHING, IRONING, AND RESTORING

After all visible traces of silver nitrate stains are bleached out thoroughly, the paper is washed exactly like any photographic paper, either in running water or in eight or ten changes of water until the bleaching solution is removed or effectively diluted. If the clearing solution is not removed from a paper, the paper deteriorates, becoming brittle and crumbly.

After a paper or document has been thoroughly cleared and washed, it is ready for ironing (Fig. 86). Ironing with a moderately hot iron is preferable to ordinary air drying in order to remove wrinkles. The secret to good ironing is to avoid overheating and to do the ironing between blotters. An electric iron with a temperature control is desirable. Ironing should not be attempted with the iron in direct contact with the document; in

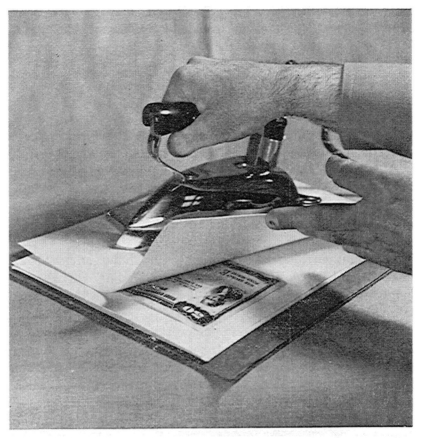

Figure 86. The bleached and washed document is ironed with a warm iron between clean blotters to complete the clearing operation.

addition to possibly scorching the paper, dirt accumulated on the iron may transfer to the paper surface.

Blotters are preferable to lightweight paper, because they absorb moisture or steam lost by the document, and they also prevent overheating. When blotters are used, the job can be done without fear of damage to the paper being restored. While a document is being ironed, the blotters may be lifted and aired or turned over; they become damp during the ironing process, and reversing sides is helpful. The ironing should be done on a table top protected with heavy cardboard or corrugated paper; otherwise, heat and moisture caused by ironing may damage it. When ironing is completed, the document should look almost as it originally appeared.

94

OSMIUM TETROXIDE TECHNIQUES

Osmium tetroxide may be used in latent fingerprint work as either a fuming technique or an aqueous solution that is brushed onto a paper surface. The fuming technique is preferable for documentary evidence, because the papers may then be subsequently processed with ninhydrin and silver nitrate. Osmium tetroxide is similar to iodine in that both substances react with the oils and fatty substances of latent print residue. The osmium tetroxide developed images are, however, gray black in color, and the coloration is permanent. Iodine is more commonly used because of the relatively higher cost of osmium tetroxide.

Several early authorities in fingerprint work referred to an aqueous solution of osmium tetroxide as osmic acid and termed the fuming technique *osmium tetroxide* (Mitchell, 1920). This is not an accurate description, but it does provide a convenient method of distinguishing between the two techniques.

Recommended concentrations for the aqueous solution vary from 1 to 3%. Considering that a 1% solution yields satisfactory results and the expense of osmium tetroxide, there is little advantage in the higher concentrations. A 1% solution is prepared by dissolving one g of osmium tetroxide in 100 ml of distilled water. The solution is then applied to a document by brushing, exercising care to evenly cover the paper. Uneven application may result in light and dark streaks across the latent image. The paper is allowed to dry naturally in direct sunlight. The solution deteriorates with age and exposure and should be stored in dark, well-stopped bottles.

Two methods may be used for fuming with osmium tetroxide: One is to simply boil an aqueous solution within a fuming cabinet, exposing the document to the vapors. The second method is to place the osmium tetroxide on a watch crystal within the fuming cabinet and add a small amount of carbon tetrachloride or ethyl ether. In this latter method, the substance must not be heated, as an explosion may result. When using carbon tetrachloride and osmium tetroxide, an investigator must be careful not to spill the solution on the skin; it is poisonous and is absorbed through the skin.

Osmium tetroxide is impractical as a regular latent fingerprint technique for many reasons; its cost is prohibitive for the results obtained; the fuming technique requires an unusually long period of development (one to twelve hours), compared with other more practical techniques; it is a laboratory technique that cannot be used effectively and conveniently by investigators in the field, and the vapors are highly poisonous.

95

RUTHENIUM TETROXIDE TECHNIQUE

Ruthenium tetroxide was suggested as a latent fingerprint technique for developing latent prints on paper by Mitchell (1920), as the reaction with fatty substances is the same as osmium tetroxide—producing a black compound. However, the substance is only slightly soluble in water, and aqueous solutions require an unusually long period of time to produce even faint images.

Rhodes (1940) recommended ruthenium tetroxide as a fuming technique. The procedure for the fuming technique is given: The crystals are heated over a water bath at a temperature not to exceed 122° F. The crystals must not be heated too rapidly nor the temperature raised too high or an explosion may occur (Kharadory, n.d.).

Considering the safety hazard and the results that may be obtained with other techniques, such as iodine fuming, ruthenium tetroxide does not provide a practical latent fingerprint technique. It is not a technique that should be tried by the average investigator. If it is used, such use should be restricted to the laboratory and by qualified personnel.

96
HYDROGEN FLUORIDE TECHNIQUES

Hydrogen fluoride is one of the most dangerous chemical substances used in latent fingerprint work—techniques involving this substance should be restricted to laboratory use. Even within the laboratory, the use of hydrogen fluoride techniques should be restricted to adequately ventilated areas (chemical exhaust hoods), and the minimum safety precautions should include a rubber apron, face shield, and rubber gloves. Hydrogen fluoride as a vapor, liquid, or solution is extremely dangerous.

Hydrogen fluoride is a gas, and when this gas is dissolved in water, a colorless solution, hydrofluoric acid, is formed. The acid must be kept in wax, rubber, lead, or plastic bottles, as it etches glass. The acid is violently corrosive and causes painful, slow-healing sores, which could result in the loss of fingers or a hand. The vapor causes ulceration of the mucous membranes and may cause chemical pneumonia. The vapors may also attack the eyes, causing inflammation of the membrane covering the surface of the eyeball and the lining of the eyelids. Inhalation of concentrations of the vapor of about 1,500 ppm in air are fatal within a few minutes (*Fires Protection Guide*, 1967).

Hydrofluoric acid may be used to develop latent fingerprints on glass by pouring the acid over the glass surface (O'Hara and Osterburg, 1949). The acid etches the glass, except for those areas protected by the waxy substances of latent print residue. The action of the acid is stopped by flooding the surface with water, and any alkali or alkaline solution stops it immediately (Cooke, 1916).

The vapor technique is considered superior to the acid technique, because there is less likelihood of damage to the ridge detail. One method of hydrogen fluoride fuming is to make a paste of powdered fluorspar and hydrofluoric acid in a rubber container and then place this container in a fuming cabinet or container. Fuming cabinets for hydrogen fluoride may be made from sheets of clear plastic. The vapors of the paste fill the cabinet and etch any glass objects placed within.

Another method of hydrogen fluoride has been described by MacDonell (1960), who suggests pouring a 48% hydrofluoric acid solution into a small polyethylene container and then placing this container and the object to be examined in a larger polyethylene container with a cover. A small paddle is fashioned from a sheet of polyethylene and fitted over a glass rod inserted into the larger container to provide circulation for the vapors. The normal developing time is two to two and one-half hours.

Considering the results obtained with hydrogen fluoride in comparison with other latent fingerprint techniques and the potential hazards involved in its use, hydrogen fluoride has limited application in fingerprint work. Latent prints with a high content of waxy and fatty substances are readily visible on glass and may be photographed without any development necessary. Powder techniques produce excellent results with latent prints on glass surfaces and, if it is determined that fuming is necessary, iodine may be used.

97
CHEMICAL TECHNIQUES FOR BRASS SURFACES

There are four chemical techniques that may be used to develop latent fingerprints on brass surfaces; two are liquid solutions and two are fuming techniques. All may be used after the surface has been examined with brush and powder. If the evidence to be examined is brass cartridge cases, which must also be examined by a firearms examiner, the firearms examiner should be consulted before using any of the techniques. None of the techniques normally destroy the chamber, extractor, or other markings essential for the firearms examiner, but they may darken or lighten the color of the metal to such an extent that the markings cannot be adequately seen for comparison purposes.

If the brass surface has a bright or polished appearance, the liquid chemical solution that produces the best results is the *liquid brass technique.* This technique was developed by Lieber (1959) during an investigation of a crime involving the sale of brass discs as dental gold. The liquid brass solution darkens all areas of brass to which it is applied and which are not protected from the solution by the latent print residue. The ridge details of the latent print, therefore, appear light against a dark background (Fig. 87).

Figure 87. Latent fingerprint on a polished brass surface, developed with the liquid brass technique.

Preparation of the liquid brass solution simply requires mixing copper carbonate (basic cupric carbonate) to excess in ammonium hydroxide. One gram of basic cupric carbonate in 100 ml of ammonium hydroxide provides sufficient solution for considerable usage. The solution remains usable as long as the ammonia does not escape from the solution; therefore, it should be stored in well-stopped bottles. The warmer the solution, the faster it oxidizes and discolors the brass surface. It should not be heated above room temperature, because too fast a reaction may result in damage to the latent print. As soon as a latent print appears, the brass must be rinsed in plain water to halt the reaction between the solution and the brass.

If the brass surface has a dark or heavily oxidized appearance, the liquid chemical solution that produces the best results is *silver nitrate* (Rhodes, 1940). The silver nitrate solution lightens or cleans the brass surface, while darkening the ridge details of the latent print. The ridge details of the latent print, therefore, appear dark against a light background (Fig. 88).

The silver nitrate technique for brass surfaces simply requires dipping the brass into a 3% silver nitrate solution for five to ten seconds or until the entire surface is coated with a light-brown crust. The brass is then removed from the solution, thoroughly rinsed in water, and the light-brown crust is wiped off very gently with soft tissue paper or a piece of cotton.

If the brass surface has a bright or polished appearance, the chemical fuming technique which produces the best results is *hydrogen sulfide fuming.* Hydrogen sulfide fumes darken all brass surfaces exposed to the fumes except those protected by the latent print residue. The ridge details of the latent print appear light against a dark background (Fig. 89).

A small amount of sodium sulfide, about 1 g, is placed in a small glass beaker. The beaker and the object to be examined are both placed in a bell jar or under an upturned wide-mouth jar. Immediately prior to placing the jar over the beaker and object, a few drops of concentrated hydrochloric acid are added to the sodium sulfide. The object may be observed through the glass jar and the brass object removed when the latent print has developed.

Figure 88. Latent fingerprint on an oxidized brass surface, developed with silver nitrate.

A note of caution is necessary when using hydrogen sulfide, as it is a poisonous gas. It should only be used within chemical exhaust hoods with adequate ventilation. This gas has the smell of rotten eggs and is very noticeable, and exposure to even small amounts may produce severe headaches.

The *nitric acid fuming technique* may be used on brass sur-

Figure 89. Latent fingerprint on a polished brass surface, developed with the hydrogen sulfide technique.

faces regardless of whether the surface is polished or oxidized. On dark or oxidized surfaces, the acid fumes lighten the brass surfaces unprotected by latent print residue, and the ridges of the latent print appear dark against a light background (Fig. 90). On polished brass surfaces, the ridge details of the latent

Figure 90. Latent fingerprint on a polished brass surface, developed with the nitric acid fuming technique.

print appear light against a dark background (Fig. 91). This technique has been successfully used on brass cartridge cases, even after the latent prints have been powdered and lifted (Given, 1976).

One method of applying the nitric acid fuming technique is

Figure 91. Latent fingerprint on an oxidized brass surface, developed with the nitric acid fuming technique.

to heat concentrated nitric acid in a flask and expose the brass object directly to the fumes. However, water vapor present in the fumes produces a mottling effect on the brass, which may obscure the ridge details of the latent print. The best method of applying this technique has been described by Given (1976) who recommends constructing an apparatus consisting of two Erlenmeyer flasks, one Erlenmeyer filtering flask, and connecting tubing (Fig. 92).

Figure 92. Example of a nitric acid fuming apparatus. This same apparatus may be used for hydrogen sulfide fuming; however, the operation should be accomplished within a chemical exhaust hood to safely remove the poisonous fumes.

A 20% nitric acid solution is heated in the first flask and piped through tubing to the filtering flask where the water vapor is removed by passing the fumes through a quantity of glass beads. The fumes are then piped through tubing from the filtering flask to a flask in which the brass object has been placed. Normal exposure time to develop latent prints is twenty to forty seconds. However, the object may easily be viewed through the flask and exposure halted whenever development occurs.

A 40% to 60% nitric acid solution was used by early investigators to develop latent prints on practically every type of metal and for wood and paper (Cooke, 1916). The acid discolored or blackened the surfaces, while the latent print residue protected the surface underlying the ridge details. Today, more successful results may be obtained from other techniques. Except as a fuming technique for certain metallic surfaces, nitric acid is not a practical latent fingerprint technique.

Nitric acid is a powerful oxidizing agent, and extreme care should be exercised when handling and using this acid to avoid contact with the skin and to avoid inhalation of the fumes. Use of this technique should be restricted to adequately ventilated chemical exhaust hoods within a laboratory.

The two fuming techniques described above are, perhaps, the best techniques for developing latent fingerprints on brass surfaces. Fuming techniques are less likely to damage latent prints, and the entire process is readily visible, thereby providing greater control over the action of the fumes. After using any of the techniques for brass surfaces, oxidation of the brass by prolonged exposure to air may result in loss of the latent prints developed. After photographing, the latent prints may be protected by lightly spraying with a thin coat of clear lacquer.

98

CALCIUM SULFIDE TECHNIQUE

A significant problem is presented to fingerprint technicians when very dark or black papers are encountered for examination for latent fingerprints. Magnetic powders develop fresh prints, while prints developed by normal chemical techniques, such as iodine fuming, ninhydrin, and silver nitrate, are usually obscured by the background color. One approach to this problem is to use a *calcium sulfide solution* (Robinson, 1935). Latent prints developed with calcium sulfide appear white or light gray in color (Fig. 93). The calcium sulfide reacts with the sodium chloride in latent print residue; however, it is not normally as successful a technique as silver nitrate.

A 1% calcium sulfide solution is prepared by dissolving 1 g of calcium sulfide per 100 ml of distilled water. The solution appears milky in color. The paper to be examined is submerged completely in the solution for thirty to sixty seconds. While the paper is in the solution, the tray must be continuously agitated; otherwise, a white residue is deposited over the entire paper sur-

Figure 93. Latent fingerprint on fibrous black paper, developed with the calcium sulfide technique.

face. Submersion for periods longer than sixty seconds and solutions stronger than a 1% solution also deposit a white residue over the entire paper.

Upon removal from the solution, the paper may be blotted and dried at room temperature for about one hour or it may be dried with an air gun. Heat should not be applied to the paper, such as blowing a stream of hot air over the paper, as this also causes a whitish discoloration of. the entire paper. The white color of the ridge details of the latent prints may not appear very intense to the naked eye but can be photographed satisfactorily.

99

TANNIC ACID TECHNIQUE

Bridges (1942) lists tannic acid as a chemical technique that may be used for developing latent fingerprints on paper. The acid reacts with the albumin, simple proteins, present in latent print residue, coagulating the albumin and producing dark-gray lines. A 10% solution is used; it is prepared by dissolving 10 g of tannic acid in 100 ml of distilled water. Tannic acid is not a practical technique for developing latent prints on paper; far better results are to be obtained with the ninhydrin technique.

100

INK, DYE, AND STAIN TECHNIQUES

The use of inks to develop latent fingerprints on paper was suggested by early authorities (Forgeot, 1891, and Faulds, 1905), and the use of dyes and biological stains has also been tried (O'Neill, 1937). Inks, dyes, and stains are not practical latent fingerprint techniques, as their use generally results in damage to documents with little success in developing latent prints. However, in some instances, these techniques may be used to provide greater contrast for oily or greasy prints, which are, at least, partially visible. Every effort should be made to photograph even these partially visible prints prior to applying any latent technique. However, an oily or greasy print may often appear partially visible to the naked eye when viewed with oblique lighting but does not record photographically and disappears when viewed through a magnifier.

There are two methods by which inks, dyes, and stains may develop latent fingerprints on paper: The latent print residue may repel the solution and the paper is discolored, or specific substances in the latent print residue may combine chemically with the solution and retain coloration when the excess solution is rinsed off of the paper.

Inks generally provide the least desirable results of all the techniques that may be used in this category. The greatest disadvantage of inks is the number and types of inks available and, therefore, the inability to predict the behavior of an ink with latent print residue—whether or not the ink will be repelled by the residue. The theory behind the use of inks is that the ink is repelled by the oils and fatty substances of latent print residue while the paper is discolored. This is not always the case; for example, black drawing ink diluted in water is absorbed by the latent print residue. If the paper is rinsed immediately, the paper appears clear and the ridge details of the latent print black.

Mitchell (1920) suggested the use of a dilute solution of osmic pyrogallate, which is at first violet but almost immediately becomes greenish blue and, when applied to paper, gives a rich violet black coloration. The solution is prepared by adding 2 ml of a 1% osmic acid solution to 2 ml of distilled water and then dissolving 0.05 g pyrogallic acid (pyrogallol or 1,2,3-trihydroxy-benzene). The solution should be brushed over the paper with one broad sweep of a soft camel's hair brush.

Dyes and biological stains may also be used to develop latent fingerprints on paper when there is an indication of greasy or oily fingerprints. Water-soluble dyes and stains produce the best results with less damage and diffusion of ridge details. An example of a dye that may be used is Rit Liquid Dye®, manufactured by Best Foods and available in almost all retail department and food stores. It is a textile dye which is poured over the surface of the paper being examined; the paper is then immediately rinsed in running water to remove the excess dye. The paper remains clear, and the latent print retains the color of the dye.

Aniline blue, eosin, and basic fuchsin are examples of biological stains that may be used to develop latent prints on paper. These stains must be rinsed off immediately with running water and stain the latent image. However, like inks, the staining solution must be diluted; otherwise, the entire paper surface may be discolored.

101

TECHNIQUES FOR LATENT PRINTS IN BLOOD

Prior to applying any chemical techniques for developing latent prints to suspected blood stains, the evidence should first be examined by a serologist (*see* Sec. 44). This policy is advisable even in cases where the identification and grouping of the blood stains to be examined is of secondary importance to any latent fingerprints. Many substances may give the appearance of blood and, without confirmation that a particular stain is in fact blood, the application for chemical techniques to enhance bloody prints may result in complete loss of any possible fingerprint evidence. Further, even if a latent print is developed and identified, only a serologist can testify that the print was in blood.

Photography is another aspect that must be considered prior to applying chemical techniques to blood stains. The size, shape, and appearance of the stain should be recorded photographically prior to the application of any technique that may alter the stain. Quite often, ridge details of latent prints that cannot be seen with the naked eye can be visualized in a photograph by proper film selection or the use of filters. Whenever a latent print is suitable for identification purposes without treatment by latent fingerprint techniques, it is usually best to proceed without resorting to these techniques. Consideration of all possible factors and examinations regarding bloody prints may prove to be of extreme importance during any subsequent legal proceedings, particularly when questions may arise regarding the completeness or thoroughness of the investigation.

All bloods consist of two principal parts: The liquid intercellular material, the plasma, and the cells suspended in it. The chemical composition of blood is a complex and extensive mixture of inorganic and organic substances of which only two are of interest insofar as latent fingerprint techniques are concerned. Blood plasma contains a higher percentage of proteins than sweat. Therefore, the ninhydrin technique may be used for bloody prints on a porous surface. The other chemical techniques for bloody prints are modifications of chemical tests for the activity of iron porphyrin enzymes, peroxidases, which catalyze reactions between hydrogen peroxide and other substances.

THE NINHYDRIN TECHNIQUE

Ninhydrin is the best technique available for developing latent prints, including bloody prints, on porous surfaces—paper, cardboard, unfinished wood, surfaces painted with an absorbent water-based paint, and bloody prints on cloth. A regular ninhydrin solution may be used and applied by spraying, swabbing, or dipping. No additional or special procedures are required, except for prints on cloth. Better results may normally be expected with ninhydrin than with other techniques reacting solely to blood, because ninhydrin develops both the ridge details due to blood on the fingers and those deposited by sweat. Frequently, because of insufficient blood on the fingers or some other failure to transfer a complete latent image onto the receiving surface, bloody prints may not be sufficient for identification purposes.

When examining cloth for bloody fingerprints, it is necessary to fix the prints onto the surface of the cloth by running a solution of 70% ethyl alcohol over the surface and allowing it to dry. This solution is prepared by mixing 30 ml absolute ethyl alcohol with 70 ml distilled water. After applying the alcohol solution, the cloth must be thoroughly dried before applying the ninhydrin solution. This fixing is necessary to prevent the ridge details from running and blurring the image. The ethyl alcohol solution precipitates the protein material from the blood plasma and binds it to the fabric.

Bloody prints developed with ninhydrin generally have a more intensive coloration and appear much darker than those developed solely by the reaction between ninhydrin and the amino acids of sweat.

LEUCOMALACHITE GREEN TECHNIQUE

Leucomalachite green is a sensitive reagent which has been used for a considerable time by criminalists as a chemical test for blood (Kirk, 1953). This colorless leuco base of the dye malachite green, produces an intense malachite green coloration when oxidized in the presence of peroxidase as a catalyst. Bloody fingerprints and heavy deposits of blood appear a dark greenish blue not more than a minute after application, and the entire treated surface is stained a light green.

The stock solution for this technique is prepared by dissolving 1 g of leucomalachite green in 70 ml of ether and adding 1 ml (10 drops) of glacial acetic acid. A working solution is prepared for immediate use by placing a small portion, about 5 to 10 ml, in a test tube and adding a few drops of 25- to 30-volume hydrogen peroxide (Svensson and Wendel, 1965). The solution is applied by allowing it to flow over the area being examined while a stream of heated air is directed against the treated surface. All latent prints developed should be photographed as soon as possible.

Synonyms for leucomalachite green are: 4,4′-bisdimethylamino-triphenylmethane; 4,4′-tetramethyldiaminotriphenylmethane; and p,p′-benzylidenebis-N,N-dimethylaniline.

BENZIDINE TECHNIQUE

Benzidine has been identified as a carcinogenic substance that may be absorbed through the skin and may cause cancer of the bladder. Exposure times as short as 131 days have been demonstrated to be associated with the subsequent development of cancer, although the usual latent period is generally accepted to be fifteen to twenty-five years.

The *Federal Register* (Jan. 29, 1974) established guidelines for specific safeguards that must be made when exposed to concentrations of benzidine of 0.1 percent or more. The concentration used in latent fingerprint techniques is about ten times that amount. The safeguards provide that use of benzidine in concentrations greater than 0.1 percent must be with either a closed-system operation or an isolated system.

The closed-system operation is one wherein the benzidine is stored and used only within a regulated area with filtered ventilation. Only authorized personnel may enter the room, and they must wear protective outer clothing, which must be discarded upon exit. They must wash their hands, forearms, face, and neck immediately upon exit. The isolated system is a glovebox with air locks for placing and removing items within the box. The problem exists, in both systems, that once an item is treated with benzidine it is contaminated and, therefore, must be placed within a sealed container when removed from the system.

The benzidine test, although not specific, is considered by criminalists to be the most positive chemical test yet discovered for blood (Culliford, 1971). Although there are potential health hazards associated with the use of this chemical, it does provide the best technique available for developing and enhancing bloody fingerprints on nonporous or nonabsorbant surfaces (Fig. 94). All nonporous surfaces that are to be examined with this technique must first be treated with a 70% solution of ethyl alcohol to fix the impressions, in the same manner as described for the use of ninhydrin to develop blood prints on cloth.

Bloody fingerprints developed with benzidine appear blue or bluish green in color with a light-brown discoloration of the background. Background discoloration is dependent upon the amount of blood present on the background surface, but any

Figure 94. Latent partial palmprint on a knife handle, developed with the benzidine technique.

discoloration is generally negligible in comparison to that of leucomalachite green. The background of a print located on top of a blood smear is naturally discolored to a greater degree than those which are not, but the degree of development may be controlled by immediately washing the benzidine solution off of the surface when it appears that sufficient development has been achieved.

The benzidine-free base technique for developing latent fingerprints in blood was developed by Conley and Andes (1959), and its preparation and use has been best described by Moenssens (1971).

A stock solution is prepared by making a saturated solution of benezidine in 70% ethyl alcohol and allowing this solution to stand for at least one hour to insure total saturation. This saturated solution may be easily prepared without reference to exact weights and temperature by simply adding small amounts of benzidine to the alcohol solution until the solution does not dissolve the benzidine, or 0.5 g of benzidine may be added per 100 ml of the ethyl alcohol solution. After a saturated solution is obtained, it is mixed with an equal volume of 70% ethyl alcohol; this final solution provides the stock solution. The stock solution should be stored in a dark-brown bottle and may be stored as long as a month. However, it is not advisable to keep the solution in excess of a week for best results.

Immediately prior to use, three parts of the stock solution are mixed with one part of 20- to 30-volume hydrogen peroxide. The solution may be applied by dipping, spraying, or by pouring it over the surface. Due to the potential health hazard of the benzidine, spraying does not appear to be a wise choice as a method of application. After the prints develop, the surface is immediately washed with cold water and air dried. Any latent prints developed should be photographed as soon as possible, because the prints may fade in less than half an hour, although they have also been known to last for weeks.

Nariyuki, Ueda, and Sasaki (1971) developed a method for spraying benzidine solutions, the *blood spray technique,* which also provides an excellent means for lifting any latent prints developed. The solution is prepared by dissolving 1 g of benzidine in 10 ml of glacial acetic acid, allowing the solution to stand for a few minutes for the undissolved particles of benzidine to settle, and then mixing 1 ml of the supernatant fluid (liquid portion at the top only) of this solution with 20 ml of collodion ether solution. The 0.5 ml (5 drops) of 30-volume hydrogen peroxide is added. The solution is well stirred and placed within a spray bottle for application. Aerosol spray kits generally used for thin-layer chromatography are well suited for use with this technique.

If the investigator wishes to lift any impressions that may be developed with this technique, the collodion solution is increased from 2.5 to 5%. After the sprayed solution has dried, the impressions are lifted with regular lifting tape.

Harrell (1973) developed a modification to the blood spray technique, a means for using the technique at crime scenes without requiring chemical apparatus or equipment. Harrell's approach is to premeasure all the necessary ingredients and package each separately for immediate mixing and use. The solution used in this technique differs from that previously described for a blood spray and requires the preparation of two separate stock solutions, one a collodion and the other a buffer.

A dilute stock solution of collodion is prepared by mixing 5 ml of collodion in 2 ml of ethyl alcohol and then adding 20 ml of ethyl ether. The buffer solution is prepared by dissolving 10 g of sodium acetate in 100 ml of distilled water and then adding 86 ml of glacial acetic acid. Both of these stock solutions should be stored under refrigeration, and the collodion solution is highly inflammable.

The working spray solution is prepared by dissolving 50 mg of benzidine and 100 mg of sodium perborate in 2 ml of the acetate buffer. One ml of the supernatant fluid of this solution is then mixed with 20 ml of the diluted collodion solution and sprayed. Stored in their separate containers, the reagents may last for periods estimated up to six months.

The continuing availability of benzidine for purchase may be limited. Due to increased federal regulation of this substance, many chemical supply companies have stopped stocking. Synonyms for benzidine are: benzidin; 4,4'-biphenyldiamine; 4,4'-diaminodiphenyl; p-diaminodiphenyl; 4,4'-diphenylenediamine; CI Azoic Diazo Component 112; and Fast Corinth Base B.

LUMINOL TECHNIQUE

Luminol is a highly sensitive chemical test for blood which produces a chemiluminescence of fifteen minutes duration or more. Old bloodstains react more strongly to this technique than fresh ones. However, if it is known that the stains are fresh, the surface to be examined may be sprayed with 1% to 2% hydrochloric acid to partially decompose the blood (Kirk, 1953). Except for the ninhydrin technique, use of the luminol technique does not preclude subsequent use of other chemical techniques for blood.

The standard luminol spray reagent is an aqueous solution prepared by dissolving 0.1 g of luminol and 5 g of sodium carbonate in 100 ml of distilled water. Immediately prior to use, 0.7 g of sodium perborate is added to the solution. Zweidinger, Lytle, and Pitt (1973) developed a modified solution using 95% ethyl alcohol as the solvent and making the solution 0.02 M in potassium hydroxide. This solution produces a bright luminescence for several minutes with lower background than that of the aqueous solution.

Several disadvantages are associated with luminol as a latent fingerprint technique: A darkened area is required, the duration of chemiluminescence is limited, and photographic equipment must be set up and ready for use prior to its application.

102

FLUOROGENIC CHEMICAL TECHNIQUES

Fluorescent chemical techniques are, at this time, still in the research and developmental stage insofar as applications as a latent fingerprint technique. Although a satisfactory technique has not yet been developed, there are significant indications that fluorogenic reagents hold considerable promise as a means of developing latent fingerprints (Kerns and Turbyfill, 1976).

The fluorogenic reagents are themselves nonfluorescent but react with primary amino acids to form highly fluorescent products that give an intense blue fluorescence under long-wave ultraviolet radiation. The reagents are about 100 times more sensitive to amino acids than ninhydrin, but their greatest advantage as a latent fingerprint technique is their use on multicolored and black paper surfaces.

The primary obstacle to developing a satisfactory latent fingerprint technique using fluorogenic reagents is determining an appropriate buffer solution, as amino acid fluorescence is generally maximum at pH 9. The use of 0.2 M sodium borate as a buffer, used by biochemists, is not satisfactory in latent fingerprint work, as the buffer tends to "bleed" or spread the amino acids on the paper, thereby causing a blurring of ridge details.

Ohki (1976) has reported the successful development of latent fingerprints using the fluorogenic reagent fluorescamine, the trivial name for the compound 4-phenylspiro[furan-2(3H),1′-phthalan]-3,3′-dione, which is marketed under the trade name Fluram® by Roche Diagnostics, Nutley, New Jersey. Ohki's experience is slightly at variance with that of other researchers in that he reported a white yellow rather than a blue fluorescence.

Ohki's technique is to dissolve 15 mg of fluorescamine in 100 ml of acetone and, immediately prior to use, add 0.1 ml of triethylamine. The solution is sprayed onto the paper surface, allowed to dry at room temperature for a few minutes, and the latents are then viewed and photographed under long-wave ultraviolet light. The reaction time between fluorescamine and amino acids occurs with a half-time of milliseconds, and the fluorescence may continue for several hours, although Ohki reported that the fluorescence was stable for a few days.

Another fluorgenic reagent that may hold promise as a potential latent fingerprint technique is o-Phthaladehyde, which is marketed under the trademark Fluorōpa® by the Durrum Corporation, Palo Alto, California. When using fluorogenic reagents, care should be exercised to keep the reagents free from contamination; laboratory equipment must be clean and the room air free from smoke.

103

AUTORADIOGRAPHY

Autoradiography is simply the use of radioactive compounds or elements to develop and record latent fingerprints on surfaces such as paper and fabrics. The radioactive materials react with substances in latent print residue, and the latent print image is recorded by bringing the treated surface in direct contact with a photographic film. Such techniques are not within the capabilities of the average investigator or police laboratory; their use is restricted to highly specialized laboratories (Moenssens, 1971).

The mechanism of the reaction between radioactive substances and latent print residue varies according to the nature of the substance used and may involve either chemical reaction, absorption, and exchange or activation of atoms (Takeuchi, 1959). An aqueous solution of radioactive silver, 110 silver nitrate, for example, produces a chemical reaction. Other radioactive materials that have been tried with this technique are carbon-14 formaldehyde, carbon-14 stearic acid (Takeuchi, 1959), and sulphur-35 dioxide (Godsell, 1973).

Autoradiography is still an experimental technique having little or limited practical application in fingerprint work. It is a time-consuming technique requiring exposure periods between the radioactive materials and the evidentiary item from thirty minutes to twelve hours and fifteen hours to one week for the photographic recording (Grant, et al., 1963).

Ordinary x-ray plates may be used for recording the latent image. The treated surface is placed in direct contact with the film, and because of the long exposure time required, both are placed within a cassette or similar light-tight container. Kodak fine-grain autoradiographic stripping plates, 4¾-by-6½ inches, may be used for small surfaces, and these plates may be used as negatives for photographic printing.

QUESTIONS

TRUE-FALSE QUESTIONS

1. When determining which technique to use, the chemical composition of the latent print is not normally one of the factors considered (Sec. 88).
2. The silver nitrate technique reacts with the salts in latent print residue (Sec. 88).
3. The ninhydrin technique reacts with the amino acids of latent print residue (Sec. 88).
4. Chemical solutions used in latent fingerprint work are not difficult to prepare (Sec. 89).
5. Successful results in developing latent fingerprints with chemical techniques are dependent upon unequivocal accuracy in the preparation of solutions used (Sec. 89).
6. Ninhydrin is the most consistently successful technique available for developing latent fingerprints on paper (Sec. 90).
7. Papers with a glutinous sizing may discolor when treated with ninhydrin solution (Sec. 90).
8. It is not necessary to mask out questioned writings on documents to be treated with ninhydrin if the writings have been adequately photographed (Sec. 90).
9. Recommended postprocessing treatment of documents processed with ninhydrin includes both heat and humidity (Sec. 90).
10. As a general rule, it is not recommended that ninhydrin stains be cleared from documents (Sec. 91).
11. Ninhydrin clearing solutions will not damage inked writings (Sec. 91).
12. Silver nitrate stains are not particularly difficult to remove from the skin and clothing (Sec. 92).
13. The most commonly used silver nitrate solution is an aqueous solution (Sec. 92).
14. Alcoholic solutions of silver nitrate may be used to develop latent prints on waxed papers (Sec. 92).

15. When a paper is removed from a silver nitrate solution for the purpose of developing the images with light, the excess solution must be removed from the paper (Sec. 92).

16. The longer silver nitrate stains remain on a paper and are exposed to light, the lighter they become (Sec. 93).

17. Always add acid to water and never water to acid (Sec. 93).

18. Osmium tetroxide may be used as a solution or as a fuming technique (Sec. 94).

19. Ruthenium tetroxide is not a practical latent fingerprint technique (Sec. 95).

20. Hydrogen fluoride, as a vapor, liquid, or solution, is extremely dangerous to use (Sec. 96).

21. Nitric acid fuming may be used to develop latent prints on glass surfaces, as it etches the glass not protected by the latent print residue (Sec. 97).

22. Liquid brass is the only technique available for developing latent prints on brass (Sec. 97).

23. Inks provide a very effective and desirable technique for developing latent prints on paper (Sec. 100).

24. Ninhydrin is the best technique for developing bloody prints on porous surfaces, such as paper and cloth (Sec. 101).

25. Benzidine has been identified as a carcinogenic substance which may be absorbed through the skin (Sec. 101).

26. The federal government has established guidelines for specific safeguards that must be made when exposed to concentrations of benzidine of 0.1% or more (Sec. 101).

27. The blood spray technique provides a means for both developing and lifting bloody fingerprints (Sec. 101).

28. Luminol reacts with blood to produce a chemiluminescence (Sec. 101).

29. Autoradiography is a time-consuming technique having compounds and elements to develop and record latent fingerprints (Sec. 103).

30. Autoradiography is a time-consuming technique having little or limited practical application (Sec. 103).

COMPLETION QUESTIONS

31. The primary source of oils and fats found in perspiration is sebum, a secretion of the . . . . glands (Sec. 88).

32. If all solutions prepared within an agency are of the same quality, the results obtained with the solutions will be more . . . . (Sec. 89).

33. In a solution of one substance in another, the dissolved substance is called the solute. The substance in which the solute is dissolved is called the . . . . (Sec. 89).

34. The concentrations of most chemical solutions used in latent fingerprint work are expressed in terms of . . . . (Sec. 89).

35. No single latent fingerprint technique has . . . . application under all circumstances (Sec. 90).

36. Ninhydrin should be used . . . . the iodine technique and . . . . the silver nitrate technique (Sec. 90).

37. Of all the solvents used for ninhydrin solutions, ... , ... , and . . . . result in the greatest damage to inks (Sec. 90).

38. The development of latent prints with ninhydrin may be accelerated by using an . . . . (Sec. 90).

39. An investigator may determine that it is necessary to remove ninhydrin stains, either to . . . . excessive discoloration or to . . . . deposits of ninhydrin crystals from the document (Sec. 91).

40. . . . . provides the simplest and most effective ninhydrin clearing solution (Sec. 91).

41. Silver nitrate reacts with the salts of latent print residue, ... and . . . . chloride (Sec. 92).

42. Generally, ...% to . . . .% silver nitrate solutions are used in fingerprint work (Sec. 92).

43. Silver nitrate solutions may be acidified by adding 1 ml of . . . . or concentrated . . . . for 100 ml of solution (Sec. 92).

44. A . . . .% solution of mercuric nitrate provides a very ef-

fective clearing solution for silver nitrate stains on materials (Sec. 93).

45. Osmium tetroxide is .... as a regular latent fingerprint technique (Sec. 94).

46. Hydrogen fluoride .... glass (Sec. 96).

47. Hydrogen fluoride is considered superior to hydrofluoric acid because there is less likelihood of .... to the ridge detail (Sec. 96).

48. .... fuming is, perhaps, the most preferable chemical technique for developing latent fingerprints on brass (Sec. 97).

49. Prior to applying any chemical techniques for developing latent prints to suspected blood stains, the evidence should first be examined by a .... (Sec. 101).

50. When examining cloth for bloody fingerprints, it is necessary to .... the prints onto the surface of the cloth by running a solution of 70% .... over the surface and allowing it to dry (Sec. 101).

REFERENCES

Bridges, Burtis C.: *Practical Fingerprinting.* New York, Funk and Wagnalls, 1942.

Brownlie, A. R., and D. Patterson: "Crime detection at a premium," *Journal of the Forensic Science Society.* vol. 2 (1962), p. 77.

"Chemical development of latent impressions," *FBI Law Enforcement Bulletin,* vol. 42 (Aug., 1973), p. 9.

Conley, B. J., and J. F. Andes: "A test for bloody latent palm prints and finger prints," *Fingerprint and Identification Magazine.* vol. 40 (Mar., 1959), p. 16.

Conway, J. V. P.: *Fingerprints and Documents.* Paper presented at joint meeting of the American Society of Questioned Document Examiners and the Crime Detection Laboratories, Royal Canadian Mounted Police, Ottawa, August 20, 1965.

Cooke, Thomas G.: *A Study of Finger Prints: Their Classification and Uses.* Chicago, University of Applied Science, 1916.

Crown, D. A.: *Non-polar Solution of Ninhydrin for Developing Latent Fingerprints.* Paper presented to California Association of Criminalists, Redwood City, October 26, 1963.

Culliford, B. J.: *The Examination and Typing of Bloodstains in the Crime Laboratory.* Washington, D.C., Law Enforcement Assistance Administration, 1971.

Cuthertson, F.: *The chemistry of fingerprints.* A.W.R.E. Report 013/69. Aldermaston, U.K., United Kingdom Atomic Energy Authority, 1969.

"Developing latents made in blood," *Fingerprint and Identification Magazine.* vol. 43 (Nov., 1961), p. 11.

Eriksson, S. A.: "Ninhydrinmethoden for framkallning av fingeravtryck paa papper," *Nordisk Kriminalteknisk Tidskrift.* vol. 31 (1961), p. 81.

Fargeot, R.: "Étude medico-legale des empreintes peu visibles ou invisibles et revelees par des procedes speciaux," *Archives d'Anthropologie-Criminologie.* vol. 6 (1891), p. 387.

Faulds, Henry: *Guide to Finger-Print Identification.* Hanley, U.K., Wood Mitchell, 1905.

39 Fed. Reg. 3779 (1974).

"Finger print detection by chemical means," *Scientific American.* vol. 109 (Nov., 1913), p. 367.

Fire Protection Guide on Hazardous Materials, 2nd ed. Boston, MA, National Fire Protection Association, 1967.

Forgeot, Rene: *Les Empreintes Latentes.* Lyon, A. Rey, 1891.

Foster, H. H.: "Ninhydrin development of latent impressions," *Fingerprint and Identification Magazine.* vol. 57 (June, 1976), p. 3.

Fritz, H., and H. Jordan: "Combination of U.V. irradiation and ninhydrin method for fixation of fingerprints," *Archiv fur Kriminologie.* vol. 145 (1970), p. 163.

Ganson, A.: "Latent fingerprints on paper and fabrics," *Identification News.* vol. 23 (Feb., 1973), p. 3.

Given, B. W.: "Latent fingerprints on cartridges and expended cartridge casings," *Journal of Forensic Sciences.* vol. 21 (1976), p. 587.

Gidion, H. M., and G. Epstein: "Latent impressions on questioned documents," *Police Chief.* (Aug., 1972), p. 30.

Godsell, J.: "Fingerprint techniques," *Journal of the Forensic Science Society.* vol. 3 (1963), p. 79.

Grant, R. L., F. L. Hudson, and J. A. Hockey: "A new method of detecting fingerprints on paper," *Journal of the Forensic Science Society.* vol. 4 (1963), p. 85.

Green, W. D.: "Modified chemical and physical methods for the detection of latent fingerprints," *Criminologist.* vol. 5 (May-Aug., 1970), p. 54.

Harrell, J. R.: "Recovering the bloody fingerprint," *Criminologist.* vol. 8 (Summer, 1973), p. 49.

Hathaway, J. A., and J. A. Thomasino: *Interim Report: Carcinogens and Hazardous Chemicals, U.S. Army Criminal Investigation Laboratory,"* Occupational Health/Industrial Hygiene Special Study No. 32-1308-

77. Aberdeen Proving Ground, MD, U.S. Army Environmental Hygiene Agency, 1976.

Kerns, J. A., and R. T. Turbyfill: Fluorescamine. Personal communication. September, 1976.

Kharadory, M. N.: *Law and Technique Relating to Finger Prints and Suspect Documents.* Allahabad, India, Central Law Agency, n.d.

Kirby, F. J.: "Use of chemicals in developing latent prints," *Identification News.* vol. 18 (1968), p. 3.

————: "Don't neglect the silver nitrate process," *Fingerprint and Identification Magazine.* vol. 53 (Dec., 1971), p. 13.

Kirby, F. J., and R. D. Olsen: "A modified silver nitrate formula for intensifying faint ninhydrin prints," *Fingerprint and Identification Magazine.* vol. 54 (Mar., 1973), p. 3.

Kirk, Paul L.: *Crime Investigation: Physical Evidence and the Police Laboratory.* New York, Interscience, 1953, chap. 28.

Kirkland, R.: "Use of ninhydrin spray is described," *Fingerprint and Identification Magazine.* vol. 53 (Mar., 1972), p. 6.

Lenental, E., and A. Szuchnik: "Detection of fingerprints by autoradiography," *International Journal of Applied Radiation and Isotopes.* vol. 15 (1964), p. 373.

Lesk, J. A.: "Post-processing humidification in the development of latent fingerprints with ninhydrin," *Newsletter, American Academy of Forensic Sciences.* Rockville, MD, January, 1971, p. 7.

Lieber, Z.: "Developing prints on brass," *Fingerprint and Identification Magazine.* vol. 41 (Oct., 1959), p. 16.

Linde, H. G.: "Latent fingerprints by a superior ninhydrin method," *Journal of Forensic Sciences.* vol. 20 (1975), p. 581.

MacDonell, H. L.: "The use of hydrogen fluoride in the development of latent fingerprints found on glass surfaces," *Journal of Criminal Law, Criminology and Police Science.* vol. 51 (1960), p. 465.

————: "Recent developments in processing latent fingerprints," *Fingerprint and Identification Magazine.* vol. 44 (Aug., 1962), p. 3.

————: "Recent advancements in the processing of latent fingerprints," *Identification News.* vol. 18 (Jan., 1968), p. 4.

McLaughlin, A. R.: "Developing latent prints on absorbent surfaces," *Finingerprint and Identification Magazine.* vol. 42 (Feb., 1961), p. 3.

————: "Chemicals and their application for developing latent prints," *Fingerprint and Identification Magazine.* vol. 43 (July, 1961), p. 3.

Moenssens, A. A.: *Fingerprint Techniques.* New York, Chilton, 1971.

Mooney, D. G.: "Development of latent fingerprints and palmprints by ninhydrin," *Identification News.* vol. 16 (Aug.-Sept., 1966), p. 4.

————: "Additional notes on the use of ninhydrin," *Identification News.* vol. 23 (Sept., 1973), p. 9.

Morris, J. R., and G. C. Goode: "NFN—An improved ninhydrin reagent for detection of latent fingerprints," *Police Research Bulletin.* (Autumn, 1974), p. 45.

Moretti, C.: "Nouvelle methode pour reveler les empreintes digitales," *Revue Internationale de Criminologie de Police Technique.* vol. 19 (1965), p. 63.

Nariyuki, H., K. Ueda, and T. Sasaki: "A new method for the detection of bloody latent finger prints," *Fingerprint and Identification Magazine.* vol. 52 (June, 1971), p. 3.

"New method develops years-old fingerprints," *FBI Law Enforcement Bulletin.* vol. 23 (Nov., 1954), p. 14.

Nicoletti, R. E.: *Process for Developing Latent Prints on Dynamite Wrappers.* Interdepartmental correspondence, Denver Police Department, Mar. 25, 1974.

Oden, S., and B. von Hofsten: "Detection of fingerprints by the ninhydrin reaction," *Nature.* vol. 173 (1954), p. 449.

O'Hara, Charles E.: *Fundamentals of Criminal Investigation.* Springfield, Thomas, 1970, Chaps. 7, 31, 32, 33.

O'Hara, Charles E., and James W. Osterburg: *An Introduction to Criminalistics.* New York, Macmillan, 1949.

Ohki, H.: "A new detection method of latent fingerprints with fluorescamine," *Reports of the National Research Institute of Police Science.* vol. 29 (May, 1976), p. 46.

Olsen, R. D.; "The chemical composition of palmar sweat," *Fingerprint and Identification Magazine.* vol. 53 (Apr., 1972), p. 3.

————: "Fingerprint techniques (health and safety hazards)," *The Detective.* vol. 5 (Summer, 1975), p. 20.

O'Neill, M. E.: "The development of fingerprints on paper," *Journal of Criminal Law, Criminology and Police Science.* vol. 28 (1937), p. 432.

Rhodes, H. T. F.: *Forensic Chemistry.* New York, Chemical Pub. Co., 1940.

Robinson, Henry M.: *Science Catches the Criminal.* New York, Blue Ribbon Books, 1935.

Seaborn, J. T.: *Report of Industrial Hygiene Survey, U.S. Army Criminal Investigation Laboratory, Fort Gordon, Georgia.* Department of Environmental Engineering, U.S. Army Medical Laboratory, Fort McPherson, Georgia, 1974.

Silliman, J. R.: "Developing latent fingerprints: the ninhydrin process," *Forensic Science Digest* (USAFOSI). vol. 2 (Dec., 1975), p. 118.

Shulenberger, W. A.: "Present status of the ninhydrin process for developing latent fingerprints," *Identification News.* vol. 13 (Mar., 1963), p. 9.

Speaks, H. A.: "The use of ninhydrin in the development of latent finger prints," *Fingerprint and Identification Magazine.* vol. 45 (Mar., 1964), p. 11.

———: "Ninhydrin prints from rubber gloves," *Fingerprint and Identification Magazine.* vol. 48 (Sept., 1966), p. 3.

———: "Ninhydrin development of latent prints," *Fingerprint and Identification Magazine.* vol. 52 (Aug., 1970), p. 14.

Takeuchi, T.: "The application of autoradiography to the detection of latent finger prints," *Fingerprint and Identification Magazine.* vol. 40 (May, 1959), p. 3.

Turbyfill, R. T.: "The development of latent fingerprints using non-flammable ninhydrin mixture (London Method)," *Crime Laboratory Digest.* Issue 76-1 (Jan., 1976), p. 6.

Wagenarr: "Method of rendering latent fingerprints visible," *Analyst.* vol. 61 (1936), p. 131.

Watling, W. J.: "Process for developing latent fingerprints on cow horns," *Identification News.* vol. 24 (June, 1974), p. 3.

Zweidinger, R. A., L. T. Lytle, and C. G. Pitt: "Photography of bloodstains visualized by luminol," *Journal of Forensic Sciences.* vol. 18 (1973), p. 296.

Chapter VIII

Latent Fingerprint Electronic Techniques

104

ELECTRONICS

THE TERM *electronics* may be technically defined as the science concerned with devices involving the flow of electrons within a vacuum, gas, or solid. However, the term is generally used to distinguish between equipment or systems in which electric circuits make use primarily of electronic devices instead of relays and similar electromechanical devices.

Electronics is a comparatively new and fast-growing field that has already had a considerable impact on modern life. Almost every segment of modern industrial society makes extensive use of electronics—communications, transportation, construction, manufacturing, both the life and physical sciences, and even leisure activities. Electronics brings music and pictures into homes, sets the shutter speed or f-stops of automatic cameras, controls the speed of power tools, and regulates the fuel-air mixture in some automobile engines. Significantly, many of the recent advances in the life and physical sciences could not have been possible without analytical electronic devices and laboratory automation.

It is not surprising that a technology which has had so great an influence on the world today should also have applications in fingerprint work. Facsimile transmission of fingerprints and the use of electronic computers to file and search fingerprint records are two applications of electronics in fingerprint work that have gained wide recognition. A significant amount of research has also been expended to develop computers that identify latent fingerprints by comparison with files of inked impressions. Less generally recognized are the potential uses of electronics in the detection and development of latent fingerprints and their application to enhance the images of latent prints developed by conventional techniques.

The purpose of this chapter is to merely acquaint the reader with various electronic techniques and their actual and potential applications in fingerprint work. A more detailed treatment of these techniques would not be within the scope of this book and could be the subject of a separate text. Furthermore, many electronic techniques are not within the capabilities of the average law enforcement agency. However, all investigators should be aware of these techniques and that they may be available in many large crime laboratories or identification bureaus.

105

X-RAY TECHNIQUES

X-ray techniques employ essentially powder techniques, as finely powdered lead, 200- to 400-mesh, is used to develop the latent prints, and x-rays then used to visually record the latent print image. X-ray techniques are not normally within the capabilities of most law enforcement agencies and investigators due to the expense of the equipment, the highly technical nature of the field, and the specialized training required for safe and effective operation of x-ray machines.

X-rays are electromagnetic radiations of extremely short wavelength, extending from the extreme ultraviolet into the gamma-ray region of the spectrum. X-rays are produced in an x-ray tube by bombarding a metal target, usually tungsten, with a stream of electrons accelerated to high energy. The energy of the x-ray is determined by the energy of the electrons, which, in turn, is determined by the voltage applied across the tube. The voltage applied to an x-ray tube is expressed in terms of kilovolts (kV) and the amount of current is measured in milliamperes (ma). Therefore, the energy of x-rays is expressed in terms of the voltage and current settings of the x-ray apparatus.

At low voltages, 5 kV to 35 kV, x-rays have low energy and little penetrating power. These low-energy x-rays are referred to as *soft* x-rays. X-rays produced by medium voltages, 35 kV to 150 kV, are used for medical diagnostic purposes. At higher voltages, 150 kV to 500 kV, x-rays possess greater energy and have much more penetrating power. X-rays produced at these higher voltages are referred to as *hard* x-rays.

A radiograph is the picture (or photograph) made by x-rays on special photographic film. When an object is x-rayed, some x-rays are absorbed as they pass through the object. The percentage of the x-rays absorbed is determined by the thickness, density, and atomic number of the materials through which the x-rays pass. The unabsorbed x-rays strike the film, producing a physical change in the emulsion coating the film. Changes in film emulsion cause film darkening on areas of the film exposed to x-rays, with the degree of darkening dependent upon the amount of radiation received.

The method of producing conventional radiographs, as described above, may be referred to as *transmission radiography*, because the x-rays are transmitted directly from the x-ray tube port, through the object, onto the film. There are also other methods of producing radiographs.

Electronography is a method wherein certain metallic elements can be made to produce recordable emissions of electrons when irradiated by hard x-rays (Graham, 1973). Electron radiography, or *transmission electronography*, is an electronographic technique wherein a lead foil is placed between the x-ray source and the object being examined. The radiation passing through the object and striking the film is the electrons emitted by the lead foil (Kodak, 1969). This technique has little practical application in fingerprint work. *Electron-emission radiography*, or *auto-electronography*, is an electronographic technique wherein the object being examined is irradiated from the film side with hard x-rays that pass through a series of filters (Fig. 95). The advantage of this latter technique in fingerprint work is that only the surface of an object is recorded on the radiograph.

Graham and Gray (1966) have suggested the possibility of using x-ray techniques to recover latent fingerprints on human skin. To date, such a technique has not been fully perfected, but research is continuing in this area (Lail). X-ray techniques have also been suggested for use in cases where latent prints developed on paper by conventional techniques would be obscured by writing or printed matter. However, such difficulties may fre-

Figure 95. A fingerprint examiner adjusting the controls of a Hewlett-Packard Faxitron® cabinet model x-ray system. The object to be examined and the film are placed in the lower compartment of the cabinet. This instrument may be used for fingerprint techniques involving electron-emission radiography.

quently be overcome with special photographic or lifting techniques, rather than using x-ray techniques; for example, filters to remove specific colors or the iodine-silver transfer method.

Although the concept of using x-rays as a latent fingerprint technique is relatively new, x-rays have long been used in fingerprint work for the postmortem recording of fingerprints when inking is impossible due to advanced putrefaction or charring of the skin. Castellanos (1939) credited Henry Beclere with originating, in 1920, the concept of using x-rays to record skin details. The procedure for the technique, which uses medical diagnostic x-rays, has been described by Padron (1963), who recommended a mixture of 20 parts of lead carbonate and 100 parts of melted paraffin, which is applied to the fingers in a smooth, even coat. This masking substance coating the fingers fills the furrows between the ridges and masks out the x-rays.

The ridges appear as white lines on the radiograph, which may then be used as a negative to make a photographic print wherein the ridge structure appears dark.

Due to the dangerous nature of x-rays, safety must be a consideration of paramount importance to anyone using an x-ray apparatus. Living persons should never be x-rayed except by a fully qualified x-ray technician, and then only for valid medical purposes. All personnel operating x-ray machines must have adequate training in both the theory and operation of the equipment; operation of an x-ray apparatus by an unqualified person can be extremely dangerous for all persons near the equipment. Everyone near an x-ray machine in operation should wear film badges, and the operator should, in addition, wear a pocket dosimeter.

106

LASER TECHNIQUE

The laser technique for visualization of latent fingerprints is, simply, the direct viewing and photography of laser-induced luminescence of latent fingerprint residue. The technique was developed by a team of Canadian researchers, and it holds considerable promise as a practical and effective latent fingerprint technique. The principle of this technique is not dissimilar to that of viewing all fingerprint evidence under a strong light prior to the application of powder or chemical techniques.

The objective of the laser technique is to observe and photographically record a latent print image by the natural luminescence of various chemical substances from sweat, which may be found in latent print residue and which are luminiferous only under extremely strong light. A laser produces a beam of coherent (nonspreading) monochromatic visible light. However, in this technique, a dispersion lens is inserted into the optical path of the laser to expand the beam and the area of illumination.

Laser radiation is extremely dangerous. Therefore, direct exposure to the beam must be avoided, and everyone working with or near the laser must wear protective laser safety goggles. Even the bright light reflected from the surfaces under examination may cause eye damage. The laser safety goggles are required under the Radiation Safety Act of 1968, and the goggles must meet the specifications for the particular type of laser being used. When photographing laser-induced luminescence of latent fingerprints, a filter must also be placed on the camera lens to block out the strong visible light reflected from the surface under examination.

In the laser technique (Dalrymple et al., 1977), the latent prints are illuminated with a continuous wave, 1.5-watt, argonion laser with a wavelength of 514.5 nm. The filters for the camera and safety goggles must have an optical density of 7 at 514.5 nm. Satisfactory results have been obtained on various surfaces: stainless steel, styrofoam, glass, paper, and living human skin. The technique may be used both before and after application of powder and chemical techniques. However, luminescence is reduced by silver nitrate and powder. The advantages of this technique are that the evidence is not altered in any manner, and if unsuccessful, powder and chemical techniques may still be used.

107

SCANNING ELECTRON MICROSCOPE TECHNIQUE*

G. E. Garner
C. R. Fontan
D. W. Hobson

When fingerprints are found in the course of a major crime scene investigation, often attempts are made to photograph latent fingerprints without first processing them with powder or chemical agents. These photographs are made to record minute fingerprint characteristics before they are destroyed or obscured by a processing method and to record evidence in its original form. Often it is extremely difficult to arrange lighting conditions both to eliminate glare and to emphasize the ridge pattern of fingerprints in the photograph. This report documents efforts

---

Figure 96. A scanning electron microscope (SEM) and components. This is a very expensive instrument which should be operated only by trained personnel and which is not normally found in most police laboratories.

to apply the scanning electron microscope (SEM) to the initial problem of photographing patent fingerprints before they are processed (Fig. 96).

Owing to its exceptional depth of field, great resolution, and high magnifications, the scanning electron microscope has been applied to many other areas in forensic science. Plant material, hair, toolmarks, and paint are just a few of the recent examples of the application of the SEM to these fields.

SCANNING ELECTRON MICROSCOPY

The SEM uses a narrow (20Å to 100Å diameter) focused beam of electrons (accelerated from 1,000 V to 50,000 V), which is scanned over a sample surface in a square pattern similar to the picture generated in a television tube. When this beam impacts the sample surface, several things occur that can yield information about the surface. Electrons from the structure of the sample (secondary electrons) can be collected at each point of the scanned pattern (raster), and the intensity of secondary electrons at each point can be amplified by a photomultiplier tube and subsequently displayed on a cathode-ray tube whose phosphor surface is scanned in synchrony, with the beam scanning the sample surface. The result is a topographical picture of the sample area being scanned.

The advantage of this kind of visualization system is that high magnifications (up to 50,000 diameters) can be achieved in scanning a smaller area by reducing the size of the raster. In addition, a depth of field approximately 300 times greater than with a light microscope can be obtained.

Other informational modes are commonly used with the SEM. High-energy electrons from the primary beam or probe, which are reflected from the sample surface (called *backscattered* electrons) can be collected and are of particular value to fingerprint work, because these electrons are less susceptible to charging artifacts that occur on nonconductive or poorly conductive surfaces where prints are often found.

Usually, samples are coated by evaporating gold or one of its alloys on to the sample surface in a vacuum. The gold coat makes the surface conductive and gives higher numbers of secondary electrons with which to form the picture.

Materials and Methods

Two types of surfaces were used in scanning electron microscopy: nonconductive (glass) and conductive (aluminium). Fingerprints (consisting mostly of body oil) were deposited on glass (coverslips, microscope slides, or window glass), which were then cemented to SEM stubs with silver conducting cement. They were examined in the SEM before and after aging, weathering, and heating, with and without gold coating. Fingerprints placed on aluminium surfaces were photographed without gold coating. The fingerprints were treated or allowed to age as follows: heat, 260° C for one hour; time, ten days in a closed chamber exposed to sunlight (21° C to 40° C) and ten days out-of-doors exposed to light rain. Photographs were made with an ETEC R-1 Scanning Electron Microscope®.

CONCLUSIONS

Under certain conditions, fingerprints can be successfully recorded using the SEM where extreme difficulties are encountered using traditional methods.

The SEM works well in photographing fingerprints both on conducting and nonconducting surfaces after aging and heating. However, there are three general areas of difficulty which presently limit the usefulness of the method.

Surface Charging

On nonconductive surfaces (e.g. glass), when the surface of the print has not been coated with gold, a surface often builds up such that the print cannot be properly photographed. However, prints on conductive surfaces lend themselves particularly well to SEM examination.

Coating Material

A coat of material is deposited on the print when the fingerprint is left exposed to the elements. In the samples left exposed to the sun and light rain for ten days, the ridge pattern was clearly visible under light optics, but the SEM view was obscured, probably because electrons could not penetrate the overlying material.

Sample Size

The size of the sample placed in most SEMs is limited to an object less than 10 cm (4 inches) in any dimension. The lowest magnification permits an area approximately 2.5-by-2.5 cm to be photographed.

108

THE METAL-EVAPORATION TECHNIQUE

This technique involves the evaporation of certain metals within a vacuum chamber in such a manner that the metallic particles adhere to the surface of an object, while the latent fingerprint ridge structure remains relatively free of the particles. Although metal evaporation is not actually an electronic technique, it does involve the use of an electronic apparatus, and it cannot be properly classified under the other categories listed in other chapters in this book. At this time, and because of the equipment involved, metal evaporation is an experimental technique restricted to laboratory use. However, research has indicated that this technique may have potential as a means for developing latent prints on fabrics (Thomas, 1973).

The apparatus for metal evaporation is a vacuum chamber, such as a bell jar, a vacuum pump, and a means for evaporating the metal. The metal is evaporated from cups at the base of the vacuum chamber by using two electrodes designed to accept a tungsten cup containing the metal to be evaporated. Research conducted on plastics and fabrics with this technique used gold and cadmium (Thomas, 1975a), but research conducted on paper used a mixture of zinc, antimony and copper (Theys et al., 1968).

The metal-evaporation technique remains, for the present, an experimental technique, but one which shows considerable promise as a possible means for developing latent prints on fabrics, even after their exposure to inclement weather. It is doubtful whether this technique will prove practical for paper or plastics, considering the time and expense involved and the relative success of other techniques.

109

MICROWAVE VACUUM-DRYING TECHNIQUE

Occasionally, an investigator may encounter a situation where papers of evidentiary value have been water-soaked and it is necessary to dry them prior to any processing for latent fingerprints. Evidence of this type may frequently be found in arson cases, where documents pertaining to the financial status of a company, and which have not been destroyed by the fire, are damaged by firefighting efforts. The problem lies in drying the papers without exposing them to excessive heat, and, at the same time, keeping the individual sheets of paper from sticking together.

The microwave vacuum-drying technique was developed by the McDonnell Douglas Corporation to salvage veterans' records seriously damaged in a fire at the Military Personnel Records Center, St. Louis, Missouri. The water-soaked papers were dried by placing them inside a vacuum vessel inside a microwave oven. The papers are dried rapidly, and the moisture released into the vacuum protects the papers from excessive heat.

Amino acids are water soluble. Therefore, the ninhydrin technique does not normally produce satisfactory results on papers that have been water soaked. However, the iodine fuming and silver nitrate techniques may yield good results if the papers have been properly dried.

110
IMAGE-ENHANCEMENT TECHNIQUES

Many latent fingerprints recovered during the course of an investigation must be discarded as insufficient for identification purposes, because the latent print image lacks sufficient clarity or contrast with the background or because the texture of the underlying surface obscures much of the detail of the ridge structure. The use of high-speed general-purpose digital computers to enhance such latent prints, so that they may be viewed and photographed, is a relatively new concept which holds considerable promise as an effective latent fingerprint technique.

Much pictorial data in photographs cannot be readily observed because of the limitations of the human eye. The eye is sensitive to wavelengths between approximately 400 nm and 700 nm, but it can only differentiate between about sixteen and thirty-two levels of brightness. In other words, while the human eye can separate thousands of colors, it can distinguish between only two or three dozen shades or levels of brightness. The loss of pictorial data, therefore, is not due to a failure of the photographic film to record the data, but the inability of the eye to observe it.

The enhancement of photographic images for the purpose of observing data not visible in the original is not an unusual application of computer technology. Computerized image-enhancement techniques have been successfully employed in space exploration programs, medical diagnosis, environmental pollution monitoring, and many other fields.

One approach to image enhancement by computer is scanning the image with a recording device sensitive to levels of brightness or shades of gray beyond the range of the human eye. The signals from the recording device are then fed into a computer that assigns visible brightness levels to those previously beyond human vision. In addition, each point in the image is compared with its local average level of brightness to determine its appropriate relative brightness level.

This approach is part of the image-enhancement technique used by the Federal Bureau of Investigation in its FINDER automatic fingerprint reader (Banner and Stock, 1975). However, this is only part of the FINDER image-enhancement technique; another function of the computer is to follow the continuity of ridge structure by linking up points in the direction of ridge flow, removing small breaks or other imperfections in the fingerprint image.

Another approach to computer enhancement of latent fingerprints lacking sufficient clarity or contrast is a technique involving the use of color. The principle of this technique, called *density slicing* and *color coding*, is based upon the fact that the eye can distinguish colors better than different levels of brightness. Although there is no instance on record of this technique ever being applied specifically to latent fingerprints, its successful application in other fields indicates that it is a potential latent fingerprint technique.

The method used in density slicing and color coding has been described by Edelson (1973). The image is scanned by a television scanning camera. The scanner examines each point in the image and determines its photogenic density or brightness level

—hence, density slicing. The signal from the camera is fed into a computer that converts each slice of photographic density to a color. This is a *pseudocolor,* as the color is generated by the computer and is not in the original image. The amount of information that may be obtained from an image with this technique may be expanded more than 4,000 times that of the pictorial data in the original image (Andrews, 1972).

Another application of computer image enhancement is in cases where the ridge structure of latent fingerprints is visible but the texture of the underlying surface obscures the ridge characteristics essential for identification. It is sometimes possible in such cases for a computer to identify and remove or reduce in intensity the pictorial information on an image that is a result of the texture of the underlying surface. An example of an actual case in which such a technique was used is cited in Section 132. The case is significant because it represents the first successful application of computer technology in image enhancement of latent fingerprints.

111

COMPUTER IDENTIFICATION OF LATENT FINGERPRINTS

A long-established goal in fingerprint work has been the use of automated systems to assist in the classification, filing, searching, and retrieval of fingerprint records. The attainment of this goal has been achieved to a remarkable degree through the efforts of many agencies and manufacturers. Several automated systems are now in use throughout the nation, some of which involve the use of electronic computers. Automated systems are essential in agencies maintaining large files of fingerprint records. The initial cost of automated systems may appear extremely expensive, but such costs, in the long run, prove much cheaper than the annual salary expense of personnel required to maintain large nonautomated fingerprint files.

The successful employment of electronic automated systems in the classification, filing, searching, and retrieval of fingerprint records does not, in itself, prove readily adaptable to identifying latent fingerprints. Fingerprint files and classification systems are based upon the fingerprint card. The primary purpose of the fingerprint card is to record the pattern areas of the fingers, which may be classified according to ten-finger, five-finger, or single-print classification methods. The difficulty of searching such files for comparisons with latent prints, either manually or with an automated system, is that a great many latent prints are not classifiable.

Classification and identification of fingerprints are based upon two related, but distinct and separate, concepts (Moenssens, 1969). While identification must consider pattern types and classification focal points (cores and deltas), whenever they are present, it is based upon individual ridge characteristics and their relationship, one to another (*see* Secs. 11 and 12). Classification, on the other hand, is not concerned with ridge formations outside the pattern area on the balls of the fingers, even in those classification methods that do take into account ridge characteristics.

Latent fingerprints are also of generally poor quality in comparison to inked impressions taken expressly for recording the individual's identity. This does not imply in any way that poor-quality latent impressions are not suitable for identification purposes, only that inked impressions are purposely made as legible and complete as possible. Many factors may affect the legibility of latent fingerprints (*see* Sec. 37), any one of which may seriously impair successful identification by automated systems.

In addition to their fragmentary nature and generally poor quality, latent fingerprints are also frequently distorted in their appearance due to pressure, the angle of touch, and curvature of the receiving surface. Flesh is resilient and elastic; therefore, excessive pressure applied at an angle on a curved surface, such as a doorknob, may distort the general overall appearance of the fingerprint. Distortions do not result in an erroneous identification. Individual ridge characteristics and their relationship to each other can still be established even though the appearance of the print is distorted. However, the distortion in appearance may result, particularly in an automated system, in the latent print being unidentified even though the inked impression of the finger is on file.

Computers used for the identification of latent fingerprints must include image-enhancement techniques and, in addition to pattern type and ridge flow, a point-by-point comparison of individual ridge characteristics. The FINDER system of the Federal Bureau of Investigation is such a computer system. Although much research and development effort still remains to develop a fully automated fingerprint identification system applicable to large fingerprint files, agencies maintaining relatively small files may find such systems advantageous. There are many companies, each with different types of systems, involved with electronic automation of latent fingerprint identification. They assist an agency in determining its actual needs and requirements, whether or not their particular system will benefit the agency.

Automated fingerprint identification systems aid investigators by expediting their searches of fingerprint files and, thereby, limiting the number of inked impressions that must be compared with a latent print. Automated systems do not, however, replace the qualified latent fingerprint examiner who must make the final comparisons and verify all identifications. Also, it must be recognized that any negative response to a file search by a computer cannot be accepted as proof that the inked impressions of the individual are not in the files. Any of the factors affecting the quality of latent fingerprints may cause a negative response.

QUESTIONS

TRUE-FALSE QUESTIONS

1. Electronics may be technically defined as the science concerned with devices involving the flow of electrons within a vacuum, gas, or solid (Sec. 104).
2. Electronic computers may be used to file and search fingerprint records (Sec. 104).

3. Only a limited amount of research has been expended to develop electronic computers capable of identifying latent fingerprints by comparison with inked impressions (Sec. 104).

4. X-ray techniques employ essentially electronic techniques to develop latent fingerprints (Sec. 105).

5. Soft x-rays possess greater penetrating power than hard x-rays (Sec. 105).

6. The energy of x-rays is expressed in terms of the voltage and milliampere settings of the x-ray apparatus (Sec. 105).

7. A photograph made by x-rays is called a radiograph (Sec. 105).

8. Electron-emission radiography is the term applied to the conventional method of making radiographs (Sec. 105).

9. The use of x-rays in fingerprint work is a relatively recent concept which was first advocated in 1967 (Sec. 105).

10. The object of the laser technique is to observe and photographically record a latent print image by the natural luminescence of various substances in the latent print residue (Sec. 106).

11. Laser radiation is extremely dangerous (Sec. 106).

12. The laser technique may be used to visualize latent fingerprints both before and after processing by powder and chemical agents (Sec. 106).

13. Often it is extremely difficult to arrange lighting conditions both to eliminate glare and to emphasize ridge pattern when photographing latent fingerprints (Sec. 107).

14. Owing to its exceptional depth of field, great resolution and high magnifications, the scanning electron microscope has limited applications in forensic science (Sec. 107).

15. Usually samples prepared for examination in the SEM technique are coated with gold to make the surface conductive (Sec. 107).

16. The size of the sample placed in most SEMs is limited to an object less than 10 inches in any dimension (Sec. 107).

17. The lowest magnification of an SEM permits an area approximately 2.5-by-2.5 cm to be photographed (Sec. 107).

18. The metal-evaporation technique involves the evaporation of certain metals within a pressure chamber in such a manner that the metallic particles adhere to the surface of an object, while the latent print ridge structure remains relatively free of the particles (Sec. 108).

19. Metal evaporation has proven to be an effective and practical technique applicable to routine fingerprint work (Sec. 108).

20. It is necessary to dry water-soaked papers prior to processing them for latent fingerprints (Sec. 109).

21. Amino acids are water soluble (Sec. 109).

22. The iodine fuming and silver nitrate techniques may develop latent fingerprints on papers that have been water soaked (Sec. 109).

23. Much pictorial data in photographs cannot be readily observed because of the limitations of the human eye (Sec. 110).

24. The use of high-speed general-purpose digital computers to enhance latent fingerprints that lack clarity or are obscured by the underlying surface, is a concept which holds little promise (Sec. 110).

25. One approach to image enhancement by computer is to scan the image with a recording device sensitive to wave lengths between approximately 400 nm to 700 nm and convert different colors to various brightness levels (Sec. 110).

26. A long-established goal in fingerprint work has been the use of automated systems (Sec. 111).

27. Latent fingerprints are of generally poor quality in comparison to inked impressions (Sec. 111).

28. Classification is not concerned with ridge formations outside the pattern areas on the balls of the fingers (Sec. 111).

29. In contrast to classification, identification is concerned with individual ridge characteristics and their relative positions (Sec. 111).

30. Distortion of fingerprints due to pressure and other factors does not have much effect on identification of latent fingerprints by automated systems (Sec. 111).

COMPLETION QUESTIONS

31. The term electronics is generally used to distinguish between equipment or systems which in their electric circuits make use primarily of electronic devices as opposed to .... and similar .... devices (Sec. 104).

32. X-rays are electromagnetic radiations of extremely .... wavelength (Sec. 105).

33. At higher voltages, 150 kV to 500 kV, x-rays possess .... energy and have .... penetrating power (Sec. 105).

34. Due to the dangerous nature of x-rays, ... must be a consideration of paramount importance to anyone using an x-ray apparatus (Sec. 105).

35. The laser technique for visualization of latent fingerprints is, simply, the direct .... and .... of laser-included luminescence of latent fingerprint residue (Sec. 106).

36. Direct exposure to a laser beam must be .... (Sec. 106).

37. The advantages of the laser technique are that the evidence is not .... in any manner, and .... and .... techniques may still be used (Sec. 106).

38. The scanning electron microscope uses a narrow focused beam of .... which is .... over a sample surface in a square pattern similar to the picture generated in a television tube (Sec. 107).

39. In the SEM technique, samples are usually coated by evaporating .... or one of its alloys on to the sample surface in a vacuum (Sec. 107).

40. The SEM works well in photographing fingerprints both on conducting and nonconducting surfaces after .... and .... (Sec. 107).

41. The metal-evaporation technique involves the evaporation of certain metals within a vacuum chamber in such a manner that the metallic .... adheres to the surface of an object (Sec. 108).

42. In the metal-evaporation technique, the metal is evaporated from tungsten .... in two electrodes at the base of the vacuum chamber (Sec. 108).

43. The metal-evaporation technique remains, for the present, an .... technique (Sec. 108).

44. The problem in drying papers for latent fingerprint processing lies in drying the papers without exposing them to excessive ...., and, at the same time, keeping the individual sheets of paper from .... (Sec. 109).

45. While the human eye can separate .... of colors, it can distinguish between only .... or .... shades or levels of brightness (Sec. 110).

46. An image-enhancement technique is used by the Federal Bureau of Investigation in its .... automatic fingerprint reader (Sec. 110).

47. The primary purpose of the fingerprint card is to record the .... of the fingers (Sec. 111).

48. Many factors affect the .... of latent fingerprints, any one of which may seriously impair successful identification by automated system (Sec. 111).

49. In addition to their fragmentary nature, and generally poor quality, latent fingerprints are also frequently .... in their appearance (Sec. 111).

50. Automated fingerprint identification systems assist investigators by .... their searches of fingerprint files (Sec. 111).

REFERENCES

Andrews, H. C.: "Image restoration, enhancement, and detection," *USC Engineer.* vol. 24 (Dec., 1972), p. 15.

Angst, E., and A. Leibacher: "Computerized dactyloscopy and personal description," *Kriminalistik.* vol. 24 (1970), p. 495.

Angst, E., and F. Frieden: "The application of electronic data processing to fingerprint comparison," *International Criminal Police Review.* vol. 26 (1971), p. 230.

"Automation and the fingerprint expert," *Identification News.* vol. 16 (Oct.-Nov., 1966), p. 10.

"Automation and information sharing in New York: Major breakthrough in electronic handling of finger prints," *Fingerprint and Identification Magazine.* vol. 50 (July, 1968), p. 3.

Banner, C. S., and R. M. Stock: "The FBI's approach to automatic fingerprint identification," *FBI Law Enforcement Bulletin.* vol. 44 Part I (Jan., 1975), p. 2, Part II (Feb., 1975), p. 26.

Barth, K.: "Datengerechte Klassifizierung der Fingerabdrucke fur Programmgesteuerte Rechenanlage," *Kriminalistik.* vol. 21 (1967), p. 225.

———: "Daktyloskopische Spurenauswertung mit Hilfe Elektronischer Datenverarbeitung," *Kriminalistik.* vol. 23 (1969), p. 315.

———: "Praktische ergebnisse mit der 'Elektronischen Daktyloskopie,'" *Kriminalistik.* vol. 23 (1969), p. 597.

Bewsher, M. R.: "A topological approach to fingerprint classification," In Yefsky, S. A. (Ed.): *Proceedings of the First National Symposium on Law Enforcement Science and Technology.* New York, Thompson, 1967, p. 479.

Castellanos, Israel: *Identification Problems, Criminal and Civil.* Brooklyn, Basuino, 1939.

Cherrill, F. R.: "Transmission of finger-prints by radio," *Nature.* vol. 158 (1946), p. 525.

Cooke, T. D.: "The Russak system is rough on Miami crooks," *Fingerprint and Identification Magazine.* vol. 43 (Mar., 1962), p. 3.

Cunn, A. L.: "Use of x-ray and other techniques to visualize and reproduce fingerprints from living human skin as developed by A. L. Cunn," *Identification News.* vol. 19 (Aug., 1969), p. 4.

Dalrymple, B. E., J. M. Duff, and E. R. Menzel: "Inherent fingerprint luminescence—Detection by laser," *Journal of Forensic Sciences.* vol. 22 (1977), p. 106.

The Demonstration System for Latent Fingerprint Recognition. McDonnell Douglas Electronics Co., St. Charles, MO, June, 1971.

Edelson, E.: "Gaudy new way to see things you cannot see," *Smithsonian.* vol. 4 (Aug., 1973), p. 22.

An Experiment to Determine the Feasibility of Holographic Assistance to Fingerprint Identification. Technical Report No. 6. Sacramento, CA, Technology Committee, Project Search, June, 1972.

Fingerprint and Firearm Recognition Systems. Conductron Corp., Ann Arbor, MI, May, 1970.

Fingerprint Identification Systems. Rockwell International, Anaheim, CA, Sept., 1975.

"Fingerprints transmitted by television," *Popular Science.* vol. 135 (Sept., 1939), p. 111.

Fitzmaurice, J. A.: *Automatic Single Fingerprint Identification.* Paper presented to the Forty-fourth Annual Conference of the International Association for Identification, Pittsburgh, PA, July, 1963.

Garner, G. E., C. R. Fontan, and D. W. Hobson: "Visualization of fingerprints in the scanning electron microscope," *Journal of the Forensic Science Society.* vol. 15 (1975), p. 281.

Graham, D.: "Some technical aspects of the demonstration and visualization of fingerprints on human skin," *Journal of Forensic Sciences.* vol. 14 (1969), p. 1.

Graham, Daniel: *The Use of X-Ray Techniques in Forensic Investigations.* London, Churchill Livingstone, 1973.

Graham, D., and H. C. Gray: "The use of x-ray electronography and auto-electronography in forensic investigation," *Journal of Forensic Sciences.* vol. 11 (1966), p. 124.

Guide for Estimating Latent Search Responses. Ampex Corp., Sunnyvale, CA, July, 1974.

Harasym, W. M.: "The Videofile fingerprint storage and retrieval system," *Identification News.* vol. 23 (Sept., 1973), p. 3.

Horvath, V. V., J. M. Holeman, and C. Q. Lemmond: "Fingerprint recognition with holographic techniques," *Police.* vol. 12 (1967), p. 45.

Kent, T., G. L. Thomas, and T. E. Reynoldson: "A vacuum coating technique for the development of latent fingerprints on polythene," *Journal of the Forensic Science Society.* vol. 16 (1976), p. 93.

Kingston, C. R.: "Problems in semi-automatic fingerprint classification." In S. A. Yefsky (Ed.): *Proceedings of the First National Symposium on Law Enforcement Science and Technology.* New York, Thompson, 1967, p. 449.

——: "Progress and research in the automation of fingerprint files," *Identification News.* vol. 18 (Sept., 1968), p. 4.

Kodak: *MIRACODE.* Police Information Package. Eastman Kodak Co., Rochester, NY, Nov., 1968.

Kodak: *Photography in Modern Industry.* Eastman Kodak Co., Rochester, NY, 1969.

Leser, F.: *Automated Identification of Latent Fingerprints,* Metropolitan Atlanta Council of Local Governments, Inc., Atlanta, Georgia. Apr 1970.

Lail, H.: *Electron-emission Radiography.* Unpublished dissertation.

Marom, E.: "Fingerprint classification and identification using optical methods." In Yefsky, S. A. (Ed.): *Proceedings on the First National Symposium on Law Enforcement Science and Technology.* New York, Thompson, 1967, p. 481.

McAlvey, G. D.: "A review of Project Search activities in identification 1969-1974," *Identification News.* vol. 24 (Dec., 1974), p. 3.

Moenssens, Andre A.: *Fingerprints and the Law.* New York, Chilton, 1969.

Padron, F.: "Necrodactylography," *Fingerprint and Identification Magazine.* vol. 45 (Dec., 1963), p. 3.

"Research projects test ways to speed fingerprint transmission," *Identification News.* vol. 22 (Jan., 1972), p. 14.

Schwartz, R. E.: "System considerations in automated fingerprint classification." In Yefsky, S. A. (Ed.): *Proceedings of the First National Symposium on Law Enforcement Science and Technology.* New York, Thompson, 1967, p. 511.

Search Group Masterplan for Identification Systems Upgrade. Sacramento, CA, Search Group, Inc., Mar., 1975.

Shelman, C. B.: "Machine classification of fingerprints." In Yefsky, S. A. (Ed.): *Proceedings of the First National Symposium on Law Enforcement Science and Technology.* New York, Thompson, 1967, p. 467.

SIFTER: An Experimental Computerized Fingerprint Technical Search System for State Identification Bureaus. Technical Memorandum No. 10. Sacramento, CA, State Identification Bureau Project Committee, Project Search, Apr., 1974.

Spiva, W. E.: "Microfilmed fingerprints: Automated systems for latent fingerprint files," *Police Chief.* vol. 38, no. 2 (1971), p. 34.

"State organization installs computerized system," *Fingerprint and Identification Magazine.* vol. 57 (Apr., 1976), p. 3.

"The state of development of the FBI's automatic fingerprint system," *Identification News.* vol. 23 (Aug., 1973), p. 5.

Stroh, H. D.: "The identification unit and the MIRACODE retrieval system," *Fingerprint and Identification Magazine.* vol. 56 (Nov., 1974), p. 11.

Suzuki, T.: "Standard rules for the single fingerprint classification for processing fingerprints by computer," *Identification News.* vol. 24 (May, 1974), p. 3.

Theys, P., Y. Turgis, A. Lepareux, G. Chevet, and P. F. Ceccaldi: "New technique for bringing out latent fingerprints on paper: Vacuum metallization," *International Criminal Police Review.* vol. 23 (1968), p. 106.

Thomas, C. E.: *An Experiment to Determine the Feasibility of Holographic Assistance to Fingerprint Identification.* KMS Final Report No. 2071-F. KMS Technology Center, Van Nuys, CA, Mar., 1972.

Thomas, G. L.: "The physics of fingerprints," *Criminologist.* vol. 8 (Autumn, 1973), p. 21.

————: "Physical methods of fingerprint development," *Canadian Forensic Science Society Journal.* vol. 8 (1975a), p. 144.

————: "The resistivity of fingerprint material," *Journal of the Forensic Science Society.* vol. 15 (1975b), p. 133.

"Transmission of fingerprints by facsimile," *Royal Canadian Mounted Police Quarterly.* vol. 15 (July, 1949), p. 14.

Van Emden, B. M.: "Advanced computer based fingerprint automatic classification technique (FACT)." In Yefsky, S. A. (Ed.): *Proceedings of the First National Symposium on Law Enforcement Science and Technology.* New York, Thompson, 1967, p. 493.

Verruso, J. F.: "NYSIIS: A new era in law enforcement," *Fingerprint and Identification Magazine.* vol. 48 (Apr., 1967), p. 3.

Wegstein, J. H.: *A Computer Oriented Single-fingerprint Identification System.* Technical Note 443. Washington, DC, National Bureau of Standards. Mar., 1968.

————: *A Semi-automated Single Fingerprint Identification System.* Technical Note 481. Washington, DC, National Bureau of Standards. April, 1969.

————: *Automated Fingerprint Registration.* Technical Note 538. Washington, DC, National Bureau of Standards, Aug., 1970.

————: *Manual and Automated Fingerprint Registration.* Technical Note 730. Washington, DC, National Bureau of Standards. June, 1972.

Wegstein, J. H., and J. F. Rafferty: *Matching Fingerprints by Computer.* Technical Note 466. Washington, DC, National Bureau of Standards. July, 1968.

Chapter IX

Latent Fingerprint Lifting Techniques

112

LIFT LATENT PRINTS ONLY WHEN NECESSARY

IT MAY BE IMPOSSIBLE to forward to the laboratory or identification bureau the object upon which a latent fingerprint is found, or it may be impossible to photograph the latent print effectively because of its location or other factors. In such cases, the fingerprint may be preserved by lifting, which is the process of transferring a fingerprint from its original surface. At this time, only latent prints developed by powders or iodine fuming may be satisfactorily lifted. Research has been initiated to develop methods of lifting chemically developed latent prints, such as with ninhydrin or silver nitrate, but an effective method has not yet been achieved (Green, 1970).

Every latent print should be photographed before any attempt is made to lift it. The photograph records the original location of the latent print, in addition to preserving the latent image in the event of loss or destruction in the lifting process. The investigator's initials, date and time of photographing, and location or latent number corresponding with the investigator's notes should all be marked near the latent, to be included in the photograph. The data may also be marked on a card and placed next to the latent in the photograph.

Every lift should be marked for identification at the time it is made. Persons lifting impressions should place their initials, the date, time, and place of lifting, and the investigation case number either on the lift or a card affixed to the lift. Investigators should also keep notes to record the exact place on an object or surface from which a print is lifted, as well as other pertinent details.

Fingerprints should never be lifted merely as a matter of convenience or routine. Latent fingerprints developed on objects of evidentiary value which may be transported to the crime laboratory or police evidence room should be protected and left on the objects. It may become a critical point in subsequent legal proceedings for the court to view the print in its original location. If an object is too large or heavy to be moved in its entirety, sometimes the section bearing the latent print may be moved. This latter action may involve cutting and otherwise damaging the object; therefore, the investigator must weigh the importance of the latent print against such damage. For example, a bloody print on a wall in a murder case is of greater importance than any damage to the wall by removing that section.

Instances have been reported where an unscrupulous investigator has falsified fingerprint lifts—marking the lifts as latent prints found at a crime scene when, in fact, they were found on an object to which the suspect had legitimate access (Bonebreak, 1976). One such case, which received national publicity, resulted in the false imprisonment of an innocent man (Blank, 1975). Such cases do not reflect the integrity, dedication, and professionalism of the thousands of investigators involved in fingerprint work. Fortunately, such cases are extremely rare and, when found, the offenders should be prosecuted to the fullest extent of the law.

However, because of the actions of a few in falsifying fingerprint lifts, some courts are reluctant to accept this type of evidence. As in all professions, the actions of a few unscrupulous individuals tend to cast aspersions on the integrity of the entire profession. Therefore, to preclude any question as to the authenticity of a fingerprint lift, the actual lifting should be witnessed and a full and complete chain of custody maintained for the lift. The investigator's notes should also reflect why it was necessary to lift the latent impression.

113

THREE TYPES OF LIFTING DEVICES

Three types of lifting devices are commonly used to lift powdered latents: rubber lifters, lifting tape, and hinge lifters. Other devices may also be found, but they are not in common usage, as they are not as practical or versatile as the three listed.

RUBBER LIFTERS

The original fingerprint lifting device was a tire patch, and many investigators still refer to rubber lifters as tire patches. Rubber lifters are made of high-quality, elastic sheet rubber with sufficient adhesion on one side to pick up powder particles and hold the transparent acetate cover onto the surface to protect the lifted impressions. The adhesion, however, is not so great that the lifter sticks to a surface.

Rubber lifters are not as commonly used as lifting tape and hinge lifters, but they are far more versatile. Rubber lifters are particularly useful when lifting latent prints from uneven surfaces, especially prints on multidirectional, curved surfaces, such as doorknobs or the ridged sides of Coca-Cola® bottles.

Rubber lifters are available in two colors, black and white, and a variety of sizes from all major suppliers of fingerprint equipment. The most commonly used sizes are 2-by-2-inches and 2-by-4-inches; however, 3-by-4-inch and 4-by-9-inch sizes are also available. A 6-by-15-inch rubber footprint lifter is available from one manufacturer. This lifter may be cut in half and used for large palmprints also. When lifting latent impressions, the lifter should always be a little larger than the area to be lifted, to ensure that all of the latent print is lifted.

White rubber lifters may be marked for identification with any good-quality ball-point pen or felt-tip pens with permanent ink. Black rubber lifters, however, present marking problems. Some investigators use a white grease pencil to mark black rubber lifters, but such markings rub off easily. Another approach to marking black rubber lifters is to use ⅜-inch self-adhesive correction tape of the type for Spirit Duplicator Masters® and for blockouts, graphs, and charts. A short piece of this tape may be placed on the transparent acetate cover, or even under it, and the identifying data marked on the tape. Correction tape may be purchased from almost any office supply store.

Rubber lifters may last for years if stored away from excessive heat. Heat tends to harden and dry the lifters, which then lose their elasticity and adhesion qualities. Law enforcement agencies of the United States Department of Defense have successfully used all types of fingerprint lifting devices under the most extreme climatic conditions, from the arctic to the tropics. All yield satisfactory results if properly stored and protected from exposure to excessive heat.

LIFTING TAPE

Regular household and office cellophane tape should not be used for lifting latent fingerprints. Such tapes do not generally produce optically clear lifts, and pockets of trapped air, referred to as "fish-eyes," are common. Fingerprint lifting tapes are specifically designed for fingerprint work and are manufactured from tough hydrocarbon plastics, such as polyethylene and polypropylene. Such tapes have the exceptional strength and durability required for fingerprint use. Further, fingerprint lifting tapes are pressure wound to eliminate moisture, air pockets, and adhesive streaks.

Fingerprint lifting tape may be transparent or translucent and black or white opaque. The difference between transparent and translucent tapes is not particularly important from a fingerprint mechanics standpoint. Translucent tapes have one practical advantage over transparent tapes in that notations may be easily written directly on the tape surface. Another advantage of translucent tape is its use as an aid to photograph latent prints on highly reflective surfaces, such as polished brass. Often, by simply covering that latent print with a piece of translucent tape, the lighting may be adjusted to obtain a clear image of the latent print.

Transparent and translucent lifting tapes may be used to simply protect latent prints on the surface of an object, rather than lifting the prints. The tapes protect the latent prints from accidental damage or loss by handling and transportation. If it is later determined that the prints should be lifted, the pieces of tape may be removed and mounted on an appropriate backing.

Opaque lifting tapes must be mounted on clear pieces of acetate, but transparent and translucent lifting tapes may be mounted on a variety of covers: pieces of black or white vinyl, clear acetate covers, black or white photographic papers, special cards designed for mounting lifts, or even sheets of plain, unruled paper. One of the most convenient mounting materials an investigator may carry in a fingerprint kit is sheets of fully developed, fixed, washed, and dried photographic papers. Both black and white paper should be prepared for use. Kodak double-weight Dye Transfer Process® paper provides an excellent material for mounting lifting tapes.

All lifting tapes are sold in 10-yard rolls. Tape widths are available in any of four sizes; 1, 1½, 2, and 4 inches. The most commonly used width is 1½-inch tape.

HINGE LIFTERS

Fingerprint hinge lifters are sheets of .005 Mylar with special clear adhesive surfaces. The lifters are attached to their covers by a hinge on one side of the lifter. A thin plastic separator covers the adhesive side of the lifter and this separator is marked with removal instructions. When using the lifter, the separator is removed and thrown away. Hinge lifters may be purchased with black or white rigid vinyl covers or with transparent acetate covers. There are three sizes of hinge lifters: 1½-by-1½ inches, 2-by-4 inches, and 4-by-4 inches. The hinge of the lifter is marked as to the proper viewing side so that hinge lifters with transparent covers are not mistakenly viewed from the wrong side.

FOOTPRINT LIFTERS

Footprint lifting devices are similar to the other types of lifting devices, only larger. In addition to the rubber footprint lifter, which has already been mentioned, 6-by-15-inch transparent lifters called *footprint-residue lifters* and *evidence-collection lifters* may be purchased. White rigid vinyl and transparent acetate covers are available for these lifters. These large lifters may also be used to lift large areas of latent fingerprints where the latents are so numerous that smaller lifts may result in damage to some of the prints.

114

TRANSPARENT AND OPAQUE LIFTS

Transparent lifts, whether tapes or hinge lifters, offer several advantages in comparison to opaque lifters. Lifts made with transparent tapes and lifters can be compared directly with inked impressions, whereas opaque lifters must be reversed. Transparent lifts mounted on transparent covers may be used as photographic negatives (*see* Sec. 118). Another advantage of transparent lifting devices is that one type of lifting material may be used to lift latent prints developed with any color of powder.

An investigator must always remember that *latent prints lifted with opaque lifting devices are reversed.* These lifts must be photographed and the image reversed for proper viewing and comparison with inked impressions. However, by using a right-angle prism, it is possible to directly compare latent prints on opaque lifters with inked impressions. The lifter is pressed against one side of the prism and a fingerprint magnifier is placed on the other side. The latent print may then be viewed in its proper perspective.

Right-angle prisms from Army tank periscopes can be obtained rather inexpensively from military surplus stores. These prisms are available in two different sizes of viewing surfaces, 38-by-146 mm and 49-by-167 mm. For best use, the prism may be glued to a piece of wood cut to the same dimensions as the prism. The fingerprint magnifier may then be placed on top of the prism, while the opaque lifter is held vertically against the other side of the prism.

115

WHAT SIZE LIFT TO USE

The legible and readable ridge detail shown by the average latent fingerprint developed at a crime scene varies somewhere between ½ and ¾ of an inch in width. Latent palmprints are wider, but they seldom exceed 4 inches. The majority of palm-prints recovered are partial prints, rarely the entire palm. Scores of fingerprints are developed at crime scenes for every palm-print; therefore, it appears logical to choose for general use a tape wide enough to accommodate the majority of latent finger-prints without crowding the image or having the lift give the impression that a part of it may have been missed in the lifting process.

Tape rolls are available in various widths. The minimum width for fingerprint work or for lifting individual images should be 1 inch. A more practical all-around width is 1½ inches. However, the wider the tape, the more unwieldy it becomes and the more carefully it has to be handled.

Sufficient area to lift the majority of latent prints with adequate clear space around the latent to place identifying data is provided by 1½-inch tape. Identification marking may be placed on the cover or other mounting material on which the tape is mounted, but placing the markings directly on the lifting tape has two distinct advantages in respect to later identification of the latent print as having come from the crime scene. Any photographs of the lifted print may be readily identified and associated with a specific crime scene without further identification markings when the data is marked directly on the left. One look at the photographic negative or print and the investigator knows with which crime scene it is associated. There will never be a mix-up of latent prints in two separate cases. Another advantage in marking all identifying data directly on the lift, immediately at the time of lifting, is that such a routine practice may help to forestall any claims that the print was lifted at another location.

If two or more simultaneous fingerprints are developed in a group, the best procedure is to lift the impressions as a group. The relative position of the prints may provide the latent fingerprint examiner with a clue of which fingers of which hand made the impressions. Such data greatly expedites any search of a fingerprint file. If it is more advantageous to lift such prints individually, they should be mounted on the same cover or card with their relative positions unchanged.

Relative position of prints should never be changed; relationship of the prints one to another is important, it reveals how objects have been handled and frequently which hand was used. A skilled fingerprint examiner can in a majority of cases, where two or more prints are found, determine with considerable accuracy which fingers made the impressions, the *types of patterns*, their *positions with respect to each other*, and their *position with respect to the object* are clues to the identity of the fingers that made them.

Sometimes, when lifting palmprints, it is necessary to use two or more strips of lifting tape to lift the entire impression. In such cases, each strip of tape is applied carefully to the print with the edges of the second and succeeding strips overlapping the preceding strip. The strips are not lifted individually, but as a group. Before lifting the tape, the thumbnail should be run down the edge of all overlapping strips of tape to remove any streaks that may be caused by the overlapping. The group of strips are then lifted together as one piece and mounted on a single cover or card.

116

APPLYING LIFTS TO POWDERED PRINTS

Lifting tape should be applied to individual prints to the best advantage, usually lengthwise rather than crosswise. If a group of prints are developed, for example, three fingers of one hand, each impression may be lifted separately without endangering adjoining impressions. It may be necessary to alter the procedure to fit varying situations. If images overlap, the only recourse may be to take all prints in one lift, in which case the "direction of lift" is of secondary importance. If wide tape can be successfully applied without developing wrinkles in the tape, the prints should be lifted that way.

Tape should be applied to powdered impressions in such a way that perfect contact is obtained. If the surface bearing a print is pebbled or rough, contact may be forced with the ball of a finger or a soft pencil eraser. Air pockets between the tape and the film base of a lift should be carefully avoided; when photographic prints are made from lifts containing air pockets, the effect is exaggerated. An air pocket disperses light rays, causing a light spot in the print. Pockets may be eliminated by sliding a finger along the tape when it is applied. Pockets reflect careless workmanship, they detract from appearance, and they make identification more difficult—and they may occur at a critical point in a lift. A pocket may be deflated by puncturing the tape with a pin, but a better practice is prevention.

Rounded surfaces, like shoulders on bottles, make application of tape difficult, if not impossible (Fig. 97). Rubber lifts are better for such surfaces. The wider the tape and the rounder the corner, the harder it is to obtain a satisfactory lift; tape obviously works best on flat surfaces.

When a strip of tape is cut from a roll, both ends must be kept under control, and the strip should not be permitted to roll back on itself or to become fastened to another surface. Tape has a way of becoming entangled or attached where it is not wanted. Tape should be pulled off a roll in one continuous motion; if it is pulled a little at a time, the adhesive side may show marks where pulling started and stopped. Marks detract from the appearance of a lift. Likewise, when tape is pulled away from a powdered latent, both ends must be held securely.

Prints may be lifted without cutting the tape; the roll may be held in one hand and the free end attached to the object near the print to be lifted. The tape is severed from the roll after the print is lifted and placed on a card or cover. A person should try both methods and use the one he finds most advantageous or the one which serves his purpose best under a particular set of circumstances.

If tape is "fouled" or finger marked to the extent of interfering with a lift, it should not be used; in fact, one should go even further, a lift should be completely free from finger- or foulmarks. Fingermarks on tape in places where they may be confused with fingerprint evidence not only detract from appearance of a lift and reflect poor workmanship, but they may

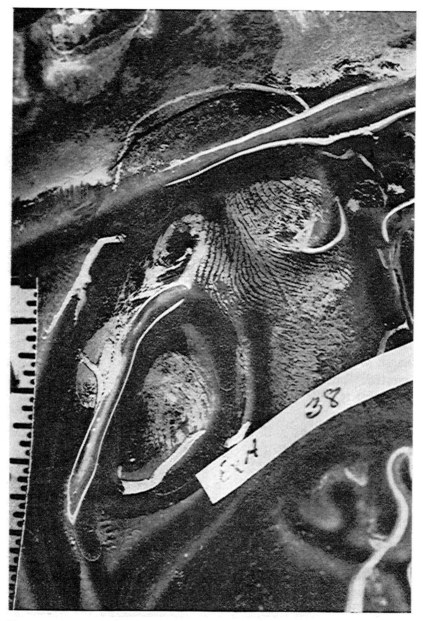

Figure 97. Latent fingerprint developed with powder on a coffee mug which has a surface with a high relief. Lifting tapes and hinged lifters cannot be used to lift this print; rubber lifters must be used if the print is to be lifted. The best procedure in such cases is to photograph the latent print and retain the mug after spraying the print with clear lacquer.

call for an explanation, should the lift become evidence in court. They provide an opportunity for the defense to becloud and confuse the issue.

Lifting tape is tough, and it is difficult to tear off the roll. Scissors should be carried in a fingerprint kit where they are within reach when working with tape. After a roll of tape is used, the free end may be folded back on itself a short distance to provide a tab by which the tape may be started again; this makes continued use of a roll easier.

A clear, flat working space such as a tabletop should be readied for laying a card or cover for receiving a lift; this should be done before the latent is lifted. One end of the tape bearing a lift may be attached to a tabletop and the card or film intended to receive the impression may be placed in position under the tape. The tape is then pressed onto the card by sliding a finger along it with the free end of the tape elevated slightly.

Every fingerprint examiner has, at one time or another, looked at a partial print lifted and submitted by another person, and was unable to decide which was top or bottom. If a partial pattern can be "oriented" to position, the task of comparison is simplified, and the time required to establish identity may be greatly expedited. The position of a finger in respect to an object can usually be determined when a latent is developed, even though a pattern is incomplete or absent. If the finger position can be determined accurately and the print is lifted lengthwise, the task of the latent fingerprint examiner in making comparisons is made that much easier. If lifts are taken lengthwise as a matter of procedure, the position of fragmentary and partial prints may be more readily established.

117

LIFTING POWDERED PRINTS

When a fingerprint is powdered, the ridge pattern is built up by minute powder particles; when lifting tape is pressed evenly and smoothly over the powdered image, the adhesive substance of the tape traps the powder particles. The thickness of the powder film is not great enough to alter the ridge detail even though the tape is firmly pressed onto the impression. When the tape is pulled away, a near-perfect powder reproduction of the ridges is obtained. It adheres to the sticky side of the tape, and detail is recorded with great accuracy (Fig. 98).

A latent print itself is not removable from a surface by the lifting process. The oils and moisture simply hold powder grains, which are in turn picked up by the adhesive tape. A powder and not the latent image is lifted; the latent undoubtedly loses some of its substance. If the process is repeated, each lift becomes progressively weaker simply because the latent image has a diminishing capacity for holding powder grains. Latents may under some circumstances be repowdered and lifted two or more times; each time, the amount of powder which adheres decreases, because the adhesive properties of the latent are dissipated.

Some fingerprints may appear to improve, especially on a second lift, because the tape removes excess powder or foreign substances detracting from clarity of the pattern, thereby giving the impression that the latent holds powder better on the second development. As a matter of fact, the second lift may be more

Figure 98. Transparent tape is used universally to lift powdered latents. The lifted prints may be preserved on a card of contrasting color to the powder or on sheets of clear plastic.

legible because it has been cleaned, but the amount of powder which adheres decreases with each succeeding lift.

In actual practice, latent fingerprints are, perhaps, lifted with tape more often than by any other method. Hinge lifters are, however, becoming more and more popular because of their convenience. A hinge lifter is applied to a latent print by removing the plastic separator from the adhesive surface and placing the adhesive side of the lifter over the latent print. The lifter is rubbed with the ball of the finger, lightly and evenly, to ensure that the powder is picked up by the adhesive and to remove pockets of air. The lifter is then removed in a steady, even motion and covered with the hinged cover. The best way to cover a latent print after it has been lifted is to place the lifter on a flat surface with the adhesive side facing up, then form a curl in the hinge cover and "roll" on the cover.

To apply a rubber lifter to a latent print, first remove the cover by grasping it at one corner and removing it in one even motion. Any hesitation in removing the cover may result in a streak across the surface of the lifter. The lifter is then placed on the latent print by placing one edge of the lifter at the bottom of the latent, holding the upper edge of the lifter between the thumb and index finger. Holding the lower edge of the lifter with a finger of the opposite hand, the slightly curled lifter is rolled slowly over the impression by moving the finger across the lifter in a firm, even manner. The lifter is removed from the latent print in a single, smooth motion and the cover replaced.

When replacing the cover on rubber lifters, the cover should be applied to the lifter in the same manner that the lifter was applied to the latent print. This procedure is important to avoid air bubbles.

Adhesive substances on all types of lifters sometimes absorb or obscure light-colored fingerprint powders. Therefore, it is usually advisable to select dark-colored powders when the print is to be lifted. As previously stated in Section 66, the selection of a powder that contrasts with the surface being examined is not of any importance if the primary intention is to lift the latent impression. If it is known before processing that the print is going to be lifted, it is conceivable that a black powder could be used on a black surface.

How many times can a latent fingerprint be developed, lifted, and redeveloped with powder—how many times can the process be repeated on one and the same latent? The answer to this question is important, for it sometimes happens that a lift is lost or damaged through carelessness, haste, or perhaps for reasons beyond the operator's control. Fingerprint evidence is very delicate evidence; if it were not possible at times to get a second lift, the attempt to recover the evidence would be a failure. An investigator has to develop evidence in various locations and under many different circumstances, and many of them are very unfavorable.

Prints in some cases can be lifted more than once, and under favorable conditions, a series of lifts may be made. Theoretically, each succeeding lift is progressively weaker than the preceding one. The latent impression retains less and less powder each time it is redeveloped until it is finally exhausted.

Figure 99 is a succession of lifts made under laboratory conditions. The original impression was made on glass by a person whose hands made particularly strong impressions. The first print was heavily powdered and care was taken with each succeeding redevelopment to force the powder to adhere to the

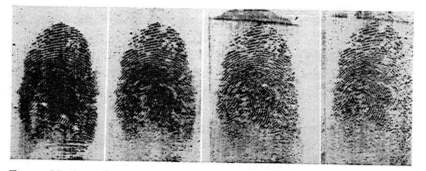

Figure 99. Some latent prints may be powdered and lifted two or more times. A series of lifts is shown; the impressions become progressively weaker. In some instances, when excessive powder has adhered to the latent, greater detail may be found in the succeeding lifts.

image. Four lifts are shown in the figure, but a fifth was obtained, and still others could have been obtained which might have been identifiable, if only in part. It is noted that the barren areas appearing in the pattern increase in size with each redevelopment. All four impressions are suitable for identification and even the fourth is better than the average latent print recovered in actual fingerprint investigations.

A second lift in many cases reveals better ridge detail and tone quality than the first lift. The first application of tape removes superfluous dust and foreign particles sometimes clinging to areas between the ridges, which light brushing does not remove. A first lift may serve in the capacity of a cleaner without detracting from pattern quality. Conversely, a second lift is not always assured because perspiration or moisture may be insufficient to hold powder more than once. Obtaining a lift from a powdered latent impression is like firing the first shot in a timed-fire string in a pistol match—it should never be a miss. When lifting fingerprints, always take particular care to preserve the first lift; it may be the last.

An attempt at a second lift is sensible if it appears that improvement can be made. The possibility of securing second, third, and even fourth lifts from one impression depends upon the many conditions affecting the quality of the original impression, such as skin condition, surface of the object, perspiration, and humidity, etc. In actual practice in the great majority of cases, the fingerprint man is gratified to obtain a good lift on the first attempt—second lifts are infrequent and they are not depended upon. Particular care is taken to develop the first image to maximum quality, but if, after the first lift is made, it appears a better one can be obtained, it is only sensible to attempt it.

118

USING FINGERPRINT LIFTS AS NEGATIVES

If dark-colored, opaque, or metallic powders are used as developing agents, and the resulting powdered images are lifted with transparent lifters and attached to transparent covers, the lifts may be used as ordinary photographic negatives. Either contact or projection prints may be made from them. If the ridges of the lifted prints are too light in color to make satisfactory prints, the colors may be reversed and intensified by contact printing the lift on a photographic film. The film may then be used as a negative for making either contact or projection prints.

An explanation of the use of a lift as a negative at this point is appropriate. A lifted fingerprint on a transparent sheet is a positive reproduction of the powdered image; it corresponds to a print of the same finger taken on a card with ink. If the image is reproduced on a photographic film by contact printing, ridges and spaces are reversed in color; the image then becomes a negative. When a photographic print on paper is made from the negative, the result is once again positive; it is a true black-and-white reproduction of the original.

When a photographic print is made directly from a black-powdered lift, the ridges of the fingerprint are white and the background is dark (Fig. 100). Reversal of colors makes comparison difficult for some persons; they prefer to compare black ridges with black, gray with gray, or white with white. If an exhibit is made for court purposes, ridge color should be the same in the known and questioned prints to avoid confusion in the minds of those inexperienced in fingerprint comparisons.

In some cases, for example when using fine aluminum lining, if the lift is used as a photographic negative for making photographic prints, the color of the gray ridges in the print may be very much like the lift in appearance. The ridges in both are gray, the powder on the tape may transmit enough light to make the ridges of the photographic print gray, although in fact, the colors are reversed. The reason for this illusion is that gray is a neutral color and it is still gray, even when reversed. Powders like lampblack and ferric oxide are sufficiently opaque to light that the lift is a positive, and a print made from that shows the ridges in reverse color—white ridges with black spaces.

Color reversal may be accomplished by placing the lift in contact with a photographic film, the emulsion side of the film in contact with the tape of the lift, and exposing the film to light

Figure 100. A latent print is developed with black powder, lifted with a hinge lifter, and the photograph made by using the lifter as a negative. The line across the lower right corner was caused by the investigator tearing the plastic lifter.

through the lift. This operation should be done in a dark room. If orthochromatic or color-blind film is used, the job may be done under a red safelight. If panchromatic film material is used, reversal must be done in total darkness, except for the actual exposure. Use of film materials like contrast-process ortho is preferable, because one does not have to work in total darkness. By using the above-named film materials, one may develop by inspection under a red safelight to good advantage.

A suggested exposure is as follows: When using contrast-process ortho film, with the film and lift in a printing frame, adhesive side to emulsion side, exposure may be made 6 feet from an open 15-watt lamp for one-half second with the emulsion side of the film material toward the light. Develop and clear in the normal manner. No reflector is used with the globe. Increased light resulting from use of a reflector shortens the exposure time noticeably.

For persons familiar with photographic processes in a dark-room, exposure may be made under the light of an enlarger. Intensity of light may be controlled by the lens diaphragm. Either of the above methods is satisfactory; it is a matter of choosing the more convenient one.

The technique of affixing lifted prints to acetate sheeting and using the lift like a photographic negative speeds up fingerprint work greatly. It saves much time in handling the evidence, and the fingerprints are well preserved and protected on sheeting. Prints may be removed from sheets if the occasion requires. A lift once affixed to a paper base cannot be effectively removed, and it cannot be used as a negative. If anything further is done with it, the image has to be photographed.

The prints in Figure 101 were developed by the powders indicated in the lettering under each print left to right: (A) manganese dioxide, (B) a special formula containing a large percent-

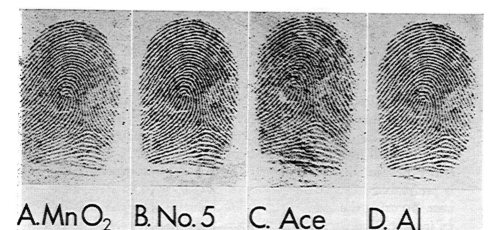

Figure 101. Nearly all powders provide lifts suitable for use as photographic negatives. (A-D) The above impressions were each developed with a different powder, as described in the text. Photographic negatives were made from each lift and the photographic prints above were in turn made from the negatives.

age of black magnetic iron oxide, (C) Ace® black and (D) aluminum fine lining. The impressions were lifted with tape and affixed to translucent film. They were placed in a printing frame in contact with a sheet of contrast-process ortho film and exposed simultaneously for ½ second at 6 feet from a 15-watt open lamp. The prints are excellent reproductions of the original powdered images. The impression second from the left, made from a black magnetic iron oxide powder shows better detail and more even development than the other three.

Opaque lifters cannot be used as photographic negatives, but the images and color of these lifters can be easily reversed for quick comparisons with inked impressions, by inserting a piece of photographic paper into the film holder of the camera and using the paper as a film. A more permanent photographic record can be made later with film.

119
LIFTING IODINE-DEVELOPED LATENT PRINTS

The iodine-silver transfer method of developing and recording latent fingerprint evidence was first publicized by McMorris of Pasadena in the middle 1930s. It is based on the principle that silver subjected to iodine vapors forms silver iodide, which darkens when subjected to a strong light or light with high-actinic qualities. The color of the iodide changes to a dark brown or nearly black color in a manner similar to the tarnishing of silverware. Development is simply accelerated by exposure to sunlight or a photoflood.

The preliminary steps in the silver transfer technique embody the same methods used in the iodine cabinet or the fuming pipe; the latent image is developed by iodine vapors. Images developed in the iodine cabinet are photographed directly after removal from the cabinet. In the silver transfer method, an intermediate step has been introduced, which makes it possible to record latents that cannot be photographed directly because of the absence of contrast for convenience. After a latent print has been developed by iodine vapors, a silver sheet is pressed against the image for a brief period of time, sometimes for several seconds if the image is weak. The iodine retained by the moisture of the ridges of the latent reacts chemically with the silver of the sheet, forming silver iodide. Where there is no contact between the iodine and the silver, for example in the intervening spaces between the ridges, there is no chemical reaction, although a prolonged contact may permit iodine vapors to spread and block out the spaces, with the result that the image is blurred.

When the silver sheet is removed from the iodine-developed latent, a faint reversed image may show on the sheet—it may or may not be visible. When the image is exposed to strong light—sunlight or a photoflood—the impressions darken perceptibly. As it is a reversed image, it must be photographed to serve as a basis of comparison or identification. It may be photographed and handled in the same manner as described for the tire-patch method of handling fingerprint evidence.

Good contact between the silver sheet and the surface bearing the developed image must be obtained to insure transfer of the best possible image. Space separating the latent image and the surface of the silver sheet results in a blurred or otherwise indistinct image. Silver sheets are inflexible. Accordingly, only objects having flat surfaces or surfaces that may be adjusted to the surface of the sheet are susceptible to the iodine-silver transfer technique.

The silver sheet must be kept clean; if allowed to tarnish or to become discolored, it will not serve. A satin finish is suggested as preferable to a bright finish, as the latter presents photographic obstacles the same as a mirror. Proper care of the silver sheet is extremely important; if it is kept in the same kit as a fuming pipe, it is difficult to keep it from being attacked by iodine vapors.

The iodine-silver technique has one advantage over direct photography. When images are developed on a surface that does not provide color contrast, it is possible to transfer the image to a silver sheet and obtain the contrast. It is a technique investigators should explore and determine for themselves, whether or not it can be employed to good advantage.

The iodine fuming and iodine-silver transfer techniques have been reported as a successful method for developing latent fingerprints on human skin (Foley, 1971). The method of application and lifting is the same as that for any other type of surface and may be used on both living and deceased persons. The area of skin is fumed with an iodine fuming pipe, and a darkened area appears where the latent print is located—the ridges of the print are not readily discernible. The silver plate is applied to the darkened area in the same manner as for any other surface, with a moderate amount of pressure for about fifteen seconds. The plate is then carefully lifted and placed under a heat lamp.

Foley reported successful results on living skin for periods up to 1.5 hours and on deceased persons for periods up to 105 hours. Another researcher (Mooney, 1977) reported essentially the same time-frame for deceased persons, but found that prints could be developed on living skin for periods up to about 8 hours.

120

CHEMICAL SOLUTIONS FOR LIFTING LATENTS

Chemical solutions that harden into a transparent film have been suggested for lifting latent prints developed with powders. Advocates of this method of lifting prints have claimed that the advantages in their ease of application, particularly on curved and irregular surfaces, outweigh any disadvantage. However, no chemical solution lifting method has ever gained wide acceptance with investigators. Lifts made with chemical solutions have a marked tendency to curl and, therefore, must be kept between two pieces of flat material to prevent curling. Also, since it is difficult to mark or mount the lifts, they must be placed in a container and all identification marking placed on the container.

Leung suggested a mixture that has a base of collodion, amylacetate, acetone, and ether (Mirzaoff, 1932). The mixture is poured over the dusted impressions, dries in a few seconds, and is ready for lifting. A more recent chemical lifting method was nylon spray (Ray, 1961), which was marketed in an aerosol container. The area to be lifted was marked off with masking tape and the solution simply sprayed on. Nylon spray had a tendency to stretch when the lift was being removed and, because the film, was so thin, the spray had to be applied at least a second time. It is doubtful if either method is in use today.

121

LIFTING VISIBLE AND PLASTIC FINGERPRINTS

Fingerprint impressions in dust usually prove to be one of the most difficult types of fingerprint evidence that an investigator may be called upon to recover. The visibility of such impressions is due to the reflection of light by the undisturbed dust particles. Lifting devices may be used to lift impressions in dust. Actually, the undisturbed dust is lifted, but successful results are usually by chance. If the layer of dust is too thin, it may be absorbed into the adhesive of the lifter, and the image of the impression disappears. If the layer of dust is too thick, the pressure required in applying the lifter usually obscures ridge structure.

Fingerprint impressions in dust must always be photographed before any attempt is made to lift the impressions. In the majority of cases, photography is the only method by which the impression is adequately recovered. When photographing impressions in dust, oblique lighting must be used and the light moved around until the right degree of illumination and pictorial detail achieved.

One technique for lifting dust impressions, called the *Müllner process*, was reported by Robinson (1935). In this process, an atomizer is filled with fine plaster, and the plaster is sprayed at a piece of cardboard held over the impression. The plaster is not sprayed directly at the impression, as the force of the spray may disturb the dust. The sprayed plaster strikes the piece of cardboard and falls gently over the impression. A finely nebulized cloud of alcohol is then sprayed into the air directly above the imprint. The layer of plaster absorbs the descending alcohol. The process is repeated until a fragile but serviceable cast is obtained and, if conditions are favorable, the dust impression adheres to the cast. The cast can be strengthened afterward by applying successive coats of plaster to the back of the cast.

One investigator has reported making successful lifts of impressions in dust by using silicone rubber (Cooper, 1977). A retaining wall of clay or putty is built around the impression, and the silicone rubber casting material is poured adjacent to the impression and allowed to flow over the impression. Silicone rubber compounds provide an excellent contrast with the lifted dust impressions.

Harrell (1973) developed a benzidine solution modified for lifting bloody fingerprints. The basic ingredient of this solution as a lifting technique is a 5% collodion solution, which is prepared by adding 5 ml of collodion in 2 ml of ethyl alcohol and then adding 20 ml of ethyl ether. A benzidine spray solution is then prepared by first adding 2 ml of an acetate buffer to 50 mg of benzidine and 100 mg of sodium perborate, and shaking vigorously. One milliliter of the supernatent solution from the foregoing solution is then added to 20 ml of diluted collodion and mixed thoroughly. The resulting solution is then sprayed onto the bloody fingerprint and, when dry, may be lifted.

Considering the health hazard of benzidine (*see* Sec. 101) as a carcinogen, it is questionable whether or not this substance should be used in a spray technique. As a minimum, all use of benzidine should be restricted to use within a glovebox. Benzidine should not be used at crime scenes, as other persons may unknowingly come into contact with items contaminated with the substance.

Plastic fingerprints, particularly those in soft substances, such as grease, soap, semidry paint, soft putty, and chocolate candy, have posed unique problems for investigators. Since these types of fingerprints cannot be preserved by normal powder and lifting techniques, the recommended procedure has been to photograph the plastic impressions, using oblique lighting.

There are several disadvantages to this photographic technique. Due to the soft nature of the receiving medium, the surface of a plastic impression is normally concave. This physical feature usually makes it impossible to distribute the light evenly over the entire surface area of the impression, resulting in different representation of ridge details in different areas of the same photograph. The ridges may appear dark in some areas and light in others.

Another difficulty encountered is the failure of the photographic technique to adequately record ridge details parallel to the beam of light and ridges leaving only a faint impression. Another disadvantage of the photographic technique is the tendency of many substances to melt upon exposure to heat. Many soft substances in which plastic fingerprints may be found

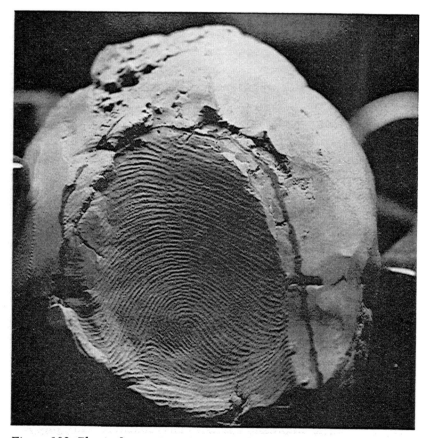

Figure 102. Plastic fingerprint impression taken in clay. This print was intentionally made for demonstration purposes.

Figure 103. A lift of the plastic impression shown in Figure 102. The impression was cast in silicone rubber, and the cast was lightly dusted with fingerprint powder. The print above was lifted from the cast using opaque lifting tape. The print will make a better-quality fingerprint chart than a photograph of the plastic impression.

readily melt above normal room temperatures, and photographic lights may produce too much heat for these substances. Also, conditions at a crime scene, such as the time required and weather conditions, may preclude adequate photographing of plastic impressions at the scene.

Silicone rubber casting provides the best technique for accurately recording and permanently preserving plastic fingerprint impressions, and it also provides a means for rapidly reproducing the impressions for direct comparison with inked impressions (Figs. 102 and 103). Several other casting methods have been tried for casting plastic impressions, but none of the other methods are adequate for impressions in soft substances.

Silicones have extremely low surface tension, and can, therefore, flow into the minutest cracks and crevices without destroying or distorting ridge details, even in such soft substances as grease or butter. Water does not affect the application of the silicone rubber, and, since no heat is involved in either its prep-

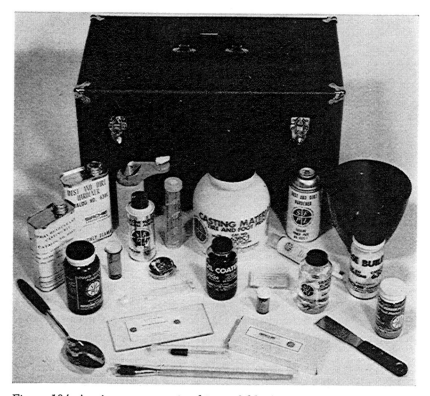

Figure 104. A crime scene casting kit available from a major manufacturer of fingerprint equipment. This general-purpose kit contains the materials necessary for lifting plastic impressions.

aration or formation, there is no damage to the impression from these two factors. The resilient casts may be easily removed from the most sticky substances, and they are extremely durable.

Upon removal of the silicone rubber cast to the laboratory, or at the crime scene if necessary, detailed reproductions may be made by lightly dusting the cast with black fingerprint powder and a fiberglass brush. After dusting, the fingerprint is recorded by pressing white opaque lifting tape against the cast and lightly rubbing to insure that all surfaces are recorded. The lifting tape is then mounted on a transparent cover, and the lifted impression can be compared directly against an inked impression. Ink should not be used to record the impression of the cast, because ink has a tendency to fill in and obscure ridge structure in the cast. Also, excessive ink on the cast is difficult to remove, but fingerprint powder is easily washed off.

QUESTIONS

TRUE-FALSE QUESTIONS

1. All latent fingerprints may be preserved by lifting, whether developed by powder, iodine fuming, or chemicals (Sec. 112).

2. Crime scene searches may be expedited without any potential loss or damage to latent fingerprints, if the latent prints are lifted as a matter of routine (Sec. 112).

3. Investigators should keep notes to record the exact place on an object or surface from which a latent print is lifted (Sec. 112).

4. Rubber lifters are particularly useful when lifting latent prints from flat surfaces (Sec. 113).

5. Fingerprint lifting tapes are specifically designed for fingerprint work (Sec. 113).

6. Opaque lifting tapes must be mounted on pieces of black or white vinyl (Sec. 113).

7. Lifts made with transparent tapes and lifters can be compared directly with inked impressions (Sec. 113).

8. An investigator must always remember that latent prints lifted with opaque lifting devices are reversed (Sec. 114).

9. Latent palmprints are larger than fingerprints, but seldom exceed 4 inches (Sec. 115).

10. The ratio of latent fingerprints to palmprints developed at crime scenes is one to one (Sec. 115).

11. If two or more simultaneous fingerprints are developed in a group, the best procedure is to lift each single print individually (Sec. 115).

12. The relationship of latent fingerprints, one to another, is important (Sec. 115).

13. Tape should be applied to powdered impressions in such a way that perfect contact is obtained (Sec. 116).

14. Rounded surfaces, like shoulders on bottles, make application of tape difficult, if not impossible (Sec. 116).

15. If a tape is "fouled" or fingermarked to the extent of interfering with a lift, it should not be used (Sec. 116).

16. When a latent print is lifted from a surface, it is the oils and moisture of the latent print which adhere to the lifting device (Sec. 117).

17. In actual practice, latent fingerprints are, perhaps, lifted with rubber lifters more often than any other method (Sec. 117).

18. It is rarely possible to lift a powdered impression more than once (Sec. 117).

19. Only transparent hinge lifters may be used as photographic negatives (Sec. 118).

20. When a lifter is used as a photographic negative, the colors on the photographic print are reversed (Sec. 118).

21. The image and color of opaque lifters can be reversed by inserting photographic paper in the camera in place of film (Sec. 118).

22. Silver subjected to iodine vapors forms silver iodide, which darkens when exposed to a strong light (Sec. 119).

23. The color of the ridge structure of iodine-developed latent prints lifted with the silver transfer technique are dark brown or nearly black (Sec. 119).

24. One advantage of the silver transfer technique for iodine-developed latent prints is that background surface color does not interfere with photographic efforts (Sec. 119).
25. Chemical solutions for lifting latent prints have gained wide acceptance and are commonly used (Sec. 120).
26. The nylon spray method of lifting latent prints covers the impression with a tough, nonstretching film (Sec. 120).
27. Fingerprint impressions in dust usually prove to be one of the most difficult types of fingerprint evidence that an investigator may be called upon to recover (Sec. 121).
28. When photographing impressions in dust, oblique lighting must be used (Sec. 121).
29. Plastic fingerprints in soft substances are normally concave (Sec. 121).
30. Ink is the best medium for recording impressions from silicone rubber casts of plastic fingerprints (Sec. 121).

COMPLETION QUESTIONS

31. At this time, only latent fingerprints developed by . . . . or . . . . may be satisfactorily lifted (Sec. 112).
32. Every lift should be . . . . for . . . . at the time it is made (Sec. 112).
33. Three types of lifting devices are commonly used to lift powdered latents: . . . . , ... , and . . . . (Sec. 113).
34. Footprint lifters may also be used for lifting latent . . . . (Sec. 113).
35. Transparent lifts mounted on transparent covers may be used as photographic . . . . (Sec. 114).
36. An advantage of transparent lifting devices is that one type of lifting material may be used to lift latent prints developed with any . . . . of powder (Sec. 114).
37. The legible and readable ridge detail shown by the average latent fingerprint developed at a crime scene varies somewhere between . . . . and . . . . of an inch in width (Sec. 115).

38. When a strip of tape is cut from a roll, both ends must be kept under .... (Sec. 116).
39. Lifting tape is tough and it is difficult to .... (Sec. 116).
40. When a fingerprint is powdered, the ridge pattern is built up by minute powder .... (Sec. 117).
41. Adhesive substances on all types of lifters sometimes ...... or .... light-colored fingerprint powders (Sec. 117).
42. When a photographic print is made directly from a black powdered lift, the ridges of the fingerprint are .... and the background is .... (Sec. 118).
43. Opaque lifters .... be used as photographic negatives (Sec. 118).
44. When the silver sheet is removed from the iodine-developed latent, a faint .... image may show on the sheet (Sec. 119).
45. The iodine fuming and iodine-silver transfer techniques have been reported a successful method for developing latent fingerprints on .... skin (Sec. 119).
46. Chemical solutions that harden into a .... film have been suggested for lifting latent prints developed with powders (Sec. 120).
47. The visibility of fingerprint impressions in dust is due to the reflection of light by the .... dust particles (Sec. 121).
48. Lifting devices may be used to lift impressions in dust, but successful results are usually by .... (Sec. 121).
49. A modified .... solution may be used for lifting bloody fingerprints (Sec. 121).
50. Plastic fingerprints cannot be preserved by normal .... and .... techniques (Sec. 121).

REFERENCES

Blank, J. P.: "The fingerprint that lied," *Reader's Digest*. vol. 107 (Sept., 1975), p. 119.

Bonebreak, G. C.: "Fabricating fingerprint evidence," *Identification News*. vol. 26 (Oct., 1976), p. 3.

Boyer, J.: "Nouveau procede de transfert des empreintes digitales," *La Nature.* vol. 60 (1932), p. 51.

Braught, L. R.: "Lifting latents for keeps and for court," *Fingerprint and Identification Magazine.* vol. 41 (Oct., 1959), p. 6.

Cooper, C. E.: *Casting Techniques.* Unpublished dissertation. USACIL-CONUS, Fort Gordon, GA, April, 1977.

Corr, J. J.: "Tips on tape," *Military Police Journal.* vol. 5 (July, 1956), p. 23.

Couch, S. H.: "Latent fingerprint processing: iodine-silverplate transfer method," *Identification News.* vol. 27 (Jan., 1977), p. 9.

Dellaria, J. F.: "Silicone rubber for crime investigation." *Proceedings of the Forty-fourth Annual Conference of the International Association for Identification.* Pittsburgh, 1959, p. 51.

Development of Polymer-Solvent Systems for Lifting and Preserving Latent Fingerprints. Feasibility report. Atlantic Research, Alexandria, VA, Jan., 1971.

Foley, J. F.: "Development of latent fingerprints—Iodine silver transfer method," *Ontario Provincial Police Review.* vol. 6 (July-Aug., 1971), p. 7.

Hanggi, G. A., and H. M. Alfultis: "Improved technique in the development and lifting of latent fingerprints," *Identification News.* vol. 19 (June, 1969), p. 5.

Harrell, J. R.: "Recovering the bloody fingerprint," *Criminologist.* vol. 8 (Summer, 1973), p. 49.

The Iodine-Silver Transfer Method for Recording Latent Finger Prints. Technical information leaflet. Sirchie Finger Print Laboratories, Moorestown, NJ, n.d.

Jordan, H., and H. Fritz: "Die Fingerabdrucksicherung von Aluminium und anderen polierten Metalloberflachen," *Archiv fur Kriminologie.* vol. 145 (1970), p. 101.

Lentsch, K., and H. Jordan: "Sicherung latenter Fingerabdrucke von stark gekrummten und elastischen Spurentragern," *Kriminalistik.* vol. 21 (1967), p. 237.

"Lifting latent fingerprints," *FBI Law Enforcement Bulletin.* vol. 34 (June, 1965), p. 14.

"The liquid silicone casting of plastic impressions," *Fingerprint and Identification Magazine.* vol. 56 (Oct., 1974), p. 10.

Method of Lifting Latent Impressions from Skin. Latent Print Unit, Missouri State Highway Patrol, 1977.

Mirzaoff, A. N.: "A new finger-print method," *Literary Digest.* vol. 113 (May 7, 1932), p. 22.

Mooney, D. J.: "Fingerprints on human skin," *Identification News.* vol. 27 (Feb., 1977), p. 5.

"A new British copier for latent lifts: The Camtac 121 system," *Fingerprint and Identification Magazine.* vol. 53 (Dec., 1971), p. 3.

"New casting material lifts latent prints," *Fingerprint and Identification Magazine.* vol. 40 (June, 1959), p. 6.

"New spray will lift latent and record dead prints," *Fingerprint and Identification Magazine.* vol. 40 (May, 1959), p. 20.

Olsen, R. D.: "Lifting plastic fingerprints," *Journal of Police Science and Administration.* vol. 3 (1975), p. 29.

Ray, D. N.: "Use of nylon spray as a lifting medium for latent impressions," *Journal of Criminal Law, Criminology and Police Science.* vol. 51 (1961), p. 661.

Robinson, Henry M.: *Science Catches the Criminal.* New York, Blue Ribbon Books. 1935.

Ruesch, S.: "Sicherung von Fingerabdruckspuren in kitt oder anderen weichen Massen," *Kriminalistik.* vol. 20 (1966), p. 296.

"Silicone—A new material for identification work," *Fingerprint and Identification Magazine.* vol. 41 (Jan., 1960), p. 7.

"Silicones for sleuthing," *Industrial and Engineering Chemistry.* vol. 52 (Mar., 1960), p. 37.

Turbyfill, R. T.: "Fingerprint evidence," *Military Police Journal.* vol. 21 (Sept., 1971), p. 12.

"Wet print lifted," *FBI Law Enforcement Bulletin.* vol. 19 (Dec., 1950), p. 19.

Chapter X

Fingerprint Cases

122

REPRESENTATIVE FINGERPRINT CASES

Eᴀᴄʜ ɪɴᴠᴇsᴛɪɢᴀᴛɪᴏɴ involves circumstances and situations unique to that specific case, although many situations may appear to be the same. Techniques and methods employed to recover latent fingerprints must, of necessity, fit each situation. The circumstances under which the latent prints were made, and many other variable factors, alter each case. Investigators should always familiarize themselves with a case as completely as possible *before* making any attempt to recover latent prints: Failure to do so may result in the irretrievable loss of valuable evidence.

The cases discussed and illustrated in this chapter have been selected from thousands. They are representative of a cross section of techniques, types of evidence, and results. The cases may supply an inexperienced investigator with a knowledge of techniques and methods applicable to certain types of fingerprint evidence gained only by long experience. These representative cases are not, however, applicable to every case involving the same type of evidence. They fit the circumstances of the specific case in which they were used and may or may not be successfully used in a similar case. It is misleading to state that any specific technique or method must be used for particular types of evidence. The proper technique and method must be the judgment of the investigator after weighing all known factors.

Cases involving fingerprints, as in all investigations, range from the ridiculously simple to the most exceedingly complex. Not all perpetrators of a crime can be expected to be as obliging as the burglar who, after cutting his way into a store with a welding torch, left a library book on welding with his equipment at the scene. The investigator simply checked with the library and determined to whom the book had been loaned and arrested the suspect. The fingerprints of the suspect were found on the welding equipment and in the chapter of the book pertaining to cutting with a welding torch. It is not possible to com-

403

pare a case such as this with those where the investigation may take months or years to bring to a successful conclusion.

Investigators have no way of knowing that their efforts to recover latent prints in a specific case will be productive of the best possible results or whether another person could have done better. Powdering a latent print is like taking a parachute jump; if it is not successful, one does not get another chance. The chances of success are enhanced in cases where the evidence can be processed by chemical techniques applied in their proper sequence. If one technique is not successful, the next may be. However, there is no guarantee of success with any technique.

Testing affords the best method for determining the applicability of a particular latent fingerprint technique, but it cannot be accomplished in all cases. Investigators may be assured of one thing when they make a test; if they cannot make and develop their own prints on a similar surface under favorable conditions, their efforts in developing latent evidence are destined to failure.

Cases in which useful fingerprint evidence is obtained by the use of light and photography are a challenge to investigators, both old and new. To obtain a good photograph of a latent print, it may be necessary to take many photographs, each with a different angle of light and camera settings. The general rule should be, "If you can see it, you can photograph it."

It is obvious that the illustrations in this chapter have been selected primarily because of their ability to reproduce well in the printed media. Certainly many clear and well-defined latent prints are recovered in investigations, but the majority have less clarity and contrast than those in the illustrations. It is misleading to include only the best illustrations of latent prints, but it is an even greater misrepresentation to include illustrations that reproduce so poorly they are completely illegible.

The cases cited in this chapter illustrate two important objectives in recovering latent fingerprints: (1) recovery of fingerprint evidence without detracting from its value and (2) improvement of the evidence. The first objective has obviously been achieved; otherwise, the cases could not be used. In many cases, the latent prints have been improved by the techniques used. It is not enough to recover the latent prints regardless of quality; they should be improved in the process. Latents in many of the cases are untouched and undeveloped, and improvement is achieved solely through light and photography. It is not always possible to improve upon a latent print by physical development; in fact, an attempt at development may result in damage or loss. A fingerprint case may often look hopeless at the outset, but patience, imagination, and testing bring satisfactory results.

123

FINGERPRINTS ON CLOTH

Latent fingerprints on cloth are about the most difficult for an investigator to detect and develop, regardless of the technique used. Even when the print is a visible impression, the weave and texture of the cloth may obscure ridge structure and details (*see* Sec. 132). There are techniques still in the experimental stage of development as latent fingerprint techniques which may prove to be successful techniques for cloth (*see* Secs. 103 and 108). At this time, however, there is no practical technique for cloth that provides consistently good results in the same respect as techniques for paper.

In some cases, latent prints have been developed on cloth by spraying the cloth with a silver nitrate solution. If an alcoholic solution of silver nitrate is used, the cloth can be dried rather quickly with a stream of compressed air. If an aqueous solution is used, the cloth must be placed within a light-tight container or in a darkroom to dry. The drying time for the latter method is much longer. After the cloth is dried, it is processed in the same manner as other silver nitrate treated evidence (*see* Sec. 92).

When silver nitrate solutions are sprayed, the investigator should wear a mask or respirator to filter out any silver particles that may enter the lungs. The metallic particles may be hazardous to the health of anyone breathing the spray.

Cloth to be treated with chemical techniques to develop or enhance bloody fingerprints should first be processed with a 70% solution of ethyl alcohol to fix the prints (*see* Sec. 101).

124

FINGERPRINTS ON TAPES

Recovering latent fingerprints on tapes generally presents a challenge to the resourcefulness and ingenuity of an investigator. It is difficult to develop latent prints on the adhesive side of any tape and even on the nonadhesive side of cloth, masking, and medical adhesive tapes. The nonadhesive side of smooth surface tapes, such as cellophane, plastic, and PVC (polyvinyl chloride) electrical tapes, can be processed effectively with brush and powder techniques, particularly magnetic powders.

A visual inspection with the aid of a strong light should be made of all evidence prior to applying any powder or chemical technique. This procedure is particularly applicable when examining tapes for latent prints. Cases have been reported where an investigator has carefully removed tape which was wrapped tightly around an object, such as a baseball bat, and a useful plastic impression was recovered from the adhesive side of the tape. Many less-persevering investigators have discarded such evidence in the belief that the pressure of wrapping the tape would destroy any possible impressions in the adhesive. An investigator should always assume that latent prints are present on an evidentiary item and make every effort to recover them.

Latent fingerprints on the adhesive side of tapes is not an uncommon occurrence. Many cases have been brought to a successful conclusion in which the primary evidence was the print of a burglar on the adhesive side of tape applied to a window to keep the glass from shattering when it was broken to gain entry to a building. Generally, latent prints on adhesive surfaces of tapes are the result of dirty fingers, but plastic impressions are not rare. The best procedure in such cases is to protect the impressions until they can be photographed.

It is sometimes possible to develop latent prints on the adhesive surfaces of light-colored tapes (Fig. 105). Iodine and osmium tetroxide fuming and silver nitrate techniques often yield satisfactory results (Smith, 1977). A 10% calcium sulfide solution sometimes yields adequate results on the adhesive of black tapes, but this technique does not work on friction tape (Fig. 106).

Ninhydrin techniques may be used on the nonadhesive side of paper tapes, and, if a transparent tape is on a document, a paper may be submerged in the ninhydrin solution until the solu-

Figure 105. Latent fingerprint on the adhesive side of white medical adhesive tape, developed with osmium tetroxide.

Figure 106. Latent fingerprint on the adhesive side of a black cloth tape, developed with calcium sulfide.

tion has penetrated the surface under the tape. Ninhydrin should not be used on adhesive surfaces or cloth and masking tapes, as it has a marked tendency to discolor such surfaces and obscure any latent prints that may be developed.

125
FINGERPRINTS IN DUST

A burglar raised a window by light, upward fingertip pressure on the dusty glass. At first glance, it may appear to an investigator with little experience that this type of evidence that recovery of the latent prints is difficult, if not impossible. The images are faint, the glass is very dirty and dusty, and the impressions cannot be successfully powdered. The glass bearing the latent prints has been exposed to the weather for a long period of time, and it bears evidence of dust, rain, and dew. Many cases of this kind come to the attention of investigators.

The correct procedure to recover latent prints on surfaces such as described above is the proper use of lighting and photography. Excellent results may be obtained by concentrating a beam of strong light at a low angle and almost parallel to the glass. Illuminated dust particles outline the ridges and spaces of the print in a striking manner. In many cases, it is possible to illuminate the latent prints on glass either from the back (transmitted light) or front (reflected light). The photographic result is usually better than the latents appear to the eye, as photographic film is more sensitive than the eye (Fig. 107).

If the opposite side of a glass windowpane is dusty or dirty, and it is does not show any evidence of a fingerprint, it should be wiped clean. This procedure is essential when photographing a print with transmitted light. If reflected light at an oblique angle is used, a dark cloth placed at a distance behind the glass

Figure 107. Fingerprints in dust on a piece of glass from a broken window. Photographed with transmitted light, the ridges appear as white lines. The detail of these prints could not be enhanced with powder or chemical techniques.

Figure 108. Partial fingerprint in fireclay dust on a paper found at the scene of a safe burglary. The print is suitable for identification. Such prints are extremely delicate and must be photographed as soon as possible, as handling may destroy the print.

provides greater contrast between the ridge structure of the latent and the dust particles. Cleaning the back side of any glass or transparent surface is a good practice if it is free of fingerprints. It eliminates the possibility of stray dust particles showing through the glass and interfering with the legibility of the latent print.

If latent prints are located on both sides of a glass pane, directly opposite each other, it is possible to photograph each print and eliminate the print on the reverse side from the photograph.

The latent print is illuminated with reflected oblique lighting, and a dark cloth is placed behind the glass at a distance. The camera is focused precisely on the latent print on the side of the glass facing the camera, and the exposure is made at the f-stop setting which provides the least depth of field. This procedure is then repeated to photograph the latent print on the reverse side of the glass.

The challenge that fingerprint impressions in dust and dirt may present to an investigator is typified in a burglary case received by the U.S. Army Criminal Investigation Laboratory. The window through which the burglar gained entry into a home was covered with a thin layer of dirt which, through weathering, was hardened onto the window frame. The investigator at the scene found a fingerprint impression on the window frame; the moist finger of the suspect had, in this case, removed the layer of dirt touched by the ridge structure of the finger. The entire window was submitted to the laboratory for examination.

The window had been painted a medium-gray color and the layer of dust was so thin that attempts to photograph the impression met with negative results. The fingerprint examiner attempted to powder the impression, but powder would not adhere to either the impression or the dirt. Chemical techniques could not be used because the paint was enamel, and fuming techniques failed. As a last resort, the fingerprint examiner sprayed the print with a saturated solution of alizarin and alcohol, dried the surface with a stream of hot air, and then sprayed it with a 25% solution of ammonium hydroxide. The dirt was stained a reddish violet color, while the ridge structure of the latent print was not stained. A satisfactory photograph suitable for identification was then obtained of the latent print.

126

FINGERPRINTS ON GLASS AND METAL

Glass, particularly clean glass, is an excellent receiving surface for latent fingerprints. Frequently, latent prints on glass may be detected by viewing the glass under a strong light. By moving the glass or light source at different angles to the line of vision, the latent print residue is easily detected and the ridge structure of the latent print clearly visible. Such undeveloped latent prints, as all visible fingerprints, should be photographed before any attempt is made to enhance the prints by applying powder (Figs. 109 and 110).

The procedure for photographing visible latent print residue on glass is the same as that previously described for photographing impressions in dust on glass surfaces, reflected light with a black cloth in the background (*see* Sec. 125). This procedure does not, however, work well for latent prints on embossed and curved glass surfaces. Soft-drink bottles are an example of such surfaces. Embossed and curved glass surfaces present unique lighting problems for photography. The use of reflected light causes highlights that may obscure ridge structure. Transmitted light or backlights from the opposite side of a bottle may interfere with the ridge structure of the latent print.

Powdered fingerprints on a glass bottle can be easily photographed with transmitted light by using one of the following methods. One method is to fill the glass bottle with a fluorescent solution and illuminate it from the side with ultraviolet light

Figure 109. Undeveloped latent fingerprints on glass showing excellent ridge detail. These fingerprints are suitable for identification purposes, and the patterns are classifiable.

Figure 110. Partially superimposed fingerprints of two persons on a window pane. The prints were backlighted and photographed—no powder development was attempted.

(Spangler, 1975). The fluorescent solution provides an even distribution of light, and highlights from embossed and curved surfaces are eliminated. The fluorescent solution may be prepared by dissolving 0.1 g fluorescein in 1 l of ordinary tap water (Page, 1976a). This method provides satisfactory results with clear and light-colored bottles, but the glass of dark amber and green bottles acts as a barrier to ultraviolet light.

Dark amber and green bottles may be photographed with transmitted light by filling the bottle with opalescent solution and illuminating it with backlighting (Page, 1976a). The opalescent solution is prepared by simply making a very weak solution of powdered milk and water. Another method that may be used for photographing fingerprints on bottles and other curved surfaces is barrel lighting (Watson, 1971). In this method, a large cardboard barrel is used. The inside of the barrel is painted a matte white, and a slit is made in the side for the camera lens. The bottle is placed in the barrel and lighted from the top with two photographic lights which are aimed down toward the sides of the barrel. The light is bounced back on the object being photographed, giving an even distribution of lighting without highlights.

Electric light bulbs should never be overlooked when conducting a crime scene search for fingerprint evidence. Numerous cases can be cited where the only evidence connecting a suspect with the scene of a crime was a latent print on a light bulb, which was recovered only through the alertness of the investigator at the scene. It is not uncommon, for example, for burglars to loosen the bulbs of security lights to prevent detection of their activities. When conducting a crime scene search, it is a wise procedure to turn on all light switches and automatically check for latent prints on all light bulbs that fail to light when a switch is turned on.

The spherical surfaces of electric light bulbs present problems to an investigator in respect to photography and lifting. Reflected light with a black cloth in the background usually produces an adequate photograph, if the glass of the bulb is clear. The barrel method also provides good results in most cases. Transmitted light usually provides the best results for photographing prints on electric light bulbs, particularly if the glass of the bulb is frosted. If the bulb is still functional, a powdered fingerprint may be photographed by reducing the voltage to the lamp with a rheostat and using the bulb itself as a light source. In some cases, it is possible to photograph a powdered print on a light bulb by illuminating it from the back, through a hole cut in a piece of cardboard.

Fingerprints on mirrors and polished metal surfaces should be developed with light-colored powders. Metallic powders are well suited for such surfaces. It appears to be an unorthodox procedure to develop a latent print with powder that does not contrast with the surface bearing the latent print, but results are more important than techniques. One feature of metallic powders is that they are so tenacious that, in many instances, they may be brushed without fear of destroying ridge detail. When using metallic powders, it is essential that care be exercised to not apply too much powder. An excess of metallic powder has a marked tendency to paint a surface and obscure latent prints.

Using light-colored powders to develop latent prints on mirrors and polished metal surfaces suits photographic purposes. Due to their highly reflective surfaces, mirrors and polished metal surfaces appear dark in photographs. If light-colored powders are used, the image of the latent print appears light against a dark background. It is possible to use dark powders on these highly reflective surfaces and obtain a good photograph of the powdered prints by simply adjusting the lighting. The use of light-colored powders, however, greatly expedites the photographic process at the crime scene and gives the investigator more time for conducting a search.

Many metals, galvanized metals and brass, for example, may have the ridge structure of latent prints etched into the metal. Such latent prints are commonly found on the coin boxes of vending and slot machines. Prints etched into metal cannot normally be developed further with powder or chemical techniques; they must be photographed as they appear. In some cases, however, it may be possible to enhance the contrast of the latent print by using the flame technique. The soot from the flame may adhere to the corroded metal of the ridge structure of the latent print.

Latent fingerprints on brass cartridges may be developed with powder or the chemical techniques described in Section 97. The reflective and curved surfaces of brass cartridges, like glass bottles, may cause highlights which obscure ridge details. This photographic problem may be overcome by using the barrel lighting method or a technique developed by Page (1976b). The latter technique is accomplished as follows. Set the camera horizontally and stand the cartridge in front of the lens. Light the cartridge with copy lighting and focus the camera. Then make a cylinder from a sheet of white paper and cut an opening at one end. The opening should be only slightly larger than the cartridge. Place the cylinder over the cartridge with the opening between the cartridge and the camera lens. A trough is then made from a sheet of white paper and placed between the lens and cylinder, with the open side of the trough facing down. The trough is secured with masking tape. Then make a hole slightly larger than the selected aperture size in a third piece of white paper. A small aperture should be selected for greater depth of field due to the curved surface of the cartridge. This variation of the tented lighting technique virtually eliminates all lines caused by highlights, which may appear in the photograph of a latent print on a cartridge.

A gun presents many handicaps to the development of finger-print evidence, but occasionally, very good fingerprints are developed. Exposed smooth surfaces on many guns are not large enough to take latent prints sufficient for identification, if the firearm is held in the normal manner for operation (Fig. 111). Some surfaces may be checked, milled, or otherwise rough, which makes the recovery of latent prints very difficult. Latent prints are particularly difficult to develop on the Parkerized finish found on almost all military firearms. This type of finish is used on military weapons to prevent rust, and the metal surface

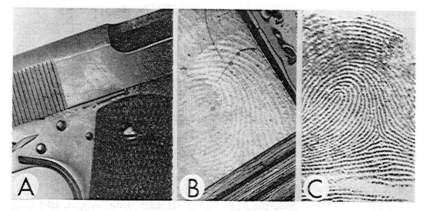

Figure 111. (A) Fingerprint in oil film on the slide of an automatic pistol as seen by reflected light. (B) Close-up of same impression. (C) Inked impression of suspect for comparison.

is usually sandblasted prior to the Parkerizing process to produce a nonreflective surface.

A firearm which has received even a minimum amount of care and maintenance usually has a light coat of oil over all the metallic parts to prevent rust. This film of oil normally prevents any attempt to develop latent prints with powder. In some cases, a visual inspection of the weapon may reveal a legible print in the film of oil. Such fingerprints should be photographed before any attempt to further develop the prints. Watson (1971) recommends chilling a firearm prior to developing latent prints in an oily film. The firearm is placed in a refrigerator and cooled to firm up the oil. The weapon is then processed with Magne Jet Black® powder. After photographing the latent print, the firearm is chilled again before the latent print is lifted.

Well-cared-for firearms in criminal cases are the exception rather than the rule. Few criminals bother to take even the minimum of care of their weapons. Every effort should be made to search for latent fingerprints on a firearm, regardless of how difficult a task it may appear to be. A thorough search should be made even when it is known that the suspect tried to wipe the weapon clean of prints. There are many cases on record where suspects have wiped firearms to remove their fingerprints, but were identified by partial prints found in the groove of a revolver cylinder, which was protected by the frame of the revolver or on the magazine of an automatic pistol. In some cases, the prints of the suspect were found on both the fired and unexpended cartridge cases from the weapon.

127

FINGERPRINTS ON WOOD

Clean painted surfaces usually afford good conditions for powder development of latent fingerprints, if the impressions are fresh (Fig. 112). Very often a visual examination of a painted surface reveals the location of latent prints, but this rule does not always hold true. Frequently, prints are developed

Figure 112. Fingerprints developed with black powder on painted window frame. Obtaining lifts on grained wood surfaces often results in some loss of ridge detail.

where they were invisible and wholly unexpected. Enamel and smooth-finished oil-based paints should always be processed with powders. All fingerprints should be photographed before any attempt is made to lift the impressions, but this is particularly true for latent prints on painted surfaces. If the paint is old, has been exposed to weathering, or has not bonded well to the underlying surface, lifting may destroy a latent print by removing portions of the paint as well as the powdered print. A test lift on a nonevidenciary area should be made before lifting prints on painted surfaces.

Latent fingerprints on unfinished wood and wood painted with water-based paints, such as latex, may be developed with chemical techniques. The same sequence of techniques may be used as for paper: iodine, ninhydrin, and then silver nitrate. The use of powders on such surfaces seldom yield good results, except for very fresh prints, and even then the powders have a marked tendency to coat the surfaces.

Wooden tool handles are rarely productive of good fingerprint evidence, but many cases have been solved by latent prints on a wooden tool handle. No possibility should be overlooked, and no portion of an object should be ignored because the chances of successful recovery of fingerprint evidence appear to be remote. A special effort should be made to locate latent fingerprints in every instance. An investigator never knows where latent prints will be found until beginning the search.

128

FINGERPRINTS ON PLASTIC

Plastic is a good receiving surface for latent fingerprints. This is true of almost all types of smooth-surface plastics: hard plastic tool handles, plastic bags, or paper and cardboard coated with a protective plastic film. Plastics are rapidly replacing glass, metal, wood, and paper and are becoming one of the most common types of materials that must be examined for latent fingerprints.

The best technique for developing latent fingerprints on plastic is magnetic powders (*see* Sec. 74). When processing some types of plastics, such as the thin plastics found in sandwich and food-storage bags, magnetic powders yield better results if they are modified by mixing the magnetic powder with regular fingerprint powder of the same color. This modified powder enables the investigator to enhance a latent print with further brushing and provides greater contrast to the ridge structure of the latent image. Transparent plastics should be processed with magnetic powders while viewing with transmitted light. A lightbox or x-ray viewer may be used, but best results can be obtained if the intensity of the light can be controlled.

Latent prints developed on pieces of very thin plastic must be photographed when they are developed. Excessive handling of the plastic after development with powder may result in loss of the latent prints. Powdered latent prints are much more fragile than undeveloped latents. Attempts to lift latent prints on sheets of very thin plastic are usually doomed to failure, and such prints must be photographed. The powder adhering to the latent print may be readily visible with transmitted light, but will not always transfer to a lifting device. Further, very thin plastics have a tendency to tear during the lifting process, and, if the area upon which the latent print is located tears and stretches, the latent is lost.

During a robbery, the thief removed the coin tray from a cash register by gripping a partition between two compartments with his thumb and the side of his index finger. The space in which the investigator had to work was very small and awkward. When a test print showed that silver magnetic powder would work well on the plastic surface, the latent was developed with silver magnetic powder and the aid of a small mirror. The latent print was subsequently lifted with lifting tape, but the investigator first photographed the print to preclude its loss during the lifting process. The print was located in a corner of a compartment, near the bottom of the tray. Due to the location of the print the camera could not be positioned properly, but the investigator solved this problem by using the small mirror. The mirror was positioned to reflect the image of the latent print upward into the camera lens, and the camera was focused on the image in the mirror.

129

FINGERPRINTS ON PAPER

Paper and paper products are, generally, excellent receiving surfaces for latent fingerprints (Fig. 113). Magnetic powders can be used to develop very fresh prints on paper, but powders should be avoided, as far better results can be obtained with iodine fuming and chemical techniques. The use of iodine fuming, ninhydrin, and silver nitrate techniques in their proper sequence normally results in the recovery of latent prints on papers. However, there are certain types of papers which respond more satisfactorily to powders than chemical techniques. Papers

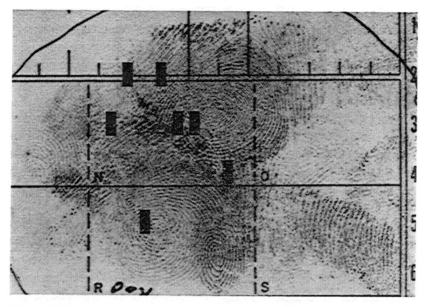

Figure 113. Latent fingerprints on a computer card, developed with ninhydrin. This is an example of the applicability of fingerprint evidence in fraud and white-collar crimes, even when the crime is committed through computers.

specially treated for resistance to grease or oils, greaseproof papers, should be examined with powders prior to the use of chemical techniques, such as an alcoholic silver nitrate solution.

Except for specially treated papers, paper sufficiently absorbs to latent print residue after only a relative short period of time. Iodine development of latent prints on paper is uncertain after several weeks. Depending upon the influence of temperature and humidity, there do not appear to be any specific time limitations for the successful development of latent prints with ninhydrin and silver nitrate.

It has been repeatedly stressed that any search for latent fingerprints must be thorough and exacting. This advice also applies to papers. In cases involving postal violations, such as the mailing of prohibited matter, suspects have been identified as a result of the recovery of their prints on the mucilage on the back of a stamp and the sealed flap of an envelope. The procedure in such cases is to completely submerge the envelope in a ninhydrin solution, and, after the paper has become completely soaked with the solution, gently remove the stamp or open the envelope without tearing the paper fibers. Of course, an edge of a sealed envelope should be slit with a sharp blade and the contents removed prior to the application of ninhydrin.

Brown craft paper and cardboard usually present problems when using the ninhydrin technique. Often a ninhydrin-developed latent print can be seen with the naked eye on such materials but disappears in photographing or when viewed through a magnifier. The next step is to apply silver nitrate, but an aqueous solution dissolves the ninhydrin image. If there is any ninhydrin-developed ridge detail at all, an alcoholic silver nitrate solution should be used to further enhance the latent image.

Glassine paper has been commonly used for the windows of business envelopes and in many cases to package small amounts of narcotics. Latent prints may be developed on this type of paper with the ninhydrin and silver nitrate techniques, but silver nitrate appears to yield the best results. Glassine is being replaced in many business envelopes with transparent plastic. Therefore, a very small amount of ninhydrin, about a drop, should be placed in a corner of the window of the envelope prior to applying the ninhydrin to the entire envelope. Most ninhydrin solutions dissolve plastics and, if a test is not made and the plastic is not removed, any dissolved plastic may adhere to the surfaces of the entire envelope.

Normally, ninhydrin-developed latent prints should be photographed using a Kodak Wratten No. 58® or No. 61® (green) filter and Kodak Tri-X film. This procedure provides maximum contrast while retaining as great a range of density of tones as possible. Contrast without density of tones usually results in the loss of visibility of much ridge structure in ninhydrin-developed latent prints. In some cases, it may be necessary to photographically remove colored writings or marks that interfere with the visibility of a latent print. For example, a ninhydrin print on the back of a bank check may be covered with a red bank stamp. The print can be photographed and the bank stamp removed with an orange filter.

130

FINGERPRINTS IN DRUG CASES

The positive identification of a suspect's latent fingerprints on items of evidence may be sufficient proof for a court to return a verdict for conviction. Modern criminal investigation is a science, and, as such, all available evidence must be methodically collected and meticulously processed and evaluated. In conducting investigations of alleged drug offenses, an investigator as a matter of routine, forwards the evidence to the crime laboratory for chemical analysis. In addition to the chemical analysis, the investigator should also request examination of the drug containers and all other related evidence for latent fingerprints.

If a suspect's latent fingerprints are found to be on any of the evidentiary items in a drug case, it may strengthen the investigator's case at the trial of the accused. In those cases where a suspect later repudiates his confession or admission and subsequently denies having knowingly possessed prohibited drugs, even though the evidence was found in his possession, the presence of his fingerprints on any of the evidentiary items may successfully refute his denials and sustain a conviction.

All narcotic and other drug evidence should always be handled with extreme care (Figs. 114 and 115). Due to its size, it should be handled like all other fragile evidence and care taken to avoid contamination or destruction. Any consideration given to fingerprint examination of suspected drug evidence should not, therefore, necessitate any additional handling procedures other than those normally required. Drug evidence may be seized in a variety of containers, and the circumstances in each case determine whether latent fingerprints may or may not be found on the evidence.

Identifiable latent fingerprints have been found on almost all types of possible drug containers: pillboxes, envelopes and other paper containers, plastic bags, dolls, matchboxes, and inside hol-

Figure 114. Bags of hashish wrapped and taped in plastic. Both the outside and inside surfaces of the plastic should be processed with magnetic powders to recover latent prints. It is possible in cases of this type to identify many persons engaged in the drug traffic, in addition to those in immediate possession of the drugs.

lowed-out candles, to name only a few. Even in those cases where more than one person is known to have handled the evidence, it is sometimes possible to develop individual fingerprints of particular individuals. To conclusively prove that an individual has handled the evidence, all that may be required is at least one identifiable latent fingerprint.

Drug offenses, such as unlawful possession, use, sale, or transfer, require that the offender has had, at some time and in some manner, possessed the drug in question. Possession implies touching. Admittedly a person may be under investigation for drug

Figure 115. Two boxes of marihuana seized during a customs inspection. The wrapping paper and the cardboard boxes should be fully processed with chemical techniques to recover latent prints. It is common in such cases to establish the identity of the person shipping the contraband through fingerprint evidence.

violations without having had direct physical contact with the drug; however, in the majority of cases, actual possession occurs. Even more important than actual conviction of the immediate offender is the identification of people engaged in the illicit traffic of drugs. It may be possible through fingerprint identification to identify suppliers and others involved in more than one case under investigation.

The examination of drug evidence should always be conducted jointly by the fingerprint examiner and the chemist. Close coordination between these two is important to preclude destruction or contamination of the evidence, which would hinder the analysis by either examiner. In this respect, an investigator in the field should not attempt to process drug evidence for latent fingerprints and should request the laboratory to do the processing.

Drug containers may be searched for latent fingerprints with techniques appropriate to the type of material involved. Plastic bags, for example, should be processed with a modified magnetic powder formula—a mixture of magnetic and regular fingerprint powders. The preliminary visual inspection for latent prints should be made with ultraviolet light, in addition to that with a strong light source, as many drugs fluoresce, and the latent print residue may retain particles of the drug.

A common material for wrapping drugs for street sale is aluminum foil. The foil is usually very wrinkled, and many investigators tend to discount the possibility of recovering fingerprint evidence from foil in this condition. However, it is possible to develop latent fingerprints on badly wrinkled foil by the method developed by Turbyfill (1976). A mixture of two-thirds gray magnetic powder is mixed with one-third regular white fingerprint powder. The drug is removed from the foil, placed in a separate, clean container, and the foil is opened gently and spread out for processing. The magnetic powder is then applied using the breath technique. If any ridge detail is detected, the foil can be smoothed out by rubbing the foil on the side directly opposite the ridge detail. After the foil has been smoothed, it should then be processed again, using the same method. The rubbing of the foil to smooth it does not destroy the developed latent print.

131

FINGERPRINTS ON SKIN

Except for visible impressions, such as bloody fingerprints, there is no case on record where a suspect has been identified and convicted on the basis of a latent fingerprint developed on human skin. Considerable research has been directed toward this goal, and considerable promise of a practical technique has been indicated, but attainment of an effective and practical technique has not yet been achieved.

The use of x-ray techniques to recover latent prints on human skin has been suggested (*see* Sec. 105), but such techniques would be severely limited in practical application because of the equipment involved and the relatively long period of time required for the technique. Several other techniques requiring less time to complete and far less expensive equipment may provide more practical results.

Development of latent fingerprints on human skin using the iodine fuming and silver transfer lifting techniques has been suggested by Foley (1971). The area suspected of bearing the latent impression, such as the neck in a strangling case, is fumed with an iodine fuming pipe. Any latent print that develops appears as a smudge; that is, the ridge structure of the latent print is not distinct. The print is then lifted with a silver plate in the same manner as any iodine-developed print would be lifted (*see* Sec. 119). Foley has reported that identifiable fingerprint impressions on living skin can be obtained for periods up to 1½ hours, and on deceased persons, the impressions were successfully developed and lifted for periods up to 105 hours. The silica gel iodine fuming technique (*see* Sec. 81) may prove more practical in the field than the fuming pipe, requiring less time at the scene for preparation.

Mooney (1977) and Reichardt (1977) have reported a lifting technique developed by Edward Stone of the Dade County Public Safety Department, Miami, Florida. In this technique, Kromekote®, a latent print card for mounting lifting tape and and marketed by the Lightning Powder Company, is applied to the suspected area for a few seconds and then the card is processed with magnetic powder and the breath technique. Mooney reports that polycontrast and Ektamatic® photographic print papers may also be used.

Another lifting technique was developed by the Latent Print Unit of the Missouri State Highway Patrol (Anon., 1977) (Fig. 116). It is similar to that described above, but almost any smooth-surfaced material may be used. A slick-finished card stock, piece of plastic, or exposed photographic paper is coated with photoprint coating of the type used in standard Polaroid photographic systems. After coating the material with a Polaroid black-and-white applicator, the coating is allowed to dry completely. The prepared surface is then placed over the skin area suspected of bearing a latent print, pressed firmly on the skin,

Figure 116. Latent fingerprint lifted from living human skin. The print was lifted using the technique developed by the Missouri State Highway Patrol and developed using magnetic powder. The lift was protected by covering with transparent tape.

and removed. Care must be exercised to avoid slippage. The coated lifter is then processed with brush and powder or magnetic powder. The developed prints can be protected with a piece of transparent lifting tape.

All the techniques mentioned for developing latent fingerprints on human skin are restricted to those skin areas relatively free of hair and relatively smooth. This indicates that the probability of success for these techniques is increased with the subject being a woman or a young person. However, the relative changes of success should not deter an attempt to recover latent prints. Successful recovery of fingerprint evidence depends on the perseverance of the investigator in seeking latent prints.

132

IMAGE ENHANCEMENT OF A BLOODY PRINT*

J. A. ROBERTS

On numerous occasions, many examiners have had to work with a bloody finger or palmprint on some type of woven cloth. All too often, any chance of an association between the print and a suspect is dissolved immediately due to (1) the absorption of the blood fluid into the cloth itself, (2) the tendency of the print to be smudged when it was placed, and (3) the usually total interference of the cloth weave with the ridge detail of the print. This article deals with the third point.

During the investigation of a murder in San Diego, California, an ordinary bedsheet was noticed to have a bloody print on it (Fig. 117). It was the only objective evidence in the case. It can be observed that ridge detail is most evident in the hypothenar area of the right palm. Although the ridges are discernible from the white background of the sheet, identification was not possible due to interference of the weave pattern with the ridge detail of the print.

At this point in the investigation, the bloody print was sent to the Jet Propulsion Laboratory in Pasadena, California, where the Space Technology Applications Office and the Image Processing Laboratory were developing a process whereby the background material, known as *interference* was entirely eliminated or as nearly as possible, thus leaving clearer ridge detail. This process is similar to that used in the enhancement of photographs obtained from the various unmanned space shots for the

* The original title of this paper was *Space Age Technology to the Aid of the Latent Print Examiner.* ©1972, The Institute of Applied Science. Reprinted with permission.

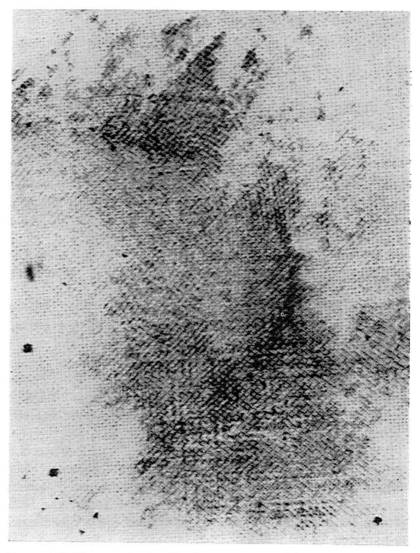

Figure 117. Photograph of a bloody print on a bedsheet. The negative of this photograph was used in the original input at the Jet Propulsion Laboratory.

exploration of the moon, Mars, and Venus under the auspices of NASA.

The technique used in separating the two patterns (the weave of the sheet and the friction ridge pattern) is one that has been used in processing television pictures sent from spacecraft in deep space. The pictures coming from the television cameras often exhibit incoherent noise patterns which interfere with the extraction of information from the picture.

In this case, a photographic transparency of the area of interest on the sheet was made and subsequently scanned with a flying spot scanner. This information was then introduced into the computer for processing.

The major processing steps undertaken were computing the Fourier transform of the image and identifying the frequency components due to the weave of the sheet and those of the friction ridge information. Following identification and verification that the correct frequency components had been selected, the components attributed to the weave pattern of the sheet were removed or reduced in magnitude, and the reverse or back Fourier transform was computed to obtain the original palm-print image, now without the weave pattern of the sheet.

Additional processing steps were taken to remove shading effects and to increase the relative contrast of the friction ridge information in the image. The area represented in the photograph of the computer-enhanced image is approximately 1 inch square in its original size, and is located in the hypothenar area of the bloody print. Noticeable is the strong ridge detail due to the partial elimination of the weave from the photograph (Fig. 118). A court chart was then prepared using the computer-enhanced image and the hypothenar area from the inked impression of the right palm of the suspect (Figs. 119 and 120). Seventeen points of comparison were marked, although there are three or four more which can be determined.

There is no doubt in the author's mind the bloody print is that of the suspect. When, however, the exhibits were offered in evidence at the trial, the Jet Propulsion Laboratory enhanced

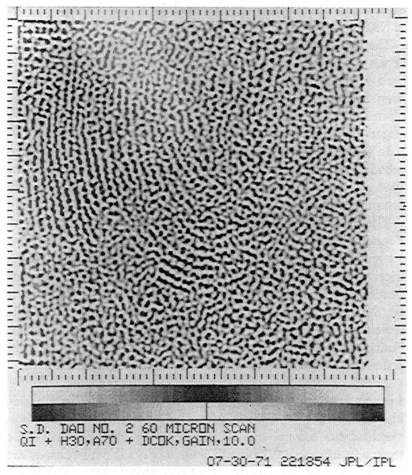

S.D. DAO NO. 2 60 MICRON SCAN
QI + H30,A70 + DCOK,GAIN,10.0

07-30-71 221854 JPL/IPL

Figure 118. Photograph of result of the process used by the Jet Propulsion Laboratory to enhance the bloody print on the bedsheet.

print was ruled inadmissible. This is the reason given by the court, as taken from the transcript:

THE COURT: Gentlemen, it is a difficult decision to make and I realize the decision I make may have considerable bearing on the case. Applying the test set forth in *Frye* vs. *Crowley*, I find that the People have failed to establish by a preponderance of the evidence any of the following:

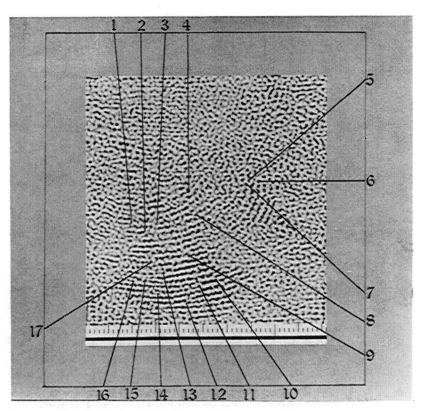

Figure 119. Enhanced image of Figure 118. The ridge characteristics have been marked off for demonstration purposes.

1. That the scientific principle used by Jet Propulsion Laboratory in the development of People's 46 (the computer-enhanced photograph) has been generally accepted among experts in the particular area involved.

2. That the technique has been accepted in the particular field of use to which it is applied in this case.

3. That there is scientific certainty about the results produced by Jet Propulsion Laboratory in this case.

I further find that the preponderance of the evidence discloses that the techniques used by Jet Propulsion Laboratory in this case to produce the exhibits are still in the experimental stage and the People's claim for the accuracy of the Jet Propulsion Laboratory

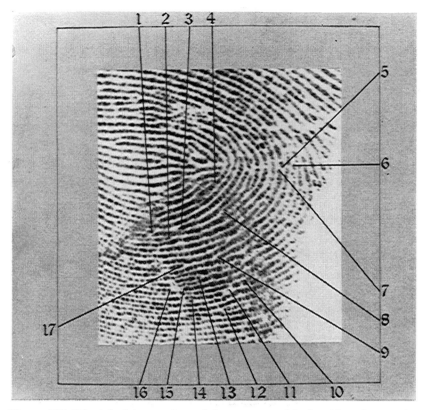

Figure 120. The inked impressions of the suspect with the ridge characteristics matching those in the enhanced print marked off. Seventeen points of similarity have been marked off in this fingerprint chart, although there are three or four more points that can be determined.

enhancement is founded on theories and conclusions which have not yet been substantiated by accepted methods of scientific verification.

I further find that the enhancement should be excluded under Evidence Code Section 352, as its probative value is substantially outweighed by the probability that its admission will create a substantial danger of misleading the jury.

I therefore rule against the admissibility of the evidence being offered in this case.

I think that is People's 1 through—which ones were they?

THE DEFENSE: 52

THE COURT: 1 through 52. The People are, therefore, directed not to mention the palmprint or anything related thereto in *voir dire* or opening statement, nor to refer to it in any other proceedings before the jury.

No latent fingerprint expert was permitted to testify to the value of the enhanced print of the Jet Propulsion Laboratory.

Subsequently, the bloody print was sprayed with benzidine solution. This process was identical to that described by Nariyuki, Ueda, and Sasaki (*see* Sec. 101). This treatment developed an area to the left of that shown in the photograph of the print on the sheet. Due in part to the admissibility of the benzidine-treated portion, a conviction was handed down after a costly and time-consuming trial.

The author believes that if the "enhanced" evidence had been admitted for its true worth, the entire case would have been expedited sooner. The jury in this case is to be commended for their thorough search between fact and fantasy.

It is the author's hope that Richard Blackwell and the Jet Propulsion Laboratory will continue their research into this valuable identification aid and that all who have or will have similar cases will become familiar with this instrument. The author feels most privileged to be the first person, to the best of my knowledge, to use this important process for print identification.

133

USE OF NEW TECHNIQUES

Judging from the failure of the court to accept the image-enhancement technique of the Jet Propulsion Laboratory described in the preceding section, it may appear that a new technique for developing or enhancing latent prints should not be used until it has gained wide acceptance. If this were true, no new technique would ever gain acceptance and there would be no progress.

In Section 89, it was stated that it is not necessary for anyone using latent fingerprint techniques to have prior training in chemistry, nor is it essential that they understand the chemical reactions involved. In other forensic sciences, such as forensic chemistry, the results of particular analyses and examinations may depend greatly upon the method and procedure involved. The use of a wrong reagent or sequence of reagents may give false indications. *This is not the case for latent fingerprint techniques.* The sole question regarding a latent print should be whether or not it can be identified, based on individual ridge characteristics and their relative position to each other. Techniques for developing or enhancing latent prints do not add ridge characteristics which are not present originally. At worst, an improperly used technique would hinder or prevent the identification of a latent print by obscuring or destroying ridge details. Such an occurrence is to the benefit of a suspect rather than his detriment.

The view that a new technique may so change ridge details that a false identification may result can be refuted statistically. The probability of two individuals having twelve identical characteristics in the same relative positions is one in ten million million (*see* Sec. 13). It may be reasonable to assume that the probability of a new technique in any way altering ridge characteristics in a manner that would result in a false identification would be even greater. However, for the sake of illustration, it is assumed that the probability is the same as that for twelve identical points, one in ten million million. The probability of a new technique changing ridge characteristics identical to those of the suspect would, therefore, be so astronomical as to be impossible.

The above can be illustrated by the following analogy. Suppose that one ticket is bought in a lottery where one million tickets are sold; obviously the chance of winning is one in one million. Suppose there are two lotteries, each selling a million tickets, and one ticket is bought in each. One's chance of winning both lotteries is not one in two million—it is one in one million million.

Any attempt by a defence counsel to make a latent fingerprint examiner explain and justify the techniques used to develop or enhance a latent print is merely an attempt to sidetrack the examiner's testimony and detract from the identification of the print. During the pretrial interview with the prosecutor, an examiner should make the prosecutor aware of the possibility of such tactics and that it is merely an attempt to cloud the issue. An investigator should not be deterred from using a particular technique simply because it is new. The technique selected for use in each case should be governed only by the investigator's decision as to which technique will provide the best results.

134

FINGERPRINT COURT EXHIBITS

In testifying to fingerprint identification before a court, a fingerprint examiner usually uses charts to visually aid the court and jury in understanding the nature of the testimony. These charts are used solely to demonstrate how an examiner arrived at a conclusion regarding the fingerprints; they are not used for the purpose of demonstrating the sufficiency of the examiner's findings. To become qualified as a latent fingerprint examiner, a person must receive intensive training and fulfill an internship of at least two years working full time as a latent fingerprint examiner. It would not be reasonable to assume that during the short period of testimony, a court and jury could become proficient in fingerprint identification. In some cases, it may be a wise decision not to prepare a chart for court. Charts in cases involving fragmentary prints, smudged impressions, and prints with ridge structure lacking good contrast may prove confusing to laymen.

Fingerprint court charts are photographic enlargements of the latent print and the inked impression of the area of friction skin identified as having made the latent print (Fig. 121). These two photographs are mounted on stiff cardboard, and each print is identified as to whether it is the latent or inked impression, and the individual matching ridge characteristics in each print are marked.

Each examiner and agency may have their own methods for preparing fingerprint court charts, but the procedures are basically the same. The latent and inked impressions should be en-

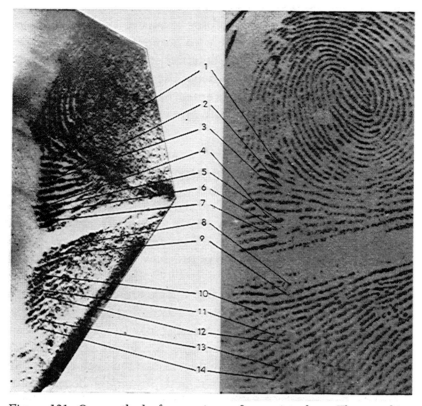

Figure 121. One method of preparing a fingerprint chart. The matching points in the latent and inked fingerprints are indicated by lines drawn to a single vertical column of numbers between the two impressions. The latent print was made on the metal foil cover on a bottle top.

larged with the same degree of magnification. The size of the final enlargements is immaterial, they may be 5-by-7, 8-by-10, or even 16-by-20 inches. However, when an image on a photographic negative is enlarged too much, there is a tendency for the image to lose clarity. Therefore, the enlargement should not be so great that details of the ridge structure may be lost.

The photographic enlargements of the latent and inked impressions may be made by first blocking off the negatives with photographic tape and then making the enlargements. Another method may be used, if a ruler or other type of measuring device has been included in the photographs to the same scale, using the ruler in the photograph. The particular area to be used for the court chart is then cut out of each enlargement.

After the enlargements of the latent and inked impressions have been prepared, they are mounted on a piece of cardboard. The cardboard should be at least 1 mm in thickness, but 2 mm provides an even better chart board. The side of the cardboard on which the photographs are mounted should be white. The positioning of the photographs, inked on the right and latent on the left, is a matter of choice of the individual examiner. Some examiners have advanced the argument that the inked impression should be on the left because people normally look at things in the same manner as they read, from left to right, and they believe it would be best if the court were to see the inked impression first. However, the standard rule in practice for most examiners seems to be for the latent print to be on the left.

After the photographs have been mounted on the chart board, each photograph is identified as to whether it is the latent or inked impression. This identification may be handprinted in ink, inked in with a lettering set, or placed on the mounting board with rub-on lettering. The exact designation of the latent and inked impressions depends upon the terminology used by the particular agency and examiner. They may be as follows: Latent and inked, latent fingerprint and inked fingerprint, questioned and known, or latent and record.

It is not necessary to chart all of the ridge characteristics in the latent and inked impressions. A sufficient number to illustrate the identification is all that is necessary. The numbers designating the ridge characteristics should be marked on the mounting board in a clockwise manner around each print, although some examiners prefer a single, vertical row of numbers between the two impressions. A line is then drawn in ink from each characteristic to its corresponding number (Figs. 122, 123, and 124). Many examiners prefer to use red tape, ⅟₁₆- or ⅛-inch wide, depending on the size of the photographs, for making the lines designating the ridge characteristics.

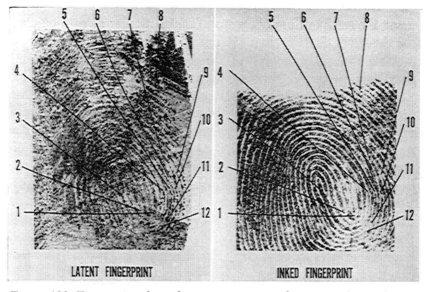

Figure 122. Fingerprint chart showing comparison between a latent fingerprint developed with powder on a metal coin box and the inked impression of the suspect.

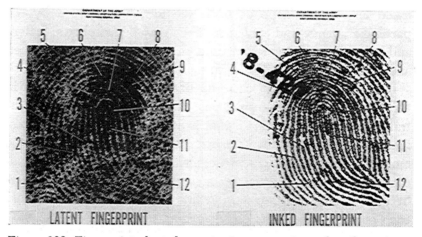

Figure 123. Fingerprint chart demonstrating comparison of a silver nitrate developed latent print and inked impression of the suspect. The latent print was developed on a cardboard box used to ship contraband.

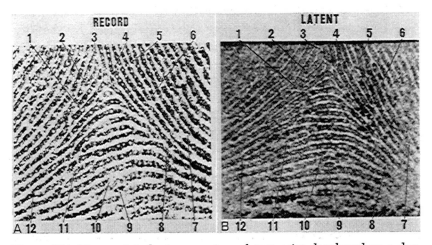

Figure 124. Fingerprint chart comparing a latent print developed on a document with ninhydrin (A) and inked print of suspect (B). There are many more points of similarity than the twelve marked. The latent print was made by the palm of the suspect, but in making the comparisons, the fingerprint examiner had to examine all delta formations, including those of the fingers. Partial or fragmentary impressions, such as the one illustrated, require a complete and thorough search of all friction skin areas of the hand.

The projection lines from the ridge characteristics should never cross one another. Extreme care should be taken to insure that each projection line in the latent print enlargement corresponds with the same projection line in the enlargement of the inked impression. For example, if the projection line of point number 1 in the latent print ends exactly on the end of an ending ridge, the projection line of point number 1 in the inked impression should end on exactly the same point. It may be misleading to the court and jury if one were to end a little short or a little beyond the same point at which the other projection line ends. The advantage of using tape for projection lines is that if the examiner makes an error in preparing a chart, the tape may be easily removed and repositioned.

Many examiners take photographs of their court charts and make smaller copies for the court, jury, and attorneys. These additional copies have several advantages: It is easier for the court to follow the examiner's demonstration of the large chart when they have a copy in front of them, they may be used by the jury in their deliberations, and the small copies are easily included in the court record in lieu of the larger chart.

It must be remembered that fingerprint charts are merely an aid to fingerprint examiners in presenting their testimony in court. Charts may supplement an examiner's testimony, but they do not conceal an examiner's lack of qualifications or preparedness. Before testifying in a case, the examiner should review all notes and other records pertaining to the case and, during the pretrial interview with the prosecutor, the line of questioning and all aspects thoroughly discussed. At the request of a defense counsel, an examiner should make himself available to the defense counsel for pretrial interview. If the defense counsel wishes to have the identification verified by another examiner, this request should be complied with without hesitation. There is rarely a difference of opinion regarding the identification of a fingerprint between two qualified fingerprint examiners.

QUESTIONS

TRUE-FALSE QUESTIONS

1. The circumstances under which the latents were made, and many other variable factors alter each case with respect to the techniques and methods used to recover latent fingerprints (Sec. 122).
2. Cases involving fingerprints, as in all investigations, range from the ridiculously simple to the most exceedingly complex (Sec. 122).
3. Investigators know beforehand whether or not their efforts to recover latent prints in a specific case will be successful (Sec. 122).
4. Testing provides the best method of determining the applicability of a particular latent fingerprint technique, and it may be done in all cases (Sec. 122).
5. Latent fingerprints on cloth are about the most difficult for an investigator to detect and develop (Sec. 123).

6. Powders cannot be used to develop latent fingerprints on any tape surfaces (Sec. 124).

7. An investigator should always assume that latent prints are present on an evidentiary item and make every effort to recover them (Sec. 124).

8. The correct procedure to recover latent prints in dust is the use of lifting devices (Sec. 125).

9. Latent fingerprints on glass can rarely be detected until developed with powders because of the transparent nature of glass (Sec. 126).

10. Latent fingerprints on embossed and curved glass surfaces are best photographed with reflected light (Sec. 126).

11. Electric light bulbs should never be overlooked when conducting a crime scene search for fingerprint evidence (Sec. 126).

12. Latent fingerprints etched into metal can normally be developed further with chemical techniques (Sec. 126).

13. Latent fingerprints on unfinished wood and wood painted with water-based paints may be developed with chemical techniques (Sec. 127).

14. Wooden tool handles are very good receiving surfaces for latent fingerprints (Sec. 127).

15. The best technique for developing latent fingerprints on plastic is magnetic powders (Sec. 128).

16. Powdered latent prints are more fragile than undeveloped latents (Sec. 128).

17. All papers and paper products should be examined with latent fingerprint chemical techniques and never with powders (Sec. 129).

18. Most ninhydrin solutions will dissolve plastics (Sec. 129).

19. Drug evidence should always be processed for latent fingerprints before the drugs are submitted to the crime laboratory for chemical analysis (Sec. 130).

20. All narcotic and other drug evidence should always be handled with extreme care, only to prevent possible loss of the drugs (Sec. 130).

21. The preliminary visual inspection of drug evidence for la-

tent prints should be made only with a strong light (Sec. 130).

22. Except for visible impressions, such as bloody fingerprints, there is no case on record where a suspect has been identified on the basis of a latent fingerprint developed on human skin (Sec. 131).

23. Latent fingerprint techniques that have proven practical for developing latent prints on skin include x-ray techniques (Sec. 131).

24. The use of the iodine fuming and silver transfer techniques for developing latent prints on skin has limited practical application because of the expense of the equipment involved (Sec. 131).

25. Successful recovery of fingerprint evidence depends on the perseverance of the investigator in seeking latent prints (Sec. 131).

26. The weave pattern of cloth usually interferes with the ridge details of fingerprints on cloth (Sec. 132).

27. Improperly prepared and applied latent fingerprint techniques may result in a false identification of a latent fingerprint (Sec. 133).

28. The view that a latent fingerprint technique could change ridge details in a manner that would result in a false identification is a logical assumption based on extensive scientific research (Sec. 133).

29. Fingerprint charts serve as an aid to examiners when they are presenting their testimony to courts and juries (Sec. 134).

30. When preparing a fingerprint chart, all the matching ridge characteristics in the latent and inked prints should be marked (Sec. 134).

COMPLETION QUESTIONS

31. Investigators should always familiarize themselves with a case as completely as possible . . . . making any attempt to recover latent prints (Sec. 122).

32. The proper technique and method used to recover latent prints must be the judgment of the investigator after weighing all the known . . . . (Sec. 122).

33. A fingerprint case may often look hopeless at the outset, but . . . ., ..., and . . . . bring satisfactory results (Sec. 122).

34. Latent fingerprints on cloth are about the . . . . for an investigator to detect and develop (Sec. 123).

35. Recovering latent fingerprints on tapes generally presents a challenge to the . . . . and . . . . of an investigator (Sec. 124).

36. Glass is an . . . . receiving surface for latent fingerprints (Sec. 126).

37. Enamel and smooth-finished oil-based paints should always be processed with . . . . for latent prints (Sec. 127).

38. Plastic is a . . . . receiving surface for latent fingerprints (Sec. 128).

39. Transparent plastic should be processed with magnetic powders while viewing with . . . . (Sec. 128).

40. Latent prints developed on pieces of very thin plastic must be . . . . when they are developed (Sec. 128).

41. Paper and paper products are, generally, ... receiving surfaces for latent fingerprints (Sec. 129).

42. Iodine development of latent prints on paper is uncertain after several . . . . (Sec. 129).

43. Depending upon the influence of . . . . and . . . ., there do not appear to be any specific time limitations for the successful development of latent prints with ninhydrin and silver nitrate (Sec. 129).

44. Brown craft paper and cardboard usually present problems when using the . . . . technique (Sec. 129).

45. Normally, ninhydrin-developed latent prints should be photographed using a green filter and Kodak . . . . film (Sec. 129).

46. The examination of drug evidence should always be conducted . . . . by the fingerprint examiner and the chemist (Sec. 130).

47. The view that a new technique may so change ridge details that a false identification may result can be refuted . . . . (Sec. 133).

48. The technique selected to develop latent prints must, in each case, be governed only by the investigator's .... as to which technique will provide the best results (Sec. 133).
49. Fingerprint charts are not used for the purpose of demonstrating the .... of the examiner's findings (Sec. 134).
50. At the request of a defense counsel, an examiner should make himself available for a .... (Sec. 134).

REFERENCES

Balshy, J. C.: "The charting of fingerprint exhibits," *Fingerprint and Identification Magazine.* vol. 54 (Aug., 1972), p. 14.

Beuys, W.: "Fingerspurensicherung auf der Memschlichen Haut," *Die Polizei.* vol. 57 (1966), no. 3, p. 31.

Brooks, A. J.: "Frequency of distribution of crime scene latent prints," *Journal of Police Science and Administration.* vol. 3 (1975), p. 292.

Cooper, C. E.: *Casting techniques.* Unpublished dissertation, USACIL-CONUS, Fort Gordon, GA, Apr., 1977.

"Development of latent prints on human skin," *Crime Laboratory Digest.* Issue 76-6 (Aug., 1976), p. 3.

"Fingerprint testimony," *Identification News.* vol. 24 (Mar., 1974), p. 10.

"Fingerprint charts aid court testimony," *FBI Law Enforcement Bulletin.* vol. 19 (Dec., 1950), p. 17.

"Fingerprints raised from cloth," *Scientific American.* vol. 153 (Oct., 1935), p. 200.

Fischer, K.: "Zur Sichtbarmachung von Fingerspuren auf der Haut," *Archiv fur Kriminologie.* vol. 139 (1967), p. 53.

Foley, J. F.: "Development of latent fingerprints—Silver transfer method," *Ontario Provincial Police Review.* vol. 6 (July-Aug., 1971), p. 7.

Foreman, P.: "The defense attorney views the identification witness," *Fingerprint and Identification Magazine.* vol. 51 (Dec., 1969), p. 3.

Forrest, R.: "Development of latent fingerprint impressions on skin," *Police Journal.* vol. 39 (1966), p. 539.

Giese, E. G.: "Court presentation of finger print evidence," *Fingerprint and Identification Magazine.* vol. 52 (Aug., 1970), p. 3.

Hamilton, J. L.: "Show your stuff," *Fingerprint and Identification Magazine.* vol. 55 (Nov., 1973), p. 6.

Inbau, F. E.: "Expert witness: False representations as to qualifications perjured testimony by fingerprint expert," *Journal of Criminal Law, Criminology and Police Science.* vol. 31 (May-June, 1940), p. 124.

Jensen, E.: "Fingerprint testimony in court," *Identification News*. vol. 18 (Nov., 1967), p. 5.

King, D. P.: "Scientific evidence and the courts," *Fingerprint and Identification Magazine*. vol. 45 (Sept., 1963), p. 3.

————: "Law and science: Changing standards of scientific proof," *Fingerprint and Identification Magazine*. vol. 56 (Sept., 1974), p. 16.

McLaughlin, G. H.: "The presentation of finger print evidence," *Fingerprint and Identification Magazine*. vol. 40 (Dec., 1958), p. 7.

Meadows, W.: "The prosecution views the defense witness," *Identification News*. vol. 19 (Oct.-Nov., 1969), p. 1.

Method of Lifting Latent Impressions from Skin. Latent Print Unit, Missouri State Highway Patrol, 1977.

Moenssens, A. A.: "Finger print evidence and the courts," *Fingerprint and Identification Magazine*. vol. 49 (Aug., 1967), p. 11.

————: "Testifying as a fingerprint witness," *Identification News*. vol. 22 (Aug.-Sept., 1972), p. 5.

————: "The fingerprint witness in court," *Fingerprint and Identification Magazine*. vol. 54 (Apr., 1973), p. 3.

————: "Courtroom techniques: Beware of lawyers," *Identification News*. vol. 24 (Sept., 1974), p. 7.

Mooney, D. J.: "Fingerprints on human skin," *Identification News*. vol. 27 (Feb., 1977), p. 5.

Olsen, R. D.: "Drug evidence and fingerprints," *Military Police Journal*. vol. 18 (June, 1969), p. 10.

Page, H. V.: Fingerprint Photography. Personal communication. Nov., 1976a.

————: "Photographing latent prints on cartridges," *Journal of Evidence Photography*. vol. 8 (Oct., 1976b), p. 4 (b).

Reichardt, G. J.: *A Process for Obtaining Latents from Human Skin Using Conventional Materials*. Paper presented to the Twenty-Ninth Annual Meeting of the American Academy of Forensic Sciences. San Diego, Feb. 19, 1977.

Roberts, J. A.: "Space age technology to the aid of the latent print examiner," *Fingerprint and Identification Magazine*. vol. 54 (Aug., 1972), p. 3.

Smith, D. W.: *A Practical Method for the Recovery of Latent Impressions on Adhesive Surfaces*. Unpublished dissertation. USACIL-CONUS, Fort Gordon, GA, April, 1977.

Spangler, P. F.: Fingerprint Photography. Personal communication. 1975.

Stephens, E. O.: "Fingerprints for court evidence," *Sparks from the Anvil*. vol. 4 (Dec., 1936), p. 3.

Turbyfill, R. T.: "Developing latent fingerprints on aluminum foil," *Crime Laboratory Digest*. Issue 76-5 (July, 1976), p. 3.

Tyler, J. W.: "Preparing for and presenting expert testimony in court," *Fingerprint and Identification Magazine.* vol. 47 (Mar., 1966), p. 3.

————: "You can't turn jury into panel of experts in fifteen minutes," *Fingerprint and Identification Magazine.* vol. 51 (Mar., 1970), p. 3.

Vandiver, J. V.: "Photographs latent on live human tissue," *Fingerprint and Identification Magazine.* vol. 52 (Jan., 1971), p. 12.

————: *Iodine Development of Fingerprints on Human Skin.* Memorandum for record, HQ USACIDC, Alexandria, VA, Mar. 23, 1976.

Watson, J.: "Latent print techniques for firearms," *Fingerprint and Identification Magazine.* vol. 52 (May, 1971), p. 3.

Bibliography

Adams, Arthur T.: *Adams on Finger Prints*. Buffalo, NY, Remington Rand, 1933.

Albert, Josef: *Die Daktyloskopie in Öffentlichen und im Wirtschtsleben zur Verhütung von Urkunden- und Unterschriften-Fälschungen*. Innsbruck, Austria, Gebeuder Scheran, 1933.

Allison, Harrison C.: *Personal Identification*. Boston, Holbrook, 1973.

Arias, Rafael L.: *Curso de Dactiloscopía*. Havana, Cuba, Casasus, 1956.

Arthur, Richard O.: *The Scientific Investigator*. Springfield, IL, Thomas, 1965.

Battley, Harry: *Single Finger Prints*. New Haven, CT, Yale University 1931.

Becerro de Bengoa, Miguel: *Palmografía*. Montevideo, Uruguay, El Siglo, 1938.

Beletti, F. M. G.: *Identificando a Impressáo Palmar*. Rio de Janiero, Brazil, Institute of Identification, 1934.

Block, Eugene B.: *Fingerprinting: Magic Weapon Against Crime*. New York, McKay, 1969.

Boersma, W.: *De Mono-Dactyloscopie*. Leiden, The Netherlands, Sijthoff, 1940.

Boolsen, Frank M. (Comp.) and B. C. Bridges (Ed.): *Fifty-one Fingerprint Systems*. Berkeley, CA, privately printed, 1935.

Born, Friedrich: *Monodaktyloskopie*. Bern, Switzerland, Rösch, Vogt and Co., 1926.

Bose, Rai Hem Chandra: *Finger Print Companion*. Calcutta, India, Da Gupta and Co., 1927.

Brayley, Frederic A.: *Brayley's Arrangement of Finger Prints*. Boston, Worcester Press, 1910.

Browne, Douglas G.: *Fingerprints: Fifty Years of Scientific Crime Detection*. London, Harrap, 1953.

Burns, Thomas J.: *What Are Finger Prints?* Charlotte, NC, privately printed, 1932.

Calaber, P.: *La Dactyloscopie en Belgique*. Brussels, Belgium, Bruylant, 1951.

Calico, José: *La Identificación Personal*. Barcelona, Spain, Bosch, 1941.

California Department of Education, Bureau of Trade and Industrial Education: *Fingerprint Identification and Classification*. Sacramento, CA, 1949.

Carus, Karl G.: *Uber Grund und Bedeutung der Verschiedener Formen der Hand*. Berlin, Germany, Breslaver, 1927.

Castellanos, Israel: *Dactiloscopía Clinica*. Havana, Cuba, La Propagandista, 1935.

———: *Diccionario de Dermopapiloscópis; Impresiones Digitales, Palmares y Plantares*. Havana, Cuba, Montero, 1952.

———: *El Investigador Dermatoscópico en el Lugar del Suceso*. Havana, Cuba, Fernandez, 1957.

Cataldo, Louis: *A New Approach to Single Finger Prints: The Revised Cataldo System*. Barnstable, by the author, 1958.

Chapel, Charles E.: *Fingerprinting: A Manual of Identification*. New York, Coward-McCann, 1941.

Chatterjee, Salil K.: *Finger, Palm and Sole Prints*. Calcutta, India, Artine Press, 1953.

Christensen, Herbert E. and Thomas L. Luginbyhl (Ed.): *The Toxic Substances List*. U.S. Department of Health, Education and Welfare, Washington, D.C., U.S. Govt. Print Office, 1974.

Cherrill, Frederick R.: *Fingerprints Never Lie*. New York, Macmillan, 1954.

Collins, Charles S.: *A Telegraphic Code for Fingerprint Formulae and A System for Sub-Classification of Single Digital Impressions*. London, Police Chronicle, 1921.

———: *Fingerprint Clues*. London, H.M.S.O., 1930.

Colmenares del Castillo, Rafael: *Identificación personal, dactiloscopía*. Bogotá, Columbia, Editorial Voluntad, 1949.

Cromwell, Oliver: *Finger-Print Photography*. London, Stock, 1907.

Crosskey, Walter C. S.: *The Single Finger Print Identification System*. San Francisco, privately printed, 1923.

Daae, Anders: *Identifizierung von Personen Speziell Durch Fingerabdrucke*. Kristiania, Norway, Thronsen, 1905.

———: *Fingeraftryk-Signalementer*. Kristiania, Norway, Thronsen, 1907.

Deuel, Joseph M.: *Finger-Prints*. New York, Brown, 1917.

Dillon, Lester R.: *Scientific Fingerprints*. San Antonio, TX, privately printed, 1940.

Duncan, J.: *An Introduction to Fingerprints*. London, Butterworth, 1942.

Duhamel, Roger: *R.C.M.P. Fingerprint Textbook*, 3rd ed. Ottawa, Ontario, Queen's Printer and Controller of Stationery, 1966.

Dunlap, Charles B.: *The Science of Finger Printing*. Chester, PA, Grieco-Miller, 1932.

Engeset, Senar: *Prakist Fingeravtrykkslare*. Oslo, Norway, Politiskolen, 1967.

Evans, Emmett: *Finger Print Instruction Book*. Chicago, Evans National Manufacturing and Supply Co., 1917.

Faulds, Henry: *Dactylography*. Halifax, England, Milner, 1912.

————: *The Hidden Hand.* Hanley, England, Wood Mitchell, 1920.

————: *A Manual of Practical Dactylography.* London, Police Review, 1923.

Ferrer, R.: *Manual de Identificacion Judicial.* Madrid, Spain, Reus, 1921.

Field, Anita T.: *Single Hand Classification and Filing.* Los Angeles, Los Angeles Police Department, 1954.

————: *Fingerprint Handbook.* Springfield, IL, Thomas, 1959.

Forgeot, Rene: *Des Lignes Papillaires et des Empreintes, au Double Point de Vue Medico-Legal et Ethnographique.* Lyon, France, Rey, 1892.

Frankel, Harold A.: *Finger Print Expert.* Philadelphia, Nandor-Wilson, 1932.

Garson, John G.: *A System of Classification of Finger Impressions.* London, British Association for the Advancement of Science, 1900.

Gayer, G.: *Foot Prints.* Nagpur, India, Law Publishers, 1909.

Gladkova, T. D.: *Kozhnye Uzory Kisti i Stopy Obez' iân i Cheloveka.* Moscow, USSR, Hayka, 1966.

Goicouria, Wilfredo de: *Impresión digital e identificación.* Havana, Cuba, Montiel, 1936.

Gómez Osorio, Cipriano: *La Identificación Científica en Colombia.* Bogotá, Colombia, 1925.

————: *Cartilla dactiloscopía.* Ibague, Colombia. Imprenta Departmental, 1937.

Grant, Douglas: *The Classification and Identification of Palm Prints.* Glasgow, Scotland, privately printed, 1950.

Gregory, Russell A.: *Identification of Disputed Documents, Fingerprints, and Ballistics.* Lucknow, India, Eastern Book Co., 1957.

Hall, John D.: *Suggestions on Taking Finger Prints.* Washington, D.C., U.S. Govt. Print. Office, 1910.

Hansen, Waldemar: *Fingeravtrykk og signalement.* Oslo, Norway, Tanum, 1932.

Heindl, Robert: *System und praxis der daktyloskopie* 3rd ed. Berlin and Leipzig, Germany, Gruyter, 1927.

Herschel, William J.: *The Origin of Finger-Printing.* Cambridge, Oxford University Press, 1916.

Hewitt, Cecil R.: *Personal Identity.* London, Joseph, 1957.

Holloway, Harry D.: *The Science of Fingerprint Classification.* Columbus, Ohio, National Training Institute, 1941.

Holt, James H.: *Finger Prints Simplified.* Chicago, Drake, 1920.

Horoszowski, Pawe: *Daktyloskopia; Kurs Praktyczny.* Warsaw, Poland, K.G.M.O., 1947.

Inbau, Fred E., Andre A. Moenssens, and Louis R. Vitullo: *Scientific Police Investigation.* Philadelphia, Chilton, 1972.

Jackson, Richard L.: *Gross's Criminal Investigation,* 5th ed. London, Sweet and Maxwell, 1962, pp. 160-171.

Jensen, Jay R., and J. C. Ramsey: *Palm Print Identification System.* Denver, Denver Police Department, 1965.

Jiménez Jerez, José: *Análisis quiropapilar dactiloscopía.* Santander, Spain, Aldus, 1935.

Jørgensen, Hakon: *Distant Identification and One-finger Registration.* New York, International Police Conference, 1923.

————: *Einzelfingerregistrierung.* Graz, Austria, Moser, 1926.

————: *Lehrbuch des Fernidentifizierungsverfahrens.* Berlin, Germany, 1926.

————: *Kortfattet Vejledning i Daktyloskopi og Fjernidentificering.* Copenhagen, Denmark, Busck, 1916.

Kehdy, Carlos: *Elementos de Dactiloscopía.* São Paulo, Brazil, 1957.

————: *Exercicios de Dactiloscopía,* São Paulo, Brazil, 1968.

Kingston, Charles R.: *Probabilistic Analysis of Partial Fingerprint Patterns.* Ann Arbor, Michigan, Xerox® Corporation, 1965.

————: *Research Plan for an Automated Fingerprint Processing System.* Albany, N.Y.S.I.I.S., 1968.

Kuhne, Frederick: *The Finger Print Instructor.* New York, Munn, 1916.

Larson, John A.: *Single Fingerprint System.* New York, Appleton, 1924.

Lahy, Jean M.: *La Profession de Daktylographie Étude des Gestes de la Frappé.* Berlin, Germany, Preiss, 1924.

Laufer, Berthold: *History of the Finger-Print System.* Reprint from 1912 annual report of the Smithsonian Institution. Washington, D.C., U.S. Govt. Print. Office, 1913.

Locard, Edmond: *Manuel de Technique Policere,* 2nd ed. Paris, Payot, 1934.

————: *Traite de Criminalistique,* Lyon, France, Desvigne, 1914-1940. Vols. 1-2, *Les Empreintes et les Traces dans l'Enquete Criminelle;* vols. 3-4, *La Preuve Judiciaire par les Empreintes Digitales.*

Lochte, Theodore: *Gerichts und Polizeiarztliche Technik.* Wiesbaden, West Germany, Bergmann, 1914.

Lucas, A.: *Forensic Chemistry and Scientific Criminal Investigation.* New York, Longman Green, 1937.

Mairs, G. T.: *Fingerprint Study Data.* New York, Delehanty Institute, 1938.

Maravoto, Enrique S.: *La Dactiloscopía Aplicada a los Actos Civiles y de Comercio.* Lima, Peru, Imp. Americana, 1918.

Mennonno, Charles: *The Magic of Fingerprints.* Albany, NY, unpublished paper, 1940.

Morland, Nigel: *Finger Prints.* London, Street and Massey, 1936.

————: *Science in Crime Detection.* New York, Emerson Books, 1960, Chap. 1.

Moenssens, A. A.: *Fingerprint Techniques.* New York, Chilton, 1971.

Moenssens, A. A.: *Fingerprints and the Law.* New York, Chilton, 1969.

Muller, Helmut: *Die Klassifizierung der Einzelffingerabdrucke Nach dem Berliner System.* Berlin, Freiheitsverlag, 1935.

Murphy, Edward H.: *Finger Prints for Commercial and Personal Identification.* Detroit, International Title Recording and Identification Bureau, 1922.

Niceforo, Alfredo: *Die Kriminalpolizei und Ihre Hilfswissenschraften.* Gross-Lichterfelds-Ost, Germany, Langenscheidt, 1909.

O'Brien, Kevin P., and Robert C. Sullivan: *Criminalistics: Theory and Practice.* Boston, Holbrook, 1972, Chap. 13.

Olsen, Robert D., Sr.: *Program of Instruction: Latent Fingerprint Examiner.* Fort McClellan, AL, U.S. Department of the Army, Military Police School, Fort McClellan Field Printing Plant, 1976.

Ortiz Fernandez, Fernando: *La Identificación Dactiloscopía,* 2nd ed. Madrid, Spain, Jorro, 1916.

O'Sullivan, F. D.: *Crime Detection.* Chicago, O'Sullivan, 1928.

Pond, Gilbert P.: *The Palm Printing Method of Infant Identification.* Ohio, Physicians Record Co., 1938.

Protivenski, Franz: *Grundzüge der Daktyloskopie.* Prague, Czechoslovakia, Calve, 1904.

Repis, Karl: *Theoetische und Praktische Daktyloskopie; Ein Handbuch fur Sicherheitsdienst.* Vienna, Austria, Braumuller, 1957.

Roscher, Gustav T.: *Handbuch der Daktyloskopie.* Leipzig, East Germany, Hirschfeld, 1905.

Rodriguez, Sislan: *La Identificación Humana; Historia Sistemas y Legislación.* La Plata, Argentina, Taller, 1944.

Rosenfeldt, August C.: *Universal Single Print Identification.* Seattle, Washington, privately printed, 1940.

Ryan, Patrick: *The Ryan Dactyloplane for the Finger Print Expert.* New York, privately printed, 1922.

Ribeiro, Leonidio: *Dactilo-diagnose.* Rio de Janeiro, Brazil, Impresna Nacional, 1939.

Richardson, James R.: *Modern Scientific Evidence: Civil and Criminal,* 2nd ed. Cincinnati, OH, Anderson, 1974.

Schneickert, Hans: *Der Beweis Durch Fingerabdrücke in Juristischer und Technischer Beziehung; Leitfaden der Gerichtlichen Daktyloskopie.* Berlin, Germany, Hayn, 1923.

Scott, Charles C.: *Photographic Evidence.* St. Paul, MN, West Pub. Co., 1955.

Scott, Walter R.: *Fingerprint Mechanics*. Springfield, IL, Thomas, 1951.

Seymour, Lee: *Fingerprint Classification*. Los Angeles, privately printed, 1913.

Sharp, Vaughan: *Palm Prints: Their Classification and Identification*. Cape Town, South Africa, Merchantile-Atlas, 1937.

Soderman, Harry, and John J. O'Connell: *Modern Criminal Investigation*, 5th ed. New York, Funk and Wagnalls, 1962.

Spatz, Jacob W.: *Fingerprint Science*. Portland, OR, Interstate Fingerprinting Training, 1941.

————: *The Science of Fingerprinting*. Portland, OR, American Academy of Applied Science, 1946.

Stirling, William: *La Palm Parlé*. Lyon, France, Desvigne, 1932.

Taylor, J. H.: *One Finger System, for Use of Hospital Corpsmen Assigned to Duty at Recruiting Stations*. Washington, D.C., U.S. Govt. Print. Office, 1921.

Turner, William W. (Ed.): *Criminalistics*. Rochester, NY, Aqueduct, 1965.

Uffrecht, Hermann W. J.: *Uber den Nachmessen der Identitat von Finger- und Handabrücken und die Erfolge der Daktyloskopie in Bremen*. Gotha, Germany, Schmidt und Thelow, 1911.

Urbaneja, Carlos: *Identidad Personal*. Caracas, Venezuela, Garrido, 1943.

U.S. Department of the Army: *Fingerprints*. Provost Marhsal General Technical Bull. No. 7. Washington, D.C., U.S. Govt. Print. Office, 1966.

U.S. Department of the Army: *Military Police Criminal Investigations*. Field Manual 19-20. Washington, D.C., U.S. Govt. Print. Office, 1971.

U.S. Department of the Army: *Fingerprint Identification Kits*. Technical Manual 10-632. Washington, D.C., U.S. Govt. Print. Office, 1963.

U.S. Department of the Army: *Identification Still Picture Camera KE-3(1)* Washington, D.C., U.S. Govt. Print. Office, 1955.

U.S. Department of Justice, Federal Bureau of Investigation: *The Science of Fingerprints*. Washington, D.C., U.S. Govt. Print. Office, 1973.

U.S. Department of Justice, Federal Bureau of Investigation: *Correspondence with the FBI*. Washington, D.C., U.S. Govt. Print. Office, 1970.

U.S. Department of Justice, Federal Bureau of Investigation: *Fingerprint Identification*. Washington; D.C., U.S. Govt. Print. Office, 1970.

U.S. Department of the Treasury, United States Secret Service: *A Guide to Taking Palmprints*. Washington, D.C., U.S. Govt. Print. Office, 1973.

U.S. Department of the Treasury, Consolidated Federal Law Enforcement Training Center: *Taking Fingerprints*. Washington, D.C., U.S. Govt. Print. Office, 1972.

Viotti, Manuel: *Dactyloscopia e policiogia*, 4th ed. São Paulo, Brazil, Saraiva, 1935.

Vivas, Jose R.: *Dactiloscopia*. Tenerife, Spain, Sans, 1950.

Waggener, Paul N.: *The Science of Fingerprinting.* Memphis, TN, Waggener Fingerprint Corp., 1941.

Wagner, Frederick: *National Finger Print System.* New York, privately printed, 1922.

Wallace, Paul J.: *Fundamentals of Fingerprinting.* Los Angeles, privately printed, 1944.

Wentworth, Bert, and Harris H. Wilder: *Personal Identification.* Boston, Badger, 1918.

Wilton, George W.: *Fingerprints: History, Law and Romance.* London, Hodge, 1938.

————: *Fingerprints: Scotland Yard and Henry Faulds.* Edinburgh, Scotland, Green, 1951.

————: *Fingerprint Facts.* Galashiels, Scotland, Walker and Son, 1953.

Windt, Kamillo, and Siegmund Kodioek: *Daktyloskopie. Verwertung von Fingerabdrücken zu Identifizierungsweken.* Vienna, Austria, Braumuller, 1904.

Yvert, A.: *L'Identification par les Empreints Digitales Palmaires.* Lyon, France, Storck, 1904.

AUDIO-VISUAL MATERIALS

Classifiable Fingerprints. Forty-three slides, color. Walteria, Police Research Associates.

Crime Scene Search for Latents. 16-mm film, twenty-six minutes. Chicago, Chicago Police Department, 1975.

Discovery, Development and Lifting of Latent Prints. Thirty slides, color. Walteria, CA, Police Research Associates.

Fingerprint Lifting. 35-mm film strip, sixty-two frames. U.S. Army, 1954.

Fingerprint Lifting. Sixty-two slides, black and white, Walteria, Police Research Associates.

Fingerprints. Fifty-seven slides, color. U.S. Army Military Police School.

Fingerprints. Eighty slides, color, cassette. Washington, D.C., Police Science Services.

Fingerprints and Fingerprint Examination. 35-mm filmstrip, sixty-nine frames. U.S. Army, 1953.

Focus on Fingerprinting. 16-mm film, black and white, ten minutes. Ottawa, Royal Canadian Mounted Police, 1964.

Focus on Fingerprinting. 16-mm film, black and white, ten minutes. New York, McGraw-Hill, 1964.

Military Police Photography. 16-mm film, color, twenty-four minutes. U.S. Army, 1965.

Packaging of Evidence for Transmittal to Criminal Investigation Laboratories. 35-mm filmstrip. U.S. Army, 1956.

Physical Evidence. Eighty slides, color, cassette. Washington, D.C., Police Science Services.

Printing the Dead. 16-mm film, color, sixteen minutes. Chicago, Chicago Police Department, 1973.

Processing of Evidence. Part I—Preservation and Collection. 16-mm film, thirty-five minutes. U.S. Army, 1960.

Processing of Evidence. Part II—Handling, Evaluating, and Identifying. 16-mm film, eighteen minutes, U.S. Army, 1960.

Searching the Crime Scene. 16-mm film, color, twenty minutes. Tuxedo, CA, Norwood Studios, Inc., 1968.

U.S. Army Criminal Investigation Laboratories. 16-mm film, twenty-four minutes. U.S. Army, 1962.

Veriprint Systems, Inc., 94-95
Iodine fuming cabinets, 190-193
Iodine fuming pipe, 194-195, 247
Iodine techniques
    cold iodine technique, 247-248
    Driodine, 248
    fixing iodine prints, 250-255
    iodine absorption, 243
    iodine dusting, 249
    iodine saturated silica gel technique, 248
    nascent iodine technique, 248
Ironing and restoring documents, 306-308

L

Laser technique, 347-348
Lead sulfide techniques, 229
Life of latents, 123-125
Lifts, fingerprint
    as evidence, 369-370
    color reversal of, 150-151
    how many from one print, 382-383
    image reversal of, 114
    infingerprint kits, 167
    types of, 370-373
    use of as negatives, 383-387
Light source, use of strong, 127-131
Lightboxes, 184-185
Liquid brass technique, 311-313
Luminol technique, 329

M

Magnetic powder techniques, 164-165, 223-227
Magnifier, fingerprint, 171-175
Major case prints, 70-72
Major manufacturers of fingerprint supplies
    list of, 201
    superior quality of powders, 171, 212, 213, 232
Mercuric chloride, 303, 305
Mercuric nitrate, 304-305
Mercurous chloride, 303
Metal evaporation technique, 351-352
Microwave vacuum-drying of papers, 352

N

Names
    of fingerprint pattern types, 21
    of flexion creases of the hands, 41-42
    of pattern areas of the feet, 44-45
    of pattern areas of the hands, 40-41
Nanometers, 186
Ninhydrin technique
    clearing solutions, 290-291
    concentrations for, 278-282
    dry techniques, 289
    methods of application, 285-286
    postprocessing treatment, 286-288
    reaction of, 273, 277
    solvents used in, 283-285
    test solution, 289-290
Nitric acid techniques, 314-319
Notes and note taking in fingerprint work, 134-135, 369-370

O

Osmic acid technique, 295-296, *Also see* Osmium tetroxide technique
Osmium tetroxide technique, 295-296, 308-309, 407

P

Palmprints, 36-39
    flexion and tension creases, 41-42
    how to take, 72-74
    pattern areas, 39-41
Paper
    electronic drying of, 352-353
    folds, 132-133
    prints on, 420-423
    result of powder on, 219-221
    use of magnetic powder on, 220, 226
Patterns, types of fingerprint, 21
Phosphorescent powders, 229-231
Plastic, fingerprints on, 226-227
Plastic impressions, 115
    lifting, 390-395
Points, *see* Friction ridge characteristics
Porelon pad, 91
Pores, 7, 8, 30-35
Poroscopy, 30-35
Postmortem fingerprinting, 84-89

burned skin and, 89
dehydrated skin and, 87-88
loose skin and, 88-89
Powders, fingerprint, 163-165, 170-171, 189-190, 209-235
  formulas, 233-235
  superior quality of commerical powders, 212, 214-215
Pressure and the appearance of fingerprints, 23

R

Radioactive chemical techniques, 331
Relative humidity
  effect on latent prints, 120, 121-122
  effect on ninhydrin prints, 197-199, 287
  table, 198
Rubber lifters, 167, 175-176, 371-372, 374, 377, 381
Ruthenium tetroxide technique, 309-310

S

Scanning electron microscope technique, 348-351
Searching for latent prints
  large areas, 130, 221-223
  points to remember, 129-133
  special laboratory considerations
    blood and body fluids, 135-136
    firearms and toolmarks, 138-139
    hairs and fibers, 136-137
    questioned documents, 137-138, 282-283
Silver nitrate techniques
  alcoholic solutions, 293-295
  aqueous solution, 293
  clearing solutions
    acetic acid, 306
    Clorox, 305-306
    hyposodium sulfite, 306
    mercuric chloride, 305
    mercuric nitrate, 304-305

methods of application, 296
methods of developing, 299-301
preparation of solutions, 293-296
reaction of, 273, 291
Skin damage, 80-82
Skin, fingerprints on, 426-429
Space values on fingerprint cards, 19-20
Stance for taking fingerprints, 69-70
Stand, fingerprint, 183-184
Sweat
  chemical composition of, 115-117, 271-273
  glands, 7-8, 30
Steam iron development of ninhydrin prints, 287-288

T

Tape, fingerprint lifting, 167, 175-177, 372-373, 375-380
Tapes, fingerprints on, 406-408
Tannic acid technique, 321
Temperature, 120, 121-122, 286-287
Test prints, 211
Thermoplastic powders, 227-229
Toe prints, 43
Transmission radiography, 345

U

Ultraviolet
  chemical techniques, 329-331
  fingerprint powders, 171, 229-231
  light sources, 185-187
  long wave and short wave light, 186

V

Visible fingerprint, lifting, 390-395

W

Wet powder technique, 222
Wood, fingerprints on, 417-419

X

X-ray techniques, 344-347